T0284930

ENGLAND'S GREEN

ENGLAND'S GREEN

NATURE AND CULTURE SINCE THE 1960s

DAVID MATLESS

REAKTION BOOKS

To Jo and Edwyn

Published by
Reaktion Books Ltd
Unit 32, Waterside
44–48 Wharf Road
London N1 7UX, UK
www.reaktionbooks.co.uk

First published 2024
Copyright © David Matless 2024

All rights reserved

No part of this publication may be reproduced, stored in a retrieval system or transmitted, in any form or by any means, electronic, mechanical, photocopying, recording or otherwise, without the prior permission of the publishers

Printed and bound in Great Britain by Bell & Bain, Glasgow

A catalogue record for this book is available from the British Library

ISBN 978 1 78914 921 0

CONTENTS

Wellow, Nottinghamshire, 1 May 2017.

1
Six Green Decades

Not far from the middle of England, a maypole on the green. May Day 2017 at Wellow in Nottinghamshire, and a man plays a tune with melodeon and drum, not for any audience but for the day, marking the season, in suitable dress. At the base of the maypole, across the road from The Maypole pub, with the trees into leaf and the car park filling, custom is kept. Passing visitors chat, and the man plays on.

A maypole has stood on Wellow's green since at least the 1830s, likely dating back much further, initially wooden and from at least the mid-nineteenth century around 60 feet high, with replacements erected every twenty years or so due to decay, fire or vandalism. In 1976 Nottinghamshire County Council replaced a rotting wooden pole with a steel version, topped with a weather vane.[1] The current steel pole, painted red, white and blue as if streamers had twisted round in a precise pattern, with vane on top and crown fittings at intervals to hold streamers in place, has a plaque at the base: 'Wellow Maypole erected March 2011 as a result of generous donations from residents and friends of Wellow and surrounding villages, plus Nottinghamshire County Council. Supplied and erected by Abacus Lighting Ltd.'[2] Community celebrations are held annually, not on May Day but on the late May Whitsun spring bank holiday. Five minutes of amateur film from 1965, available for view online via the British Film Institute, shows a Whit Monday May Queen procession, the crown passing from old to new, one teenager to another, with stalls on the green, fashions and hairstyles marking the period, and small children dancing the red, white and blue maypole, skipping both ways, streamers twisting and untwisting.[3]

Wellow, Nottinghamshire, 1 May 2017.

Spring festivals, maypoles, village greens, turning seasons, fertility symbols, denote one variant of a Green England, with Wellow's red, white and blue paint also suggesting a patriotism that is more than just English, celebrating English customs in a British country. *England's Green* explores green varieties of England, including the folkloric green, and examines cultures of fauna, flora, land, farming and other ways in which humans engage with the natural world; or with a world whose naturalness seems increasingly pressured and in question. The structure of *England's Green* is outlined in the second half of this chapter, but Wellow provides a stepping-off point, its surrounding area offering indicative territory for the book.

Within a Five-Mile Radius of the Maypole

Take the maypole as a centre of a circle with a five-mile radius, as if it were the standing arm of a compass, with a very long streamer stretched to trace the encircling line, carried across country by a dancer, and what kinds of relationship between the human and the natural world can be caught within?

The circle gathers a green patch of rural Nottinghamshire, with modern farming, arable and pastoral, and questions arising of the greenness or otherwise of agriculture. Food is produced, livestock is raised and sent for slaughter. Just outside Wellow, Jordan Castle Farm invites school visits to see environmentally friendly mixed farming, as part of a 'Countryside Classroom' scheme fostered by LEAF, a national body dedicated to 'Linking Education and Farming'.[4] Elsewhere in the circle, modern farming makes its way, in changing agricultural times. East from Wellow, though, at Laxton, is a kind of agricultural time capsule. Laxton, as the last open field village in England, shows a country as if agricultural enclosure had never happened, albeit with adjustments over the centuries. Farmhouses stand in rather than outside the village, and large fields are farmed in strips allocated to individual tenants by an annual village court leet. A country differently farmed and differently held, land differently green.

From Laxton, return past Wellow and head west to the other end of the English landed property spectrum, to the Dukeries, that part of Nottinghamshire named for its historically high proportion of dukes per head. Within the circle lie the centres of the landed estates of Rufford and Thoresby, the estate of the former sold off in the 1930s, and Rufford Abbey and park now owned by English Heritage and Nottinghamshire County Council. Thoresby Hall was sold by the ancestral owners to the National Coal Board in 1979, and is now a Warner Leisure Hotel, but the Thoresby estate continues in family hands, with farming, business and sporting interests. Landed England carries properties of adaptability, and the green qualities of farming and other landed practice are matters of contest. Within a five-mile radius of the maypole, a rural England, green or otherwise.

Past Rufford, and for a fee, enter Center Parcs Sherwood Forest holiday village, the first of the UK Center Parcs, established in 1987 and presenting a compact of leisure and environment, commercial yet seemingly natural, cutting across conventional oppositions of popular leisure and environmental conservation. Beyond the village of Edwinstowe, with its 'Forest Corner' roadside cricket ground, ancient oaks are conserved in the Sherwood Forest Country Park and National Nature Reserve, managed by the Royal Society for the Protection of Birds, Nottinghamshire County Council, the Sherwood Forest Trust and the Woodland Trust. Birds, insects, mammals, fungi and trees mark a distinctive nature zone, green qualities symbolized by ancient oaks, including the iconic Major Oak, around 1,000 years old and supported by props. Within a five-mile radius of the maypole, the green values of conservation guard a rare ecology.

Visitors to Sherwood are attracted not only by the oaks but by the outlaws. Until a County Council redesign a few years ago, Country Park machines dispensed 'automatic outlaw' stickers, building adventure excitement as paths were walked to the Major Oak, to see where Robin Hood might have been in his greenwood hideout. An English outlaw hero, his green elements accentuated in late twentieth-century accounts, defying authority and at one with the forest, a green man who might have danced at Wellow in between fighting injustice. Within a five-mile radius of the maypole, more folkloric greenery, with an overlay of legend and mystery, as to whether it is all true, and whether its truth is historic, mythic or a bit of both.

Within a five-mile radius of Wellow's maypole, the human relationship to the natural world thus takes in farming, nature conservation, folklore and the legends of the greenwood. And a mile northwest of Wellow is the former mining village of Ollerton, the colliery closed in 1994, with Forestry England's Ollerton Pit Wood nurturing nature on the former pit site. A couple of miles beyond Center Parcs is the former Clipstone colliery site, closed in 2003, though the headstocks and winding house remain as Grade II listed heritage structures. Wellow is a village in rural England, with a maypole on the green, but also in mining country, and after pit closures the differences of settlement type across the circle remain evident. Within a five-mile radius of the maypole, the human relationship to the natural world includes mineral extraction, with its long and contested history of labour and community, private and public wealth, and the society and economy of environmental resources. Fossil fuel extraction in the middle of England, shaping an industrial world which in turn has shaped a planetary ecosystem. Pits may have closed, but the Anthropocene opens. South of Wellow, across the fields, not so long ago, donkeys could be seen, nodding, the 'nodding donkey' surface oil-well structures of the inland English oilfield at Dukes Wood near Eakring, in production from the 1940s until 1971. Over 47 million barrels of oil were produced, initially in response to wartime energy security fears. The former oilfield site is now Dukes Wood Nature Reserve, owned by Nottinghamshire Wildlife Trust, with an industrial archaeological nature trail opened in 1987, featuring restored nodding donkeys.

Beyond Eakring, on the edge of the five-mile Wellow circle, a viewpoint at Maplebeck gives wide views back towards Wellow, and on across Nottinghamshire to Lincolnshire and Leicestershire. What kind of English greenery is in view? What to take in? Within a five-mile radius of the Wellow maypole, green pleasures and green conflicts, with human relationships to the natural world encompassing farming and mining, folklore and forest leisure, ecological conservation and oil extraction, landed estates and open fields, and the workaday farming landscape. *England's Green* addresses all such themes, finding the green in all its varieties and England in all its complexity. As the streamer inscribes its five-mile circle, the maypole generates fertile green territory, not far from the middle of England.

Navigating *England's Green*

> I come quite often now upon a sort of ecstasy, a rag of light blowing among the things I know, making me feel I am not the one for whom it was intended, that I have inadvertently been looking through another's eyes and have seen what I cannot receive.[5]
>
> Roy Fisher, 'City' (1961)

England's Green traces the meeting of the English and the environmental over six decades, taking the period as a distinctive green time, effectively an environmental present. The book's title could carry two apostrophic meanings; descriptive, with a missing 'i' (*England is Green*), or possessive, suggesting England has a green something. Both meanings apply throughout, the book indicating the claimed green properties of a country.[6]

The genealogy of concern for nature, landscape and environment of course reaches back far beyond sixty years, but the 1960s gave a novel twist, with environmental concerns shaping a Green politics marked by its critique of industrial society. Pollution, pesticides, industrial farming and upset ecologies were presented as signs of a world gone wrong, all later supplemented by and gathered into narratives of anthropogenic climate change, humanity endangering its global home. The geographic scales of the global and local commonly inform environmental concern, yet the national retains a political and emotional charge as landscapes are threatened and responses mobilized.

While it traces the emergence of a new green, this book is also concerned with echoes of and continuities from older greens: the green of English pastoral, of earlier environmental and ecological campaigns, of post-war government attention to nature. In an earlier book, *Landscape and Englishness* (1998), I addressed such themes between 1918 and the 1960s, and this introductory chapter, and the excursion around the green which follows in Chapter Two, also tap into earlier examples, showing how the past six green decades are fed by earlier sensibilities of land, nation and the natural world, though with a key twist in the changing environmental status of agriculture.[7]

Six chapters follow this introduction, before a concluding chapter reflects back across the book and looks forward to possible green futures. Chapter Two, 'An Excursion around the Green', explores the complex time signatures of the green, the connections between the green and the national, the genealogies of the especially powerful English phrase 'green and pleasant', and the green's English cultural associations, qualities and varieties. The chapter opens up the green as a category, beyond the most obvious ecological reference points, stretching and enriching its remit. Along the way, notable renderings of England's green – poetic, musical, political, literary – will be considered, indicating the variety of source materials addressed in the book.

Chapter Three, 'Life, Death and the Land', examines farming. Modernized from the Second World War, notably through new technologies of production, agriculture was recast from the 1960s as a destroyer of English landscape and of the national values there enshrined. The farmer shifted from custodian to villain, whether in the pesticide treatment of crops or the factory farming of animals, agriculture not necessarily any longer a green pursuit. Agricultural revolution set off cultural argument over the greenness or otherwise of rural England. Landed property too was subject to critique, with questions asked as to whose England the country was. Agrarian voices, landed and not-so-landed, responded, with farming and other rural practices such as hunting becoming a political and cultural battleground as the twentieth century closed, rural England styled as having a distinct and ignored voice. 'Life, Death and the Land' also considers the countercultural land values proposed from the 1960s, around traditional and/or organic farming, wholefood and self-sufficiency, good living on the land retaining its charm. The chapter concludes with the departure of the UK from the European Union, and from the Common Agricultural Policy, reopening questions as to how England might be green.

Chapter Four, 'English Nature', focuses on the 1960s and '70s, and the meeting point of English landscape and environmentalism, the national and the natural in alignment. A new Department of the Environment, established in 1970, connected the green and the governmental, while radical Green campaigners indicted countries and companies. English landscape values shaped arguments for nature, with key events such as the wreck of the oil tanker *Torrey Canyon* off Cornwall in 1967 focusing concern. Arguments over landscape become, as ever, arguments about people, with human conduct a matter for ecological debate, notably in 1960s' debates around leisure and its effect on non-human species. Television transmitted green thoughts, including in programmes aimed at children, though also viewed by adults, England's green projected onto spaces inhabited by invented, inventive creatures; the blue planet of the Clangers, the urban common of the Wombles. Writers on English nature too cultivated new outlooks, building on older versions of nature and pastoral. The work of Richard Mabey, a figure of some cultural significance, here offers a bridge from the environmental moment of the late 1960s and early '70s to the nature writing of the twenty-first century. English nature, like English agriculture, moves to a new policy landscape after the UK's departure from the EU, with green futures envisaged, if not yet realized.

Chapter Five, 'England and the Anthropocene', considers connections between a green England and a new geological epoch, in a time when environmental reflection has been also under- and overwritten by climate change. The focus is on twenty-first-century preoccupations, but also their anticipation in the second half of the twentieth century. Sites of former industry feature, with Norman Nicholson's poetry and prose on the Cumbrian coastal town of Millom as a starting point, and the gravel pits of Attenborough in the Trent Valley the end point, both presenting England as Anthroposcenic. In between, the chapter explores England and the wild, with movements to rewild English landscape working alongside a common emphasis on England as long marked by human action and English nature as humanly inflected. Climate change puts English weather and climate in question, as something conventionally temperate and changeable turns capricious. The drought summer of 1976, with England barely green at all, appears in retrospect a very dry run for the future, while the hurricane of 1987 gave a taste of storms to come. Floods become iconic English Anthroposcenes for the new millennium, while the coast, already overlain with island stories, is marked by climate change as erosion quickens and clifftop structures fall. On the shore, by the river, in the relics of industry and in wilded land, England meets the Anthropocene.

Chapter Six, 'English Mystery', turns to another sense of the green, where nature and greenery denote the spiritual, the mystic, the magical. The chapter explores the mystical geographies of English nature, with 1970s countercultural fairs and festivals, notably in East Anglia and at Glastonbury and Stonehenge, presenting England as a magical alternative Albion. The 1970s and '80s saw clashes between this other England and the state regulation of travelling lifestyles. Alternative archaeologies presented England as site of ancient mystery, with stone circles and ley lines markers of green earth magic, whereby natural energies might be tapped in resistance or as antidote to modern life. The ancient past becomes an imaginative resource for thinking through the English present, whether in art, film, music or stories for adults and children.

Chapter Seven, 'Folkloric England', extends the mystical green to consider how song and dance have been presented as the route to an authentic green country. A slight diversion from the green considers how, over the past six decades, folk's claims to English national tradition have been variously renewed or critiqued. Longstanding connections of folk and nation, manifest in the work of the English Folk Dance and Song Society, are subject to new reflections on indigeneity from the late twentieth century and also take energy from an environmentalist age. The folkloric performance of the magical and mythic green proceeds from the 1960s to today, practitioners pondering and tapping folkloric mystery, with varying results, England's green led a merry dance, occasionally around a maypole. 'Folkloric England' ends with the scarecrow as an English landscape figure, linking the folkloric, the mystical, the natural and the agrarian.

As an initial illustration of the themes outlined above, two indicative examples follow to end this chapter, one from within the past six decades, the other from before. They represent too the variety of material encountered in *England's Green*, with one a piece of music, the other an analysis of farming.

The first example, a song video, opens up *England's Green*'s themes of nature, weather and mystery. An iconic English downland landscape was chosen as the video setting for Kate Bush's 1985 single 'Cloudbusting'.[8] Two figures stand on a hill operating a tubular contraption, pointing at the sky, engaging with the atmosphere and tapping landscape mysteries. The song's story, of the relationship between psychoanalyst Wilhelm Reich and his son Peter, and the 'cloudbuster' rain-making machine Reich made to point at clouds, is set in the USA; in the video, conceived by Bush with Terry Gilliam, a crop-haired Bush plays the son and Donald Sutherland the father. 'Cloudbusting' was filmed at the hill fort of Uffington, east of Swindon, with the conical Dragon Hill below the ancient chalk carving of the Uffington white horse, seen at the video's conclusion. The chalk horse, subject of G. K. Chesterton's nationalistic 1911 poem 'The Ballad of the White Horse', here oversees a tale of weather, science and authority.[9] As Donald Sutherland is arrested and driven away, Bush remains on the hill, restarts the machine, and the rain falls. The magic of an ancient English setting helps humans make the weather, nature in harness. Watching decades on, with heightened anxieties over the human capacity to make the weather, the staged rain of 'Cloudbusting' is given another twist.

Kate Bush's work is often labelled 'English' in style and sensibility, and the English green of 'Cloudbusting' ran alongside older national sentiment in her work. Bush's second album, from 1978, was entitled *Lionheart*, the effective title track 'Oh England My Lionheart', a madrigal-like ballad with piano, recorder and harpsichord accompaniment. The song played with older English cliché, but the play was not ironic, rather marked by Bush's typically sincere theatricality. Interviewed for *Melody Maker* in November 1978, Bush stated: 'Everything I do is very English and I think that's one reason I've broken through to a lot of countries. The English vibe is very appealing.'[10] 'Oh England My Lionheart' deployed wartime symbolism of Spitfire and air-raid shelter, but war was overlaid, and overcome, by English pastoral, with shepherds and roses, orchards and wassailing, and the shelters blooming with clover. In 1978, a year after the Queen's Silver Jubilee, and the Sex Pistols' declaration in 'God Save the Queen' of there being no future in England's dreaming, Bush demurred. On *Lionheart*, as in different fashion on 'Cloudbusting', England's green dreaming appeared valid.

The second introductory example, an analysis of farming first published in the 1920s, opens up *England's Green*'s themes of the rural and agrarian, and also introduces an influential phrase whose genealogy will be examined in Chapter Two. In 1925 J. W. Robertson-Scott published *England's Green and Pleasant Land*, its title simultaneously serious and ironic, invoking an ideal yet critiquing a reality: 'It is not everybody who can see through, who keenly wishes to see through, the pleasing haze of the traditional, the ordered, and the picturesque, who has the stomach for radical change *at the time it is needed*.'[11] For Robertson-Scott, rural England was often far from pleasant, and required socio-economic change and agricultural transformation. In 1947 *Green and Pleasant Land* was reissued by Penguin, and Robertson-Scott reported a 'gladdening advance' since 1925: 'I was *amazed* by the gap between Then and Now.'[12] War had brought 'technical and social advance', and an 'astonishing' advance in farming:[13]

> What do I believe as I come to the end of my manuscript? That if in rural Britain we continue to advance as far materially, intellectually, and, I will say, spiritually, as we have done in the past twenty-five years, no countryside in the world is likely to become a better place to live in, work in and hope in![14]

England's Green and Pleasant Land remained the ideal, Robertson-Scott's critique by 1947 serving less as a counter-pastoral than a sharpened pastoral, ushering a better future. The rural England that developed in the post-war decades is the agricultural starting point for *England's Green*. The technologies welcomed by Robertson-Scott would however see a green and pleasant rhetoric turned against the new farming, as the ecological effects of 'technical advance' decoupled the green and the agrarian.[15]

England's Green and Pleasant Land, as revisited by Robertson-Scott in 1947, highlights the ways in which, at particular moments, environmental outlooks are transformed by political debate, technological change and the diagnosis of crisis. England's green is refigured across historical stepping stones, moments standing out from the general flow, when environmental matters gain heightened significance and assumptions are recast. Whether examining agriculture, nature, the mysterious or folkloric, *England's Green* thereby finds parallels between the ten years around 1970 and the ten years around 2020, with green reflections matching wider debates on the country and the planet. Step back from the 2020s to the 1970s, and then another step can be taken to the Second World War, the time of the transformation of farming and much else, each stepping stone a vantage point for change, before and after. Step forward again, from 1940 to the 1970s, and on to the 2020s, and what can be seen ahead? Political and environmental uncertainties make prediction hazardous, but an England politically detached from recent European and longer-term British connections, in the changing climate of the Anthropocene, is not wholly implausible. Is England's green and possibly pleasant land still rock solid? Are we on shaky ground? And is that a worry, or a relief?

The next chapter examines the green and pleasant within a wider excursion around the green, but to conclude this account, another perspective on this book's time period. If the apostrophic title of *England's Green* might suggest a missing 'i', there is also a present 'I' here, the six green decades matching my own time on earth, almost all spent in England. The book includes reflection on lived encounters, whether as an adjunct to study, or from a time before study would have been imagined. On agriculture, natural history, meteorology, mystery and folk culture, however, I make no claim to technical expertise. All these things have become familiar to me in a 'green' manner, but here 'green' denotes the novice, the unexpert. Growing the odd potato, but never farming. Knowing some birds and plants by sight, but never keeping a list. Making a rain gauge for a sixth-form geography project, but never forecasting weather or modelling climate. Visiting witchcraft museums and observing Morris dancers, but never being seriously tempted. *England's Green* hears the voices of those asserting their authority over such fields, presenting a critical, close appreciation of green claims, with the 'I' of the book present across the decades, thinking about the knowledge and attending to the passion.

2
An Excursion around the Green

To take an excursion around the green in England might suggest pleasant strolling in a common space, perhaps with the odd animal grazing, or cricketer playing, and with accompanying birdsong and breeze, the leaves rustling, shade dappling, some occasional bells, and so on, and this chapter takes in such joys and harmonies, some green English dreams. The propensity for pastoral, and for dreams, to carry anxieties, to cast foreboding shadows, is however also evident. This excursion visits pleasant green fields and considers the claims made for and upon them, registering environmental worries, the concerns of an ecological Green movement. It also stretches the green beyond the obvious, exercising the complexities of English belonging, ranging across the political spectrum and registering the green as having contrarian and sinister qualities. The excursion begins with a site perhaps not obviously green, but which will feature on several occasions through the book, and which turns out to be a place generating various green reflections: the gravel pit.

The Trent Valley, 1962

In 1962, somewhere near the middle of England, geographer David Smith photographed gravel. On one picture, trucks, a works building, a foreground of fine gravel piles, and hopper signs proclaiming 'The Best For All Purposes', at Hilton Gravel's Hemington Works. Another picture shows a land surface upturned, rutted and pockmarked, with some plant colonization, and an old can lingering, pylons and cooling towers behind. The not-so-fine gravel is left behind, the excavators move on, with in the distance work ongoing.

David Smith, 'Hemington: Gravel Workings of Hilton Gravel Ltd', 1962.

Smith photographed Hemington as part of a gathering of industrial landscape images, many published in his pioneering 1965 book, *Industrial Archaeology of the East Midlands*.[1] Smith's pictures of Cromford in Derbyshire and Beeston in Nottinghamshire featured in *England's Green*'s companion volume, *About England*, standing for a neglected industrial history at a time when many of its surviving structures were running down.[2] Here were the remains of the days when England set off an industrial revolution, with global import. The gravel pictures didn't make it to Smith's publication, the book instead highlighting the relics of transformative eighteenth- and nineteenth-century transport and manufacturing, but sixty years on, Smith's gravel pictures gain a different traction.[3] In twenty-first-century retrospect, the environmental legacies of industrial heritage loom, with England the birthplace of a fossil-fuel-driven modernity, now the focus for planetary anxiety. If Smith's unpublished gravel pictures were less potent for a 1960s reclamation of the industrial past, in part for the modesty of their associated built structures, then their extractive presence, their upheaval of the earth, resonates anew today. Smith's pictures of Cromford and Beeston said something about England; Hemington's gravel works can open this excursion around England's green.

Smith's photographs, held within the University of Nottingham archive, are pasted onto A4 paper sheets. Place and catalogue number appear above the image, with explanatory text below.[4] Both images shown here are labelled 'Hemington Derbyshire'; the River Trent, whose flood plain deposits hold the gravel, here forms the Derbyshire-Leicestershire boundary, with Hemington village on the Leicestershire side, but the image may have been taken across the river. The explanatory text for each states:

> HEMINGTON: *Gravel workings of Hilton Gravel Ltd.*
>
> Part of the extensive gravel workings in the Trent Valley to the north of Hemington, between Long Eaton and Castle Donington. The buildings associated with the extraction of gravel are insignificant features of the landscape by comparison with the dereliction of the land which results.
>
> HEMINGTON: *Derelict gravel workings*
>
> This picture illustrates the after-effects of the indiscriminate extraction of gravel. The land shown has been rendered useless for any other form of economic activity. Large areas of former gravel workings, much of it under water, exist in the Trent Valley, in particular in the Hemington area and near Attenborough and Beeston. In the distance can be seen the cooling towers of Castle Donington power station.

David Smith, 'Hemington: Derelict Gravel Workings', 1962.

Smith's Midland England images signal themes running through *England's Green*, of land, nature and human earthly presence. Smith identifies dereliction, with land 'rendered useless'. A fertile flood plain, which might have been pasture or, flood-risk permitting, arable land, is disturbed. Land use becomes land loss, and the third chapter of this book will consider arguments over the use and value of land, and the erosion of the green. The captions suggest indiscriminate nature exploitation, resources plundered; the 1960s saw the emergence of an environmentalism presenting industrial modernity as ruining nature, and Chapter Four of *England's Green* traces the connections of environmental consciousness and English landscape. Smith also, however, noted gravel workings under water, including at Attenborough in Nottinghamshire, now a nature reserve, the flooded pits preserved for wildlife and valued for leisure. The human-nature story becomes one of reuse as well as loss, as land 'rendered useless' finds new purpose. Hilton Gravel were based at Hilton, southwest of Derby and around 15 miles west of Hemington; their former Hilton pits now make up Derbyshire Wildlife Trust's Hilton Willow Pit nature reserve, a 29-hectare Site of Special Scientific Interest.

The upturned earth of Hemington also anticipates the Anthropocene, the idea that humanity has made its mark on the earth such that a new geological epoch has been inaugurated, the future rock record carrying a human stamp. The meeting point of England and the Anthropocene, and the English landscapes of climate change, will be examined in Chapter Five, but Smith's gravel pictures give a glimpse. There are the background cooling towers, with coal-fired electric power a focus for climate change and Anthropocene reflection, as was discussed towards the end of *About England*.[5] The Castle Donington station, opened in 1958, closed in 1994 and was later demolished, though the nearby station at Ratcliffe-on-Soar lingers. The Hemington gravel also tells an Anthropocene story, with Cooper and Symonds, in their study of the Trent valley aggregates industry, noting how the second half of the twentieth century brought 'the transformation of sand and gravel from a minor commercial product on a local scale to one of the key constituents in the creation of the modern built environment . . . the Trent valley has been at the forefront of this revolution.'[6]

Hilton Gravel ran seven quarries in Derbyshire, Leicestershire and Staffordshire, a 1957 advertisement highlighting their gravel's use for mass and reinforced concrete, road surface dressing, footpaths and asphalt, and claiming '8,000 tons daily of Quartzite Gravel & Sand'.[7] Cooper and Symonds note the particular value of quartzite in concrete manufacture, promoting 'the extraordinary growth of the aggregates industry in the second half of the twentieth century', with notable East Midlands demand from road and motorway construction (the M1 runs close to Hemington) and the building of the Trent valley power stations.[8] The foreground of Smith's picture helps make its background. Trent gravel went to construct things that, as they eventually enfold into earth, will form Anthropocene geological signatures; concrete buildings, highways, pavements, the infrastructures of the epoch: 8,000 tons daily removed, but in the end, whenever the end is, disaggregated back into a future sign of human presence.

Smith's images from somewhere near the middle of England, six decades ago, serve as a starting point for this excursion around the green, in part for their signalling of complex green time signatures. Smith's pictures conjure questions of immediate resource use, with gravel destined for specific modern functions. They indicate near-future possibilities of reuse for the derelict and useless, whereby the spaces of extractive industry would turn into nature zones. They also carry hints of the geologically epochal, of an Anthropocene to come. The next section of this excursion takes forward these various temporal registers, exploring the various times of the green.

Green Time

England's green, like any green, carries varied time signatures. Alongside the specific decadal story of the past sixty years, and its anticipation in earlier green commentaries, different green temporal registers feature at various points in this book. Green time may be epochal on the geological scale, may be cyclical, turning with the seasons, or may signal the constant and/or eternal, a kind of green nature drone underscoring human activity. Different temporalities inform environmental outlooks.

The Anthropocene epoch, with the earth geologically stamped by the human, twists the temporally familiar. Something with, in geological time, a brief presence – the human – is registered on a geological timescale, with its units of ascending size, from epoch to period to era to eon. From a geological perspective the time of nature is enormous, yet not eternal, and can be comprehended through compartmentalization. Marking the geological time of nature with the name of the 'Anthro' jolts the human relationship to the earth, on the one hand locking the human in, on the other embedding the human in future change. One lesson of the geological timescale is that all units are finite. The Anthropocene will, at some point, close, and where will humanity be then?

From the epochal to the annual. The green carries a seasonal time signature, denoting cycles whereby humanity experiences, exploits and/or reveres the natural. The popular music of the 1980s again registered this green, as when XTC's 1986 LP *Skylarking*, with its cover drawings of male and female pan pipers, includes Andy Partridge's song 'Season Cycle', asking who pedals the cycle, with its verdant spiral and growing green. The opening LP track 'Summer's Cauldron', and the closing 'Sacrificial Bonfire', likewise approach something pagan, themes continued on other XTC records: the 1999 LP *Apple Venus, Vol. 1* includes an Odin-noting 'Easter Theatre' and the nature-spirit song 'Greenman'. As climate changes, such appeals to annual cycles grow, tapping seasonal rhythms which, in all their variation, may have lasted as long as recorded human experience, but which now appear newly fragile. Eleanor Parker's 2022 book *Winters in the World* gives an account of the seasons as shown in Anglo-Saxon poetry, histories and religious literature, moving from Midwinter to spring and Easter, through the 'blossoming summer', harvest and autumn, and back to Midwinter again. Parker describes a seasonal year where customs and commentary mixed the Christian and the pagan, expressing closeness to and dependence on the natural world. She finds a renewed contemporary interest in seasonal festivals, Christian or otherwise, and thus a new resonance in Anglo-Saxon things:

> Such festivals offer opportunities to mark the passage of time, to gather in community with others and to acknowledge the profound value of our relationship with the natural world. In a time of ecological crisis, Anglo-Saxon poems which recognize how fundamentally we are connected to the rhythms of nature – how dependent we are on the well-being of the earth, how grateful we should be for its gifts and its beauties – speak truths we still need to hear.

Parker adds: 'The cycle of the seasons, to which poets have so often turned as a reminder that nothing in this world is stable, is in fact one of the great constants in life . . . every year, when the blossom springs and the leaves fall, we see what the Anglo-Saxon poets saw.'[9]

Yet what of the common contemporary remark that the blossom and leaves seem now to appear at times when they wouldn't just a few decades ago? Living memory notices altered pattern, the quick onset of a new epoch. There is still a seasonal cycle, but is it out of kilter? The appeal of past settled cycles might derive precisely from the sense that there is something different about today. The reader of *Winters in the World*, enjoying an account of an Anglo-Saxon mead-hall in winter or the August Lammas festival of first fruits, may look outside to unsettling weather and a season cycle pedalled off course into the Anthropocene. The contemporary answer to who pedals the season cycle may be found as much in the mirror as in church, humans making the weather through something more than a cloudbuster.

Green times, whether epochal or annual, are also historical, figured through human contexts and thereby variable and contested. Even when the green is invoked as something transhistorical, as eternal and continuous, persisting through and despite history, it becomes wrapped in events, serving particular cultural and political purposes. In July 1934 an England 'green and eternal' was invoked in the Old Rectory Garden at Abinger in Surrey, through a pageant staged in aid of the Church Preservation Fund. The Abinger Pageant showed, in the words of scriptwriter E. M. Forster, 'the continuity of country life' in a distinctive parish:

> Abinger is a country parish, still largely covered in woodland. It is over ten miles long – one of the longest parishes in England – but very narrow, and it stretches like a thin green ribbon from the ridge of the North Downs right away to the Sussex border in the South.[10]

Devised and produced by Tom Harrison, the Abinger Pageant had music by Ralph Vaughan Williams from his *English Folk Song Suite*; in content and personnel this local event claimed national significance. The pageant narrator was a 'Woodman', at once clearing and caring for the trees, and telling a story of ordinary local life, from the ancient British 'beginning of history' through Saxon, Norman and medieval, with charcoal burning and iron working, farming and forestry, folk song and dancing.[11] Moving 'Towards Our Own Times', the Woodman spoke 'The Epilogue':

> Houses, houses, houses! You came from them and you must go back to them. Houses and bungalows, hotels, restaurants and flats, arterial roads, by-passes, petrol pumps, and pylons – are these going to be England? Are these man's final triumph? Or is there another England, green and eternal, which will outlast them? I cannot tell you, I am only the Woodman, but this land is yours, and you can make it what you will.[12]

A successor pageant in 1938 by Forster and Vaughan Williams, 'England's Pleasant Land', for the Dorking and Leith Hill District Preservation Society, had a developer singing 'Ripe, ripe for development/ Is England's Pleasant Land'.[13] The eternal green is mobilized in 1930s Surrey, working for particular interests in the present, defending a version of English landscape.[14] The wrapping of green in national events and emotions is the subject of the next stage of this excursion.

Provisional England: The National Green

England's Green explores the alignment of the national and the green through farming, nature conservation, climate commentary, landscaped mystery and the folkloric. Green concerns are global and local, but also national, and to indicate the variety of connections made, three examples are given here. One is from the present, and two are from the 1960s.

In May 1966 Colin MacInnes, known for his appreciative liberal commentary on England's ethnic and sexual diversity, wrote in the magazine *New Society* on 'The Green Art: Gardening'.[15] MacInnes found gardening 'a major, and widely diffused, affection' in England, connected to climate ('almost perfect for variety and subtlety in gardens'), nostalgia ('gardening satisfies an instinct for a lost rural heritage') and nature ('a direct and intimate means of communing with nature'). Gardening could also convey grandeur ('an instinct for display that is socially acceptable'), offer exercise and meditation, was of relatively low expense and satisfied 'a profound instinct for creation'.[16] MacInnes visited sample gardens in town and country, finding 'Rural

Bliss' in Thameside Oxfordshire. Here was the English green by an iconic English river, where 'two gents who live, as they say, together' kept their riverside lawn, rock garden and borders in the Gertrude Jekyll style. MacInnes took tea: 'it was one of those freak March days, and we had it under the fruit trees which were already budding.'[17] MacInnes's garden reflections draw out key elements of *England's Green*; property, the rural, the styles of human conduct appropriate to environments, the values of the natural.

Across the Chilterns from Thameside rural bliss, on 23 June 1954 John Fowles had visited a Buckinghamshire school, his daily journal noting:

> Watching a display of dancing given by children at the Little Gaddesden village primary school. They did English folk dances. It was a bright blue day, fleecy clouds, green grass. The dances sprightly, pastoral, a sad lonely ghost. I had a sudden whiff of sorrow for the past. England my England, England's mysterious deep ghost, sprightly, green; I see it in the shade of the great beeches. Very rarely. One day I must catch it in Robin Hood, the remotest and perhaps profoundest of my projects.[18]

Fowles returned to this English green in autumn 1964, in an essay in the *Texas Quarterly*, 'On Being English but Not British'. Fowles began by noting: 'For a decade now I have been haunted by the difficulty of defining the essence of what I am but did not choose to be: English.'[19] For Fowles, 'the agonizing reappraisal we English-Britons have had to make of our status as a world power since 1945 in fact permits us to be much more English again,' and positive English possibilities lay in the green.[20] Fowles made a distinction between England and Britain, proposing a retreat from a militaristic and imperial British nationalism, and the advance of a gentler Englishness. Fowles's England, 'virtually an island', sheltered an 'archetypal' concept of 'the Just Outlaw': 'What John Bull is to the Red-White-and-Blue Britain, Robin Hood is to the Green England.'[21] Here was a figure essentially '*in revolt, not in power*', his outlaw dissenting quality pulling Fowles's Green England more to the political Left than Right.[22] Fowles added transatlantic political equivalents for his *Texas Quarterly* readers: 'the Whig-Labour-Democrat movement is (or has been) more characteristic of the Green England than the Tory-Conservative-Republican.'[23]

Fowles's Green versus Red-White-and-Blue colour scheme registered themes shaping discussions of environmental England over the following decades, though this was not a simplistic opposition, with the 'indefinable' nature of Englishness deriving from Anglo-British complexity: 'The Great English Dilemma is the split in the English mind between the Green England and the Red-White-and-Blue-Britain.' Fowles insisted: 'I am emphatically not a Little-Englander,' with the UK fine as a 'federal' administrative entity: 'in the United Kingdom only a handful of lunatics in the Celtic twilight still caterwaul for home rule.'[24] Green England was ultimately 'far more an emotional than an intellectual concept. Deep, deep in those trees of the mind the mysteries still take place; the green men dance, hunt, and run.'[25]

The emotional Green might help navigate the English dilemma: 'The Green England is green literally, in our landscapes. This greenness is not very fashionable at the moment . . . But we have no choice: England is green, is water, is fertility, is inexperience, is spring more than summer.'[26] Fowles's *Texas Quarterly* evocation of an English green spring was issued two years after the publication of Rachel Carson's *Silent Spring*; a national nature spirit is called up at a time of ecological anxiety, something to harness against adverse political and commercial forces. Fowles's 1979 study *The Tree* would likewise offer an environmentalist philosophy from the greenwood, finding in trees

> their natural correspondence with the greener, more mysterious processes of mind . . . our woodlands are the last fragments of comparatively unadulterated nature, and so the most accessible outward correlatives and providers of the relationship, the feeling, the knowledge that we are in danger of losing: the last green churches and chapels outside the walled civilization and culture we have made with our tools.[27]

From 1964, at the start of this book's six green decades, Fowles sets off Green England in one direction, a nature-communing national sensibility, countering other versions of England/Britain. From 2022, at the close of this book's coverage, and in a work sharing its title, Zaffar Kunial offers a different evocation of *England's Green*. Kunial's poetry collection, following his 2018 volume *Us*, reflects on family change in passages of country and memory: on the death of his Midland

English mother, on his father living in Kashmir, having left England and family, though Kunial's maker's names are never mentioned.[28] Kunial works through languages national, local and global, with cricket offering a terminology for the post-colonial in poems such as 'Leg Glance', 'Mid On' and 'F', on winter net practice and on showing the bat maker's name in a proper straight shot.[29] 'The Groundsman' taps the English style of Philip Larkin, with mentions of 'Queen Anne's lace', matching the 'Lost lanes of Queen Anne's lace' in Larkin's poem 'Cut Grass', and its end point that 'days are a cut field, clipped and made/ to run on', echoing Larkin's 'Days', where long-coated priest and doctor come 'Running over the fields'.[30] Cricket and literature meet too in *England's Green*'s final poem, 'The Wind in the Willows', the willow the tree of book and bat.[31]

The first half of Kunial's book, 'In' (the second half is 'Out'), includes poems playing on the title words, England and Green. 'The Hedge' thus helps form England's 'green envelope', with its landscape pattern of 'Thorned blank verse'.[32] 'England' has Kunial following the other self who might have played cricket for Warwickshire and England, to unplayed-on English and Indian grounds.[33] 'Green', on Kunial's mother's grave and garden, sets plant life and human ends, the grave's grass styled as 'green hair'. Kunial's childhood home was near to Tolkien's former residence on Wake Green Road, where Tolkien 'lived and saw his Old Forest/ move'. Tolkien's home was 'off my road', and the 'off' may indicate something close, adjacent, but also a direction not taken. There is magic, if no Ents, in Kunial's green England. 'Green' projects a placed memory, and an English life and death ultimately open: 'However short the life that began with her/ a green gate will always open from a hinge in the air./ Unlatched like this now'.[34]

The variously open or closed greens of England are addressed in the remaining chapters of this book. From accounts of farming, nature, the Anthropocene, the mysterious, the folkloric, a national green emerges which is always provisional; never complete and always subject to refurbishment, yet also provisional in the sense of sustenance and nourishment. The provisional national green offers food for non-conclusive thought.

England's Green [______]?

As a book title, *England's Green* could be read as an invitation to complete a phrase, its two words the start of something longer. What follows 'England's green'? What comes to mind? England's green what?

Imagine that, in its inaugural year of 1979, the BBC game show *Blankety Blank* had staged a special St George's Day 'England' edition, with colour-related questions. First up, 'England's blue _____ ?' 'England's blue blank', says host Terry Wogan, inviting famous-ish guests to write down their answers, to see if they match those of ordinary contestants. 'Birds over the white cliffs of Dover', say some celebrities. 'Police boxes', say others, or 'bottles'. A tricky choice, nothing obvious, and the contestants write 'sea'. No points. Next is 'England's white _____ '? 'Cliffs', say some. 'Football shirts', say others. 'Cliffs' makes the match. Then comes 'England's red _____ '? 'Post boxes', say some. 'Telephone boxes', say others. 'Football shirts in the 1966 World Cup final', says another. 'Post boxes' takes it.

The final question, scores level, the decider to reach the super match: 'England's green _____ ?' 'And pleasant land', say all the celebrities. 'Though not as green as Ireland', quips Wogan. One contestant matches the panel, and goes forward. The other plumps for 'fields', and takes home the mock-silver Blankety Blank chequebook and pen. If only they had been familiar with the works of a visionary radical poet, or at least sung 'Jerusalem' at school. The contestant waves goodbye; 'And did those feet', quips Wogan, skipping across the floor to the next round, audience laughing. 'Blankety Blake', a further quip, as laughter fades.

That this might plausibly have happened indicates 'England's Green and Pleasant Land' as common knowledge, a touchstone phrase, even a slogan, for those evoking, upholding or defending the qualities of a country. Environmental campaigns, literary presentations, musical settings, have kept the phrase in circulation, a common currency unlikely to draw a blank. An examination of the genealogy of the green and pleasant shows the political and cultural variety in England's green.

Seventy years ago the green and pleasant could work in relatively straightforward fashion, allusions setting William Blake's 'green and pleasant' against his 'dark satanic mills'. The danger to the rural green appeared to come from without, from the urban and industrial; the decades since have detected danger within, in the actions of the farmer. In 1955 Dudley Barker's novel *Green and Pleasant Land* presented the construction of a coastal steel mill at 'Skelstrand', near 'Gulport', an unspecified northern location, as overturning the rural and ecological order. Sand dunes are destroyed and landed society eroded. Barker's plot, a story of planning and development in the vein of Winifred Holtby's 1936 novel *South Riding*, with added attempted mill sabotage, conveys pleasantness and unpleasantness on all sides, but the underlying opposition is clear and conveyed in the book's cover.[35] Here, industrial smoke forms an unholy grassy pattern, and the idealized English village-with-church is doomed, drawn down into satanic gloom. In 1955 the green versus industrial allusion was clear, yet even within Barker's story all sides claim to be in favour of England, and present their vision as one of environmental benefit, whether the environment is preserved wild sand dunes, fine farmed fields or a splendid and productive steel plant. Barker's title offered a seemingly simple touchstone, but the plot suggested cultural entanglement.

The green and pleasant has a complex genealogy, from its poetic appearance in the short preface to Blake's 1804 long poem 'Milton' (a still longer 1804–18 poem had the title *Jerusalem*), through its musical setting by Hubert Parry in 1916 in the song 'Jerusalem'. 'England's green' become the first two words of a poignant five, and meaning heads all ways. Jason Whittaker's 2022 study *Jerusalem: Blake, Parry and the Fight for Englishness* examines the variety of twentieth-century claims on 'Jerusalem', the song moving across cultural and political agendas, made differently instrumental: 'in the hundred years after its musical composition, "Jerusalem" came to assume the place of an English anthem while offering deeply conflicting notions of what is meant by Englishness.'[36]

'Jerusalem' becomes a moving symbol of England, and the green and pleasant gathers a range of associations. Set by Parry in 1916 for Francis Younghusband's Fight for Right organization, seeking to boost patriotic support for the First World War, the song then migrated from martial purpose. Parry, who owned the copyright, became disillusioned with Fight for Right, and gave the song to Millicent Fawcett's National Union of Women's Suffrage Societies, orchestrating it for a March 1918 Suffrage Demonstration Concert. Edward Elgar further orchestrated 'Jerusalem' for larger orchestra in 1922. Between the wars 'Jerusalem' gained association with the Women's Institute movement, moving from wartime martial male to peacetime rural community female. Political Conservatism still however made a claim. Elgar conducted his orchestration at the opening of the 1924 Empire Exhibition at Wembley, and the song played on BBC radio after Conservative Prime Minister Stanley Baldwin's speech at the end of the General Strike in 1926. Imperial Englishness, Conservative order; but 'Jerusalem' also served as an anthem of the Left, Paul Robeson recording it in 1939, and the song embraced by the Labour movement, Clement Attlee especially enthusiastic for Blake. 'Jerusalem' was sung to mark Labour's 1945 landslide election victory, and at the end of party conferences, a song for socialist sentiment; but also from 1953, with Elgar's orchestration, it became a fixture of the Last Night of the Proms, under conductor Malcolm Sargent. 'Jerusalem' shapes a mainstream flag-waving patriotism, alongside 'Land of Hope and Glory' and 'Rule Britannia' rather than the 'Red Flag'. A song for late empire, a rousing sing-song as Union Jacks were waved in the Royal Albert Hall and lowered across the globe.

By the 1970s 'Jerusalem' could also be for the culturally and musically progressive. The song opens Emerson, Lake and Palmer's 1973 LP *Brain Salad Surgery*, Parry's tune turned to progressive rock, three minutes of musical bombast on drum, bells, organ and guitars, with Greg Lake's faintly yearning vocal. ELP's 'Jerusalem' registered a typically prog mix of technical dexterity and mythic fantasy, and takes its English prog-anthemic place alongside Rick Wakeman's 1975 *The Myths and Legends of King Arthur and the Knights of the Round Table*, performed at Wembley Arena as an ice show. Blake's words can be orchestrated, embellished, sonically filled out; but they can also be stripped bare, as when Billy Bragg restated the song's socialist value on the 1990 LP *The Internationale*, singing with plain piano backing. In his 2006 book *The Progressive Patriot*, written 'to reconcile patriotism with the radical tradition', Bragg noted how 'a sense of place continued to inform my songwriting', such that even a globally political album 'still had room for William Blake's "Jerusalem"'.[37] Bragg would title a 1996 LP *William Bloke*.[38]

'Jerusalem' carried its multivalent politics into the late twentieth century, serving as both symbol for Thatcherite Conservatism and a sign of resistance to it.[39] Such sentimental complexity appears in the 1981 film *Chariots of Fire* (dir. Hugh Hudson), its title from Blake's poem and Parry's song. The film's story of British masculinity, at once invoking and critiquing patriotism, returned the tune to its origins in Parry's conflicted outlook on the First World War. *Chariots of Fire* has 'Jerusalem' playing at the 1978 funeral of English Jewish athlete Harold Abrahams before segueing back to the younger runners on a beach, Vangelis's theme tune kicking in to close the film. Oscar-winning-athletic-film watchers thus received the Blakean, and sporting crowds would also join in, 'Jerusalem' adopted by the England men's Test cricket team in 2003, achieving new prominence through the 2005 Ashes victory and played at the start of every home Test day since. Team England adopted the song at the 2010 Commonwealth Games in Delhi, England's green and pleasant land sounding in the independent economically resurgent subcontinent. When in 2006 the Labour government, concerned over a perceived political neglect of English identity in a devolved UK, revealed twelve 'Icons of England' to foster national belonging, 'Jerusalem' the song appeared, alongside Stonehenge.[40]

By now the song might have been tired of all the re-settings. Surely time to lay fallow? But no, a global event would again put the UK at the centre of things, with a national narrative projected across the world. The 2012 London Olympics opening ceremony began with an eleven-year-old boy singing the opening verses of 'Jerusalem', before a choir performed 'Danny Boy', 'Flower of Scotland' and 'Bread of Heaven', 'Jerusalem' then returning for its final verses, United Kingdom varieties sandwiched into an English anthem. Jerusalem as idea ran through Danny Boyle and Frank Cottrell-Boyce's production, the ceremony's media guide stating: 'We can build Jerusalem. And it will be for everyone.'[41] For John Higgs, in his 2019 *William Blake Now: Why He Matters More than Ever*, the Blake-inspired Olympic ceremony made for 'wild, surreal hours', an 'act of communal magic unlike anything else created in our lifetime. The country saw who they were in that ceremony, and with recognition came a sense of joy.'[42]

A few decades ago, the default English song for national events, if one was needed to mark the country out within the UK, tended to be 'Land of Hope and Glory'. By 2012 'Jerusalem' served that purpose, becoming, as reflected in the title of a 2005 BBC documentary, *Jerusalem: An Anthem for England*.[43] 'Jerusalem' and 'Land of Hope and Glory' share an Elgar connection, Elgar the orchestrator of one and composer of the other, and Elgar has his own complex connections to Englishness.[44] 'Land of Hope and Glory', though, appears monovocal in sentiment, A. C. Benson's lyric making for a song you are either with or without, not a song for everyone in an England taking pride in multi-vocality. As expansionist 'wider still and wider' imperial sentiments ebb, 'Jerusalem' rises, its several-vocal sentiments matching self-conscious national cultural variety. A country finds a song it can happily sing about itself, and to itself. Or perhaps the plurality of claims on 'Jerusalem' make it the perfect anthem for a divided country, different groups singing it for themselves, across each other, in different keys. England may be green and pleasant, but definitions of pleasantry and the green find themselves at odds.

England's Green and Quite Contrary

John Higgs begins *William Blake Now* with the unveiling of a new grave marker for Blake in London in August 2018, attended by a large and diverse crowd, the stone marked with a quotation from the long poem *Jerusalem*, about a golden string leading to heaven's gate, indicating Blake as 'a way to a numinous place'.[45] For Higgs the upheavals since the 2012 Olympics themselves have a Blakean air: 'We have caught up to him to the extent that we are now seen as an "unfortunate lunatic". Clearly, we are getting somewhere.'[46] Blake's England might usurp any lingering sense of a world-leading nation where people defer to their rulers: 'Free at last from the myth of British exceptionalism, we can at last see ourselves as we really are . . . The people on this island are a wild, psychedelic, eccentric, creative mob, as should have been blindingly obvious all along.' Blake's message of 'the importance of deep imagination' might equip the country for a better future: 'he has prepared us for the world we find ourselves in.'[47]

The settings of 'Jerusalem' noted above are largely of an overground variety, organizations and individuals making a public statement of values. There is also, however, an underground, countercultural 'Jerusalem', looking beyond the Parry setting, wary of corralling Blake, where the green and pleasant takes other hues. Blake was hardly an orthodox figure and sparks an England of dissidence, for, as Michael Bracewell puts it, 'visionary poetics and political subversion . . . the mystical, in England, has often lent itself to underground or alternative thinking'.[48] Thus in 1995 the group Dreadzone released 'Little Britain', a single from their *Second Light* LP, issued 'In memory of

William Blake'.[49] The opening lines of the song's 'Vocal Version' set things in this green and pleasant land, the song offering a dub-rave vision of a multi-ethnic, spiritually diverse inheritance, leading all a merry dance. In this particular Little Britain, Blake denotes a dissident underground harmony, an alternative pastoral, green and pleasant for an alternative country.

Blake-gone-underground can also, however, spark things less harmonious than contrary, and this section considers some recent Blakean contrariness, before ending with Blake's own poetry. Seven years after *Chariots of Fire*, a contrarian Blake appeared on stage and record, 'Jerusalem' featuring on The Fall's 1988 LP *I Am Kurious Oranj*, made alongside a ballet performance by Michael Clark and his company, for the 300th anniversary of the accession of William and Mary to the British throne. On the LP the track appears as 'Dog is Life/Jerusalem', credited to 'William Blake/M. E. Smith', with band leader, singer and lyricist Mark E. Smith offering Blake with supplements, a cerebrally caustic 'Jerusalem'.[50] Smith starts with 'And did those feet', but diverts after two Blake verses into a recalcitrant voice of complaint, satirizing those who both blame the state for their ills and demand its life support. The remaining Blake verses complete the song, a touch garbled, ending at the green and pleasant, though a little green around the gills.

Over a forty-year career The Fall were tied in upbringing, residence and lyric to Manchester and its urban hinterlands. The country tended only to feature as a site of dullness or irony; on 'English Scheme' (1980), with its jaunty citation of grassy dales and lowland scenes, and caustic asides on Greenpeace, or 'Hard Life in Country' (1982), with its accompanying LP sleeve note on 'Horrid truth behind all that romanticized green grass'. Blakean green mystery sneaks in, though. A sleeve note to the 1979 *Dragnet* LP alludes to: 'Village. Location unknown. Said to be negative Jerusalem.' The lyric of 'Before the Moon Falls' on the same record, on creating a new regime or being crushed by another man's, echoes Los early in Blake's *Jerusalem*: 'I must create a system, or be enslaved by another man's.'[51] The song 'W.B.', from *The Unutterable* (2000), has lyrics part taken from Blake's 'A Song of Liberty', with fire falling over London and Heaven and Hell arising. The Fall's 'Jerusalem' mines, and picks at, a running Blakean green seam, its pleasantries and unpleasantries. Smith's relationship with England, as with much else, was a contrarian love-hate, emotions often simultaneous rather than alternate.

The underground Blakean seam surfaced also in 1969, in Michael Horovitz's anthology of the 'Poetry of the "Underground" in Britain', *Children of Albion*, the cover showing a detail from Blake's engraving 'Glad Day'. Horovitz, with Blake 'my master', hailed 'a green and pleasant land again, suddenly, in sight of these young men of the new age who put poetry before all else'.[52] At the first International Poetry Incarnation at the Royal Albert Hall in 1965, Horovitz, Allen Ginsberg and others had 'improvised an Invocation', taking six lines from Blake's epic poem *Jerusalem* to set off thoughts of a 'Spontaneous planet-chant Carnival!', England's green gone cosmic:

> England! awake! awake! awake!
> Jerusalem thy Sister calls!
> . . .
> And now the time returns again:
> Our souls exult, & London's towers
> Receive the Lamb of God to dwell
> In England's green & pleasant bowers.[53]

The poetic style and subject matter of *Children of Albion* was varied, its landscapes urban as well as rural; again the varieties of England's green are evident. Horovitz thus quoted Gael Turnbull's 1962 commentary on Roy Fisher's 1961 Birmingham poem *City*, with its scrutiny of a suburban English back garden: 'If Wordsworth and Constable helped to establish a certain "landscape" in the last century, a work such as CITY is an effort to establish another landscape.'[54] Fisher, who termed Blake 'as near to the political position that I have as anybody', and was described by poet Denise Levertov as 'utterly and unmistakeably English', offered a different greenery, for a modernist poetry of prosaic reflection.[55] Seven Fisher poems appeared in *Children of Albion*, including two extracts from *City* (1961), 'The Entertainment of War' and 'Starting to Make a Tree'. Fisher's made tree stretches greenness and pleasantry, very differently arboreal to Fowles's unadulterated nature, being made of urban detritus, happening to be present. A 'faggot of steel stakes' is driven in the ground to frame 'an old, down-curving tree', and the work is 'done with care'. The details of bough and bole are modelled from local human anatomy, with materials gathered aplenty from nearby houses:

> a great flock mattress; two carved chairs; cement; chicken-wire; tarpaulin; a smashed barrel; lead piping; leather of all kinds; and many small things.
>
> In the evening we sat late, and discussed how we could best use them. Our tree was to be very beautiful.[56]

England's green can be quite contrary, its garden growing different beauties. Elsewhere in *City* Fisher offers hints of mystery, relating things not quite accountable, though hardly in tune, or in tone, with any 'Spontaneous planet-chant Carnival!' Interviewed by John Kerrigan in 1998–9, and asked why the shift of the 'mobile centre' of his poetry from Birmingham to Derbyshire over the past couple of decades had not produced a 'move to something like nature poetry', Fisher replied:

> I don't think there's all that much of a transition. I live on a picturesque lane driven down through his tenants' fields by the 16th century Duke of Rutland/Lancaster/somewhere else anyway – let's call it Normandy – to get the coal down from his pits on the moor 400 feet above. The house is on a field labelled at that time 'The King's Piece of Glutton'. Over the wall is a small herd of heifers bred from bulls imported as frozen embryos; they're isolated because of ringworm. The BSE incinerator's two villages away. The skyline up the road is being shipped off to underlie the second runway at Manchester Airport. Dow Low rears above us, and I'll take the dog for a walk along the edge of its Drop when I've finished this. I don't know if that's an answer.[57]

If the green always entails questions of society and economy, and if English nature and English humanity are properly entangled, it probably is.

What then of Blake's own green, beyond the pleasant green familiar from 'Jerusalem' the song? Blake's poetry is a mixture of the succinct and sprawling, its variety in part the reason for its different adoptions. Blake can be read for a few lines catching an emotion, or for a complex cosmology demanding readerly immersion in a new language of Albion. Any *Blankety Blake* spin-off might have sailed smoothly through 'Chariots of BLANK', 'Tiger, tiger, burning BLANK', or 'did those feet in ancient BLANK', but would have foundered on 'Los took his globe of fire to search the interiors of Albion's BLANK', or 'While Los sat terrified beholding Albion's BLANK'.[58]

'Green' appears twice in Blake's 'Milton' preface, in the 'green and pleasant land', and in 'England's mountains green'. Green also colours Blake's *Songs of Innocence* (1789), where 'The Echoing Green' gives a spring poem of birdsong, bell chime and youthful 'sports', all 'On the echoing green'.[59] Old folk watch, recalling their own youthful joy, and day closes, the sun descending. Here is a joyful green, the old folk and the sunset signalling a natural cycle of play and rest. A mournful counterpoint comes in *Songs of Experience* (1793), in 'The Garden of Love', where the place 'Where I used to play on the green' is debased by a chapel and graves. Priests walk, 'binding with briars my joys and desires'.[60]

Blake's shorter lyrics thereby carry green variety, and a green English Albion also runs through the epic *Jerusalem*, written between 1804 and 1820, with over 4,500 lines. Subtitled 'The Emanation of the Giant Albion', *Jerusalem* tells of the fall of Albion, as giant and country, and his/its renewal and reawakening by Los, a hero Christ figure; Christ himself appears as 'the Shepherd of Albion'.[61] Jerusalem, featuring as both city and woman, also seeks England's redemption: 'The Fifty-Two Counties of England are harden'd against me/ As if I was not their Mother.'[62] The relatively straightforward sentiments of the 'Milton' preface 'Jerusalem' are amplified manifold, as mythic characters and actual places across England, Britain and beyond convey Blake's vision. This England is at once numinously local and a shining world exemplar, requiring only redemption from industrial, militaristic, mechanistic fall. Before, 'Albion cover'd the whole Earth, England encompass'd the Nations,/ Mutual each within other's bosom in Visions of Regeneration'.[63] The early twenty-first-century governmental 'Icons of England' pairing of Jerusalem and Stonehenge hardly holds here, with Stonehenge for Blake a symbol of a cruel Druidic religion: 'The Serpent Temples thro' the Earth, from the wide Plain of Salisbury,/ Resound with cries of Victims.'[64] Blake asks: 'O when shall the Saxon return with the English his redeemed brother?/ O when shall the Lamb of God descend among the Reprobate?'[65]

The verses of 'Jerusalem' the song are echoed in the simpler interlude sections of *Jerusalem*; the 'England! awake! awake! awake!' of 'To The Christians', quoted for Albion's 1960s children by Horovitz, and in 'To The Jews' where the Lamb of God runs with 'Jerusalem his Bride' on the fields of the unfallen London, 'Among the little meadows green'.[66] At *Jerusalem*'s conclusion, Albion awakes, takes his 'breathing Bow of carved Gold', his 'Quiver of the Arrows of Love' and 'The Druid Spectre was Annihilate'. If Parry's setting of 'Jerusalem' carries green English mystery into easily sung popular song, *Jerusalem* releases 'Visionary forms dramatic'.[67]

Blake's green meadows have been projected as English cultural ideal, but so too his images of the fallen Albion have carried forward, to shame a country no longer green and pleasant. Blake's woodcut illustrations to Thornton's *Pastorals of Virgil*, published in 1830 and an important reference point for twentieth-century engagements with an ideal mystic ruralism, included 'The Blighted Corn'.[68] The image illustrates a passage from Virgil where Thenot agrees with Colinet that he was born in a 'hapless hour of time . . . when blightning mildews spoil the rising corn, or blasting winds o'er blossom'd hedgerows pass, to kill the promis'd fruits . . .'.[69] Pastoral's ever-present downsides project through Blake, and his fallen Albion was invoked when late twentieth-century farming was diagnosed as a blight on England. When in 1984 Jonathon Porritt, Director of Friends of the Earth and a leading figure in the Ecology Party (later the Green Party), published his influential *Seeing Green*, the chapter on agriculture, asking 'if there are any in the Ministry of Agriculture to whom the Earth whispers its warnings', was entitled 'A Green and Pleasant Land'. Blake's phrase served as an indictment of a fallen present, and allusion to what was, and what might be again.[70]

William Blake, *The Blighted Corn* (1830), wood engraving on paper.

Green Varieties

This excursion concludes with an examination of the complex varieties within the Green, before selected cases of greenery indicate recurrent themes for the book.

As a title, *England's Green* could be taken as simple description, green a prominent tone across English landscape, from urban and suburban parks to rural fields. Pastoral farming regions hold their green: the rougher green of upland grazing, the smoother lowland meadow. Flying in or out of the country, depending on the airport and the line of approach, passengers emerge from cloud to sights in some way green. Description is, however, never simple and the assumption of a generally green country is undercut by local and regional variation, in parts of towns where trees have been cut down or in any predominantly arable countryside where the seasonal round shows brown ploughed soil, or ripening summer gold, either side of emergent spring crops or autumnal brassicas. The loss of hedges and hedgerow trees makes arable England less green in colour, and ecological critique labels such regions less Green in environmental value.

Description as ever shades into commentary and analysis, statements of colour wriggling into symbolism, and invoking claims to value, whether of intact beauty or diminished ecological quality. The excursion around the green undertaken in this chapter has sought to go beyond obvious environmental referents, to acknowledge the powerful alignment of the green and environmentalism while also noting other green associations, indeed other senses of the word. Peter Bishop's 1990 book *The Greening of Psychology*, a study of 'the vegetable world in myth, dream and healing', seeking to counter any clichéd view of 'greening', explored the green as a complex 'root metaphor of *a* way the world is experienced, valued, and perceived, as well as of *a* way that the world presents itself'. The words for green offered Bishop a starting point: 'Olive, emerald, moss, leaf, myrtle, ivy, avocado, lime, spinach, sage, lettuce, marjoram, sea, mold, and slime present us with both radically different hues and sharply contrasting metaphors.'[71] Cautious of a 'danger in the fantasy of "pure" green or greenness', Bishop offered varieties, of 'rural green', 'fresh green', 'green passion', 'green hope', 'deathly green', 'green envy'.[72] There were mixtures too, green whitened, blackened, purpled, blued, reddened and yellowed: '"Green" is a whole world, filled with subtlety, contrast and paradox.'[73]

Add the green of naivety, and the nauseous green around the gills, and England's green gains possibilities beyond the positively pleasant. And add also a green of projected alienness, of little green men, examined by John Agard in his 2018 poetic collection *The Coming of the Little Green Man*. Agard's outsider visitor from elsewhere navigates the peculiarities of London and England, unsure which identity box to tick ('Ticking Boxes'), entranced by greens from across the world in supermarket vegetable aisles ('Amidst a Multitude of Vegetables'), throwing settled assumptions ('In a world of the plural/ being green keeps one singular' ('A Case of Mistaken Identity')), and occasionally finding affinities, as when 'The Little Green Man Goes Pub Crawling', and settles for a visit to the *Green Man*.[74]

Three cases of English greenery close this excursion, one from the early twentieth century, two from the late, but all anticipating matters running through this book: the mysteries of the green, the playful green of leisure, and variants of green patriotism, ending in slime.

In *On Living in an Old Country*, his 1985 study of the past in contemporary Britain, Patrick Wright considers the interwar modernist fictions of Mary Butts (1890–1937), noting how for Butts green becomes a substantial marker of deep meaning, signalling a mythic country:

> 'Green', for example, is suddenly a world in itself; people walk around and stand on it, just as they breathe and swim in 'blue'. Freed, if this is the word, from any simply referential relationship to a close experience, 'green' becomes the very ground of an England of the mind.[75]

Butts's great-grandfather, Thomas Butts, was a friend of William Blake, and Blake's watercolours hung in Salterns, her Dorset childhood home; in 1800 Blake wrote a visionary poem 'To my friend Butts'.[76] Living at Sennen in Cornwall from 1932, Butts took gardening as a green art with a sacred tone, tending her bungalow garden as 'a nature sacrament with the flowers and the earth and the quickening sun'. Gardening was 'the way to certain basic contacts and knowledge; the entrance to the workshop of Nature and to her altar'.[77]

Green arts went, however, beyond the garden, Butts finding nature in general a site for green English mystery. In Butts's short story 'Green', first published in 1931 in the modernist magazine *Pagany*, characteristically well-off, unworking characters find themselves somewhere magical. Ambrose Alexander visits Nicholas and Nancy Loring on behalf of Nicholas's mother, who regrets her son's marriage, sending Ambrose to upset the arrangements: 'They took him out, a tramp across green, from green to green.'[78] 'Green' carries Butts's characteristic enfolding of setting and symbol, with the colour the chief totem, in a place marked by 'the very green', where Nicholas lives 'folded up in country-quiet'.[79] Nearby is 'a shut cottage on top and a garden with tansy in it, and herbs used in magic'.[80] Butts describes the view from the Lorings' house:

> They were looking out at a green plain which lay as far as the horizon on their left, and their house stood on the shelf of a grass hill beside the plain, tilted in the sunlight to another green. High trees stood about the hill, and a short way outside, across a lawn, a copse created its last bank. The plain had once been the sea, an estuary savaged with tides, now narrowed to a river, tearing at its flow and ebb; where all winter, for every hundred yards, a heron watched its patch. There was no dust: no sound but birds and air; no colour but green. There was every green.[81]

England's green haunts, enchants, colours a country numinous in its variety.

A different set of young people gathered the green in the towns of 1960s England. Iona and Peter Opie's 1969 survey of *Children's Games in Street and Playground* included, under 'Chasing Games', 'Dead Man Arise', also known as 'Green Man Arise'. The game was 'played in the Manchester area', and also in Jersey, where it was known as 'Green Man Rise-O'. For the Opies 'Green Man Arise' was 'the most sepulchral of the games in which a prostrate figure becomes the chaser', recorded also earlier in the century in London, Durham and Glasgow, and with 'a still more ritualistic version' in wartime Manchester, with girls skipping round a recumbent figure chanting to the 'Green lady'. The Opies concluded that here was 'an example, and not the only one, of a children's diversion being the enactment of an ancient horror story', citing in support a folkloric study from the 1919 *Journal of the Folk-Song Society*, featuring a green lady dancing in a basin of blood.[82] Author Annie Gilchrist had commented in 1919 on associations of green and bad luck, manifest in stories such as 'Jenny Greenteeth', where an evil water-spirit appeared 'as the green scum on stagnant water', and the 'Green Lady', a figure 'living on or delighting in, blood'. Gilchrist also discussed the death-themed ring game 'Green Gravel', the name 'possibly a confused memory of the gravel and grass of the grave'.[83] The Opies' 1960s version of 'Green Man Arise' had the dead or green man leaping up 'when least expected', rushing after 'those who have resurrected him, trying to touch one of them, and make him the dead man in his place'. Game preparation saw scenes of mystery in 1960s England: 'One player lies on the ground and is entirely covered with a blanket or cloth, preferably green, or with a pile of coats, or, as available, with grass or hay, or with sand if the game is played on the beach.'[84]

The Opies in general admired the recurrence of the ancient in the contemporary: 'Parties of schoolchildren, at the entrance to the

Raymond Briggs, Bogey garden, from *Fungus the Bogeyman* (1977).

British Museum, secretly playing "Fivestones" behind one of the columns as they wait to go in, little think that their pursuits may be as great antiquities as the exhibits they have been brought to see.'[85] *Children's Games in Street and Playground* also celebrated the wildness of play, the attraction of children to 'the wastelands', including surviving bombsites. The Opies satirized a trend for the contrivance of wild adventure:

> Having cleared away the places that are naturally wild is it becoming the fashion to set aside other places, deposit junk in them, and create 'Adventure Playgrounds', so called, the equivalent of creating Whipsnades for wild life instead of erecting actual cages . . . In the long run, nothing extinguishes self-organized play more effectively than does action to promote it.[86]

The Opies found wild England in places far from typically green, taking nature and folkloric values beyond the obvious.

Children of the 1970s, reading indoors rather than street-playing, could also get a green surprise. Raymond Briggs's *Fungus the Bogeyman*, published in 1977, presented an England refracted through the green, and a green anti-hero, in slimy skin colour and environmental outlook.[87] Briggs's underground world of Bogeydom entailed a comic inversion of landscape values. As 'Fungus cycles on through the Bogey countryside', he admires the contentment of the 'pattyman', gathering cowpats to stack in piles to mature, for use 'in the manufacture of Bogey Face Creams and Food Colouring'. Decorative pastoral ceramics are popular: 'The Old Cowpat Gatherer with his traditional "Patty Hook" has been immortalised in story and verse for over two hundred years in Bogeydom./ No Bogey mantelpiece is complete without a Muckenware figure of a Pattyman.'[88]

Fungus also tends his garden carefully, in a green art which helps things wither: 'Bogey gardening is a strange art./ Bogeys do not like flowers. They hate their bright colours and sweet scent. They love the fading greens and pale yellows of dying leaves. They love the smell of decay.' *Fungus the Bogeyman*, published in the Silver Jubilee year of 1977, stands as an autumnal hero, with his own musty patriotic air. Briggs pictures the bogey garden, with numbered features. Number six is a 'hodden' (midden), number five the quoits of a 'popular Bogey garden game' and number two a moss bunker to ensure a damp shelter in periods of dry weather. There is decorative care, with number four the 'Bordure' ('A border composed of ordure') and number three: 'Boglet. A small decorative bog as in a Bogey suburban dwine.' Here is a sweet-stinking Bogey/English suburbia, with on the brick wall a slogan: 'Putrefaction is the end of all that nature doth entend.' And over the garden, at number one, Fungus flies the Bogey flag, fixed on its rough pole and made of stone ("These are known as flag stones') so it doesn't rustle in an irritating manner in any breeze: 'Bogey Flags. Bogeymen are patriotic and many of them fly the national flag. This has no design or colours and is a plain muddy brown – symbolic of Muck, the Bogey Stuff of Life.'[89] England is green, and also muddy brown, Bogeydom a green England as if seen through the bottom of a murky glass.

Over the remaining chapters, *England's Green* explores an England variously and provisionally green, in its nature and weather, mysteries and folklore, and in the treatment of land. The variety in England's green is aesthetic, social and political, and the cultures of green English landscape find all three entangled. There is variety too in the intended audiences for green communication: readers and listeners, the niche and the mass, politicians and playgrounds, children and grown-ups. From gravel to slime, via poem and song, this introductory excursion around the Green has ended in suburban Bogeydom. From this one emblematic English landscape, the garden, the next chapter begins with another: the farm.

3
Life, Death and the Land

On 1 June 2022 the government estimated that 301,000 people in England worked on agricultural holdings, including 180,000 defined as 'farmers, partners, directors and spouses', and 67,000 'regular workers'.[1] A small minority of working people in England thus work the land, producing things basic to life within and beyond the country. Farming has often been presented, indeed promoted, as something fundamental, dealing in the basics, and this chapter examines how such fundamentals have been contested over the past six decades, with farming both challenged and defended for its ecological effects and its cultural value.

Visions of the Basics

Is England green, is farming green and what is the place of farming in a green and pleasant land? Visions of the basics of life, death and land run through the discussion: land and living on and off it; death in the killing of creatures, deliberately for food or as an effect, intended or inadvertent, of agrarian practice; life in the sustenance provided by land's products, and land's underground and overground ecology.

The second half of the twentieth century saw farming transformed, in England as elsewhere. Commentators have termed the change a 'Real Agricultural Revolution', with an 'almost unimaginable change in English agriculture', Brassley and others suggesting that if a farmer's son serving at Waterloo in 1815 had returned to farm at the outbreak of war in 1939, he would have 'known what to do'. If, however, he had returned at the time of the Falklands War in 1982, 'he would have been completely baffled.'[2] Scenarios of bewildered return, and related hopes and fears of transformation, have their own history in rural commentary, and one such vision from 1945 anticipated the twentieth century change. C. S. Orwin's *Problems of the Countryside* began by noting Washington Irving's Rip Van Winkle, a farmer falling asleep for twenty years in eighteenth-century America and waking astonished. Orwin, Director of the Agricultural Economics Research Institute at the University of Oxford, imagined 'a latter-day Rip van Winkle' falling asleep for sixty years in rural England in 1880 and waking to find things little changed.[3] Orwin argued that the country needed shaking from torpor, and concluded *Problems of the Countryside* by imagining another figure falling asleep in 1940 and waking 'a generation later'. Orwin foresaw a new English scene:

> The landscape, as it first greeted him, would show notable changes. While the appeal of the rural scene, always fresh to the country lover, affected him as strongly as ever, there was now a spaciousness and order about it which was new. The many awkward little fields, the pastures too often full of thistles and sometimes of thorns, the overgrown hedgerows and choked ditches, all were gone. The trim hedges enclosed larger fields, more of them were in crops of various kinds, and where grass appeared, it had the strength and vigour associated more with clover mixtures than with aforetime permanent pastures and meadows. There were no horses to be seen; all the field work in progress was being carried out by the agricultural tractors, which he remembered as just coming into general use. Some of the implements were familiar, enlarged to give full scope to the power of the tractors, but others were quite new to him. Everywhere there was the suggestion of technical changes, all of which seemed to promote a greater activity on the land.[4]

Farming is new, and renewed, and with it rural society and environment, with a younger population, new roadways, community facilities, new buildings, an 'air of order and efficiency', and 'live and progressive enterprise': 'There was vigour and activity about the place which it had never suggested as he remembered it, and he found it good.'[5]

Orwin's imagined English scene, projected a generation ahead to the 1960s, would be realized, yet not all commentators 'found it good'. Doubts would emerge over the ecological effects of new farming, notably via a technology not explicitly mentioned in Orwin's vision, the use of chemical fertilizers and pesticides to increase productivity. From whatever perspective, however, later twentieth- and early twenty-first-century disputes over life, death and the land proceeded from a sense that Orwin's vision of an improved England had triumphed. An examination of that vision as it was expounded after the Second World War is therefore required to set the scene for subsequent argument, and a tour through various sources – agricultural shows, television shows, magazines – follows, conveying the modern aesthetic and popular cultural resonance of an England of new farming. Reflections on life, death and the land over the past six decades departed from an England green, pleasant and modern.[6]

Today's Country

From 1966 the BBC, in its children's 'Watch with Mother' slot, broadcast *Camberwick Green*, made by Gordon Murray Puppets. Along with *Trumpton* (1967) and *Chigley* (1969), *Camberwick Green* was set in Trumptonshire, presenting stop-motion animation stories of village characters getting along, though with occasional tension.[7] Characters, each with their own rhyming narrative theme song, represented occupations – doctor, fishmonger, postman and so on – with some of them specifically rural. *Camberwick Green* had its farmer and its miller, representing contrasting rural visions.

Farmer Bell and Windy Miller, detail from the front cover of the 1970 *Camberwick Green Annual*, illustration by Harry McGregor.

Young viewers, myself included, could follow Farmer Jonathan Bell:

> A go-ahead farmer is Jonathan Bell, who works his farm and works it well. He doesn't hold much with the good old days, in modern times use modern ways. Electric mechanical, all that is new, which does the work that men used to do. He swears by it all and he proves it too, on his modern mechanical farm.

An admiring story of modern farming emerges. Pick-up trucks, fork-lifts, indoor-laying hens; efficiency, modernity, on which we all depend. Bell as modern farmer was taking care of the country. The farmer's friendly rivalry with Windy Miller contrasted the forward-looking and the traditional, Windy's free-range hens producing a few eggs to give to friends, his home-made cider headily local, his corn milled by the wind. The cover of the 1970 *Camberwick Green Annual* pictured Bell and Windy together, Windy wheeling a sack of his flour, Bell showing papers: perhaps a business note, or a handful of money.[8]

Both Bell and Windy can be viewed as 1960s figures. Windy, with his roaming hens, personal cider and wind-power, is in tune with natural rhythms, traditional tropes at one with an emerging 1960s counterculture. Bell loves machinery, produces eggs in bulk, a new farmer at home in a '60s world of white-hot technology. Both have catchy sing-along tunes ('Windy Miller, Windy Miller, sharper than a thorn'), but if the miller is the more eccentric and amusing, the farmer is no sense a villain, rather the embodiment of careful and caring efficiency. Bell may be a touch self-regarding, but is someone for children to admire, with his scale-model machinery akin to that with which a child might play when the programme ended, produced by a flourishing British model toy manufacturing industry. Robert Newson, Peter Wade-Martins and Adrian Little's studies of *Farming in Miniature* comprehensively document such scale models of agricultural England, finding 69 companies, including Britains, Corgi, Dinky and Matchbox, producing farming toys, the British toy industry dominating the world market for thirty years after the war.[9] Toys shadowed a farming industry flourishing economically with state support and technological modernization. Combines, tractors and accessory equipment shaped children's imaginations, just as they reshaped English landscape.

As 1960s infants watched Farmer Bell, juniors could read the educational magazine *Look and Learn*, whose March 1964 issue gave a

'Summer', detail of diorama from the Science Museum's former Agriculture Gallery, photographed by the author, December 2016.

'Allman High/Low Volume Sprayer', detail of diorama from the Science Museum's former Agriculture Gallery, photographed by the author, December 2016.

'Focus on the Farmer's Year'. The magazine front cover showed a boy and girl walking their dog across fresh stubble as a combine harvested wheat, the dog spying a foreground rabbit fleeing the machine. The issue's centre spread, showing 'a typical farm of the eighteenth century', a period itself seen to represent historic progressive improvement, was surrounded by vignettes of new twentieth-century technology: tractor ploughing, seed drills, mechanical milking, muck moving, beet harvesting, hedge trimming, harrowing, pea vining, baling, combine harvesting. The densely populated eighteenth-century field contrasts with contemporary solo operatives, working 'the indispensable machinery, all colours, shapes and sizes'.[10] Labour is saved, production smoothed.

Farmer Bell, and *Look and Learn*, echoed displays celebrating farming technology. From 1951 visitors to London's Science Museum could view the Agriculture Gallery, with displays of machinery, including tractors and a combine, backed by scale-model dioramas.[11] A wrought iron cyclorama by Ralph Lavers ran the length of the gallery showing progress from ancient Egyptian techniques through medieval England to a modern country of tractors and helicopter spraying. The gallery stood until 2016 as a time capsule of a post-war outlook, celebrating the new as in harmony with the old. Agricultural machinery companies donated the diorama models, many set in Kentish landscapes, the machine happily remaking the garden of England, enhancing rather than diminishing England's green. In the 'Summer' harvest diorama, a red McCormick International combine gathered the corn; a full-size Massey Ferguson red combine stood nearby in the gallery, with buttons allowing elements of machinery to be set in motion. One 1951 diorama showed a tractor-pulled 'Allman High/Low Volume Sprayer', modern chemical farming presented as in harmony with English landscape and with little sense of risk to labour. A man is seated, entirely unprotected, on an open Massey Ferguson tractor, trees in blossom nearby. Two figures watch from an arched stone bridge, technology as novel spectacle in traditional landscape: 'Allman High/Low Volume Sprayer. This tractor mounted sprayer is for the application of selective weed killers, insecticides or fugicides [*sic*]. The drift guard on the boom prevents damage to surrounding orchards, etc. Capacity 120 gallons; operating pressure 0–600 lb. per sq. in.'

Across England, modern farming was also celebrated at annual county agricultural shows, with their particular mix of pride in achievement, trading advertisement and popular entertainment. In the context of critiques of farming, county shows continue as affirmative events, enrolling the visiting public, although also, as Lewis Holloway notes, serving to 're-image' farming to farmers, whether encouraging new technology and/or sustainable practice.[12] Growing up in suburban Norwich, in the farming county of Norfolk, the annual agricultural Royal Norfolk Show, held at the showground at Costessey, just outside the city, had a significant local media presence and occasionally we went. I retain the programme 'Catalogue' from June 1975, listing the arena displays, the hundreds of stallholders and the animals exhibited.[13] Cows loom large in the catalogue and in the memory, a lasting recollection of the event being the sight and smell of white Charolais cattle. It was one thing to climb in a tractor cab, or watch the Royal Marines Motor Cycle Team, or see the Young Farmers Clubs' pageant 'Cavalcade of Post Office Communications', but cattle in a show tent were properly impressive. Here were the animals of a rural county, on show for a suburban child, whose grandparents might have worked the land, but whose parents went to the office. Goats and cattle were paraded, sheep were sheared, hunters rode, tractors were handled, while from the bandstand by the 'Grand Ring' a regimental band played 'Strawberry Fair', 'British Grenadiers', a Carpenters medley and an arrangement of Hot Butter's 1972 electronic hit 'Popcorn'. A fitting soundtrack, popular tunes invoking past, present and future, accompanied agricultural display.

Modern farming could also claim aesthetic value. While later critiques presented agricultural revolution as destructive of amenity, it is important to register the values of beauty communicated through agricultural displays or museum dioramas. In 1970, in *New Lives, New Landscapes*, landscape architect Nan Fairbrother reflected on 'The New Farming Landscape':

> But the new open farmland, if we cease to look at it nostalgically, has its own distinctive beauties, its very openness being one . . . In large-scale arable farming we are conscious too of the land, the earth itself. We can see the shape of the ground as we never can in small hedged fields, and in our rolling landscapes the modulations of the surface are in themselves beautiful.[14]

New Lives, New Landscapes put forward an evolutionary principle whereby humanity sought control over environment, with the formula:

'Landscape = habitat + man'.[15] Farming was one of Fairbrother's 'Landscapes for an Industrial Democracy', with an appealing rural modernism, a functional beauty. Fairbrother echoed fellow landscape architects Sylvia Crowe and Brenda Colvin in the appreciation of new technologies, captioning one image: 'Modern silo and barn – as at home in the landscape as the church they resemble.'[16] On hedgerow removal Fairbrother commented: 'fields as we know them will logically disappear, and "field" return to its original Anglo-Saxon meaning not of hedged enclosure but of open space . . . we can imagine future historians studying surviving areas of the old field-patchwork as we now study Celtic lynchets and the open-field system at Axholme.'[17] The scale and openness of new arable especially suited a landscape of travel, a scene to pass through in 'a valid twentieth-century experience of landscape': 'as on a roller coaster, actually *feel* the curve and moulding of the ground as we move across it.'[18] For Fairbrother new farming, far from destroying environment, offered an appreciative return to earth, in a land restyled for today.

In Fairbrother's new landscapes, as in agricultural Toyland, or in *Camberwick Green*, agriculture is no environmental villain. By the 1960s, however, the public image of the farmer was shifting, and in subsequent decades would be fundamentally recast, with significant implications for English landscape and its cultural value. By the end of the century a default position in mainstream public commentary was to present agriculture as a source of environmental problems and landscape destruction, and one of the prime targets was new farming's chemical nature.

Death by Farmer: The Chemical Country

The 1975 Royal Norfolk Show programme shows barely a trace of environmentalism. However in the far northeast corner of the showground, on Stand number 489, in the 'Sport and Country' section, the Norfolk Naturalists' Trust (NNT) promoted their work. Conservation shared display space with field sports; the NNT were next to the Nature Conservancy Council (Stand 490) and the National Trust (Stand 491), and just along from the Coursing Supporters Club (Stand 497). Stand 489 presented 'Vanishing Norfolk', the NNT (later renamed the Norfolk Wildlife Trust) appearing with walking groups, the Norfolk Society (the county branch of the Council for the Protection of Rural England,

CPRE) and the University of East Anglia Conservation Corps.[19] The NNT sought accommodation with landed interests, indeed since their foundation in 1926 had been a vehicle for conservationist landownership, but by the mid-1970s tensions were evident, with shooting banned on NNT reserves and concerns over new farming. The NNT's 1976 Golden Jubilee volume *Nature in Trust* concluded: 'Unless a new attitude towards the countryside can be developed and fiscal incentives introduced to help farmers manage their land with some regard for conservation, the prospects for wildlife are bleak indeed.'[20] The 'Vanishing Norfolk' stand also featured ICI Plant Protection Ltd, whose claims to make things vanish were displayed in a show catalogue advertisement, stating their products had treated the showground's display rings and lawns.[21] The prevailing tone of chemical technological solution had, however, been severely challenged by 1975. The NNT increasingly regarded nature reserves as islands in a sea of agricultural problems, and conversely the Norfolk Show could itself appear an island of agrarian self-confidence washed by waves of environmental critique, levels of concern rising.

Emerging chemical concern can be traced at a prominent 1960s conservation gathering, the November 1963 'Countryside in 1970' conference, held in London under the Duke of Edinburgh's patronage. Farming was one focus for debate. For some speakers, conservation needed to allow for agricultural change, Dudley Stamp, a key shaper of post-war rural planning via his role on the wartime Scott Committee, stating that 'new farming conditions must be accepted', with the 'agricultural worker of the future' becoming 'a man in a white coat': 'The rural scene, and the rural ecology, need not be greatly altered.'[22] Others, however, aired chemical anxieties. Dr J. S. Ash of the Game Research Association spoke against 'the extensive use of chlorinated hydrocarbon pesticides', recommending 'as a matter of great urgency that the more persistent of these chemicals should be withdrawn from use'.[23] The issue even prompted a rare recorded intervention by the conference president: 'HRH The Duke of Edinburgh referred to the tragedies which had arisen from the use of thalidomide and dieldrin and said it was disturbing to hear that scientists could not predict the deleterious effects of chemicals before they were applied extensively.' The duke 'questioned whether the system was entirely satisfactory in all respects', and in his closing speech noted: 'I spoke out of turn at the different meetings yesterday', but also: 'I have a slightly awkward reputation here, and I am glad of it.'[24]

It is notable that the most forceful chemical criticism at 'The Countryside in 1970' came from game interests, reflecting existing concerns over a threat to creatures nurtured for hunting and shooting.[25] In 1957 James Wentworth Day had issued *Poison on the Land: The War on Wild Life and Some Remedies*, a critique of new farming practice from one who would elsewhere write extensively on the virtues of landownership, upholding agrarian life as the foundation of English identity. The second half of *Poison on the Land* conveyed hearty reminiscences of shooting pheasant, partridge and 'the mystical woodcock', but the first half, alongside anxieties over myxomatosis, increasing rat populations, threats to hunting and river pollution, detailed 'chemical dangers' from the 'revolution in farming': 'Who wants the Britain of broad bright fields, of tall woods brilliant against gentle hills, of water-meadows and shining rivers where birds sing and animals gladden the eye to become a silent land where no wild life stirs? It is a nightmare vision.'[26] For Day, squire and gamekeeper had been replaced by 'a race of urban-minded scientists, chemists and agricultural executive committee bureaucrats. They are remote from the soil.'[27]

Day indicates one line of country critique of chemical farming. By the time of the 'Countryside in 1970' event, another evocation of a silent land had appeared, Rachel Carson's *Silent Spring*, published in the USA in 1962 and in the UK in February 1963. *Silent Spring* went far beyond game, presenting nature disturbed, chemical farming making for a season where no birds sing. As Sean Nixon notes, Carson drew on the British experience, her work 'rooted . . . within the trans-Atlantic networks of bird conservationists',[28] but *Silent Spring* was primarily an American account, beginning with 'A Fable for Tomorrow': 'There once was a town in the heart of America where all life seemed to live in harmony with its surroundings.' Carson's idealized small town America, fallen after 'a strange blight',[29] with familiar birds dying, found English echo-locations in Lord Shackleton's introduction to the 1963 British edition of *Silent Spring*. Shackleton, a geographer and Labour peer, offered a strange English country fable of mysterious fox deaths in 1959. Reports from near Oundle in Northamptonshire had sick foxes so bewildered as 'to be found in such unlikely localities as the yard belonging to the Master of the Heythrop Hunt'. This was the wrong way for a fox to die, consuming poisoned bird life: 'Then came the spring of 1961, when tens of thousands of birds were found littering the countryside, dead or dying in agony.' Incidents were reported in

45 British counties, chiefly in eastern and southern England. Shackleton highlighted a utilitarian 'agricultural Establishment' unleashing 'havoc in the fields', with poisons also prevalent in garden chemicals, 'even our gardens are becoming extremely dangerous places for wildlife.'[30] Julian Huxley followed Shackleton's *Silent Spring* introduction with a preface emphasizing the need for an 'ecological approach' to counter an 'exaggeratedly technological and quantitative approach': 'In fact, as my brother Aldous said after reading Rachel Carson's book, we are losing half the subject-matter of English poetry.'[31]

John Betjeman nonetheless made poetry from poison, reworking the hymn 'We plough the fields and scatter' into a lyric of dystopian England. 'Harvest Hymn', first published as a letter in *Farmers' Weekly* and issued in the 1966 collection *High and Low*, began: 'We spray the fields and scatter/ The poison on the ground/ So that no wicked wild flowers/ Upon our farm be found.'[32] Concern over pesticides had developed from the early 1950s, with a committee set up in 1951, chaired by Solly Zuckerman, reporting in 1955 for the Ministry of Agriculture, Fisheries and Food on the dangers of chemical use. The British state reflected on pesticides well before *Silent Spring*, although as John Sheail notes: 'It was not until the Food and Environmental Protection Act of 1985 that the statutory regulation of pesticides was attained.'[33] Monks Wood Experimental Station, established under the Nature Conservancy in 1960, provided a research focus, its first director Kenneth Mellanby authoring the 'New Naturalist' volumes on *Pesticides and Pollution* (1967) and *Farming and Wildlife* (1981).[34] The former, covering what Mellanby's editors called 'the hottest potato in the nature business',[35] identified 'persistent organo-chlorines' as 'the villains of the piece': 'It is difficult if not impossible to find a field in England which does not contain a detectable amount of pesticide, or a bird or mammal without residues in its tissues.'[36] Mellanby nonetheless concluded that 'pesticides are essential to British agriculture to-day, and without them our present farming pattern would disappear.'[37] Mellanby presented his topic as 'the way in which man is unintentionally contaminating his environment';[38] for many critics, however, pesticides were a deliberate and in effect uncaring route to profit, whether for chemical manufacturer or farmer.

The material nature of pesticides nurtured fears and anxieties, as substances visible when sprayed but afterwards invisible, with invidious environmental effects. By the mid-1960s around two hundred pesticides were in common use. Sheail notes how the deaths of seven agricultural workers from Dinitro-ortho-cresol (DNOC) poisoning between 1946 and 1950 helped prompt the 1952 Agriculture (Poisonous Substances) Act, with regulations requiring operatives to wear protective clothing.[39] The 1951 Science Museum diorama tractor driver, blithe to hazard, has no such costume. Pesticide stories, upbeat or downbeat, crucially became landscape stories. J.F.M. Clark describes how a May 1963 toxic waste spill at Smarden in Kent became a story of 'poison in the garden of England'.[40] Fluoroacetimide, produced for insecticide and rodenticide use, was accidentally released from a Rentokil factory, contaminating water courses and killing livestock, and raising human health fears. Just as Carson wrote as a biological scientist dissenting from the products of science, so in Smarden a prominent critical voice was local veterinary scientist Douglas Good, who wrote of the 'Smarden poisoning' in the Soil Association's journal *Mother Earth*, an account also broadcast on the BBC: 'The house-martins never came this spring, and there was no bird-song in the hedgerows. The only rabbits were a few young ones, picked up dead in ditches. The subject of Rachel Carson's book *Silent Spring* had become a reality here in the heart of the Garden of England.'[41] Fluoroacetimide was banned in 1964, with soil from the Smarden factory removed in cemented oil drums and dumped in the Bay of Biscay. Clark comments, 'a parochial waste spill in Kent became evidence for a nationally significant indictment of pesticides in the English landscape.'[42] English nature, and the English village, were traduced by new farming.

At Smarden the victims of poisoning included livestock, but wild creatures became the key focus for anxiety. Bird deaths were reported from 1956, pigeons dying mid-flight from consuming seed dressed with dieldrin, but one species became the focus of English attention, Shackleton noting in his *Silent Spring* introduction, 'The story of the peregrine is particularly significant.'[43] Work by the Nature Conservancy and the British Trust for Ornithology, originally prompted by a pigeon fanciers' campaign to control peregrines thought to be killing racing birds, identified a surprise population decline, especially in southern England but affecting all areas outside the Scottish Highlands. Nature Conservancy biologist Derek Ratcliffe's research highlighted peregrine poisoning from consuming organochlorine pesticide-infected prey, notably pigeons, with a related thinning of eggs leading to breakage in the nest: 'The wave-like spread northwards of decline coincides closely with the pattern of use of organic pesticides, both geographically and in time.'[44] Ratcliffe concluded: 'Future prospects for the species are extremely bleak. This is a completely new factor in the biology of the Peregrine, against which the bird appears to be defenceless.'[45] Helen Macdonald comments: 'Suddenly, falcon and human were fellow-sufferers of the industrial disease, both at the tops of their respective food chains, and the fate of the peregrine became a parable of the effluent society, an ominous foreshadowing of the fate of mankind itself.'[46]

The peregrine survived with the regulation of pesticide use. The bird's preference for cliff nesting led from the 1980s to its encouragement to nest on high buildings, whether cathedrals or office blocks, with platforms provided, monitored by telescope and nest webcam, wildness nurtured and scrutinized.[47] Not that urban falcons are entirely novel, indeed James Wentworth Day's 1935 account of urban wildlife was entitled *A Falcon on St Paul's*, beginning with the sight of a peregrine perched on the cathedral's golden cross.[48] The renewed cultural prominence of the peregrine has come not only via nest webcams, but through a literary rediscovery from its period of decline, J. A. Baker's 1967 *The Peregrine*, on tracking falcons in the Essex countryside: 'Hawk-hunting sharpens vision . . . A vivid sense of place grows like another limb.'[49] Baker is cherished for his wild subject matter, and the intensity of his attention, characteristic of a raptor nature-culture also informing works such as Helen Macdonald's *H is for Hawk*.[50] *The Peregrine* was republished, along with Baker's 1969 *The Hill of Summer*, and selections from his diaries, in 2011, as a touchstone for the emerging publishing genre of 'New Nature Writing', an introduction by Mark Cocker presenting Baker as 'the gold standard for all nature writing'.[51] Hetty Saunders's 2017 biography of Baker, *My House of Sky*, received a foreword by Robert Macfarlane, who provided an afterword to a fiftieth anniversary edition of *The Peregrine* in the same year, had also introduced a 2005 edition and had hymned Baker in his influential 2007 nature work *The Wild Places*.[52]

The Peregrine was presented by Penguin in the cover blurb for its 1970 paperback edition as a book which 'celebrated the English countryside', indeed the wider frame of geographical reference for Baker is always England, not Britain. This England is, however, a shadowed land: 'Few peregrines are left, there will be fewer, they may not survive. Many die on their backs, clutching insanely at the sky in their last convulsions, withered and burnt away by the filthy, insidious pollen of farm chemicals.'[53] Baker's 1971 essay 'On the Essex Coast', in the RSPB *Birds* magazine, evoked a spirit of wilderness on the Dengie peninsula: 'On the east coast of England, this is perhaps its last home. Once gone, it will be gone forever.'[54] Baker lamented chemical farming, the proposal for a third London 'Maplin Sands' airport (never built), and, by the sea-wall, found an oil-stricken red-throated diver: 'It is an atrocity, a stumpy victim of our modern barbarity . . . This bird died slowly and horribly in a Belsen of floating oil.'[55]

Sean Nixon notes that, for all Baker's image as a solitary autodidact (*The Peregrine*'s Penguin author blurb stated: 'He has no telephone and rarely goes out socially'), his work emerged from an amateur natural history culture of field observation, map work and publication.[56] This was no outsider art, Baker an active member of the Essex Birdwatching Society, formed in 1949 and with close ties to the BTO, although naturalists could be sceptical of Baker's observational claims, Derek Ratcliffe's 1980 monograph *The Peregrine Falcon* highlighting Baker's 'uncertainties on facts', 'artistic licence' and 'somewhat extravagant style'.[57] Baker's writing, notably its diary format (daily October to March records in *The Peregrine*, month-by-month from April to September in *The Hill of Summer*), also echoes English natural history convention, whether the late Victorian rapt observation of Richard Jefferies, or the journalistic country diary works of mid-twentieth-century East Anglian naturalist Ted Ellis, who interviewed Baker for BBC radio in 1968.[58] Baker's modernist poetic intensity makes *The Peregrine* a visionary poisoned pastoral, a sensibility echoed in the title of *The Hill of Summer*, a quotation from A. E. Housman's *A Shropshire Lad*. Housman's late Victorian poetry, and its English pastoral musical settings around the First World War, had come to stand for a doomed country. Baker has 'On the idle hill of Summer/ Sleepy with the flow of streams' as his book's epigram; Housman's original poem moves on to evoke the drums of war and soldiers marching to die, reverie overhung by sorrow.[59] The 1960s English landscape provides for Baker an equivalent experience; beauty remains, and his visceral eye tracks a vivid ornithology, but all is shadowed: 'I have tried to recapture the extraordinary beauty of this bird and to convey the wonder of the land he lived in, a land to me as profuse and glorious as Africa. It is a dying world, like Mars, but glowing still.'[60] Baker's elevation of Essex alongside Africa may be a sardonic allusion to the contemporary work of the World Wildlife Fund, whose post-colonial nature conservation is discussed below. Baker also anticipates themes of nature mystery, his naturalism presented as a quest: 'My pagan head shall sink into the winter land, and there be purified.'[61]

Uncaring Country

Betjeman's 'Harvest Hymn' also noted 'The twenty-four-hour broiler-house' as a new source of farming income, helping 'To line our purse with pence'; 'neat electric fence' provides the rhyme.[62] New farming also became a focus for welfare critique. The sense of an agriculture industrialized registered in the critical term 'factory farming', with animals presented as units to process and an implied severing of any emotional connection between human and beast.

The Science Museum's Agriculture Gallery had from 1965 included a dairy display: 'a full-size reproduction of an early nineteenth-century dairy complete with dairymaid, and in direct contrast . . . a full-size working demonstration of a modern milking parlour and dairy'. The Gallery featured a milking cow: 'it is mechanized, giving movement to the head and tail'.[63] For some, such upbeat conveyance of modernized animal husbandry did not give a full picture of the animal farm. On 18 January 1970 P. H. Reeve, secretary of the London-based Union of Animal Societies, wrote to the Museum's Keeper of Agricultural Machinery and Implements, Lesley West, finding the museum's animal agricultural displays 'no longer up to date' and 'seriously misleading'. Reeve asked for an impartial display, and by implication an exposure of factory farming:

> Over 90% of laying poultry are nowadays kept in intensive indoor conditions; virtually 100% of broiler chickens produced in this country are kept in battery cages. This industry is very large. Yet, you have no display of poultry units or of battery cages. The majority of pigs are kept in conditions very much more intensive than those shewn in your display. You show no veal calf units at all.
>
> We make it clear that we think you should impartially represent modern farming techniques. At the moment, we consider your displays more like a public relations exercise on behalf of ideal farmers. You show the conditions of a horse

The 'traditional farm', from Ruth Harrison, *Animal Machines* (1964).

'The new type of farm is like a straggling factory', from Ruth Harrison, *Animal Machines* (1964).

> in the last century. Do the chickens justice by showing the conditions of them in the latter part of this century. I should be pleased to come and discuss the matter with you.[64]

Reeve's comment on public relations indeed echoed West's own 1967 account of the gallery, published in the U.S. journal *Agricultural History*:

> Soon after the gallery was opened a representative of the Farmers Union, which at the time had just spent the equivalent of $100,000 in an attempt at educating the British public to the fact that farming was no longer a business that technologists might hesitate to enter, on seeing the new gallery, flatteringly expressed the view that the Science Museum had succeeded better on a smaller budget.[65]

J.G.S. Donaldson, Frances Donaldson and Derek Barber's 1969 account of *Farming in Britain Today* concluded that 'Factory farming is here to stay . . . What is required is a mental adjustment to factory farming which will permit of sensible control and safeguards.'[66] For the Donaldsons and Barber, 'too much of the protest was ill-informed and emotionally charged', but controversy over animal welfare, as over pesticides, showed farming to be an emotional matter, for all sides.[67] Factory farming's textual equivalent to *Silent Spring* was Ruth Harrison's 1964 *Animal Machines: The New Factory Farming Industry*, for which Rachel Carson provided a foreword: 'The modern world worships the gods of speed and quantity, and of the quick and easy profit, and out of this idolatry monstrous evils have arisen.'[68] Humans had no right 'to reduce life to a bare existence that is scarcely life at all', and Carson hoped for 'a consumers' revolt'.[69] Sydney Jennings, past president of the British Veterinary Association, used his preface to *Animal Machines* to draw human parallels echoing Baker's comment on the sea bird in a Belsen of oil: 'Already farming is being financed increasingly by shareholders who know little of what goes on in factory farms. It is relevant that after the Second World War millions of German people asserted that they knew nothing of what transpired in concentration camps.'[70] A holocaust blithely proceeded in the British countryside.

Animal Machines, informed by the organic movement on food production and diet, and as Harrison's biographer Claas Kirchhelle highlights, weaving together 'diverse environmental, moral and welfare concerns', led to Harrison serving on government advisory committees on farm animal welfare.[71] Harrison emphasized that *Animal Machines* was based in part on farm visits, rather than secondary reports, on her first page stating: 'Let me tell you about a visit to one of the more extreme units where veal calves were reared.'[72] *Animal Machines* highlighted battery and broiler chickens, intensively reared beef cattle, pigs, rabbits and veal calves, and raised concerns over food safety and effects on human health. In 'The new factory farming – a pictorial summary', 24 pages of photographs contrasted outdoor and indoor rearing. The opening picture showed a veal calf staring forlornly from a crate, before the next two images framed an English landscape argument. On a 'traditional farm', the location unspecified but landscape and building suggesting a rolling southern England, sheep graze, contributing to 'the visual pleasure of the countryside', and denoting 'a pleasant environment for the animals', the farmer recognizing 'the animal's rights as a living creature', livestock held in 'warm regard'. New animal sheds appear by contrast 'like a straggling factory. The buildings jar on the eye and rob the countryside of much of its charm.' Structures 'completely utilitarian' are run 'by people who are businessmen rather than farmers', the animal as 'an efficient food-into-flesh converting machine. With the increasing disappearance of animals from the countryside our children lose a very precious heritage.'[73] Outdoor grazing becomes a moral and aesthetic matter, *Animal Machines* a cultural argument for an English animal landscape.

A Stolen Countryside

From pesticides to battery farms, agriculture was cast in the 1960s as destructive of the countryside and of a particular green England. Through the 1970s and '80s this argument moved mainstream. The Countryside Commission's 1974 report *New Agricultural Landscapes* indicated the scale of transformation under way, revealing 'fresh and deeply disturbing facts about the nature and scale of changes taking place in the appearance of much of the English countryside'.[74] As a government agency the commission hoped that, with sound advice, 'new landscapes no less interesting' might still be the outcome, but others presented transformation only as destruction.[75] Patrick Cormack's 1976 *Heritage in Danger*, while chiefly focused on buildings, suggested 'The Countryside We Take for Granted' was threatened by 'the industry which largely created, and still largely controls, the landscape pattern of England: farming'.[76] Taxation and subsidy meant that 'The owner-occupier, who for generations has demonstrated a sense of true responsibility, is in danger of being transformed by the actions of the State from the guardian of our agricultural heritage into a potential enemy.'[77] Cormack's blame was sympathetic, suggesting a farmer only following state orders, but others were less charitable.

On 9 December 1984 *The Observer* indicated the mainstreaming of farmer critique by devoting its colour supplement to a 'Save Our Countryside' campaign, featuring 'country lovers' including poet Ted Hughes, green campaigners Jonathan Porritt and Edward Goldsmith, actress Susan Hampshire and Conservative MP Alan Clark. The issue was framed by two images, a photograph of the 'traditional landscape' of the Wye Valley, 'an idyllic rural scene', and an illustration by Richard Clifton of 'The Making of the New British Landscape': 'the march of high-tech farming, better roads and growing towns could erode our classic landscapes. Note the loss of trees and hedges to make way for large-scale arable farming (even the river banks are neatened to allow ploughing up to the water's edge).' A dual carriageway crosses the valley, a farm occupies hedgeless fields and new houses stand in regular rows, as do the conifers in plantation behind them. The image title alludes to W. G. Hoskins's 1955 *The Making of the English Landscape*, a foundational work of landscape history, the caption paralleling Hoskins's analysis of modernity erasing meaning: 'The individual features which have graced our countryside for generations are gone for ever.'[78] The new aesthetic is of clean-lined order, efficiency and rationality, much like Orwin's 1945 dream, but here representing a dream debased.

Farmer critique was crystallized in 1980 by Marion Shoard's influential *The Theft of the Countryside*. Shoard, who had worked for the CPRE for four years from 1973, set out a crime against Englishness, beginning: 'England's countryside is not only one of the great treasures of the earth; it is also a vital part of our national identity.'[79] A foreword by sculptor Henry Moore evoked 'the special quality of the English countryside' shaping 'English character' and 'much of England's art'.[80] For Shoard, 'our English countryside has given us such ideas as we have had of what paradise might be like,' cherished in town as well as country: 'our countryside has knitted itself into our idea of ourselves as a nation.' Shoard echoes John Fowles's 1964 appeal to a Green England pre-dating and persisting through modernity, but with a mournful twist: 'Our empire may have passed away; our industrial strength may be tottering; but the matchless charm of our countryside – that was ours before imperial power or economic hegemony, and it survived them. Until now.' The English landscape was 'under sentence of death', with the 'executioner' being 'the figure traditionally viewed as the custodian of the rural scene – the farmer'.[81]

The theft of Englishness by the 'new agricultural revolution' is itemized through data on loss, of hedgerows, water meadows, down and heath, flower-rich meadows, ponds, woods and wetlands. New farming is symbolized by a monocultural 'prairie' landscape: 'This new English landscape can offer little delight to the human eye or ear.'[82] Global comparison suggests a superior Englishness under threat: 'The kind of countryside we are getting is the kind in which the people of Kansas or the Central Asian steppes live without complaint. But those people were never blessed with the good fortune to experience the rural glory of our demi-paradise.'[83] Visible destruction is accompanied by less visible inorganic fertilizers and pesticides, with flora and fauna diminished. Government support schemes following the 1947 Agriculture Act become 'subsidies for destruction', 'in effect a tax on food', and delivered since 1973 via the EEC: 'everyone has forgotten that the original reason for boosting home production – fear of a blockade of imports – is no longer very real.'[84] Citizens were in effect funding the theft of their own identity via a 'feather-bedding of British farmers': 'The English countryside can be regarded as a vast tax haven.'[85]

Shoard argued that national park planning principles, 'one of the real triumphs of post-war rural planning', should extend to the rest of the countryside, with the balance of farming and conservation reset via 'direct, surgical measures to control the fate of the landscape, coupled with a shift in the distribution of power over the countryside'.[86] A year later the Conservative government's 1981 Wildlife and Countryside Act offered a legislative gesture to conservationist concern, but for Shoard and others this fell well short, agricultural and conservation groups polarized rather than aligned. The 1981 Act, influenced by the National Farmers' Union (NFU) and Country Landowners' Association (CLA), sought a voluntary approach to conservation through bodies such as the Farming and Wildlife Advisory Group, set up in 1969. Farmers and landowners asserted a stewardship role, worthy of assistance but not deserving statutory constraint; Graham Cox and Philip Lowe presented the Act as 'a success for the astute and carefully sustained lobbying of the NFU and CLA'.[87] The plans of government conservation agencies could conversely provoke agricultural anger, as when the Nature Conservancy Council informed farmers on the Somerset Levels in 1982 that their land was now part of a Site of Special Scientific Interest. Protests included the hanging and burning of effigies of NCC and RSPB officials.[88]

Shoard's theft charges were raised to murder in Graham Harvey's 1997 *The Killing of the Countryside*. Harvey, for twenty years agricultural story editor of BBC radio rural soap opera *The Archers*, cast modern farmers (Brian Aldridge would have been Ambridge's representative) as 'rural industrialists', with conservation payments to set aside land from production appearing ecologically absurd.[89] The audit of habitat and species loss in Shoard's work continues, as in the 2013, 2016, 2019 and 2023 *State of Nature* reports issued by the National Biodiversity Network, set up in 1997 through a consortium of voluntary and public bodies.[90] England and Britain present a paradox of coexistent nature love and nature loss, the membership growth of bodies such as the National Trust (over 5 million members) and the RSPB (over 1 million) accompanying dramatic loss of bird, insect and plant life, notably farmland birds. For Mark Cocker in 2018, such figures indicated a 'nature-obsessed nation' blithely unaware of ecological catastrophe: 'In the twentieth century, the British drained their landscape of wildlife, otherness, meaning, cultural riches and hope. Yet because it is central to our purposes and to our relationships with each other, we continue in denial.'[91] Cocker suggested that conservation bodies combine in a National Environmentalists' Union, equivalent to the NFU.

Concerns for wildlife are echoed in ongoing farm welfare argument, modern agriculture presented as denatured, whether in mid-1990s campaigns against live animal exports, with national publicity for direct action in January 1995 at the port of Shoreham in Sussex, or anxieties over Bovine spongiform encephalopathy (BSE).[92] 'Mad cow disease', 172,438 cases of which were reported in Britain between November 1986 and September 1998, appeared an outcome of unnatural feeding practices in animal husbandry. Until 1988 animal remains were recycled in ruminant feed, herbivores made carnivores, with potential for disease transmission to humans via beef consumption, and a concomitant loss of public trust in farming and government. British beef exports were banned by fellow EU countries from March 1996, with 2.6 million cattle culled in an attempt to restore consumer confidence and lift the export ban, which was removed in November 1998.[93]

Farming commentary spins across orbits; the morality of the natural, the beauties of scenery, the question of Europe. Farming becomes about more than farming, and Fintan O'Toole suggests that the BSE crisis, like other EU food stories, anticipated the Brexit debates of twenty years on. Visceral themes of food put fundamental dimensions of national identity on the table, whether the ostensibly trivial, as conveyed in what O'Toole terms the 'intuitive brilliance' of a 1991 Boris Johnson column on a notional EU regulatory threat to prawn cocktail crisps, or the substantive, as in the beef ban threatening farming livelihoods.[94] Iconically British/English foods were sent into political and cultural battle, feeding Euroscepticism, storing up protein of sorts for a future struggle.

English Property

Critiques of farming conduct could become critiques of property. Cocker, for example, noting a 'land-blindness' in conservation debate, labels farm subsidies 'a feudal system of transfer from the poor to the wealthy'.[95] Shoard followed *The Theft of the Countryside* with the 1987 *This Land Is Our Land*, which likewise combined data and emotion to question landed property, itemizing sources of landed wealth, the local, regional and national scales of landed power, and the difficulties of accessing information, with no public landownership register. For Shoard the 1981 Wildlife and Countryside Act had fostered a 'conservation protection racket', with landowners compensated for restraint; Shoard proposed environmental protection, development control, reformed subsidy and a rural land tax: 'Everyone now takes it for granted that the land is far too important to be left to landowners.'[96] Shoard's scope in *This Land Is Our Land* was British, but accounts of Scotland, Wales and Northern Ireland appeared departures from a generally English analysis, with land overwhelmingly in private hands, the aristocratic landowner still 'an extremely potent force' and 'untitled barons' powerful: 'Britain remains sharply divided between those citizens who own land and those who do not.'[97] Shoard identified 'two fundamentally opposed value systems', with landowners 'motivated by whims and aspirations reflecting the peculiar national experience of their breed. Three things obsess them above all: wealth, power and privacy.'[98] Major landowners appeared a 'secret club', privacy valued especially for 'bloodsports': 'A particularly British feature of the pleasure a landowner takes in his holdings is that it is a *private* pleasure.'[99]

Public pleasure in land demanded a general right of access, a right to roam, to restore a 'broken contract' made between landowners, state and public under the 1949 National Parks and Access to the Countryside Act, an argument Shoard developed further in *A Right to Roam* (1999): 'Most of Britain's countryside is forbidden to Britain's people.'[100] The Ramblers' Association organized an annual 'Forbidden Britain' day from 1988, with mass trespasses on selected properties, part of a political lobbying which produced a limited right to roam over the 'open country' of mountain, moor, heath, down and common land (around 10 per cent of England and Wales), under Labour's Countryside and Rights of Way Act 2000.

Shoard set present claims against a heritage of dispossession. As indigenous peoples in former British colonies challenged imposed systems of land ownership, might a parallel challenge emerge at home? The Norman Conquest holds a nine-hundred-year resonance, with 'land ownership by working farmers' usurped by a feudal 'ownership by conquest', shaping a 'landowning class' whose 'attitudes and habits' lingered: 'The enduring attachment of landowners to bloodsports is a striking example of this.'[101] The 1997 edition of *This Land Is Our Land* concluded with a millenial call:

> For the first thousand years after the birth of Christ the land of Britain was effectively in the hands of its people. The last thousand years have been a kind of dark age in which the people have been shunted into a landless wilderness while the few have lorded it over their space. Let us make sure that we take the present opportunity to regain our birthright. And to hold on to it for another thousand years.[102]

Shoard incites England to throw off the Norman Yoke, itself an agricultural image of humans as harnessed oxen. As Christopher Hill argued in his essay on the often radical political genealogy of 'The Norman Yoke', the theory posited:

> Before 1066 the Anglo-Saxon inhabitants of this country lived as free and equal citizens, governing themselves through representative institutions. The Norman Conquest deprived them of this liberty, and established the tyranny of an alien King and landlords. But the people did not forget the rights they had lost.[103]

Fowles's outlaw Green England offers one variant, Shoard's access plea another. The sense of a people denied their green birthright also shaped the fictions of Paul Kingsnorth, known for his ecological and political writings on a neglected *Real England*, who in 2014 published *The Wake*, a novel written in a form of Anglo-Saxon English, set around the Conquest.[104] Kingsnorth presents a band of 'green men' resisting occupation in a fenland setting echoing the story of Hereward the Wake in the Isle of Ely, with Buccmaster of Holland the equivalent hero. Kingsnorth sought to present through language 'the sheer alienness of Old England', yet also to register connection: 'The early English created the nation we now live in. They are, in a very real sense, the ancestors of all of us living in England today, wherever our actual ancestors come from.' For Kingsnorth, 'The Norman invasion and occupation was probably the most catastrophic single event in this nation's history,' and *The Wake* sought to awaken the contemporary reader to its legacies of land inequality: 'the effects of Guillaume's invasion are still with us.'[105]

Late twentieth-century land campaigners also mobilized civil war histories, notably of Gerrard Winstanley and the Diggers with their 'advanced proposals for land reform'.[106] The 1997 edition of Shoard's *This Land Is Our Land* carried a foreword by George Monbiot, writing as founder of the land rights group The Land is Ours, who in April 1999 reprised the Diggers' 1649 communal cultivation of St George's Hill at Weybridge in Surrey, now an area of golf course and luxury property, with a rally and subsequent occupation of land. A commemorative film was soundtracked by Billy Bragg's 1985 recording of Leon Rosselson's 'The World Turned Upside Down', with the earth asserted as, in Winstanley's phrase, 'a common treasury' and the song's title matching Christopher Hill's 1972 history of the English revolution.[107] At Weybridge, histories of protest underpinned a deliberately motley invasion of a tidied, moneyed country, aligned to the road protests of the same decade and setting out a language of occupation against enclosure that would be prominent in early twenty-first-century radical movements.

Investigations into English property continue. Guy Shrubsole's 2019 *Who Owns England?* echoes Shoard, in a post-devolutionary, post-map digitization, post-Freedom of Information Act analysis of England as a country where secrecy, enclosure, and private, public and corporate power entwine. Shrubsole finds the value of UK land increasing fivefold since 1995; finds 36,000 landowners, 0.06 per cent of the population, own half the rural land of England and Wales, and within this aristocracy and gentry owning around 30 per cent of England; finds area payment farm subsidies supplementing offshore wealth. Shrubsole's subtitle is *How We Lost Our Green and Pleasant Land and How to Take It Back*. Land reform, with land treated as 'a common good', might foster 'a progressive English identity that isn't based on xenophobia, nostalgia and grabbing land off Wales, Scotland, Ireland and the rest of the world'.[108]

A politics of land also informs assertions of the public view. The act of looking at landscape, whether entailing physical access to a territory or not, can signal collective affinity, emotional possession and the right to have a say. Such questions are heightened in images of denied access, yet also register where a scene grabs the viewer and the viewer takes emotional if not proprietorial hold. The language of seeing and possession, and its underpinning of class and gender inequity, has been subject to critique, yet the imbrication of looks and claims can also be turned to critical radical effect.

The sense that looking might register an interest characterizes the photographic work of Fay Godwin (1931–2005). In 1990 Godwin's collection *Our Forbidden Land*, winner of the first Green Book of the Year award, made the camera an instrument of access.[109] Godwin was President of the Ramblers' Association (RA) from 1987 to 1990, having been a member since the mid-1950s, and dedicated *Our Forbidden Land* to the RA. The book's title was a homage to the late Tom Stephenson, access campaigner since before the war and whose *Forbidden Land* had appeared posthumously in 1989.[110] Godwin's introductory essay set her work alongside Shoard's, and within campaigns against footpath and moorland closure, loose bulls and aggressive farm dogs, militarized landscapes, transport policy, the commodification of heritage, pollution, water privatization, the nuclear industry and intensive forestry and farming. Godwin stood in favour of organic food and a

Freedom of Information Act, for an openly sustainable country. In 1985 Godwin's collection *Land* had carried an accompanying essay by John Fowles, who suggested a form of ecological genocide was under way in rural England: 'we have let scientific agriculture, or agribusiness, perform with its poisons and (idiotically so called) grass enrichers what we would call, in a human context, a holocaust.'[111]

Godwin's *Our Forbidden Land* photographs showed looking as a transgressive act, at once highlighting barriers and seeing beyond them to an accessible future. At Brassington in Derbyshire Godwin shoots especially detailed signage, forbidding climbing, camping and shooting without permission, and instructing ramblers to keep to paths. A sheep looks over the wall as if puzzled at the attention. Godwin's accompanying text described an amateur photographer facing a landowner at Rainster Rocks, the distant focal point of her image, demanding that they remove their film: 'he didn't want any publicity or any more people coming to his rocks. If he had his way, there wouldn't be any ramblers there at all.'[112] Godwin offers photography, and interested looking, as an act of defiance. *Our Forbidden Land* quoted G. S. Phillips's 1848 book *Walks around Huddersfield*:

Fay Godwin, 'Brassington, Derbyshire', from *Our Forbidden Land* (1990).

> Beauty is a kind of property which cannot be bought, sold or conveyed in any parchment deed, but it is an inalienable common right; and he who carries the true seeing eyes in his head, no matter how poor he may otherwise be, is the legitimate lord of the landscape.[113]

As in Wordsworth's formulation of the Lake District as 'a sort of national property', a phrase which became a touchstone for the national parks movement, there is a notable qualifier on the 'true seeing eyes', on ways of seeing. Phillips's legitimate lords have the capacity to see rightly; for Wordsworth it was those who had 'an eye to perceive and a heart to enjoy'.[114] Godwin's photography might shape true seeing eyes, opening up the publicly, properly viewed.

The politics of beauty and its viewing was also articulated in the 1980s by Fraser Harrison, whose *Strange Land* (1982) and *The Living Landscape* (1986) questioned ways of seeing England.[115] Writing of his home patch around Stowlangtoft in Suffolk, Harrison asserted the right to a view, his ordinary, everyday perspective over English fields as legitimate as those of their legal owners. Harrison identified a form of emotional ownership to be valued, rather than dismissed as sentimentally detached:

> I do not work on the land, or own any of it, or play any part at all in the processes which shape it. Yet I am not a tourist, and I belong to this patch of countryside as surely as the earthiest farm labourer . . . I am no different from the great majority of my neighbours, who are not farmers either.

If a lack of influence over surroundings risked turning viewers into 'voyeurs' ('We can only look on helplessly'), Harrison claimed the rights of a resident observer: 'For although nature may, in the strictest sense, belong to nobody, the countryside, which is an entirely social and cultural concept, belongs to everybody. In short, it may be their land, but it is *our* countryside.'[116]

Agrarian Voices

Or is it? From the 1990s the critique of modern farming received an organized, mobilized retort.[117] What Michael Woods terms 'the strange awakening of rural Britain' combined sociology, ecology, culture, politics and economics in claiming the countryside as something agrarian.[118] Ideas of a rural idyll were critiqued as leisure fantasies, ideals of working community were upheld and a distinctive rural voice claimed. And just as the treatment of animals had shaped farming critiques, so the animal was central to the rural retort.

In 1995 the Countryside Movement was launched, with former Liberal leader David Steel (MP for a rural Scottish Borders constituency) as Chair, projecting rural interests as under threat and with a particular focus on hunting. In March 1997 the Countryside Movement merged with the Country Business Group and the long-standing British Field Sports Society to form the Countryside Alliance. Woods notes how this rural lobby reflected in part the disturbance of Conservative hegemony in rural England, the BSE crisis leading farming groups to feel betrayed by a Conservative UK government as well as by the EU. Anti-hunting campaigns thus met a landed and farming lobby slipping its accustomed political moorings.[119] In June 1997, a month after a new Labour government took office, Labour MP Mike Foster sponsored a private member's Wild Mammals (Hunting with Dogs) Bill to ban hunting. Fisher's Bill was filibustered out at the report stage, but hunting would take seven hundred hours of parliamentary time between 1997 and 2004. Between December 1999 and June 2000 the Burns Committee of Inquiry into Hunting with Dogs in England and Wales reviewed the matter, and in July 2000 a government bill to outlaw hunting with dogs was issued. Commons-Lords conflict followed, with the Parliament Act eventually invoked to overrule Lords' objections, the ban becoming law in February 2005.

Pro-hunting campaigns articulated an agrarian England against the proposed ban. The first London Countryside Rally took place on 27 July 1997, with over 120,000 people in Hyde Park, and a Countryside March followed on 1 March 1998, 250,000 people moving through central London. A further planned march in 2001 was cancelled due to the outbreak of foot and mouth disease, but in September 2002 the Liberty and Livelihood March attracted 400,000 people, converging on Whitehall and Parliament Square. Beacons were lit across the country in advance, a gesture of both celebration and warning, the country put on alert. Protests asserted agrarian rurality over a counter-urbanized countryside, and an urban interest presented as distanced and arrogant. The National Trust and CPRE did not support the protests, the sociological pitting of rural against urban matching neither their principles nor their membership. Placards urging resistance to the 'Urban jackboot' were distributed at the Countryside March by *Horse and Hound* magazine, wartime imagery called up to project dictatorship onto a governing class priding itself on liberalism and cultural openness, the banning of hunting on the grounds of animal welfare and rights styled an illiberal act against rural humans. Some freedoms were upheld, others rejected; the Countryside Alliance opposed Labour's proposed Right to Roam.

The flags of the Countryside Marches were varied, with the Union Jack alongside Scottish, Welsh and Cornish flags, and the flag of St George. Britain, and England, were lined up against a governing class seen as unable to speak for the nation, without any affinity with tradition and fixated on the new. As public spectacle the Countryside Marches worked in counterpoint to the Millennium Dome, two London spectacles representing two national visions, with only one deemed a public relations success. As the Dome spectacle, associated with professional public relations, disappointed, the Marches' carefully staged authenticity cut through, people and their animals released onto London streets to impressive effect, whether the effect was to cheer or repulse. The sense of the country coming to London, to 'town' in the sense of the city as a site for an occasional visit, was key. London became an open space where argument might be noticed, with corporeal distinction evident in the crowd's comportment (restrained, polite, leaving no litter) and in the presence of dogs and horses, those companion animals which also participated in the hunt.

A placard at the front of the 1997 Countryside Rally carried G. K. Chesterton's line from his 1908 poem 'The Secret People': 'We are the people of England, that never have spoken yet'. 'The Secret People' is a poem of stoic grievance, presenting a voice unheard by the governing class since Norman times.[120] An anti-hunt reading of the Countryside Marches could be that here were groups historically far from powerless, who had never needed to speak up because their power had never been challenged. The placard, however, implied a people taken for granted and finally moved to anger, an England overlooked and nursing a grievance that other cultures in the UK (whether longstanding or recently migrant) received affirmative attention. Woods notes a new 'mood of defiance and belligerence' at the 2002 Liberty and Livelihood event, echoing militant activities such as the Countryside Action

Network blockading motorways and promoting civil disobedience, and the Real Countryside Alliance placing a papier mâché huntsman on the Uffington White Horse and a 'Love Hunting' banner on the Angel of the North on Valentine's Day 2003.[121] On 15 September 2004 eight men invaded the House of Commons to disrupt parliamentary proceedings, with Otis Ferry, son of singer Bryan and Master of the South Shropshire hunt, a leading player.[122] Militancy in part reflected splits within the rural movement. As the Countryside Alliance broadened its remit, some saw the pro-hunting message diluted. The Real Countryside Alliance, organized on a cell basis and with its name echoing dissident Irish republicanism, placed stickers with a green union jack logo on rural road signs. English landscape was marked with signs of a differently Green movement. The militant Farmers for Action, set up in May 2000, played a key role in the fuel price protests of September 2000, prompting a sense of crisis in a modern economy and panic in the state. Direct action more commonly associated with French agriculturalists, indeed sometimes evoked in that context in anti-European commentary, was transplanted cross-Channel.

Countryside rallies promoted field sports and national identity as somehow connected, with hunting a performance of Englishness, contentious throughout its history around issues of class and cruelty, though for some accruing in the twentieth century a charm of anachronism. Opponents too mobilized longstanding English questions, going back to the Conquest. For George Monbiot in 2004: 'By taking on the hunt, our MPs are taking on those who ran the country for 800 years, and still run the countryside today. This class war began with the Norman Conquest. It still needs to be fought.'[123] Class, like animal welfare, could be invoked to polarize, hunting becoming a matter for social as well as moral absolutism. Allyson May, however, notes complexities, notably of gender, undercutting traditional stereotypes of the hunting man. By the 1950s half of the typical hunting field were women, with by the late 1970s around seventy female Masters of Foxhounds, a significant minority; there were 175 packs in 2000.[124]

Garry Marvin, in his pre-ban anthropological analyses, conveys foxhunting as cultural performance, in the formalities of the event, unwritten etiquette, dress and vocabulary, sights and sounds, and 'the cultural elaboration of all the animals involved': 'the Hunt openly and deliberately announces itself in the countryside.'[125] Marvin suggests hunting converts the countryside into a green 'sacred space' for its adherents.[126] The sacred green is echoed in Roger Scruton's 1998 *On Hunting*, mixing autobiography, philosophical reflection and polemic in defence of something authentically English and personally redemptive. Of his initial encounter with a hunt while riding in a country lane, Scruton reflects, 'I was also discovering England.'[127] Here was 'a piece of England which was not yet alien to itself . . . And I wanted to join.'[128] Scruton hunts with the Beaufort and the White Horse, but as an academic philosopher never fully belongs, can never be one for whom this is an authentic taken-for-granted element of life. Anti-hunting is for Scruton a sentimental and majoritarian outlook, while hunting celebrates ordinary English country, with property and enclosure as the basis of good landscape. Scruton also invokes a Heideggerian sense of care as '"ahead-of-itself-Being-already-in as Being-alongside". And that, more or less, is what it feels like, jumping hedges on Barney.'[129] Hunting becomes the practice of conservative philosophy. Scruton buys his first hunting gear from Enoch Powell, whom he struggles to converse with at a dinner until hunting comes up, whereby shared love animates Powell, who sells Scruton his now-unused costume. The coat is torn on Scruton's first hunt, but Being-alongside Enoch ('one of the few politicians for whom England was still the centre of the world'), even falling to earth alongside Enoch, brings fulfilment.[130]

Marvin, scrupulously non-judgemental, conveys how landscape is 'not merely a stage or setting for the event' but rather 'essentially constitutive of foxhunting', which helps explain why foxhunting continues post-ban.[131] The Hunting Act of 2004 banned the hunting and killing of wild mammals with dogs, though exempted the use of two dogs to flush out quarry to be shot. The latter in effect allowed hunting to continue in all aspects except for the hound kill, a full pack being permitted to follow a scent trail. In 2000 there were 175 packs; 250 hunts met on Boxing Day 2005, 314 on Boxing Day 2006. Hunting as social activity was paradoxically boosted by its legal abolition. If the fox was given protection, and the nature of hunting thereby in one visceral sense diminished, appeals to the authentic in human experience were extended. The English landscaped performance proceeds, in defiant mood. Hunting despite the ban is likely to continue, though the ban is set to stay. Repeal of the 2004 Act, the restoration of what for its proponents would be hunting's full phenomenological truth, would demand a government, likely a Conservative one, to judge it worth parliamentary time and the risk of alienating a significant part

Watchtree Farm,
Cumbria,
March 2004.

of the electorate, to put forward legislation. Conservatism, even of the 'one-nation' variety, might paradoxically shy from legalizing an activity deemed of national significance by its proponents.

Alongside hunting and BSE, the cultural status of agrarian England received a further twist through the 2001 outbreak of foot and mouth disease, which prompted public sympathy rather than a polarization of opinion. Foot and mouth was detected in Essex on 19 February, with outbreaks across the country by the end of the month.[132] The EU imposed an export ban on British livestock, meat and animal products on 21 February, and the countryside went into a form of quarantine, with events cancelled, tourism restricted, footpaths closed and 7.7 million animals culled. Cremation pyres and burial sites became landscape features. Smoke rose from small piles of burnt carcasses, while mass graves facilitated bulk disposal. In the heaviest affected county, Cumbria, the former wartime airfield site at Watchtree Farm, Great Orton, between Wigton and Carlisle, was utilized for burial and later converted to a nature reserve. A memorial stone, 'The Watchtree Stone', itself an exhumed glacial erratic boulder, was placed at the perimeter, with an explanatory plaque:

The Watchtree Stone
taken from this ground
A Symbol
To the birth of
Watchtree Nature Reserve
Dedicated on this day the 7th May 2003,
the second anniversary of the final burial.
A Memorial
To 448,508 sheep, 12,085 cattle, 5,719 pigs
buried here during the
Foot and Mouth outbreak of 2001
'The tree of everlasting life takes the goodness
from the soil to sustain new beginnings'

The burial may be mass, but the figures are precise, creatures individually itemized. Visiting a year after the stone's dedication, the view was of plain grass, but in a few years Watchtree reports detailed amphibians, butterflies, dragonflies, birds, moths and bats, while hares became the reserve's signature species, life gambolling over the grave.[133]

The management of foot and mouth in part set agricultural interests above the interests of tourism, and argument followed over the economic importance of different sectors, notably in upland areas such as the Lake District. Cumbria contained 44 per cent of infected premises, with Devon the next English county on 8.7 per cent and North Yorkshire 6.6 per cent. For Woods, foot and mouth marked 'the end of farmer exceptionalism in government', with the Ministry of Agriculture, Fisheries and Food abolished and replaced by the Department for the Environment, Food and Rural Affairs (DEFRA) after the election of June 2001, the department's title pointedly not including the words 'agriculture' or 'farming'.[134] If however agriculture's political claims were undermined, in other senses farming gained public support. The diminution of tourist access during foot and mouth heightened the sense of a farming community under siege and in peril, sacrificing their flock under government order in a fight against disease. From the funeral pyres rose public sympathy, in part as this was a sector of the farming industry not conventionally associated with substantial wealth. If pesticide arguments had often focused on arable farmers and the profits of so-called barley barons, foot and mouth highlighted farmers with less income and fewer prospects.

From 2001 onwards the animal rather than the arable carries increasing prominence in agricultural discourse, in hunting rallies, yet also in other landed stories. If the Countryside Alliance made the London streets their stage, the London theatrical stage also got in on the act, seeing performances conjuring the rural and the animal, in dramatizations of farming plight such as Nell Leyshon's *The Farm* (2002, set on a Somerset farm declining post-BSE), Richard Bean's *Harvest* (2005, on a hundred years of life on a Yorkshire Wolds farm), Bea Roberts's *And Then Come the Nightjars* (2015, set on a Devon farm during the foot and mouth outbreak) and Simon Longman's *Gundog* (2018, set on a disease-stricken sheep farm).[135] Performance sometimes brought the animal on stage, whether in furs and skins or corpses, a visceral if not living presence. Livestock and hardship, groundedness and struggle, a care for the animal whose breeding and killing sustained livelihood; here were farming narratives neither idyllically pastoral nor especially critical of subsidy. The emphasis on the animal rather than the arable – on the stage, in foot and mouth reflections, on Countryside Marches – asserted an agrarian authenticity, an unsentimental country, raw not cloying. In 1995 an early Countryside

Movement full-page newspaper advertisement had presented a photograph of 'George Roberts, Head Slaughterman and Animal Lover': 'the reality of food production involves both life and death.'[136] The country ideal becomes a working farm, livelihood rather than wealth, and with a handy and humane local abattoir.

In the twenty-first century agrarian culture has been given notable public expression in the writings of James Rebanks, whose bestselling 2015 book *The Shepherd's Life* conveyed a working Cumbrian country, bringing together the agricultural and the conservationist in distinctive fashion.[137] *The Shepherd's Life* is subtitled 'A Tale of the Lake District', telling of an unstoried part of a heavily storied region, unappreciated where amenity and ecology are prioritized. By 2015 Rebanks was already a public voice, having a monthly column in *Cumbria Life* and 30,000 Twitter followers as the 'Herdwick Shepherd', having begun tweeting in January 2012. *The Shepherd's Life* tapped an expanding market for nature writing, but steered such readers into agrarian territory, critical of those who ignored working human lives: 'No one who works in this landscape romanticizes wilderness.'[138] Rebanks tells a family story, of farming generations over six hundred years, with land in Matterdale bought by his grandfather in the 1960s. Discovering literature after leaving school at fifteen, taking A-levels at twenty-one, going to Oxford University to study history and then returning home, undertaking non-farm work, including a role as expert adviser to the UNESCO World Heritage Centre in Paris, and finally building a farmhouse on Racy Ghyll Farm, where his children grow, the generational story ongoing. The book was adapted by Chris Monks as a play, premiered at Keswick's Theatre by the Lake in March 2017.

The Shepherd's Life is organized chapter-by-season, summer to spring, detailing the hard practicalities of sheep farming, with an introductory essay entitled 'Hefted'. The word refers to the ability of sheep, especially the local Herdwick breed, to know their part of the fells, to wander circumscribed, but here implies a parallel human quality, people knowing their patch through practical routine. For this particular group, the land is ours, proprietorially and emotionally. Rebanks details the practicalities of sheep farming; solitary or communal shepherding, sheep sales, prize shows, early morning feeds and inspections, no days off, the land and the sheep coming first. The literary landscape of the Lakes, including that conjured by such a self-consciously down-to-earth figure as Alfred Wainwright, is presented as excluding

'Herdy', souvenir toy purchased in Keswick, spring 2016.

history's 'nobodies', 'the forgotten people'.[139] A few authors though come into alignment with Rebanks; W. H. Hudson, whose 1910 *A Shepherd's Life* told of Wiltshire shepherd Caleb Bawcombe ('This book, in all its glory, was about us');[140] John Clare, whose critiques of enclosure lamented the loss of a common freedom which for Rebanks persisted on the northern fells; and Beatrix Potter, who of the Lake District writers had most respect for farming and shepherds. Rebanks begins with Wordsworth's passage from his *Guide to the Lakes*: 'Towards the head of these Dales was found a perfect Republic of Shepherds and Agriculturalists,' and *The Shepherd's Life* presents a good life clinging on in Matterdale.[141]

Wordsworth's republic of shepherds was one touchstone for the Lake District's successful bid for World Heritage Site status, awarded in 2017 on grounds of 'cultural landscape'. The Lakes were granted universal value from a combination of factors; centuries of pastoral farming continuity, the birth of romantic landscape appreciation and the invention of modern conservation.[142] Versions of English pastoral cohabit, not without tension, in Lakeland world heritage; workers of pastoral farms, pleasure seekers escaping the city, defenders of landscape beauty and ecology. Rebanks acknowledged UNESCO colleagues for helping him 'to understand why stories and rooted identities matter, and what a "cultural landscape" really means', and he supported the Lake District bid.[143]

When Lake District World Heritage chose a brand symbol, it echoed Rebanks's Herdwick persona. Herdy, a smiling plain-drawn sheep face, with associated cuddly toys, presented the Herdwick breed as Lakeland icon. On his Matterdale farm, Rebanks raises pure-bred Herdwicks, having restocked with the breed after foot and mouth, and he tweets as herdyshepherd1. The face of world heritage is hardy and agrarian, properly hefted, and in toy form cute and loveable, a souvenir for play and for reflection.

Good Living

Proponents and critics of the new farming of the post-war decades invoked a good life on the land; the efficient production and distribution of food, or a more natural alternative to chemical agriculture. The 'good living' examined in this section of the chapter, emphasizing work from the 1970s, considers appeals to tradition, philosophies of 'natural' and organic farming, connections of natural food and health, and experiments in land work, all forms of 'complex nostalgia' long associated with the rural, and persisting into the twenty-first century, as identified by Dominic Head in relation to the farming fictions of writers including Melissa Harrison and Sarah Hall.[144] As modern agriculture was critiqued from the 1960s, alternatives to the present were explored.

Alternatives to the Present

In 1977 Shirley Toulson's *Discovering Farm Museums and Farm Parks*, number 229 in the Shire Publications 'Discovering' series, reviewed a recent upsurge in farm museums, offering displays different to the Science Museum's Agriculture Gallery. National collections such as the Museum of English Rural Life in Reading, set up in 1951, had been supplemented by exhibits reflecting specialist interests or private passions. Thus the Riber Castle Fauna Reserve in Derbyshire showed rare breeds, a Mr Smith showed a private collection of vintage tractors near Boston, Lincolnshire, and another Mr Smith curated farm tools in Charlbury, Oxfordshire. A call to Mr R. S. Enticknap of Milford, near Godalming, Surrey (phone number provided), would allow a viewing of his threshing drum and binders. Toulson's gazetteer listed 114 sites in England, sixteen in Scotland, eight in Wales, one in Northern Ireland, two in the Isle of Man. Entries catch an emerging farm heritage culture, within and beyond the museum. At the King William pub in Ipsden, Oxfordshire, 'the landlord, Brian Penny, has covered the walls and ceiling of his bar with hand tools of various types,' while the beer garden showed wagons, carts, ploughs 'and a completely restored steerage seed-drill. These objects nearly all come from the surrounding area.'[145]

Toulson captions one photograph: 'In the Rev. Philip Wright's collection is this Maltese plough, made to be drawn by a woman and of the same pattern as the ard of the late stone age.'[146] Wright, in clerical garb, holds the plough. A woman holds the chains as if to pull, a smart check coat worn for the photograph. Neither smile, but then this is serious historic demonstration, not a piece of costume re-enactment. Toulson's gazetteer listed 'Philip Wright's Collection of Bygones' at Roxwell, near Chelmsford in Essex. Wright, a Suffolk farmer's son, had 'worked with many of the old implements': 'The exhibition is arranged in three huts containing respectively agricultural hand tools, farmhouse and dairy implements, and horse gear.'[147] Wright was a notable contributor to an emerging heritage publishing industry, his books including *Traction Engines* (1959), *Old Farm Implements* (1961), *Old Farm Tractors* (1974) and *Salute the Carthorse* (1971). Wright helped found the National Traction Engine Club in 1955, serving as president, and also acted as commentator at the annual Easter London Harness Horse Parade.[148]

As farming modernizes, interest in historic farming emerges in counterpoint, for some a fondly remembered sign of the world we have progressed from, for others a traditional indictment of the present. In 1967, in *Pesticides and Pollution*, Kenneth Mellanby, commenting on conservationist lament for weed loss after herbicide use, had stated, 'there may be a case for a "museum" farm where bad husbandry is practised to allow weed species to perpetuate themselves, but it is obviously unwise to try to persuade farmers to encourage weeds in their crops.'[149] Ten years later Toulson suggested:

> The 1970s may well go down in history as the time when town dwellers returned to the countryside, with an upsurge of interest in the traditional production of food, and with a nostalgia

> for those simpler years when the energy used in farming was supplied by men, horses and oxen.[150]

From the late 1960s, visions of good living, around food production, food consumption and attempts to sidestep the system, take as their point of departure a sense that modern agriculture is awry. Scrutiny of the 1960s and '70s shows a new counter-modern English landscape of food and farming, which continues to shape twenty-first-century debates over good living.[151]

English Organics

Environmentalism gave new energy to the organic movement, which from the 1930s had presented itself as offering an alternative, though not a museum, English farming landscape. Organic production indeed shaped a key environmentalist text, E. F. Schumacher's 1973 *Small Is Beautiful*, meeting 'small' criteria of human scale, decentralization and the local, with techniques akin to those intermediate alternative technologies Schumacher promoted in non-Western contexts.[152] Like the organic movement, Schumacher could mix the radical and conservative, seeing for example in the medieval concept of the Great Chain of Being lessons in hierarchy as well as interdependence. From the 1950s Schumacher worked as an economist for the National Coal Board in London, but lived and gardened on four acres in the Surrey countryside, practising organic cultivation, joining the Soil Association in 1951, helping found the journal *Resurgence* in 1966 and becoming Soil Association President in 1971. *Small Is Beautiful* presented industrial agriculture as anti-natural, denying life through mechanical process, part of a wider environmental crisis whose solutions were spiritual rather than technical.[153]

In its cultural politics the organic movement could appear at once dissident and establishment, personified in the role of Charles, the former Prince of Wales, who from 1985 converted the Home Farm of his Highgrove estate in Gloucestershire to organic production, and whose organic food brand Duchy Originals, set up in 1990, combined the alternative and the conservative for commercial effect. The prince styled himself as 'dissident' in his environmental views, as in his architectural interventions, challenging orthodoxy to reassert a balanced order. Philip Conford suggests that emphasis on the distinctiveness of a new 'Seventies generation' of organic activists, and their associated claims to radicalism, may play down continuities with the organic movement's earlier conservative history, although new organicists seldom shared the social conservatism, Christian philosophy and sometimes politically far-right politics of the movement's founders in the 1930s and '40s.[154] Some older figures however retained a presence, with Lady Eve Balfour, in effect the founder of the Soil Association in 1946 after her 1943 book *The Living Soil*, taking on the presidency after Schumacher's death in 1977 until 1982. Balfour remained active until her death in 1990, though less influential after the Soil Association's 1985 move from her base in Haughley, Suffolk, to Bristol.

Key early figures such as Rolf Gardiner and Gerard Wallop (who also wrote as Viscount Lymington and the Earl of Portsmouth) also remained active, both showing the shaping of English cultures of landscape by global connections, pursuing agricultural interests in post-war Africa in a kind of organic parallel to the wildlife conservation work of the World Wildlife Fund. Wallop moved to Kenya after the war, acting as government advisor and buying a 10,000-acre estate, and when this was nationalized at independence, he advised the new Kenyan Ministry of Agriculture.[155] Gardiner wrote in the journal *African Affairs* in 1958 on his family tea and tung oil plantations in Nyasaland, which became Malawi on independence in 1964. For Gardiner, soil-conservation efforts could counter laissez-faire exploitation and maintain social order: 'A demoralised rural proletariat squatting on denuded, impoverished land: is there drier tinder for agitation and revolt than this?'[156] In 1961 Gardiner helped host a British Council-sponsored visit of twelve African farmers, active in African Farmers' Unions in Nyasaland and Rhodesia, to England, staying on farms in Yorkshire and the West Country, including Gardiner's Dorset estate at Springhead, in a form of transcontinental interracial agrarian exchange: 'The Africans have been warmly welcomed as civilised countrymen passionately concerned with land . . . Working alongside such practical people and sharing their meals and table-talk made the Africans feel truly at home in rural England.'[157]

For Conford the shift in editorship of the Soil Association's journal *Mother Earth* in 1963 on the death of Mosleyite Jorian Jenks, editor since 1946, to the liberal Robert Waller, marked a 'significant change'.[158] Waller, also involved with the *Ecologist* magazine, remained editor until 1972, after which *Mother Earth* was renamed the *Journal of the Soil Association*. Waller sought to emphasize ideas of human ecology, and the diminished agricultural labour force in modern farming, reduced by around two-thirds between 1949 and 1980, meant that small-scale, more labour-intensive organic producers could be presented as a re-peopling of the fields.[159] From 1972 the Soil Association had defined its own organic food standards, with an associated product symbol, and would shape the 1987 UK Register of Organic Food Standards.[160] From the early 1980s the Soil Association became more commercially focused and public-oriented, joined in the organic movement by new organizations, the Organic Growers Association (1981) and British Organic Farmers (1982); the three bodies would merge in the mid-1990s. Consumer concern for food quality increased the urban demand for organic products, which gained a presence in supermarkets (first in Safeway in 1981), its products gradually becoming mainstream rather than eccentric. In 2006 the Organic Growers Alliance was formed in response to a sense that the Soil Association had itself become too commercially oriented, Conford commenting that 'a paradox is perhaps discernible in the fact that members of the counter-culture helped make organics part of the mainstream of the capitalist market system from which they once tried to escape.'[161] In 1984 the organic movement reached *The Archers*, Tony Archer converting his farm, a seriously minded, non-eccentric radio soap character marking the organic as something not strange.

In what sense was the organic movement of the later twentieth century English as well as Green? The earlier movement prided itself on being about, in the titles of two key works, *England and the Farmer* (edited by H. J. Massingham, 1941), and *England Herself* (by Rolf Gardiner, 1943).[162] In the later movement English nationalism was overtaken by a concern for an England whose distinctiveness derived from being a place of localities, with organic production setting local origin at a moral and financial premium, products trumpeting location. Conford notes that in 2008, when the Soil Association held a celebrity fund-raising dinner, they called it the 'Feast of Albion', with menu by River Cottage chef Hugh Fearnley-Whittingstall and products sourced within 25 miles of London's Guildhall.[163]

Gardiner died in 1971, but his later work continued to indicate the complexities of organic England. Gardiner addressed the 1965 'Countryside in 1970' conference (a follow-up to the 1963 event noted earlier), promoting farming as 'a National Service', if 'biologically sound', while in April 1969 the Epsom Soil Association heard his lecture 'Is England being poisoned?'[164] Before his death Gardiner, who from 1963 had coordinated with German colleagues a European Working Party for Landscape Husbandry, left a synopsis for a contracted book on 'England, Europe and the Land'. As Andrew Best notes in a 1972 anthology of Gardiner's writings: 'The book was to have offered a policy for agriculture and the landscape for the Common Market countries, and would have shown the relevance of the English experience to Europe.'[165] Jefferies and Tyldesley reflect on whether Gardiner, with all his sometimes controversial history, stands in the early twenty-first century as, in Patrick Wright's term, an '*eminence vert*'.[166] After Gardiner's death Schumacher, a friend from the mid-1960s, encouraged his widow Marabel to establish the Springhead Trust to further his ideas. The Trust still manages Gardiner's former Springhead, Dorset, home as 'a rural centre for creative and sustainable living', with patrons including Jonathon Porritt and Gardiner's son John Eliot Gardiner, organic farmer and conductor, his musical practice pioneering the use of period instruments to render historic sound in authentic form, echoing his father's preoccupation with cultural authenticity.[167] In 1957 Gardiner wrote of a musical tour of Hesse, including John Eliot and fellow future-conductor Roger Norrington, the Springhead group sharing English polyphony and country dance with their German hosts, and acquaintances renewed from pre-war visits: 'I danced, twice through, the Morris jig "Ladies Pleasure", with which I had first greeted Goetsch in 1926.'[168]

Gardiner's late work also connects the landed and the countercultural, via one of the less familiar variants of postmodernism. The organic movement is, always, about more than crops and livestock, and in his Harvest Thanksgiving sermon in Cerne Abbas church in Dorset on 6 October 1968, Gardiner warned of the exhaustion of Creation by resource exploitation in an artificial, mechanized 'discarnate' world.[169] Gardiner projected a different future, 'the Post-modern age, which will be different, and based on laws of true sanity and thrift': 'the Aquarian or post-modern Age of man the gardener and husbandman, watering the earth with the gift of the Holy Spirit'.[170] Gardiner's 1970 company report on his family's Malawi tea and tung oil estates, which had received backing from President Hastings Banda for a catchment plan for peri-urban development, claimed: 'The Aquarian Age of husbandry and the Holy Spirit will dawn in Africa.'[171] At the dawning of the Age of Aquarius, organic England might anoint the world.

Taste and Place

Visions of the good life also entailed a geography of food, whereby localized production and consumption denoted quality, health and taste. An organic emphasis on the biological quality of food was set against modern chemical placelessness. As with critiques of farming, however, it is important to acknowledge the aesthetic and moral arguments within as well as against progressive positions. Just as Farmer Bell offered a joyous sense of productive efficiency in contrast to Windy Miller's crafted cider and eggs, so proponents of modern consumption found delight as well as profit in convenience. Alternative and mainstream consumption make relational sense, and discussion of the work of two public figures from the same generation, prominent through the post-war decades into the 1970s and beyond, can illustrate the cultures of taste and place.

The public voice of chemical, placeless nutrition was Magnus Pyke (1908–1992), biochemist and food scientist.[172] Pyke, who had worked on nutrition for the wartime Ministry of Food, became a public figure in his retirement from industry. After becoming secretary of the British Association for the Advancement of Science in 1973, and appearing from 1974 on Yorkshire Television's science programme *Don't Ask Me* (and its successor *Don't Just Sit There*), Pyke became a fixture on adult and children's science television, caricatured as an arm-waving eccentric but also a figure of knowledge; he was awarded Expert of the Year by the BBC's Saturday morning *Multi-Coloured Swap Shop* in 1977–8, matching its presenter Noel Edmonds's combination of earnestness and eccentricity. For Pyke, the popularization of science involved the promotion of new food technologies, and scepticism over alternative methods. In popular scientific writings such as *Townsman's Food* (1952), *Food and Society* (1968) and *Man and Food* (1970), Pyke emphasized that 'life is a chemical process', normalizing the deployment of chemicals in food production, in contrast to the organic movement's biological focus.[173] Pyke envisaged the new geography of a well-fed world:

> the tendency of advancing technology is for a larger and larger proportion of the human race to move from the countryside and congregate in towns. And in such towns, in whatever part of the world they may be, citizens expect to be able to obtain the same processed foods, the same canned meat and fish, the

> same products of the great processing plants which already distribute their goods world wide. It is my contention that this expectation is a reasonable one and will, in fact, be fulfilled.[174]

The security of global sameness offered an opposite geography to the organic ideal of local wholefood variety. Pyke's organic counterpoint in outlook and persona was Doris Grant (1905–2003), active in the organic movement from the 1930s and publishing from the 1940s to the '70s. Grant set female domestic wisdom above corporate science, with her own easy-to-make, no-knead 'Grant Loaf' wholemeal bread at the heart of good eating. Amy Whipple notes how as a middle-class housewife Grant both personified the target of convenience food and styled herself as leading the resistance to it. Grant, active in the anti-state British Housewives League, pursued a conservative reassertion of the active domestic authority of women, yet also anticipated 'anti-establishment activism'.[175] Whipple concludes that for Grant, 'baking organic, wholemeal bread was . . . a political act directed at both the modern food supply system and the powerful elite that had allowed such a system to emerge in the first place.'[176] Grant's 1958 *Housewives Beware*, written against the 'chemical assaults' on food 'from the soil to the table', was dedicated 'to all the Saint Georginas who having read this book will help slay The Chemical Dragon'.[177] Hope was at hand: 'The Organic Movement is gaining momentum all over the world. "Free of all chemical additives or contaminants" will be the biggest selling point of a food in the future.'[178]

Some of Grant's 1958 examples of 'Food for Health' would not be out of place in an alternative store a decade or two on: yoghurt, sunflower seeds, watercress, oatmeal ('preferably straight from the mill . . . Also obtainable from Health Food Shops'), brown rice ('From Health Food Shops'), mung beans, dandelion coffee, rosehips and brazil nuts, 'specially recommended because they are still produced without the help of fertilizers and poisonous sprays. Nuts are best eaten raw. Although more digestible when cooked, says Dr. Dudley Wright, they tend to be rather constipating.'[179] The family resemblance of Grant and alternative wholefoods indicates how the radical counterculture of the late 1960s and early '70s carried strains of conservatism, whether in its affection for certain pasts or its prescriptions for present conduct. Freedom carried strictures.

On 13 January 1976, on BBC1, the vogue for wholefoods, nutty or otherwise, received popular satire. Mike Leigh's *Nuts in May*, an English Regions Drama production in the *Play for Today* series, and watched by 9.5 million viewers, featured Roger Sloman and Alison Steadman as Croydon couple Keith and Candice-Marie Pratt, camping near Corfe Castle in Dorset in search of something natural, in a comedy of middle-class manners; Keith is a social services pensioners' holiday organizer, while Candice-Marie works in a toyshop.[180] The suburban comedy *Abigail's Party*, also starring Steadman, would follow in 1977, another of what Andy Medhurst terms Leigh's 'indigenous tragicomedies', exploring 'the horrors and humours of being English'.[181] Keith and Candice-Marie's landscape and campsite activities echo contemporary commentaries on leisure, but with added countercultural themes, all filtered through Keith's organizing principles. Keith explains the virtues of unpasteurized milk, which they buy in their health food shop at home, to a dairy farmer, who finds his analysis 'all bollocks'. Health regulations prevent purchase, but they find some from an accredited herd nearby. In an echo of Grant's advice, Keith insists that nuts should be chewed 72 times for proper digestion, and the couple lecture a fellow camper on vegetarianism; the suburban party snacks of *Abigail's Party* would symbolize other claims to cultural distinction via food. On the campsite tensions grow over someone playing pop radio, Keith and Candice-Marie's acoustic banjo and guitar singalong not counting as equivalent noise, before all erupts over the lighting of an irregular fire. Keith loses control of the terms of freedom, as their good life, their healthy alternative, is stymied by others. The Pratts leave the site and end up pitched in the dairy farmer's field, without facilities, alone together. Candice-Marie sings an anti-pollution song as Keith walks off, spade in hand, to find a natural toilet. One of Leigh's later, bleaker films was entitled *Life Is Sweet*; the concluding motto of *Nuts in May* could be 'Life Is Shit', although Keith would point out that excreta is a part of the circle of life, and if processed and deployed correctly can be invaluable in encouraging new growth.

Broadcasting The Good Life

The conservative and countercultural met also in a figure central to 1960s and '70s commentary on good living. John Seymour (1914–2004) grew up in Essex, worked in southern Africa, served in wartime in Sri

Lanka, where he admired peasant life, and became a writer and broadcaster. Seymour admired organicist writers including Massingham and L.T.C. Rolt, providing an introduction to Rolt's 1947 philosophical *High Horse Riderless* on its reissue in 1988.[182] Like Schumacher, Seymour embraced Roman Catholicism in later life, attracted by the Distributist thought associated with early twentieth-century writers such as G. K. Chesterton and Hilaire Belloc.[183]

After marrying potter Sally Medworth in 1954, Seymour settled in rural Suffolk in a remote long-lease low-rent estate cottage. *The Fat of the Land*, illustrated by Sally, describes the Seymours' attempts at self-sufficiency, 'living in the highly civilised county of Suffolk very much as if we had been cast up on a desert island'.[184] The Seymours get a cow, pigs and a horse, gather wild food, and rear chickens, geese and ducks. Stock is cared for and killed: 'We are not vegetarians.'[185] The book is part memoir, part advice guide, part generator of writerly income, presenting a move 'from an industrial to a peasant economy', generating resource resilience: 'If the rest of the world blew itself up tomorrow we could go on living quite happily here and hardly notice the difference.'[186] The theme of local life continuing, whatever global change might come, also hints at a possible mode of life for England after empire, of self-sufficiently surviving without dominating others. Earlier imperial experience frames Seymour's organic English life: 'I had spent most of my life in Africa, where there was always a nice African man to do anything I wanted doing.' Now 'unfamiliar jobs' had to be learnt, and done.[187]

In a 1973 afterword, 'Thirteen Years After', Seymour linked self-sufficient prospects to challenges of land acquisition: 'I would like to start a society, the object of which would be to find out *who owns England* and then to make the ordinary Englishman take an interest in the ownership of his country.'[188] Seymour envisioned a differently settled land, in ten-acre plots, generating more food and life than any monocultural agribusiness, a 'diverse countryside, of orchards, young tree plantations, a myriad small plots of land growing a multiplicity of different crops, farm animals galore, and hundreds of happy and healthy children'.[189] By 1973 Seymour had moved to Pembrokeshire, helping establish the West Wales Soil Association group in 1975, countercultural back-to-the-land philosophy having a strong presence in West Wales. In 1973 Seymour also published *Self-Sufficiency*, followed in 1976 by *The Complete Book of Self-Sufficiency*. Seymour reflected that when they were in Suffolk, 'we were probably the only family in England living in this way,' but many had followed: 'Of course nearly all hippies have as part of their philosophy the ideal of becoming self-sufficient. Few of them have achieved it as yet because they cannot tear themselves away from their guitars long enough. But many of them have had a try.'[190]

Self-sufficiency might have remained a specialist lifestyle interest were it not for a situation comedy, the first point of reference for the phrase 'The Good Life' for many who lived in 1970s Britain. *The Good Life*, first broadcast in 1975 and written by John Esmonde and Bob Larbey, took self-sufficiency as its plotline, indeed helped make Seymour's *Complete Book* a bestseller. The show title puns a surname, Tom and Barbara Good pursuing self-sufficiency in the south London suburbia of Surbiton, Tom quitting his draughtsman's job with enough to live on, a mortgage paid and their garden a decent plot. The Goods' neighbours, Tom's ex-work colleague Jerry Leadbetter and snobbish wife and self-styled community pillar Margo, are puzzled but sympathetic. The four characters, played respectively by Richard Briers, Felicity Kendal, Paul Eddington and Penelope Keith, dominate a comedy of neighbourly friendship.

What could have been a comedy ridiculing suburban daftness became instead a sympathetic portrayal of a couple dropping out of conventional work but remaining in their suburban home. The Good garden sustains two adults (there are no children), with vegetables, pigs and chickens, a goat and a cow. Over three years and four series, with the 1977 Christmas special viewed by 21 million, *The Good Life* made self-sufficiency a common term among millions who would never contemplate it, but who could admire an ethos of growing your own, making and mending, caring for each other, dropping out without offending and living more sanely than the suburban norm. The suburban setting made the comedy; a village setting would have made for different humour. Suburbia also allowed the radical and the conservative to intertwine. The Goods turn their world upside down, but with relatively little disorientation. Self-sufficiency in Surbiton is incongruous, yet garden cultivation attends to the land beneath suburban homes, denoting a different kind of domestic care, less concerned with appearance (whether in the look of house and garden or the dress of its residents) than practical worth, and with its own aesthetic of scruffy charm, personified in the contrasting looks of Tom and

Jerry, Barbara and Margo. Homespun appeal deepened the home's emotional and indeed financial ties. Occasional minor tradesmen characters consistently empathize with the Goods' working wisdom, not the Leadbetters' superior airs. Departure from employment frames a programme which celebrates graft, as suburban land is put to work. Nobody in Surbiton really drops out. *The Good Life*, founded on a radical gesture, offers an ultimately conservative fable, a not uncommon blend in 1970s environmental commentary, as the next chapter of *England's Green* explores.

Where England Has Landed

From Farmer Bell to *The Good Life*, from the chemical to the organic, England since the 1960s sees varieties of food-producing greenness. For some the newest technology shapes a green and pleasantly productive land. For others the green nature of the country is traduced by its landed custodians. Different visions of the basics, of life, death and the land, broadcast across country and town, and informed by narratives of past farming, have shaped English agriculture.

Farmer Bell went on his efficient way in a country which had tried but failed to join the European Economic Community. From 1973, however, arguments over English farming were also arguments over European farming, with the UK agricultural sector falling under the Common Agricultural Policy, with its initial aim to increase production. The post-war transformation imagined by Orwin in 1945, and celebrated by the mainstream farming community, continued with EEC membership. Emergent environmental critiques of the revolution in farming were deepened by a sense of EEC productivist excess, symbolized by European butter mountains and wine lakes. As production targets were exceeded, surpluses became fabulous in public commentary; fabulous in their supposed extent, and in their narrative qualities. Here were fables of excess in the wealthy world while others starved, and/or fables of excess at the expense of a denuded environment, all gathered into the styling of farming as counter-natural, whether in its treatment of animals or land. Alternatives to the present were put forward, and a countercultural world of wholefoods and organic philosophy gained mainstream purchase.

And then Farmer Bell's descendants find themselves outside the EU. From 2016 agricultural policy gained the potential to move in different directions, and other possible English and UK futures opened up, if not independent then entailing new kinds of interdependence. As with other aftermaths of Brexit, clarity has taken a while. Despite policy documents, white papers and new visions, at the time of writing things are not wholly resolved. The aftermath of 2016 has perhaps seen an exponential growth in sentences including the phrase 'at the time of writing', and if you add in 'at the time of editing' and 'by the time of publication', prediction from an unclear present seems futile. All that can be gone on are government statements made since 2016 which, if present or future governments do not take another path, indicate possible futures.

The Common Agricultural Policy made land one area where departure from the EU had very clear implication, making significant change possible, if desired. With agriculture a devolved matter within the UK, agricultural and environmental policy statements from DEFRA, initially under Secretary of State Michael Gove (2017–19), sketched out a greener Brexit England. Farmers would receive public support not for their size of landholding but for the production of public goods, a category including environmental benefits, with environmental schemes an underpinning philosophy rather than an optional bonus. The Agriculture Act 2020, receiving Royal Assent on 11 November, stated: 'In England, farmers will be paid to produce "public goods" such as environmental or animal welfare improvements.'[191] Doubts remained as to whether food and animal welfare standards might be compromised in future international trade deals, the aims of one part of government potentially stymied by the actions of another.

The language of the Agriculture Act was green, with Environmental Land Management (ELM) schemes 'a mainstay of future support'.[192] DEFRA's November 2020 'Agricultural Transition Plan 2021 to 2024' outlined *The Path to Sustainable Farming*, with the three components of ELM being the 'Sustainable Farming Incentive', 'Local Nature Recovery' and 'Landscape Recovery'. DEFRA presented ambitious aims by 2028 for 'a renewed agricultural sector, producing healthy food for consumption at home and abroad, where farms can be profitable and economically sustainable without subsidy', and with 'farming and the countryside contributing significantly to environmental goals including addressing climate change'.[193] Introducing the sustainable path, the then Secretary of State George Eustice ('My family have farmed in West Cornwall for six generations'), who would relinquish his role in the political chaos of summer 2022, set out a vision which in effect inverted Orwin's 1945 generational prospect, noted at the start of this chapter, while still claiming aspects of modernity. Progress in a post-Brexit environmental age would entail a different English country:

> In this moment of change, where, for the first time in fifty years, we have a chance to do things differently, we should think through from first principles what a coherent policy actually looks like and chart an orderly course towards it.
>
> Over the last century, much of our wildlife-rich habitat has been lost, and many species are in long-term decline. I know that many farmers feel this loss keenly and are taking measures to reverse this decline; but we cannot deny that the intensification of agriculture and the bureaucratic Common Agricultural Policy have taken their toll on wildlife. To address this, we need to rediscover some of the agronomic techniques that my Great Grandfather might have deployed, but then fuse them with the best precision technology and plant science available to us today. I am confident that the changes set out in this document will help us deliver for nature.[194]

Eustice hoped that 'a decade from now the rest of the world will want to follow our lead.'[195] At the time of writing, the leadership qualities of the UK remain in doubt, and trade deals remain to be negotiated, but another country will emerge, on transition's other side.

4
English Nature

A young woman emerges from a lake, hair lank, hands open, inviting a question: *How Do You Want to Live?* The unnamed woman was photographed by Lord Snowdon, the cover image for a Department of the Environment report on 'The Human Habitat', prepared for the June 1972 United Nations Conference on the Human Environment.[1] Imagery akin to a progressive 1970s LP cover comes to Her Majesty's Stationery Office.

Inside, beyond the foreword by Secretary of State Peter Walker, the contents page and the commendation by the committee of authors, is Philip Larkin. 'Prologue', printed over a black-and-white prospect photograph of the ICI chemical works on Teesside, is an early version of Larkin's poem 'Going, Going', written in January 1972. Larkin gathers pollution, mass leisure and speculative development to suggest a country sold for pleasure and profit, England the 'first slum of Europe', with 'filth in the sea'. The auctioneer title of 'Going, Going' suggested inexorable trajectory, the final hammer-down word appearing at the penultimate verse, 'And that will be England gone.' The England going is one of lanes and meadows, guildhalls and 'shadows', a dappled world contrasting with the stark clarities of modern life. English landscape here carries an ecological burden, and any faith in the sea's capacity to take our waste diminishes, with 'doubt' over the cleanliness of the tides. Will earth still respond, 'However we mess it about'? Perhaps 'it isn't going to last'? England and nature, or at least the nature to which we have become accustomed, is going.

The poem's final verse begins 'Most things are never meant,' and ends 'I just think it will happen, soon.'[2] The trajectory echoes Larkin's 1977 poem of death, 'Aubade', with its line 'Most things may never happen: this one will.'[3] As an opening statement on the *Human Habitat*, Larkin's 'Prologue' pushes England down a parallel chute. 'Going, Going' was published in 1974 in Larkin's collection *High Windows*, with amendments to the 1972 'Prologue' version. The first verse, evoking a world beyond the town which the poet had thought would last his time, has a minor amendment, with 'sports from the village' changed to 'village louts'; a less polite, rough-and-ready English country vernacular, with syllables cut to accentuate the downbeat. More significant change comes halfway. A transitional line in 'Prologue' where 'The pylons are walking, the shore', had replaced a verse cut because of its seeming criticism of business and government, profiteering via 'Grey area grants' in 'unspoilt dales' and with 'five percent profit (and ten/ Per cent more in the estuaries)'. The Department of the Environment deemed the verse unsuitable and asked for removal; Larkin complied, but restored the verse for lasting publication in *High Windows*.[4]

Front cover of *How Do You Want to Live? A Report on the Human Habitat*, Department of the Environment (1972).

'Going, Going' evokes the auctioneer, selling nature, selling England, a country almost, though still not quite, gone. Between 'Prologue' and 'Going, Going', between *How Do You Want to Live?* and *High Windows*, came another rendition of England under the hammer. In October 1973 Genesis released the LP *Selling England by the Pound*, whose first track, 'Dancing with the Moonlit Knight', has the album title as its refrain. Singer Peter Gabriel presents an eight-minute lament, which returns at the album's end in the track 'Aisle of Plenty'. Lyrical puns carry a sardonic vision of England diminished; the moonlit knight's Arthurian green shield meets Green Shield Stamps, then given away as a dividend with supermarket goods. Reward and redemption become commercial transaction, chivalry is gone. The final track works in store names: Safeway, Co-op, Fine Fare, aisles of plenty shaping consumer life. The aisle/isle pun wraps island, church and shopping in a diagnosis of decline. Gabriel asks where his country lies, hope and glory ring hollow, and Father Thames has drowned. A nation goes under from the weight of money, England sold by the pound.

Gabriel performed the song as Britannia in Union Jack costume. Larkin looked from the high windows of his Hull flat, and his Hull University Library office, on a world diminished. In different form, to different audience, yet with parallel sentiment. Nature goes, and England goes, Gabriel and Larkin in unlikely duet. In that sentimental sense, if in no other, it would have been plausible for Gabriel to pause mid-song to introduce a poetic guest, Larkin intoning 'Going, Going' over a Phil Collins drum solo. Larkin was an enthusiast for, and reviewer of, trad jazz rather than progressive anything, and politically the duetters would have pulled apart, Larkin's Conservatism far from Gabriel's promotion of World Music and his anti-apartheid lauding of black South African activists such as Steve Biko. In sentimental terms, however, the plausibility of such a meeting, Gabriel and Larkin in duet on a sold England, indicates the capacity of environment to cross cultural and political divides, catching emotional hold for the conservative and the radical, the traditionalist and progressive. National and natural could align in plural fashion.

Something to Govern

Eight years before 'Prologue' and nine before *Selling England by the Pound*, John Fowles produced his 1964 essay 'On Being English but Not British'. Fowles stated: 'The Green England is green literally, in our landscapes. This greenness is not very fashionable at the moment.'[5] The not-very-fashionable in 1964 would proliferate in the next decade, as an environmental 'Green' movement emerged to challenge the priorities of the modern world. Fears of pollution and resource depletion, and Apollo images of a fragile Earth from space, galvanized green action international and local, yet also national.[6] A few years after 1964, it was not unusual to reflect on Green England, and even government joined in.

How Do You Want To Live? was one of four reports issued by the Department of the Environment for the United Nations Conference on the Human Environment in June 1972, held in Stockholm. The Department of the Environment, with Peter Walker as Secretary of State, was the world's first government department with a specifically environmental remit, combining the former Ministries of Transport, Housing and Local Government, and Public Building and Works. *How Do You Want To Live?* outlined conservation challenges for transport, industry, recreation and the built environment, seeking to balance architectural modernism and environmentalism. The report's authoring committee was chaired by the Countess of Dartmouth, who would fulfil a similar role for the Department of the Environment's 1975 architectural report *What is Our Heritage?*[7] Of the other three 1972 reports, *Sinews for Survival* covered natural resources, *Nuisance or Nemesis?* addressed pollution and *50 Million Volunteers* reviewed organizations and youth.[8] A further document, *The Human Environment: The British View*, offered a summary position: 'We have only one world to pollute; if this one is ruined, we have no other.'[9] A colour landscape photograph of a valley farm, with mixed arable and pasture, and hills behind, captioned as 'the well-planned and efficiently managed rolling landscape of the lowlands', showed the unruined country: 'Despite intense competition for rural land for new towns and highways, there is still the England of the leafy lanes, the villages and market squares, the churches and timbered houses which give the land its distinctive character.'[10] Whatever the changes, 'England, for the most part, is still "a green and pleasant land".'[11]

The 1972 Department of the Environment reports convey what Matthew Kelly and others have termed the 'nature state', with government aspiring to be 'nature's manager'.[12] This could also embrace rather than reject elements of modernity, another *Human Environment* illustration showing an aerial view of the M62 passing along the Scammonden Dam, built in conjunction with the motorway, a combination showing 'brilliantly what Britain is doing to use her limited resources to the full'.[13] The Department's general aim was less to assert control than to invoke humility, acknowledging the limits of state capacity where nature's complexities and powers were concerned. This was not a new position, as shown for example in histories of coastal defence where, from the nineteenth century, the language of defiant engineering was balanced by a concern to work with natural process.[14] The 1970s, however, saw governmental environmental humility gain new prominence, although state bodies could pull in different directions; the Department of the Environment, the Nature Conservancy Council and the related Natural Environment Research Council were in tension with the Ministry of Agriculture, Fisheries and Food, whose priority was food production. Governmental departments with formal nature designations were often in a position of relative weakness against state infrastructural initiatives on transport, housing or energy.

The cover images of the four 1972 Department of the Environment reports offer a striking gallery of nature governance. *Sinews for Survival* shows William Blake's 'The Ancient of Days creating the World', and begins with a quote from the 'last debate' chapter of Tolkien's *The Return of the King*, the final book of the *Lord of the Rings* trilogy, on inheritance, responsibility and the limits of power:

> It is not our part to master all the tides of the World, but to do what is in us for the succour of those years wherein we are set, uprooting the evils in the fields that we know, so that those who live after may have clean earth to till. What weather they shall have is not ours to rule.[15]

The words are Gandalf's, addressing an assembly near Minas Tirith in Gondor before the final battle against the forces of Mordor. The wizard is unnamed in *Sinews*, but for Gandalf, perhaps in all humility, read Peter Walker. Tolkien, a common reference point for 1960s and '70s countercultural environmentalism, is claimed for good government:

'A theme which runs through all our evidence is that our management of our limited non-renewable natural resources is wasteful and often profligate; and that this is economically stupid and ethically indefensible.'[16] *Nuisance or Nemesis?*, its cover by Michael Peyton in the style of a child-drawn United Nations sandcastle, assessed the pollution of air, rivers, seas and land, including by agricultural DDT and other pesticides. Without pollution control, 'the downfall of civilisation will not be a matter of science fiction. It will be the experience of our children or grandchildren.'[17] Government reports of the early 1970s anticipate warnings of civilizational extinction fifty years on.

The broad sense of 'environment' informing the Department of the Environment publications comes through clearly in *50 Million Volunteers*, on 'Voluntary organisations and youth in the environment'. A chapter-length 'Survey of Voluntary Activities in the Environment' begins with a curious subheading: 'Spiders to spaceships; lichens to liquor; pot-holing to pornography'. The authors comment: 'Twelve months ago none of us could have conceived of the sheer variety of voluntary movements with environmental activities that we now know to exist in the United Kingdom.'[18] The heading is peculiar; the survey which follows covers natural history and recreation, but there is no evidence concerning the second term in each pair. Volunteering was, however, becoming 'the natural way in which citizens can be involved in the community', with membership increases at 30 per cent per annum for the RSPB and from 160,000 in 1968 to 278,300 in 1971 for the National Trust.[19] There had been 'a remarkable and unprecedented upsurge of voluntary activities concerned with the environment over the past two or three years'.[20] The 'human environment', as 'our surroundings', was defined: 'not only does it include the biophysical environment, but it involves a series of complex social and cultural relationships as well. These in turn affect our behaviour, attitude and relationship to our biophysical environment.'[21] England as human environment entwines culture and ecology.

The front cover of *50 Million Volunteers* showed a map of the British Isles with chains of words running diagonally northwest to southeast across the UK. A close look revealed the message 'you and

How Do You Want to Live?: A Report on the Human Habitat; *Sinews for Survival: A Report on the Management of Natural Resources*; *50 Million Volunteers: A Report on the Role of Voluntary Organisations and Youth in the Environment*; *Pollution: Nuisance or Nemesis? A Report on the Control of Pollution.*

HUMAN HABITAT:
HOW DO YOU
WANT TO LIVE?

Documents
AL RESOURCES
SINEWS FOR
SURVIVAL

ORGANISATIONS AND YOUTH
50 MILLION
VOLUNTEERS

POLLUTION:
NUISANCE
OR NEMESIS?

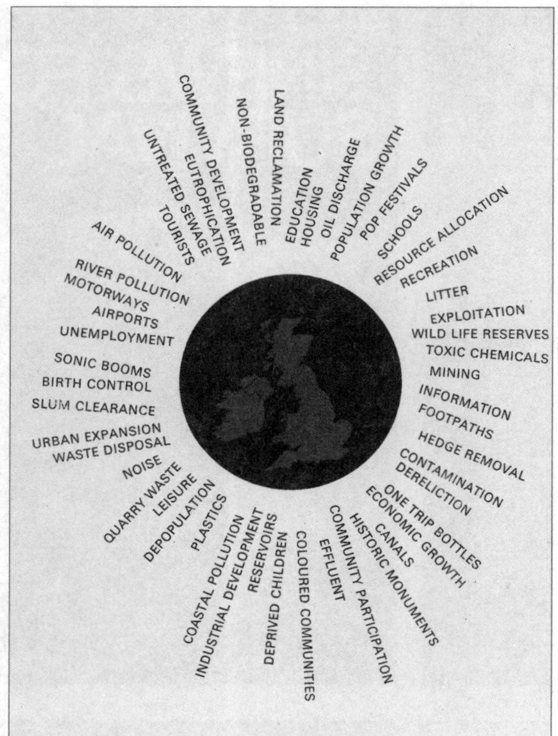

Back cover, *50 Million Volunteers: A Report on the Role of Voluntary Organisations and Youth in the Environment*, Department of the Environment (1972).

you and you and you'. The back cover had a central outline map encircled by word rays, showing the issues to be addressed, ecological and social, amenity and cultural. The 'human environment' thus encompassed 'plastics' and 'one trip bottles', 'deprived children' and 'coloured communities', 'airports' and 'toxic chemicals', 'pop festivals' and 'sonic booms', 'oil discharge' and 'hedge removal', and much more. The nature state attends to more than the natural world.

The establishment of the Department of the Environment connected to a broader concern in government for technocratic nature thought, if not nature confidence. Jon Agar highlights 1970s governmental concern for assessing future trends, focused on Department of the Environment Research and Policy units, and on the Official Committee on World Trends set up by Peter Walker and Prime Minister Edward Heath in 1972, to take a fifty-year view.[22] Governmental work on anthropogenic climate change began in the early 1970s, with experts advising on the scientific plausibility of claims. Climate concern accompanied fears over resource depletion, as in the

Club of Rome's influential 1972 report on *The Limits to Growth*.[23] Government becomes not only projector but stocktaker, with the oil crisis of 1973, when OPEC dramatically raised the price of crude oil, enfolding anxieties over energy resources and diminished Western power. Sinews for survival needed strengthening, and voluntary effort was required, if pollution was not to be nemesis. How Do You Want to Live?

For the UK, seventeen years after the 1956 Suez crisis, the shock to Western economies from decisions taken in the Middle East carried a specific post-imperial inflection. Alongside 'Going, Going', Larkin's 1974 collection *High Windows* included the 1969 poem 'Homage to a Government', lamenting the replacement of an imperial with a commercial ethos. Troops had vacated imperial postings east of Suez for 'lack of money', yet money ruled at home.[24] The Department of Environment, defending England's leafy lanes, sought to project a post-imperial global environmental influence, but for Larkin, the commercial erosion of landscape chimed with imperial loss. England was going, going, and the auctioneer's litany could go only one way.

Looking Forward to the 1970s?

The governmental hopes and fears of 1972 reprised earlier 1960s official and unofficial worries over wildlife, pollution and leisure. Debate in each field in the 1960s shaped a new form of environmentalism, but also carried forward legacies of earlier argument on the relationship of the modern and traditional, and the regulation of human conduct. As in debates before, during and after the Second World War, stories of past and present informed future projections, and national, local and global scales were enfolded. Matthew Kelly, in his insightful study of *The Women Who Saved the English Countryside*, shows how the post-war landscape campaigning of Pauline Dower and Sylvia Sayer moved into a new context, 'towards an environmentalism more strongly predicated on nature conservation, ecology and the shared vulnerabilities of all life on Earth'.[25] Consideration of 1960s debate around leisure and conservation shows how established discourses of English nature met new formulations of threat and crisis.

Looking ahead from the 1960s, were the 1970s something to look forward to? In November 1963 the Nature Conservancy, directed by Max Nicholson, hosted a major conference on 'The Countryside in

1970', held at Fishmonger's Hall in London, and chaired by the Duke of Edinburgh, with representatives of ninety organizations attending. The conference's consideration of agriculture was discussed above. A second 'Countryside in 1970' conference was held in 1965, a third in October 1970, part of European Conservation Year, attended by Edward Heath and exploring the government's environmental remit. The duke chaired the events as a figure personifying both tradition and the modern, associated with field sports and landed property, but with a dynamic personal image, committed to wildlife, and to youth environmental education through the Duke of Edinburgh Award scheme, established in 1956. Looking ahead to 1970 from 1963 suggested both prospective analysis and something practical and achievable, within seven years. In his closing speech the duke detected 'a determination that we are going to be in control of our own habitat'.[26] A world undergoing change might be steered in an appropriate direction, though the duke's comments opening the third 1970 conference indicated the scale of environmental challenge: 'The search for an exploitation of resources to feed this insatiable technological monster, the exploitation of human resources to manage it and the mountains of waste it produces all result in the gradual erosion of our whole living environment.' The English countryside had prompted a global vision: 'What started as an exercise in co-operation to control abuses and plan development in our own countryside is now seen to be part of a much more extensive campaign to save the world from human exploitation.'[27]

The 1963 conference was wide-ranging, conveying expert overview of industrial location, energy generation, nature conservation, amenity, telecommunication, landownership and forestry. The emphasis was on urban forces meeting the country, indeed National Farmers' Union representative R. Saunders 'expressed disappointment at the comparative neglect of the farmer and of farming interests in the arrangements for the conference'.[28] A prominent urban-rural theme was leisure, with concern over a potential leisure society marked by material affluence, the extension of leisure time to the mass of the population and the increase in car ownership democratizing unchecked mobility. Kelly notes of 'The Countryside in 1970', 'most rural interests, the tourist industry excepted, found a common enemy in the leisure motorist.'[29]

In a 1965 Civic Trust survey Michael Dower coined the term 'fourth wave'. After the three waves of industrial towns, rail development and car-based suburbs, leisure was breaking on the country: 'Now we see, under the guise of a modest word, the surge of a fourth wave which could be more powerful than all the others. The modest word is *leisure*.'[30] Dower's survey first appeared in the *Architects' Journal* for 20 January 1965, and was reissued as a pamphlet entitled *The challenge of leisure*, its cover showing beach crowds: 'If everyone in England and Wales went to the seaside at the same time, each would get a strip of coast three-and-a-half inches across.'[31] English landscape was open to leisure on a new scale. Debates paralleled those in the interwar and immediate post-war years, but here were new numbers, Dower evoking 'weekend multitudes', a metaphorical 'juggernaut in English lanes', congesting roads and leaving litter, 'their chalets and caravans threaten all parts of our coast, their cars and motorboats echo in quiet valleys and lakes.'[32] The their/our phrasing is telling, the collective national 'our' threatened by some of its own, who are not quite 'us'. Around three years after *The challenge of leisure* I would have my first holidays, in a small caravan owned by an aunt, on the cliffs at Hopton-on-Sea in Suffolk. Here were low-cost delights, staying without a car, walking into the resort of Gorleston, enjoying some bingo, spending time on the beach. Toes were dipped in the fourth wave. Was I part of Dower's problem? On whose coast were we caravanning?

A stock image in 1960s and '70s leisure literature is of cars drawn up on open ground to admire a view; the implication is of a diminished landscape experience, indeed a diminished view. The opening image in Dower's *The challenge of leisure* shows 'Bank holiday crowds by the Thames at Runnymede', cars parked to the river, leaving picnic space between bonnet and bank.[33] Family groups relax in temporary territory, in their own afternoon bit of England. Geographer J. Allan Patmore's 1970 *Land and Leisure*, issued as a Pelican paperback in 1972, conveyed similar imagery, and its corresponding investigative technique, the visitor survey. In a footnote Patmore records 22 recreational surveys between 1964 and 1970, plus two 1970 Countryside Commission guides to surveying sites.[34] The Countryside Commission (an expanded version of the National Parks Commission) had been set up under the 1968 Countryside Act, extending amenity and conservation concerns beyond national park boundaries. Patmore's graphs itemize 'Numbers of visitors present on Sunday afternoons at sites in Hampshire (upper) and at Box Hill (lower)', 'Length of stay of visitors to recreational sites in Staffordshire and Worcestershire', and 'Observed activities of visitors to open spaces'.[35] People sat in cars, sat near cars, picnicked, walked and strolled, played games and sometimes studied nature: 'The inherent reluctance to move far from the car is a continuing theme.'[36]

Patmore included, in pictures of 'Getting away from it all', alongside queueing holiday traffic, a film still: 'Equipment for the picnicker, a scene from the BBC TV play *The Gorge*.'[37] Patmore noted that Peter Nichols's satirical 1968 play had 'devastatingly parodied' the accompaniments to relaxation: 'rural amenities seem to many to need immoderate supplement'.[38] Nichols, whose 'childhood excursions' from Bristol were 'often to Cheddar Gorge', presented in *The Gorge* a lower middle-class Bristol family on a day trip to Cheddar via Wells. Nichols later commented: 'I suppose all my other television plays have been wiped to allow expensive videotape to be used again. *The Gorge* however is not a tape and one copy lies in the vaults of the British Film Institute, presumably as a record of British picnic customs in the mid-twentieth-century.'[39] *The Gorge* was filmed on location, the comedy inter-generational, and sometimes farcical, with lost jeans and torn trousers. The play intercuts the trip with the characters watching a home movie of the excursion, relative Jack having returned from Canada, to be reshown the sights after thirty years away. The party drive north from Cheddar to Burrington Combe for a picnic, with table and chairs, a tent put up for shelter, plastic vase and plastic flowers, pressure cooker and pans, kettles and pinafores, Liebfraumilch and liqueurs, napkins and lilos. A smaller tent conceals a chemical lavatory. The picnic is domesticated, in an outdoor home from home. Sixteen-year-old son Mike meets with Chris, the daughter of a middle-class family at the picnic site, and Nichols explores cross-class leisure sociology. While Mike, in reaction to his parents' approval, has found Cheddar grotty, Chris has delighted in kitsch amusement. The family consider returning from Cheddar via the Bristol Channel coast, taking in a view of the Severn Bridge, and mentions Peter Scott's Slimbridge wildfowl centre: 'Perhaps a dekko at the Wildfowl Trust. Don't want to miss that, eh, Jack?'[40] Nature is on the tour list, with Scott by 1968 a nature celebrity, a fame indicated when the Bonzo Dog Doo Dah Band's 1967 song 'The Intro and the Outro', with its roll call of spoof guest performers, included, alongside John Wayne on xylophone and Billy Butlin on spoons, 'Peter Scott on duck call'.

In 'Going, Going', Larkin evoked a young crowd in the M1 café, bound for more caravan sites, in an England almost gone. For others the solution was to channel leisure, and thereby conserve a diminishing countryside, with the leisure user also potentially educated into undestructive access.[41] At the 1963 'Countryside in 1970' conference Lord Molson of the CPRE described 'the menace of car and caravan', presenting a traffic-in-country analysis paralleling that in Colin Buchanan's influential 1963 report on *Traffic in Towns*: '"Access in excess" destroyed natural beauty, just as unrestricted access by cars to towns choked them up. The Buchanan Report (soon to appear) would state unequivocally that motor cars obscured the view.'[42] Molson's tone of restriction was countered, however, by Lord Mabane of the British Travel and Holidays Association, who noted visitor increase 'was due to a general rise in the standard of living, a matter for which one should thank Providence',[43] and by Tom Stephenson of the Ramblers' Association: 'one could not cage four fifths of the population in the towns, nor could one canalize them along selected tracks. Sometimes one was tempted to think that man was the only animal that the Nature Conservancy did not wish to conserve.'[44] The opportunities of freedom were contested, with the country's future at stake.

Commentary on 1960s landscape and '60s people merges, as in Garth Christian's 1966 book *Tomorrow's Countryside*, subtitled 'The Road to the Seventies', with a foreword by the Duke of Edinburgh. Christian presented education, 'the one unifying force capable of transforming the outlook of a whole nation', as the only answer to a 'hooliganism' produced by social instability and individual lack of purpose.[45] Christian offered a vignette of fires in Ashdown Forest, lighting 'the night sky to the north' and started by 'highly mobile young hooligans'.[46] Christian considered the possible role of 'field studies in preventing delinquency and hooliganism'.[47] Hooligans he had found to be 'potentially decent and enlightened citizens . . . Indeed, I once encountered a group of rockers struggling to extinguish a heath fire.'[48] The word 'struggling' may here suggest admiration for effort, and/or sympathy for lack of ability. From rockers on the heath to New Town streets, a pair of photographs compared two ways of spending 'Saturday Afternoon', a conservation work party contrasting with leather-jacketed teenagers, one V-signing the camera: 'Youth needs a challenge (Crawley, above) and often only finds it in destruction. A constructive alternative is demonstrated by the Conservation Corps (Woodwalton Fen, below).'[49] Instructive landscapes were required to redirect the fourth wave, and Christian welcomed the development of nature trails, as 'an ecological walk, an open-air tour of an area

'Saturday Afternoon', from Garth Christian, *Tomorrow's Countryside: The Road to the Seventies* (1966).

of scientific interest'.[50] Nature trails were promoted by the Council for Nature, formed in 1958 with over three hundred member bodies, with the Duke of Edinburgh as patron, and which launched the Conservation Corps in 1959, and organized National Nature Weeks in 1963 and 1966, with Wild Life Exhibitions in London sponsored by *The Observer*.[51]

Nature trails could be instructive, yet also part of a regulation of conduct designed to forestall the picnic practices satirized in *The Gorge*. Thus at East Wretham Heath in Breckland in Norfolk, the nature trail established in 1972 formed part of a newly regulated nature reserve, usurping a different kind of social space. The heath had been an unwardened site, used by residents of nearby Thetford, a town expanding through London overspill, and a Norfolk Naturalists Trust Easter Sunday 1969 visitor survey estimated over 1,000 cars, with picnicking, football, transistor radios, and swimming and canoeing on the mere. Fencing and zoning, and a ditch to prevent car access, was the response, plus the nature trail. Environmental education projected nature on a cleaned slate: 'From this it is deduced that the public as a whole are law abiding, and will respond favourably to firm instructions properly promulgated in unequivocal terms.'[52] Conservation success entailed a depopulation and repopulation of landscape, space made for new conduct.

The instructional, policing ethos of such commentary received sardonic comment from Nan Fairbrother in her 1970 book *New Lives, New Landscapes*. For Fairbrother, the emerging 'urban-rural countryside' demanded subtler appreciation of the motives for rural leisure:

> For though there are lively groups for preserving every aspect of our rural past, and protecting everything from birds to mountains, yet we also need equally articulate groups for what will be the main body of future users – a Council for Better Caravan Sites, societies for More and More Attractive Car Parks, for Country Playgrounds, for Motoring for Pleasure, and for Enjoying the Countryside without Feeling Virtuous.[53]

Fairbrother raised a moral geographical challenge for conservation, to regulate without disdain, and to acknowledge, even to experience, unelevated, unvirtuous pleasure.

Reflections on English nature also took global reference points. The language of environmental stewardship informing events such as 'The Countryside in 1970' drew on colonial experience, and post-colonial nature conservation initiative. The 1963 Conference treasurer was Aubrey Buxton, co-founder with Max Nicholson, Peter Scott and others in 1961 of the World Wildlife Fund (WWF), based in Switzerland and linked to the International Union for Conservation of Nature, with the Duke of Edinburgh as President of the British WWF branch. The WWF projected an English nature conservation ethos across the world, including in countries newly independent from British rule, English nature thereby a post-colonial story.[54] In 1978 Richard Fitter and Peter Scott produced *The Penitent Butchers*, a history of the Fauna Preservation Society, until 1950 the Society for the Preservation of the Fauna of the Empire and whose outlook ran parallel to the WWF.[55] The 'penitence' is for the slaughter of wildlife, but there is no sign of penitence for empire, only concern for the policies of the newly independent.

Global nature was invoked at the 'Countryside in 1970' conference in the summary address by Lord Howick of Glendale, Chairman of the Nature Conservancy. Howick stressed the need to demonstrate practical achievement, and recounted 'my African experience. We never got any progress among African agriculturalists when we tried, as we often used to do in Britain's colonial days, to spread our efforts equally over each region.'[56] Howick mixed global retrospect and global prospect, countering the impression of 'having lost an empire and not found a role' by emphasizing Britain as intellectual leader, somewhere looked to by others for environmental ideas: 'Ours is a country which has ideas, a country which can anyway produce the first application of these ideas.'[57] The Duke of Edinburgh regretted that 'we could not get Lord Howick to describe the way in which the conservation of nature was carried out in the Colonies over which he presided. I think it was slightly differently managed and would have provided an interesting comparison.'[58] Howick's final post had been as governor of Kenya from 1952 to 1959, overseeing suppression of the Mau Mau uprising, and using the emergency legislation thereby developed to push through agricultural reform, encouraging self-sufficient African farmers alongside the European settler community.[59] What for Howick was a liberal imperialism might also shape the environment of post-imperial Britain, Africa and England in dialogues of governmentality.

The View from the Seven Stones Reef

In 1967 an accidental event off south-west England brought a collision of environmental and economic anxieties, posing questions of nature governance, of Britain's global position and of the reliance of modern society on the international trade in fossil fuels. Scrutiny of a high-profile wreck offers another perspective on the ways in which concern for English nature were shaped by global forces and worries.

On 18 March 1967 the tanker SS *Torrey Canyon*, travelling to Milford Haven with 117,000 tons of Kuwait crude oil, ran aground on the Seven Stones reef between Cornwall and the Isles of Scilly. The ensuing oil spill, the attempts at dispersal by detergent, the bombing of the slick by the RAF with high explosive, rockets and napalm on 28–30 March, the pollution over five days from 25 March of 140 miles of Cornish beaches by 14,000 tons of crude oil, and the use of detergents to break down oil onshore ('Operation Mop-Up'), became an instant environmental fable. Here was disaster, the (mis)management of disaster, tensions between tourism, fisheries and ecology, a tense relationship between central government and territorial periphery, and the spectacle of distressed nature.[60] The vivid, multi-sensory presence of oil made this pollution of a different order to that of, say, pesticide residues. *Torrey Canyon* was pollution with presence. The 1968 report by the Plymouth Laboratory of the Marine Biological Association of the United Kingdom (hereafter MBA), on *'Torrey Canyon' Pollution and Marine Life*, described 'Arrival of the Oil':

> An account by a resident of Marazion stated that there was a smell of oil for a day before any actually arrived on the shore on 25/26 March. Dark blobs were seen silhouetted in crashing waves, and close inshore there was so much oil on the sea that the waves were smoothed, while elsewhere it was choppy with tan-coloured instead of white breakers.

The result was a 'ghastly mess . . . like thick blankets of "chocolate mousse"'.[61]

The *Torrey Canyon* story unfolded on the waves, on the beach and on television. Media rendition shaped an environmentalist as well as environmental spectacle, with figures who would become key televisual voices heard on behalf of nature: Tony Soper co-authored a key early book on the *Torrey Canyon*, while David Bellamy appeared following co-authorship of a scientific study of pollution effects in *Nature*.[62] The MBA report conveyed the scientific story, monitoring the effects of oil and detergents around the Cornish coast, Guernsey and Brittany. *Torrey Canyon* prompted an experimental field observation, on and below the land and sea surface, and the MBA concluded with 'Some Lessons Learnt': 'We are progressively making a slum of nature and may eventually find that we are enjoying the benefit of science and industry under conditions which no civilized society should tolerate.'[63]

Torrey Canyon conveyed the risks of big technology, and the failures of aggressive technology. The scale of tankers, grown 30-fold since 1945, meant that one accident might be environmentally catastrophic, and the wreck of the *Torrey Canyon* could be seen less as accidental than inevitable, a sign of things on the wrong track. The government's response to bomb the wreck, attempting to burn the oil, could appear a misguided faith in hard technology. The application of detergent to clean beaches before the summer tourist season seemed to prioritize economic amenity over ecology: 2½ million gallons of detergents, toxic to marine organisms, were applied at sea and ashore. Shore fish and crustacea, echinoderms and molluscs, suffered, green algae proliferating with the loss of browsing fauna. The MBA concluded that the oil itself, though killing thousands of sea birds, had 'little biological effect' beyond this.[64] Limpets, for example, survived and even grazed upon an oil covering, Bellamy and colleagues noting that in October 1967, 'The green carpet at Porthleven was variegated with patches of bare rock each supporting a new colony of limpets.'[65] The MBA stated 'the second, man-applied pollutant was far more damaging than the accidental one.'[66] Oil may have destroyed shore and beach 'amenities', but detergents were 'destructive of life'.[67]

Combined oil and detergent made for vivid beach colours, the MBA account, with its colour plates, displaying a kind of dystopian land art. The first plate in the book showed three images, illustrating that 'Treatment of oil with detergent may give varying results and mixtures of varying colours.' The top image showed Watergate Bay with oiled sand adjacent to rocks. On the middle image, 'Booby's Bay, 8 April: orange-brown partially emulsified oil floating on detergent solution in a high-water rock pool.' On the lower, 'Kynance Cove, 20 April: orange-brown oil emulsion after detergent treatment oozing down from boulders near high-water mark.'[68] In some ways, however, Cornwall had a narrow escape, and things could have been, and in future might be, far worse. A change in wind direction in early April, after a further 40–50,000 tons of oil spilled after the tanker broke up, prevented far more extensive landfall of oil: 'almost at the last moment, it was deflected seawards by the backing of the wind to the north.' The wind remained northerly 'most uncharacteristically for a full 30 days, and the British coastline was relieved from further serious threat'.[69]

Torrey Canyon prompted arguments over environmental governance, with tensions between central and local government, and between London and Cornwall, with its sense of distinct identity beyond or alongside Englishness. English environment was at full stretch, from Whitehall to the Scillies, the geographical convolutions indicated by Labour Prime Minister Harold Wilson directing operations not from Whitehall but, from 24 March, from his regular holiday home on the Scilly Isles. The experience prompted governmental reflection, with the Department of the Environment established in part in response. *Torrey Canyon* also signalled geopolitical stories. The MBA's frontispiece map of 'The wreck and its oily aftermath' showed oil spreading to Brittany and Guernsey as well as Cornwall, the approaches to northwest Europe vulnerable, accidents of import possible.[70] The geopolitics of oil dependency are evident, notwithstanding prospective North Sea production, oil imported from a Middle East where the UK was withdrawing from its imperial role, British troops evacuated from Aden later in 1967.

Torrey Canyon also reprised wartime actions; in the naval and air force organization of the clean-up effort, the largest peacetime combined forces operation in the UK; in the political classification of the event as a national emergency; in the attempted rescue of seabird casualties; in the rhetoric of combatting invasion, the fighting of oil on the beaches. Twenty-two years after the end of war, eleven years after Suez, four years after *Silent Spring*, five years before *How Do You Want to Live?*, six years before the oil crisis. *Torrey Canyon*'s broken back serves as an environmental and political hinge point, the Seven Stones reef a spot for retrospective and prospective view over England's nature.

Doom Days

If 'The Countryside in 1970' sought to nurture optimism for the coming decade, the *Torrey Canyon* helped foster anticipations of doom. When in 1971 Friends of the Earth issued *The Environmental Handbook: Action Guide for the UK*, edited by John Barr, the back cover stated, '1970s – Your last chance to act to make Britain worth living in.'[71]

Friends of the Earth was founded in the USA in 1969, with its UK organization established in 1970, making its name in May 1971 with the dumping of 1,500 throwaway non-returnable bottles on the doorstep of Cadbury Schweppes. Greenpeace was founded in 1971. A distinction emerges between an environmentalism of controlled concern, where the response is to assert government and elite leadership, and an environmentalism of alarm, even panic, where the desired response is disruptive action, and government is a complicit and/or complacent part of the problem. Meredith Veldman highlights the suspicion of nationalism in such environmentalism, with its calls for connection between the local and global, but national government could, as noted above, embrace environmental concerns, with key policy actors themselves asserting the need for dramatic action.[72] In 1970 former Nature Conservancy Director-General Max Nicholson published *The Environmental Revolution*, a work criticizing the actions of some government departments and promoting conservation as a holistic idea whose time had come. Nicholson subtitled his book 'A Guide for the New Masters of the World'.[73] *The Environmental Revolution* was reviewed by Ted Hughes, who found a 'crisis' demanding swift action, where England might take a global lead with a 'crash programme': 'It could be dealt with, as it should be dealt with, as a war. It will transform England, and that example would go a long way to alter the world.'[74]

Questions of national identity continued to shape even the most self-consciously radical environmental debate. National sentiment featured in part through the complex mix of radicalism and conservatism in Green politics, evident in one of the most influential ecological works of the early 1970s. In January 1972 the *Ecologist* magazine, founded by Edward Goldsmith in 1970, issued *A Blueprint for Survival*, mainly written by magazine editors Goldsmith and Robert

The Ecologist, *A Blueprint for Survival* (1972), front cover.

Allen. Another *Ecologist* editor was John Davoll, director of the Conservation Society, concerned with population control, who also contributed to the Department of the Environment's 1972 *Pollution: Nuisance or Nemesis?* The cover of *Blueprint for Survival* showed not the whole earth from space but a prospect view of a patch of countryside, unspecified in location but possibly Yorkshire or an edge-of-moorland Devon or Cornwall, similar to that featured in the Department of the Environment's *Human Environment* summary as the 'England of the leafy lanes', noted above, but chosen here to suggest a precarious agricultural living, settled but near the edge of cultivation, carefully tending its resources, an allegory for the human planetary position. Here was a resilient but threatened England, a blue-tinged landscape with 'A Blueprint for Survival' stamped over the fields.[75]

Blueprint quickly sold out, received extensive press and broadcast coverage, was reissued as a Penguin Special and its editors met Peter Walker and officials at the Department of the Environment.[76] In *The Ecologist*, and *A Blueprint for Survival*, while the nation-state is not the answer, the national helps style the argument. *Blueprint* set projected resource depletion, food shortage and chaos against an alternative 'stable society', living with ecological process, in population equilibrium, conserving energy and with a different new geography: 'Perhaps the most radical change we propose in the creation of a new social system is decentralization.' The editors used clichés of Englishness as counterpoints to their own revolutionary realism: 'We do so not because we are sunk in nostalgia for a mythical little England of fetes, olde worlde pubs, and perpetual conversations over garden fences.'[77] A different new England was envisaged, a 'diversified urban-rural mix' of small communities: 'we suggest neighbourhoods of 500, represented in communities of 5,000, in regions of 500,000, represented nationally, which in turn as today should be represented globally.'[78] England would be decentralized, but still interconnected, after a 'change-over', where an unspecified strong form of governance would direct change and reorganize the world.[79] The process and outcome of 'change' here differs from earlier variants of eco-transformation, such as William Morris's 1891 *News from Nowhere*, where after the revolution things effectively settle into anarcho-harmony.[80] The sketch of a future London in *Blueprint* does, however, share some of Morris's 'dream of London, small, and white, and clean,/ The clear Thames bordered by its gardens green':[81]

> Those regions which still have or are close to having a good urban-rural mix will be able to effect a relatively smooth transfer, but highly urbanized areas like London, the Lancashire conurbation, and South Wales will find it much more difficult to re-create communities. Nevertheless, even in London the structural remains of past communities (like the villages of Putney, Highgate, Hackney, Islington, etc.) will provide the physical nuclei of future communities – the means of orienting themselves so that they can cut themselves away from those deserts of commerce and packaged pleasure (of which the most prominent example is the Oxford Street, Regent Street, Piccadilly complex) on which so much of London's life is currently focused.[82]

From December 1972 *The Ecologist* was produced from somewhere more akin to *Blueprint*'s cover image, Wadebridge in Cornwall. An editorial piece in January 1973, headed 'And now, live from Cornwall . . .', reflected on the move, the title playing on the opening of the contemporary popular ITV game show *Sale of the Century* ('And now, live from Norwich . . .').[83] The new base, and the theme of decentralization, registered in an article in the same issue by Henry Pool and John Fleet, members of Cornish national movement Mebyon Kernow, on 'The conservation of Cornwall'. Pool and Fleet made 'a plea for greater autonomy': 'Indeed allowed proper scope, Cornish Nationalism, in the form of concern for a healthy organic community, integrated into its natural environment, could serve as a blueprint for areas with similar problems.'[84]

Notwithstanding *The Ecologist*'s move from Richmond in Surrey to Wadebridge in Cornwall, Goldsmith's own persona and interests aligned ecology with a particular English class identity. From a well-off background, and the older brother of financier James Goldsmith, who would through his 1990s Referendum Party place the idea of an EU referendum on the British political agenda, Edward Goldsmith was a close friend of maverick gambler and zoo-owner John Aspinall, their African wildlife trips generating enthusiasm for the supposed environmental wisdom of hunter-gatherer 'traditional' societies. An English upper-class post-colonial safari anthropology, pursued by figures for whom orthodoxy, in lifestyle or governance, was an unwelcome constraint, shaped radical environmentalism. Confidence in an ability to reorder geography followed. In *The Ecologist*, as in the World Wildlife Fund, Green England and a Green World met.[85] *Blueprint* appeared at a moment of concern and controversy around population growth, and Veldman notes that on the same day that *Blueprint* was reported in the press, American population campaigner Paul Ehrlich gave a presidential address to the Conservation Society, stating, 'England is still looked to as a standard setter in the world . . . educated people look a great deal to England to lead the way.'[86] *Blueprint* carried notice of 'The Movement for Survival', a new group to lobby for *Blueprint* principles, supported by the Soil Association, the Henry Doubleday Research Association, Survival International, the Conservation Society and Friends of the Earth.[87]

'Survival' as a word and topic would also have been familiar at this time from a pioneering nature television series. *Survival* was made from 1961 by Anglia Television, the regional television company for East Anglia established by WWF co-founder Aubrey Buxton. The term carried a sense of vulnerability, but also a robustness of response, just as the natural world presented was a space of red-in-tooth-and-claw vigour. Buxton brought a naturalist ethos happy to coexist with field sports, and likewise Goldsmith, *Blueprint* and *The Ecologist* could mix eco-activism with established conservationism. The listed supporters of *Blueprint* included leading conservation voices such as Peter Scott, Julian Huxley and Frank Fraser Darling, BBC Reith lecturer in 1969 on *Wilderness and Plenty*.[88] This tonal mix would also shape the emergence of ecology into British politics. Goldsmith served on the executive of the People Party, founded in Coventry in 1973 and renamed as the Ecology Party in 1975. A further renaming in 1985 produced the Green Party. Goldsmith stood for the People Party in Suffolk at the February 1974 general election, in an area where his father had been a Conservative MP, campaigning with a camel from Aspinall's zoo, bearing the anti-intensive farming slogan 'No Deserts in Suffolk. Vote Goldsmith'.[89]

Ecological concern blends global analysis with national languages of landscape. Goldsmith's editorial in the first issue of *The Ecologist* was preceded by an image of Earth from space, centred on North Africa and Arabia, with the caption: 'The Planet Earth is unique in our solar system in displaying those environmental conditions required to sustain complex forms of life.'[90] At the end of the editorial appeared a cartoon by Richard Willson, who would become a regular *Ecologist*

Cartoon by Richard Willson, from *The Ecologist* (July 1970).

contributor. Two children look at one flower in an industrial mess of pylons, power stations and road signs, the caption suggesting not only a global but a national crisis. Shakespeare is quoted to suggest a fallen state, 'this sceptred isle, this earth of majesty . . . this other Eden, demi-paradise, this fortress built by Nature for herself . . . this precious stone set in the silver sea . . . this blessed plot, this earth, this realm, this England'.[91]

The Comedy of the Commons

Environmental joys and anxieties were also broadcast to English children in the 1970s, notably via televisual stop-motion animation. Rachel Moseley notes how such programmes were 'typically structured by their interest in green space', and as noted earlier in relation to farming, children's television gave a distinctive perspective on the grown-up world.[92] Environmental messages could be transmitted, with animations such as *The Clangers* and *The Wombles* projecting televisual fables. *The Clangers* offered interplanetary conversation, *The Wombles* lessons in waste. Scrutiny of both offers another route into the emergence of environment as a public concern, via the most mainstream 1970s medium.

The Clangers was made by Smallfilms, set up by Oliver Postgate and Peter Firmin in 1957, and operating from a converted cowshed in Kent. Postgate and Firmin were already known for *Ivor the Engine*, *Noggin the Nog* and *Pogles' Wood*.[93] First broadcast in 1969, in Moon landing year, and running for two series until 1972, the Clangers occupied a small planet, bare surfaced, with dustbin lids covering the entries to cave living space. Earth's blue planet appeared as a distant neighbour. Postgate's autobiography recalled, 'there they were, somewhere out in space, the Clangers, a small tribe or extended family of civil mouse-like persons living their peaceful lives on, in and around a small, undistinguished moon.'[94] Knitted pink puppets inhabit a handmade world, a craft landscape of innocence and occasionally interrupted joy. Postgate's narration reflected on interplanetary difference, the Earth a busy and noisy place, with comment made on the space race and pollution, technology and modernity, *The Clangers* offering a prelapsarian commentary. The rockets of humankind or Major Clanger's intermediate technology? Machineries of destruction or arts-and-crafted delight? Restless galactic exploration or local planetary self-sufficiency? *The Clangers* set the child's imagination against the grain of earthly progress.

From a shed in the garden of England, cosmic environmental fables unfold. The Clangers have occasional encounters with Earth, as when, in 'The Rock Collector', broadcast in April 1971, a spaceman lands, departing in confusion. When in the second episode of Series 1, 'The Visitor', broadcast in November 1969, the Clangers net a television orbiting their world as space-junk, its crowd-noise, talk and rock music sends them scurrying to the caves. The soundworld of the Clangers (which television noise here rudely interrupts) complemented Postgate and Firmin's vision, Vernon Elliott's gentle soundtrack providing small-planet-sized chamber music and electronica to accompany the Clangers' swannee-whistling speech.[95] In 'The Seed', broadcast in June 1971, a seed lands and Small Clanger is excited at the prospect of a garden, like those they have seen on Earth through Major Clanger's telescope. Tiny Clanger summons the Cloud to water the seed, and it germinates and flowers, and proliferates, making their world less bare. But the new plants have taken over and become a problem, such that the Sky-moos, hippo-like creatures with enormous ears for flying, are called to clear the vegetation, the world chomped back to normal, in a cautionary tale of alien species and of not caring for what you have. Postgate and Firmin's book version of the story, *The Sky-moos*, conveys how when your cherished home is a bare blue planet, greenery can be scary: 'The Clangers backed away from the wall of bright greenery as it grew all around them. They backed away right around their world until they met the wall of greenery coming around the other way!' Major Clanger leads the retreat underground, and the Sky-moos are summoned to the rescue: 'The Sky-moos munched and scrunched and chomped and swallowed and munched again, working their way methodically around the planet, eating up every shred of greenery in their path.'[96] Postgate tells a green fable, albeit with the conventionally positive qualities of greenery inverted.

In 2000 Postgate published his autobiography, *Seeing Things*, conveying a life of activism alongside animation. Born in 1925, grandson of George Lansbury, Labour leader in the 1930s, Postgate's animated worlds expressed a progressive sensibility. Sent from north London to the safety of progressive Dartington Hall School in Devon at the outbreak of war until 1942, from late 1943 Postgate was a conscientious objector, and he would be active in the 1980s peace movement. In the mid-1970s he patented a solar heating system. The hand-made ethos of Postgate and Firmin's animation matched a politics critical of the modern military-industrial order. At the second general election of 1974, exasperated by party political conflict, and feeling that 'moderation and common sense must be a passion as real as any fanaticism,' Postgate made 'Vote for Froglet', a *Clangers* film to 'expose some of the absurdities of political electioneering'.[97] The BBC broadcast 'Vote for Froglet' on election night, its Soup Dragon-versus-Froglet campaign only producing futile division. On the Clangers' planet, in its uncorrupted state, no one was in charge. Clanger environmentalism would be mobilized in October 2006 when Postgate placed press advertisements, 'sponsored by The Clangers', with a Clanger pictured, asserting that 'global warming is a global emergency.'[98] The Clangers were revived in 2015, the new series closely echoing the original, with Firmin still involved. Postgate's narrator place was taken by Michael Palin, by then not only an ex-Python and televisual traveller but a recent president of the Royal Geographical Society. Explorations, as ever, are shaped by and speak to their places of departure.

Stop-motion techniques animated a tactile world of bodged objects and textured surfaces, the antithesis of an emerging plastic age. If *The Clangers* gave English lessons in outer space, *The Wombles* offered a grounded story, in a specific part of London, Wimbledon Common. The first of Elisabeth Beresford's six Womble books, *The Wombles*, appeared in 1968: 'it was during a walk on Wimbledon Common with her children Kate and Marcus that the Wombles suddenly came to life.'[99] The Wombles lived in an intricate burrow under the Common, 'and it is their special responsibility to "tidy up" everything that untidy Human Beings leave behind them'.[100] If Clangers encounter space junk, Wombles recycle suburban detritus:

> the wind had driven across the streets and gardens of South London before it reached the Common and on its journey it had picked up everything in its path. There were newspapers and paper bags, handkerchiefs and hats, scarves and gloves, bus tickets and shopping lists and notes left for milkmen, and a lot more besides, all scudding happily across the grass and through the bushes.[101]

Television adaptations, made by FilmFair with puppets by Ivor Wood, appeared between 1973 and 1975, the puppets less teddy-bear-like than the illustrations in the original books. Bernard Cribbins, known as a children's television storyteller as well as for his acting and singing, narrated the series, lending each character a distinctively accented voice. The Wombles thus became social creatures not only in their mode of life but in standing for kinds of human, via gentle national stereotyping. There is French cook Madame Cholet, the visiting bagpiping Scottish Cairngorm MacWomble the Terrible, and variants of English social class; well-spoken *Times*-reading head of the burrow Great Uncle Bulgaria, scholarly young Womble Wellington, workmanlike Tobermory, comical Orinoco and down-to-earth young Bungo and Tomsk.[102] As in earlier children's literature such as *The Wind in the Willows*, social anthropomorphism is clear, although *The Wombles* contrasts with the divergent species of the riverbank in offering a convergent common collective.

The Wombles' television theme song became a hit single for writer and performer Mike Batt, 'The Wombling Song', the first of eight hit singles, performed by Batt and others on *Top of the Pops* in full

Womble costumes. From a 1968 book, the Wombles became a 1970s phenomenon, a common cultural reference point. Aged nine, 'The Wombling Song' was my first pocket-money-purchased single. The B-side declared there were 'Wombles Everywhere', and a great-aunt made me a Tomsk, old materials recycled for the perfect gift. The title of one of Batt's major hits, 'Remember You're a Womble' (1974), needed no explanation to its millions of listeners. And what was the listener to remember? That humanity was a rubbish-creating species, and that the Wombles offered exemplary recycling, reusing human discards, putting us to shame. If humans, via what Garrett Hardin had in 1968 influentially termed 'The Tragedy of the Commons', struggled to care for collective resources (even, it seemed, those London commons preserved from development in the conservation campaigns of the late nineteenth century), the Wombles (also first appearing in 1968) showed the way with a comedy of the commons.[103]

Womble Greenness chimed also with an older environmental preoccupation, that of litter. If the Clangers echo an environmentalist

Tomsk, made by Great-Aunt Alice, *c.* 1974.

critique of industrial capitalism which might dream of overthrowing the existing order, the Wombles match a concern for ameliorating pollution, restoring an order lost. In *The Wombles at Work* (1973), when Bulgaria reads in *The Times* that 'We are facing Doomsday', he institutes a medal for Womble Conservation Year, resolving 'to make Britain – indeed the whole world – clean and beautiful again'.[104] The Wombles of Wimbledon Common nurture an open space for all maintained in good order, 'for the Wombles are the tidiest creatures in the world'.[105] Bulgaria comments that: 'People are strange because they are untidy,' and the tidying Wombling ethos matched campaigns to 'Keep Britain Tidy', with litter the focus for conservation at its most conservative, curbing the acts of those deemed irresponsible. 'Now remember, young Womble, it's our duty to keep the Common tidy,' says Tobermory.[106]

Keep Britain Tidy was initiated after a 1954 Women's Institute resolution to keep Britain tidy, and registered as a charity in 1960, funded in part by government and industry, including manufacturers and commercial users of packaging such as Cadbury Schweppes, who Friends of the Earth had targeted in 1971 for their single-use plastic bottles.[107] Mainstream celebrities were enlisted in 1970s litter campaigns. The Wombles, with a sew-on Womble patch saying 'I Keep Britain Tidy', lined up alongside Morecambe and Wise, the New Seekers and ABBA. On a poster, glam pop star Marc Bolan was quoted as saying: 'The pollution problem is in our hands. Keep Britain Tidy,' while a short 1975 promotional film included Harry Secombe belting out 'Jerusalem', exalting the green and pleasant land, with the tagline: 'Britain is a beautiful country, not a litter bin.' If the Clangers inhabited an off-kilter world, the Wombles found themselves in a celebrity mainstream, enlisted for tidiness, their underground overground.

Humanly Natural: Richard Mabey

An underground overground mix also characterizes the most influential English nature writer of recent decades, Richard Mabey, whose work carries a kind of wombling spirit; making good use of things that he finds, things others often overlook, moving with an intellectual freedom across the mainstream and the margins, picking up pieces along the way, and, Tobermory-like, making something new. Mabey's work, with its criticism of the ecological consequences of human action, yet also its appreciation of the meeting points of the human and natural, demonstrates key facets of the cultures of nature in England since the 1960s. As a figure of cultural significance, Mabey thus warrants detailed attention. Mabey's writings move from the 1970s to the 2020s, acting also as a bridge to the following chapter and show a variety of themes marking landscape as humanly natural.[108]

In 1973, the year of the Wombles TV debut, Mabey published *The Unofficial Countryside*, documenting nature's adaptation to human intervention, finding conservation value in spaces usually overlooked, with a focus on London and its region. Favoured here were those sites pictured at the beginning of *England's Green*, gravel pits: 'many pits, torn as they are out of monotonous rough pasture in the suburbs, have added a new element to the landscape.'[109] For some wildlife a working pit was a special attraction, with 'the greatest success story' the little ringed plover, nesting on the flat shingly terraces of active excavations.[110] *The Unofficial Countryside* was dedicated to Kenneth Allsop, whose 1949 *Adventure Lit Their Star* told of little ringed plovers migrating to Home Counties reservoirs and gravel pits. Allsop wrote from the birds' perspective, showing the appeal to other species of sites overlooked by humans as unnatural, 'my canvas is a scrappy bit of outer-Outer London, my subject an immigrant which picked that part to settle in.'[111]

The Unofficial Countryside began with a habitat not commonly associated with naturalists, the office commute, during which Mabey noticed birds and plants: 'Every patch where the concrete has not actually sealed up the earth is potential home for some living thing.'[112] Mabey found here less a story of 'survival' than 'co-existence', something 'amazingly cheering', and part of 'common, everyday experience'.[113] Observing *The Unofficial Countryside*, Mabey enacts Walter Benjamin's literary metaphor for the urban flaneur, 'botanising on the asphalt'.[114] Mabey chose not to style *The Unofficial Countryside* as a walking tour around outer London: 'It tempts you to try and make an adventure out of something whose most important meaning is altogether intimate and homely.'[115] Not that Mabey was inattentive to the strange or exotic. Arguing against the 'biological censorship' of plants hazardous to humans, Mabey considered the giant hogweed, spotting forty square yards of it between a factory and a road. Here was 'Britain's most notorious plant', subject of a popular scare in 1970 when children, attracted to touch by size and strangeness, developed rashes: 'Never before had I seen it in such profusion, or pressing so rampantly close to the polite and orderly life of the suburbs.'[116] Mabey's readers might at this point have put on the 1971 Genesis LP *Nursery Cryme*, featuring 'The Return of the Giant Hogweed', on a plant immune to herbicidal treatment and threatening to the human race, Peter Gabriel's lyrics giving an eight-minute progressive rocking botany fable.

Mabey was also sceptical of those upholding native species over the alien, and welcomed the presence of 'immigrant plants' in an open, hospitable ecology. Unlikely sites are also welcomed into natural history; gravel pits and roadsides, golf courses and railway tracks (where Mabey follows Richard Jefferies's 1879 *Nature near London* in tracking plant migration), sewage farms and rubbish dumps.[117] *The Unofficial Countryside* describes a botanists' coach outing to South Essex tips, where a layered 'geology' of waste and soil makes for 'a huge compost heap . . . mightily congenial to plant growth'.[118] Common species proliferated, with rarities among them, including those from domestic birdcage seeds:

> Here, the sunflowers, products of the plumpest and most favoured seeds, outshone everything else, awkward though they looked thrusting out of this flat and derelict field. Then there were the deep purple cascades of love-lies-bleeding; countless breeds of millet and canary grass from Australia, Morocco and South America; niger from India; yellow safflowers, blue flaxes, and most curious of all, a shoo-fly plant from Peru, with pale lilac flowers tightly closed in the gloom and Chinese lantern fruit cases.[119]

Budgerigar sweepings turn Essex exotic. *The Unofficial Countryside* ends in an abandoned brickyard beyond an executive estate, Mabey opening an old iron gate to find a car carcass grown over with spotted orchids: 'Not many planned reserves could re-create the feeling of coming upon this place by accident.'[120]

Echoing Allsop, and pioneering works such as Richard Fitter's 1945 *London's Natural History*, Mabey was not the only practitioner of urban ecology.[121] In the same year as *The Unofficial Countryside*, John Betjeman's film on London suburbia, *Metro-land*, journeying out along the Metropolitan line, alighted at Neasden to find naturalist and broadcaster Eric Simms, author of the 1971 *Woodland Birds* in the

'New Naturalist' series and later of *The Public Life of the Street Pigeon* (1979).[122] Simms is treated by Betjeman as a curious species in his own right, appearing in Gladstone Park with his binoculars, accounting for the species on the Neasden Nature Trail, spotting everything but Wombles in London's common green space. Like Simms and Fitter, Mabey explored the urban and suburban, and the often indeterminate space of the rural-urban fringe, where 'the labels "urban" and "rural" by which we normally find our bearings in a landscape, just do not apply'.[123] In 2000 Marion Shoard would likewise seek to reclaim such 'Edgelands of Promise', an urban-rural 'interface' of gravel pits, sewage plants, golf courses and wasteland, an 'anarchic mix of unloved land-use functions' offering recreation potential and wildlife refuge, as unmanaged space away from intensively farmed countryside.[124] The word 'edgelands' has since become commonplace for those pursuing unlikely nature attractions, notably in Paul Farley and Michael Symmons Roberts's 2011 *Edgelands*, a collection of 'journeys into England's true wilderness'.[125] There is a shift in tone, however, from 1970s Mabey to such twenty-first-century work. *The Unofficial Countryside* may have highlighted the wild in the overlooked, but did not present intrepid adventure. The intent was rather to familiarize, to make friendly, that which might at first surprise, Mabey's work less an intrepid venture out than a great cultural gathering-in.

Mabey's intertwining of nature and society in *The Unofficial Countryside* reflected his sociological interests. In 1967 Mabey edited a 'symposium' on *Class*, a 'predominantly radical collection',[126] including Stuart Hall (on 'Class and the Mass Media'), Raymond Postgate (founder of the *Good Food Guide* and father of Clangers-creator Oliver) and Kenneth Allsop, whose essay 'Pop Goes Young Woodley' considered pop music as 'a factor in our whole man-made environment'.[127] Allsop effectively writes as a pop naturalist, his relentless detailing of styles and performers carefully anatomizing contemporary pop species, just as he might otherwise attend to birds. Allsop concluded that the anatomy of pop put class markers in question: 'the old class ready-reckoner, which docketed a person socially as the first words leaked from his lips, became blurred and scrambled.'[128] Nature writers are social writers, Allsop billed in *Class* as someone also 'completing a social history of the American hobo and migrant worker' (the 1967 book *Hard Travellin'*), to go alongside his earlier 'story of an immigrant bird', *Adventure Lit Their Star*.[129] In Allsop, as in Mabey, there is a reciprocity in social and ecological frames of reference, identifying a humanly shaped nature and a naturally shaped human.

Mabey's first 'nature writing' success was the 1972 *Food for Free*, in print ever since and an inspiration for later revivals in wild food foraging. Mabey explored 'the edible wild plants of Britain', whether shellfish, nuts, fungi, roots, herbs, vegetables, seaweeds, flowers, fruits or spices. *Food for Free*, expanding what food might be, helped critique the outputs of modern agriculture, the required perfection of supermarket fresh produce. For Mabey, 'modern attitudes' meant that 'the most natural-looking foods are the ones that seem least "naturally" desirable.'[130] *Food for Free* taught that 'those old robust tastes, those curly roots and fiddlesome leaves, are still there for those who care to seek them out.'[131] Knowledge of wild plants was a social as well as biological matter:

> To know their history is to understand how intricately food is bound up with the whole pattern of our social lives. It is easy to forget this by the supermarket shelf, where the food is instantly and effortlessly available, and soil and labour seem part of another existence. We take our food for granted as we do our air and water, and all three are threatened as a result.

Gathering wild food would help 'deepen respect for the interdependence of all living things'.[132]

In 1980 Mabey published *The Common Ground*, written in association with the Nature Conservancy Council. As with Shoard's *The Theft of the Countryside* in the same year, Mabey presented new farming as ecologically destructive. In an additional 1981 preface Mabey praised Shoard's book, and saw the 1981 Wildlife and Countryside Act as offering little protection, indeed as heightening the antagonism between conservation and agriculture. Mabey, however, argued that while 'the radical changes brought about by the new agriculture' challenged assumptions of the 'naturalness' of landscape, they also demanded reflection on the naturalness of conservation measures: 'conservation may be looked at as much in terms of styles of human behaviour as in the maintenance of species.'[133] If agriculture generated newly artificial landscapes, was the nature conserved in reserves or SSSIs also a matter of artifice? And was that a problem? Mabey concluded, 'always the argument ends with questions of value and meaning which, like all such questions, can only be answered in a social context by a continuing *cultural* debate.'[134] Mabey took nineteenth-century poet of enclosure John Clare to show agricultural transformation as emotional attack, an 'invasion of personal territory by forces beyond our control'.[135] New farming matched old enclosure, and deserved equivalent cultural retort. As with Clare, Mabey laments the cutting of continuities, agriculture 'severing irrevocably' the 'unbroken links with the past' that create 'richness and individuality' in habitat: 'In contrast to their predecessors, modern farmers and foresters are not creating new landscapes but ephemeral sceneries.'[136]

As *The Common Ground*'s title suggested, Mabey argued that conservation should attend to the common and everyday: 'it is the *common* species that keep the living world ticking over and provide most of our everyday experiences of wildlife, and I would argue that maintaining the abundance of these is as important a conservation priority as maintaining the existence of rarities.'[137] Conservation should combat 'small erosions', 'the process by which what is common becomes scarce', maintaining the 'small links in the chain, ecologically, but the largest of all in terms of the human meanings that attach to them'.[138] For Mabey 'place', more than 'site' and 'habitat', caught 'the element of human significance' and Gilbert White's 1789 *The Natural History of Selborne* offered a model of placed nature observation and parochial allegiance.[139] Mabey edited a new edition of *The Natural History of Selborne* in 1977, and produced a biography of White in 1986.[140] Mabey noted White's annual looking out for the return of swallows and swifts, and finished *The Common Ground* with the view from his window, swifts milling above a Hertfordshire village church for autumn departure, to return in May, 'a symbolic reminder – as the whole natural world is, in a way – that the alternative to progress is not stagnation but *renewal*'. Mabey ended by quoting, as elsewhere in his work, Ted Hughes's 1974 poem 'Swifts', that 'They've made it again,/ Which means the globe's still working'.[141] The returning swift marks a seasonal intersection of dwelling human and migratory bird, a reassuring conjunction. Renewal could also, however, entail mortality, Hughes's 'Swifts' poem beginning with the birds' exultant return, only to end with the death of a crashed bird.

From *The Common Ground* in 1980, Mabey became a prominent supporter of environmental arts group Common Ground, founded in 1983 by Sue Clifford, Angela King and Roger Deakin.[142] Common Ground took forward Mabey's emphasis on place and the common via conservation initiatives informed by the arts. Several Common Ground projects encouraged nature appreciation, including 'Trees, Woods and the Green Man' (1986–9), which included land artist Andy Goldsworthy's 'Leaves' exhibition at the Natural History Museum, connected to a six-week 1986 Common Ground residency on Hampstead Heath. Common Ground issued two related publications, the poetry anthology *Trees Be Company*, edited by King and Clifford, and the practical tree 'manifesto' *In a Nutshell* by Neil Sinden, with a foreword by Mabey and drawings by land artist David Nash.[143] Goldsworthy and Nash featured too in *Second Nature*, a 1984 Common Ground anthology edited by Mabey, who chose the writers, with Clifford and King choosing contributing artists, including Goldsworthy. Mabey sought to bring the argument 'in a very literal sense back home, to the local landscapes that are most people's first-hand experience of nature'.[144] Jos Smith notes that as a place-focused collection, *Second Nature* was careful to avoid 'nostalgic nationalism', but England remains a reference point for Mabey and Common Ground, less as a source of unified belonging than an accumulation of valued local and regional particulars, all making up a distinctive country, warranting appreciation.[145] In the title of Clifford and King's later 2006 compendium, here was an *England in Particular*.[146]

Mabey chose to begin *Second Nature* with poet Norman Nicholson's 'Ten-yard Panorama', on the view from a house in the middle of the small Cumbrian iron-working town of Millom, where Nicholson had spent his life. Nicholson reflects on the images 'collected in the course of looking at that particular scene on – at a rough calculation – nearly twenty-five thousand days'.[147] *Second Nature* thus opens with an oblique choice, beyond obvious nature sites, in keeping with Mabey's editorial suggestion that 'the immense range of experiences of natural life and landscape reaching back through our history and often beyond any narrow definition of rural traditions, is part of a *common* culture.'[148] In his 1954 poem 'Weather Ear', Nicholson had described how, lying in bed in the dark, he could tell wind direction and strength, and thus likely weather, from the sonic carry of furnace hooter and market clock, the gusts on roof slate, or the rain drip from gutters in still air: a common dozing small town man attuned to the air, his weather ear second nature.[149]

Common ground, common culture, but what place for agriculture? Of contributing artists in *Second Nature* only James Ravilious, in photographs of sheep farming, and Henry Moore, in a drawing of sheep, feature farming, and Mabey notes of the essay contributors that 'none of us works the land as a first occupation.'[150] Agriculture features in *Second Nature* as either a site of a nostalgia deemed awkward, or as a modern problem, as in Raymond Williams's concluding essay 'Between Country and City'. Williams, whose essay began on a page adjacent to 'March', a woodcut of daffodils by Robin Tanner, reflected back on his 1973 critical analysis of linked rural and urban ideals in *The Country and the City*, seeing such linkage intensifying, with 'a more fully organised agrarian capitalism, ever more closely linked with the money market'.[151] For Williams, criticism of farm intensification needed to be embedded within 'a new kind of political ecology . . . which can reasonably propose alternative kinds of social and economic organisation', and new understandings of the 'real relations of nature and livelihood'.[152]

Common Ground would address the agricultural landscape through their mid-1990s Field Days project, with an exhibition at the 1996 Royal Agricultural Show, a 1998 *Field Days* anthology of poetry edited by Clifford and King, and a *Manifesto for Fields* urging that land be farmed holistically.[153] The nature values of Common Ground align with traditional farming practice, but not with chemical farming or agribusiness. Clifford and King's *England in Particular* would thus include celebratory entries on agricultural shows, drystone walls, fields, gates, hedges, scarecrows, sheep and shire horses.[154] Goldsworthy's art too demonstrates such alignment, engaging with land work through drystone walling artworks, as in the *Sheepfolds* project, where Goldsworthy worked with wallers to reinstate in variously practical form a series of sheepfolds across northern England. For Goldsworthy, Sheepfolds was as 'a monument to agriculture', a land art down to earth rather than rarified, land work valued against both intensive farming and metropolitan artistic detachment.[155]

In 1980 Mabey produced not only *The Common Ground*, but *The Flowering of Britain*, with photographer Tony Evans, on plants and their human connections across woods, fields and the 'waste lands' of mountain, moor, marsh and abandoned quarries. Mabey and Evans began their work in 1973, 'a collection of photographs showing wild flowers growing in their natural settings'.[156] Human associations and local names gave 'glimpses not just of an external landscape but of the culture of flowers which we still carry with us in our folk memories'.[157]

Having reviewed plant history from pre-glacial times, Mabey compared 'modern agriculture' to 'a glacier in permanent, animated advance', with only flora able to adapt to 'such conditions of turmoil' surviving.[158] Mabey had originally hoped his text might offer 'a comprehensive history of our flora in terms of the landscape in which it grew and the human beings who had shaped it', but a 'more modest and variegated commentary' resulted.[159]

The Flowering of Britain was, however, a precursor to Mabey's 1996 *Flora Britannica*, a compendious 1,000-species account, supported by Common Ground, of a 'lively popular culture of plants . . . informed by popular ecology and a sense of social history'.[160] From 1992 Mabey and Common Ground invited people to convey their own plant stories, 10,000 respondents making the resulting *Flora* a 'post-modern folklore' detailing plant habitats, past and present uses, and the continuing presence of 'plant rituals and mystical gestures'.[161] Mabey essayed each species, family by family, with added accounts of churches and churchyards, hedges, plants, places and names, spring festivals, wild foods, midwinter greenery, urban commons, plant medicine and meadows. Mabey found 'little evidence of nationalism in our modern cultural attitudes to plants', rather an emphasis on the 'overriding importance' of the 'local patch', the greenness of England a matter of local particularity, making a variegated national whole, embracing the native, the naturalized and the introduced.[162] Mabey delights in local English 'vernacular names', given in the *Flora* alongside the common and Latin.[163] When, of the ninety historic vernacular names recorded for the plant lords-and-ladies, Mabey gave the nine in current use, a bawdy botanics resulted: 'VN: Cuckoo-pint, Cuckoo flower, Jack in the pulpit, Parson in the pulpit, Devils and angels, Red-hot-poker, Willy lily, Snake's meat, Cows and bulls'.[164] Vernacular names appear as poetic lists, in culturally assonant, sometimes rhyming, variety: 'Marsh-marigold, *Caltha palustris* (VN: Kingcup, Mayflower, May-blobs, Mollyblobs, Pollyblobs, Horse-blob, Water-blobs, Water-bubbles, Gollins, the Publican)'.[165]

Nature has since nurtured a twenty-first-century publishing boom, the 'new nature writing' hailed in a 2008 issue of the magazine *Granta*, which included Mabey along with Mark Cocker, Kathleen Jamie, Robert Macfarlane and others, editor Jason Cowley hailing a genre 'urgent, vital and alert to the defining particulars of our times'.[166] A commercially and culturally dormant natural history book market has revived, with Mabey providing a breakthrough big-seller with his memoir 2005 *Nature Cure*, an account of combating depression after the completion of *Flora Britannica* and the sale of his lifelong Chilterns home. Mabey wrote on resettling in Norfolk, notwithstanding the 'awful sterility of East Anglia's farming landscape':[167]

> And in an odd way I was feeling patriotic, not in some brainless nationalistic way, but from a growing fondness for my *patria*, my new home country. I don't think that a love of one's own place that bears no hostility to others is a bad emotion. It is a truly ecological one, and all living things are loyal to their own patch without being disrespectful of others.[168]

Mabey cited John Clare's outlook on commons as a model of living: 'on them humans lived in the same system of mutually considerate coexistence as their fellow creatures'.[169] *Nature Cure*, as all of Mabey's work, becomes personally cultural, individually collective, humanly natural.

N is for Natural, E is for England

The title of this chapter, English Nature, was once the name of a government agency, and nomenclatural history can serve to indicate some of the complexities concerning the public care for nature in England.

The Nature Conservancy (NC) was established in 1949, one of a range of post-war bodies extending the environmental role of the state.[170] In 1966 the NC was incorporated into the new Natural Environment Research Council (NERC), from which the Nature Conservancy Council (NCC) was separated in 1973. The NCC operated until 1991, when its Scottish, Welsh and English parts were divided as Scottish Natural Heritage (SNH), the Countryside Commission for Wales (CCW) and English Nature (EN). In nomenclatural, governmental terms, English Nature signals nature devolved, in advance of the devolution of political powers later in the 1990s. In 2006 EN was amalgamated with the Countryside Agency (CA), itself established in 1999 from a merger of the Countryside Commission (CC) (set up in 1968 in part to oversee rural leisure), the Rural Development Commission (RDC) and the Rural Development Service (RDS), which carried out DEFRA's environmental land management role. The result was Natural England (NE), sponsored by DEFRA and concerned for the protection of the natural environment and its public enjoyment. To put it more succinctly:

NE = EN + CA + RDS
where CA = CC + RDC
and EN = NCC – (SNH + CCW)

Nature and its human care and appreciation navigate a forest of acronyms. A sometimes fraught institutional history, conveyed with diligence in works by John Sheail, sees nature gathered under public jurisdiction.[171] Pressures public and private are fended off, designated nature patches are defended, and attempts are made to inculcate ecological principles into wider policy, all the while adapting to altered political circumstance. The sense of the natural world as something distinct from the human, but with which the human is entangled, and which the human can impact to the point of destruction, shapes government as it shapes wider public debate. From the twenty-first century English nature is overwritten too by narratives of global climate change, considered in the next chapter, and by geopolitical shifts, not least with the departure of the UK from the EU, which generates challenges for nature policy as for agricultural policy. The first major post-Brexit piece of environmental legislation was the 2021 Environment Act, which created an independent Office for Environmental Protection. Natural England Chair Tony Juniper, a former director of Friends of the Earth and Green Party candidate, foresaw the Act as 'enabling us to have more, better, bigger and connected areas of natural habitats, bringing a range of practical benefits and permitting more people to enjoy the wonders of the natural world, while improving wider environmental quality at the same time'.[172]

From *Selling England by the Pound* to *Flora Britannica*, from 'Going, Going' to climate emergency, from UN conferences to EU departures. The 1970s set a nature tone of continuing resonance, where the cultural and governmental enfold and hopes and anxieties cross scales from local to global. If the 1970s saw a new consciousness of the earth as a whole, prompted by views from space, the twenty-first century brings another global framing via the Anthropocene. Any public body called English Nature, or Natural England, inhabits however national cultural and political complexities, signalled by events and commentaries as various as the 'Countryside in 1970' conferences, the reports of the Department of the Environment (one of DEFRA's precursors), the spillages of wrecked tankers, ecological blueprints, activist campaigns, environmental fables and nature writings.

Just as nature policy swings between parties of government, so the politics of English nature shuttles across ideologies, as demonstrated in another prominent example of recent nature writing, which can conclude this chapter. Helen Macdonald's 2014 *H is for Hawk* achieved notable publishing success from its mix of the personal and cultural, in a story of personal bereavement, falconry knowledge and literary history. Macdonald had earlier published a cultural historical study of falcons, and her work attends to the cultural and political complexities of nature, English or otherwise.[173] Nature exploration navigates an emotional economy far beyond the gently pastoral, Macdonald examining atavistic forms of nature appreciation and what for some are sinister histories. The chief human reference point in *H is for Hawk* is T. H. White and his 1951 book *The Goshawk*. Through White, Macdonald shows political outlooks on nature tracking all ways. In a chapter on 'Apple Day', a festival invented by Common Ground in 1990 to promote English apple varieties, Macdonald takes her own goshawk for display at a farm's Apple Day celebration. The Apple Day chapter follows one discussing Nazi falconry, and Macdonald reflects on the Common Ground-inspired show of apples and raptors: 'In Germany, falconry had fed into the terrible dreams of an invented Aryan past. Yet here we are now in all our variousness.'[174] If some attention to English nature is unvariously consolatory, resting on a benign sense of natural place, Macdonald acknowledges harder edges of nature belonging and different ways of being humanly natural.[175] The examples in this chapter, like the preceding analysis of agriculture, show nature mingling the radical and conservative, concern moving across the political spectrum. Oliver Postgate and the Duke of Edinburgh, Peter Gabriel and Philip Larkin, Elisabeth Beresford and Edward Goldsmith, Nan Fairbrother and Richard Mabey, stretch the politics of nature, all caring for the non-human world, in all their variousness. English nature, in the Wombles' Wimbledon or *The Ecologist*'s tainted other Eden, shows contested variety. If N is for Natural and E is for England, the formula of acronyms generating Natural England also sends cautionary letters: EDEN SCARS/ EDEN WARNS.

5
England and the Anthropocene

At the time of writing, the Anthropocene remains an unofficial geological epoch. Revision of the geological timescale awaits approval by the adjudicatory International Commission on Stratigraphy (ICS), but the word, put into scientific circulation by Paul Crutzen and Eugene Stoermer in 2000, has caught hold.[1] The Anthropocene has become common cultural currency for a planet stamped by humanity, and scientific confirmation of its epochal status appears likely, soon. This chapter explores the meeting point of England and the Anthropocene, examining the national refractions and inflexions of a global classification. Given, however, the novelty of Anthropocene terminology, some initial analysis of general definitions is required.

Definitions and Anticipations

Twenty-first-century nature concern has been both underwritten and overwritten by narratives of climate change, reinforcing and tweaking the nature outlooks considered in Chapter Four. The Anthropocene has emerged as a distinct but related frame, geological rather than atmospheric, but likewise denoting the anthropogenic. Within the proposed Anthropocene geological epoch, the human stamp on the planet will be indelible, in the rock record as in climatic systems. The Anthropocene Working Group reporting to the ICS has proposed that the term be adopted, succeeding the Holocene. The idea of the earth entering a time where not only its land surfaces and sea waters, its air qualities and climatic systems, but its rock records are irredeemably marked by human activity, has become scientifically and culturally familiar.[2]

'An English Landscape in Coal Measure Times', illustration by Maurice Wilson, from H. H. Swinnerton, *Fossils* (1960).

Alec Finlay, in his *A Place-Aware Dictionary*, gives a succinct definition, 'ANTHROPOCENE: us being too much for everything else'.[3] Inaugurating the Anthropocene may suggest human culpability or guilt, or human capability and power. Pinning such a label on the earth may for some indicate human hubris, for others recognizes blame and thereby spurs remedial action; not that such action could ever remove the label, everything becoming Holocene again. Even an Anthropocene made less transformative would remain an Anthropocene, the remedial action itself signifying the human capacity for earth effects.

The Anthropocene entails a complex temporality, not least as, unlike any other geological epoch, it is prospective as well as retrospective. Even if humans or their antecedents were around at the time, no one announced the beginning of the Holocene, or the Pleistocene. Geologists seek a 'golden spike' in the sediment record to mark the stratigraphic beginning of the Anthropocene, with the current favourite the post-1945 global traces left by atmospheric nuclear weapons tests, but processes making the Anthropocene were evidently set in train long before. A range of start dates have indeed been proposed, for an Anthropocene beginning around 1800, in the sixteenth century or in prehistory. The chosen inaugural events will help shape Anthropocene meaning: the beginnings of farming, the colonial exploitation of the Americas, the Industrial Revolution, the bomb. Different 'Anthro' stories proceed from different Anthropocene openings.

Like any other geological terminology, the Anthropocene is a piece of wordplay and one that has stuck precisely for its provocative conjunction of the human and the geological. As a complimentary play on words, the 'Anthroposcenic' can be taken to denote the ways in which landscape, in all its cultural complexity, might figure a coming epoch, becoming emblematic of processes marking the Anthropocene.[4] Particular scenes and sites gain prismatic quality, concentrating attention and articulating a natural world whose naturalness is increasingly put into question. Across the wild, the weather and the shore, 'England and the Anthropocene' explores the make-up of an Anthroposcenic England.

The Anthropocene was also anticipated before it was coined, and an English landscape image from 1960, around the time of the likely 'golden spike' for the new epoch, can illustrate the genealogy of a meeting of the human and the geological. H. H. Swinnerton's 1960 book *Fossils*, published in the popular scientific Collins 'New Naturalist' series, had as its frontispiece a picture of English landscape. 'An English Landscape in Coal Measure Times' was produced for Swinnerton by Maurice Wilson (1914–1987), known for Natural History Museum work on reconstructing the look of dinosaurs from their fossils. In 1964 Wilson would be a founder member of the Society of Wild Life Artists, and in 1972 provide the illustrations for Brooke Bond's *Prehistoric Animals* collection of picture cards. In the *Fossils* Coal Measure English landscape, an *Eogyrinus*, 15 feet long and amphibious, emerges from shallow water. Trees and tree ferns, the source of future coal, stand behind, and a *Meganeura*, a giant dragonfly, flies over. This is England, around 300 million years ago, in a picture for Swinnerton 'scientifically accurate as well as aesthetically beautiful'.[5]

Labelling a Carboniferous scene as 'English Landscape' might seem absurd. Whoever saw an *Eogyrinus* in England? In what sense did giant dragonflies fly through English tree ferns? Is this a Blakean projection back millions of years, making the Carboniferous a green and pleasant land, laying down the coal that one day would fuel satanic mills?[6] Patriotic curiosity might also be detected in Swinnerton's

'Idealised Map of the British Area in Carboniferous Times', where the land mass still above Carboniferous sea level, whose surrounding shallow waters would nurture future coal measures, is labelled 'St George's Land'.[7] In the nineteenth century Roderick Murchison had named the Silurian after a Romano-British tribe, marking the geological timescale with British patriotic meaning.[8] Does St George's Land find Swinnerton playing at Carboniferous patriotism?

Or is this less a territorial claim on the Carboniferous than a way of registering time and place as relative? A little reflection on map and painting might suggest that all things and all lands, including England, are ultimately mobile and passing, however solid and stable they seem.[9] Labelling the ancient as English opens up a dialogic seam between then and now, and for the now of 1960 the Carboniferous connections were vivid. *Fossils* appeared when the coal industry remained central to English and British economy and society. Swinnerton noted coal tips as useful fossil hunting sites, carrying traces of ancient green: 'The commonest fossils found on colliery tip-heaps are plant fragments which even beginners recognise as "fern leaves".'[10] Swinnerton, who had been Geological Society President in 1938–40, and a recipient of the Murchison Medal, was by 1960 Emeritus Professor of Geology at

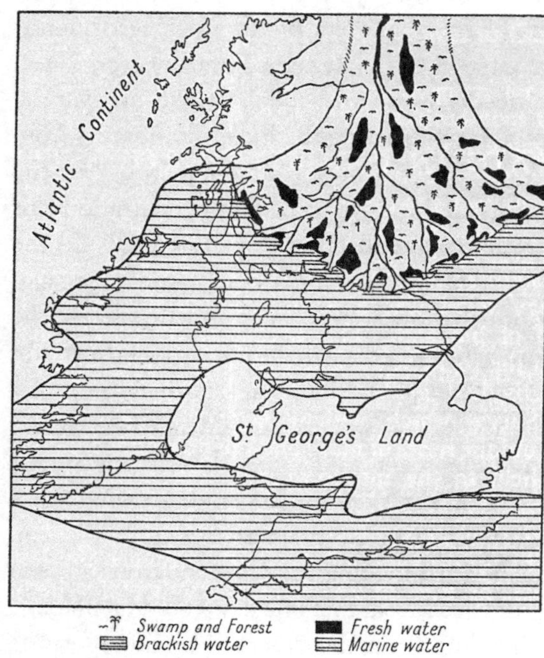

'Idealised Map of the British Area in Carboniferous Times', from H. H. Swinnerton, *Fossils* (1960).

the University of Nottingham, where he had taught since 1902. On its publication *Fossils* was reviewed by some as scientifically a little behind the times, but in the context of twenty-first-century Anthropocene science, it can be read as a prescient articulation, from the new epoch's likely inaugural years. In the Midland coalfields, and also the inland oilfields in Nottinghamshire and Leicestershire, Swinnerton saw geological science put to economic fossil fuel use, Carboniferous geology identifying the coal measures, whose exploitation fuelled the modern industrial processes that would transform human society and leave a geological mark. The green England of the Carboniferous made the blackest rock, which fuelled the England that helped make the Anthropocene.

The Anthropocene is anticipated in *Fossils* not only through Carboniferous reflection, but in discussion of the human geological legacy. From the nineteenth century geologists had anticipated the possibilities, Charles Lyell in *Principles of Geology* commenting, 'The earth's crust must be remodelled more than once before all the memorials of man which are continually becoming entombed in the rocks now forming will be destroyed.'[11] Swinnerton likewise reflected on the human modification of earth materials:

> upon a scale vastly exceeding that produced by any other organism. Today that scale has increased to such a degree that man is beginning to rival in effectiveness some of the normal geological agencies. Thus one Trent valley colliery may during the time of its existence shift as much material as the adjoining river itself. But at this point we begin to break into the precincts of geography. On the other hand the colliery shaft and tip-heaps are as truly fossil in significance as a worm-burrow or casting found in the Permian rocks, or in the basal beds of the Cambrian.[12]

Writing in 1960, Swinnerton anticipates the Anthropocene. Carboniferous England and the English landscapes of Carboniferous exploitation become Anthroposcenic.

An English Anthroposcenery

The Anthropocene jolts nature as a category, and in doing so meets different national imaginaries. There is a geography of national dispositions towards the Anthropocene, as towards climate change, and any coordination of understanding and action needs to work through rather than bypass such variation. England, like any other country, remains a scale at which climate change and the Anthropocene are distinctively lived.

Geologists have begun to examine what might signify an English Anthropocene landscape. In 2018, in the *Proceedings of the Geologists' Association*, Jan Zalasiewicz, Colin Waters, Mark Williams, David Aldridge and Ian Wilkinson explored 'the stratigraphical signature of the Anthropocene in England', tracing deposits carrying pesticide residues, microplastics and artificial radionuclides, in 'an initial sketch of how the Anthropocene might be recognized in England'.[13] With its history of human activity and geological study, Zalasiewicz et al. conclude: 'England is an ideal laboratory for this new kind of geology.'[14] From the geologists' stratigraphical signatures, the English Anthropocene field laboratory might take in upland farms affected by Chernobyl fallout, fly ash particles and pesticide residues in lake sediments, or seasides marked by microplastics, 'an unambiguous identifier of Anthropocene strata'.[15] At coastal landfill sites, marine action exposes an archaeology of 'technofossils' of late twentieth-century consumption: 'the temporal resolution attainable using such evidence is geologically precise'.[16] The wider cultural landscapes of coastal loss are examined below, but landfill erosion opens the prospect of plastic human figures, from precisely dateable Christmas toy crazes, tumbling to the beach, in a reprise of longstanding tropes of clifftop cemetery bones falling to the shore. More general processes of coastal change may also expose dateable Anthropocene ephemera, as when in May 2023 the BBC reported 'Norfolk beach walker finds crisp packet from 1960s'.[17] Erosion of dunes around Hemsby had churned old detritus, and things dropped fifty or sixty years ago had washed up nearby. Pre-decimal pricing marked brands since defunct, the plastic litter of seaside snacking barely degraded.

In natural history terms, as the work of Mabey, whose 1973 examination of landfill ecology was noted earlier, has emphasized, English nature commonly carries a human imprint. In a country accustomed to the enfolding of the human and natural, the Anthropocene as an idea becomes more readily adhesive. In such a context, relict iconic industrial landscapes, especially those associated with the Industrial Revolution, can become Anthropocene sites. *About England*, the companion volume to *England's Green*, traced the English cultures of industrial heritage over six decades, their standing given an environmental twist if England appears the birthplace of the Anthropocene, kick-starting the acceleration of carbon emissions as fossil fuels powered technological change.[18] An industrial World Heritage Site indeed features in thin disguise in a 2020 novel that might be read as an Anthropocene allegory, M. John Harrison's *The Sunken Land Begins to Rise Again*. Harrison's plot shuttles between London and a town very like Ironbridge in Shropshire, with its World Heritage Site bridge and gorge. Victoria Nyman has moved there, and strange water creatures are emerging, fish-like people. There is also something strange about a pool in the fields above the coal-fired power station. November rains fall, the land is sodden, and water percolates everywhere, even 'through the demented, unpredictable, immeasurably fortunate geology, fuel for the industrial light and magic that had once changed the world'.[19] Harrison's 'green children',[20] spied outdoors and in bathrooms, form figures of an epochal English uncanny, their time plotted in a manner akin to Victoria's view, in a dream, from the gorge's edge:

> She was to understand, Victoria knew, that she was seeing a future. People had found fresh ways to live. Or perhaps it wasn't, as far as the Gorge was concerned, a future at all, only an intersection of possibilities, unconformable layers of time, myths from a geography long forgotten or not yet invented.[21]

Anthropocene stories can also gain purchase at former industrial sites less colonized for heritage, indeed more re-colonized by flora and fauna, with new natural histories overtaking human works. The writings of Norman Nicholson, noted in the previous chapter for his contribution to Mabey's Common Ground 1984 collection *Second Nature*, indicate some narrative possibilities. Nicholson's home town of Millom in west Cumbria, north of the shipbuilding centre of Barrow and south of the nuclear centre of Sellafield, was for a hundred years dominated by iron ore mining and ironworking. Visiting the town on a midweek March day in 2004, all that was gone. Arriving in the town centre before lunch, all was quiet. A few shops were open, but the museum was closed for the season and the streets were deserted. Sudden shouts echoed the terraced streets at school lunch break, children rushing for shop snacks, before all was again quiet. Above a shop door, behind a flag of St George, limp on a still day, a plaque announced 'Home of Cumbrian Poet Norman Nicholson Man of Millom 1914–1987', just visible in a murky pre-digital photograph, the high dormer window his regular lookout over life. Driving out of town to the site of the former ironworks and mines at Hodbarrow, a new ecology appeared, old workings growing over, the odd chimney left standing. A former industrial centre, peripherally overgrown. The Irish Sea to the west, old industrial lagoons, gorse and scrub, and, as in Millom, nobody else around, the car parked furtively in the wide open. The ironworks site is a Local Nature Reserve, with Nicholson's poem 'Scafell Pike' on an interpretation plinth, and Hodbarrow is a Royal Society for the Protection of Birds reserve, purchased in 1986, and part of the Duddon Estuary Site of Special Scientific Interest, but on a dull March day twenty years ago, nature designation did not register.

Nicholson lived almost all his life in the house with the plaque, and his poetry and topographic writing helps explain the place as it stood in 2004, with its empty midweek streets and diminished employment. Nicholson, a poet of industry and geology, of working lives and rock types, and who documented Millom life in his 1959 book *Provincial Pleasures*, conveys a landscape which might be called Anthroposcenic.[22] The poem 'On the Closing of Millom Ironworks', dated 'September 1968', begins with Nicholson turning to see which way the wind is blowing, by 'the feathered/ Weathercock of the furnace chimneys', but no smoke shows the wind. Pollution – slag dust, soot and sulphur – will go, and so will work, and Nicholson conveys social loss, unemployment reprising interwar depression, with few prospects: 'On the ebb-tide sands, the five-funnelled/ Battleship of the furnace lies beached and rusting.'[23]

The economic tide gone out, Nicholson returned to the works site in 1981, in his collection *Sea to the West*, with 'On the Dismantling of Millom Ironworks'. The shock of closure grows over, and another landscape appears. Nicholson begins with a quote from Wordsworth on the adjacent River Duddon being remote from sordid industry, words at which he 'laughed once', but which now redescribe a post-industrial place, 'the Duddon rediscovers/ Its former channel almost

St George's Terrace, Millom, March 2004.

Hodbarrow, Millom, March 2004.

unencumbered'. Plants colonize, birds feed in the lagoons and views of the nearby mountain of Black Combe, a looming presence throughout Nicholson's poetry, open up: 'The wind resumes its Right of Way.' The ironworks site is smoothed, and Nicholson taps glacial imagery to set the grassing over of the works, the embedding of industry into earth, as a process of geomorphological import:

> Slagbanks ploughed down to half their height, all cragginess,
> Scrag-end and scree ironed out, and re-soiled and greened over
> To long sulky drumlins, dumped there by the look of them
> An ice-age ago.

The 'scrag-end' invokes a poor cut of meat, and Nicholson continues with a butchery theme, the works 'carcass' cut up, as 'they shovelled my childhood/ On to a rubbish heap'.

The ironworks, an industrial site working natural forces, its old fiery process compared by Nicholson to the volcanic, quietens. Igneous turns to sedimentary. The ironworks dismantled, Millom 'shrinks and/ dwindles', as 'An age/ is pensioned off.' The works become 'archaeological data'. Nicholson presents Wordsworth's ghost seeing 'a peninsula bare as it used to be', and a river 'untainted', though flowing in the poem's final words to 'a bleak, unpopulated shore'. A workforce gone, what Millom gains, though this may be scant compensation, are new strata. The relics of things that were once someone's childhood, and provided livelihood for 'five generations', are something for a future geologist to core and they might call them 'Anthropocene'. In 1981, 'On the Dismantling of Millom Ironworks', with its sulky drumlins, anticipates the English Anthroposcenic.[24]

Wild England?

In 1980 Richard Mabey had quoted Ted Hughes's poem 'Swifts' for reassurance on nature's continuing seasonal cycles. In 2005 Mabey's *Nature Cure* reprised the quotation, indeed the book began with Mabey rescuing a fledgling swift, Mabey's message from Hughes and the swifts being that 'the globe's still working'.[25] That message was, however, becoming less straightforward by 2005, with considerable doubt as to whether the globe was still working. Twenty-first-century naturalists are pulled and torn between the wild and the Anthropocene, between tracking non-human species who we can never fully know and finding the human stamp on everything. English nature as framed by climate change is discussed below, but here the focus is on England, the Anthropocene and the wild.

We Have Never Been Wilderness

To paraphrase Bruno Latour's influential phrase 'We have never been modern,' which challenged the supposed separation of human and non-human in narratives of modernity, it could be said of English natural history that 'we have never been wilderness.'[26] For as long as English 'nature' has been a concern, the human presence has been acknowledged, Jonathan Raban noting, 'in England, nature and culture are so intimately entwined that their categorical separation is a false distinction.'[27] Trails of humanly natural association carry forward into the Anthropocene; of human impact which may not be detrimental, may even be a cause for celebration and of the impossibility of disentangling human and nonhuman. The Anthropocene may be novel in its planetary and geological scope, but when scaled down meets familiar English landscape stories where the human and natural are not opposed, and where wilderness makes little sense.

If English natural history has never done wilderness, the wild nonetheless does English cultural work, whether as a mode of encounter with the non-human in a human-shaped landscape, or as a quality registered in places and creatures. Wild, or wilder creatures could be found, and there are also English echoes of North American wilderness narratives in the deployment of the wild as a dehumanizing category. Just as in North America a reverence for nature could overlook and erase indigenous capacity, so English narratives within and beyond the British Isles could project the wild onto people as well as landscapes, relishing the latter while neglecting the former and social clearance might follow. Enthusiasms for the wild, and for wilding, should be conscious and cautious of such cultural geneaologies.

The place for the wild in Anthropocene English nature can be pursued via the work of naturalist Tim Dee. In 2018 Dee edited *Ground Work*, a collection of 'writing on places and people' for Common Ground, a successor to Mabey's 1984 *Second Nature*; Mabey was the only author common to both collections. Dee argued, 'We are living – many believe – in the Anthropocene, an epoch where everything of Earth's current matter and life, as well as the shape of things to come, is being determined by the ruinous activities of just one soft-skinned, warm-blooded, short-lived, pedestrian ape.'[28] For Dee, turning away from the human to a wild nature made no sense, but attention to place did, with places as 'anthropogenic creations' offering human-natural common cooperative ground. Here were 'cultural landscapes . . . vital for life': 'All of our habitat is relevant: not just the pretty bits.'[29]

The same year as *Ground Work*, Dee published *Landfill*, exploring a site indicative of the Anthropocene: 'Landfill means more than just a tip for the end of things. It is also a description of how we have worked the rest of the living world, learned about it, named and catalogued it, and have thus occupied or planted our planet, filling the land.'[30] Dee's focus was a now common habitué of the dump, the gull, again following Mabey's reference in *The Unofficial Countryside* to gulls as 'winter opportunists' scavenging rubbish tips.[31] *Landfill* thus explored 'strangely lively' places, where waste could 'nourish and sustain', where 'in-between birds' inhabited 'an in-between world'.[32] Life cycles shifted with waste management policies, the increasing recycling of food waste making 'edible trash' rarer and landfill gull numbers subsequently falling.[33] Dee reports a rare English sighting of an American herring gull:

> in February 2016, a juvenile was reported feeding in a 'chip skip' at a McCain's potato-processing factory at Whittlesey in Cambridgeshire. This record – a rare gull, a 'new' species, making its way in the Anthropocene by stealing chips from a dump – might in a single moment have floodlit everything that I am in pursuit of here.[34]

A humanly natural history comes to the dump, one of the geologists' 'signature' Anthropocene sites. Yet the gulls in *Landfill*, whatever they feed on, remain wild creatures. In 1953 Niko Tinbergen produced *The Herring Gull's World*, a classic study of 'the social behaviour of birds', and if the Anthropocene gulls' world is increasingly connected to human waste, that does not lessen the gulls' gullness, does not reduce their species' otherness.[35] At the landfill, as at the seaside, humans and gulls cohabit their different worlds. The sense of species differently cohabiting indeed gives the wild continuing Anthropocene purchase, such that to talk of 'wildlife' in a city, or a carefully managed nature reserve, is not oxymoronic. The naturalist can pursue the 'wild' as a non-human quality apart from and threatened by human civilization, even if wilderness as intact purely non-human ecology makes little sense in England or the wider British archipelago. In *Nature Cure* Mabey, reflecting on a U.S. nature trip, concludes he was touched less by wilderness than 'the quality of *wildness*', 'the untidy, energising edge of all living systems'.[36]

The wild can also carry consolatory quality, conveyed in a poetic citation rivalling Hughes's 'Swifts' in frequency. Gerard Manley Hopkins's characteristically alliterative 1881 poem 'Inversnaid', written on a place near Loch Lomond, includes the lines: 'What would the world be, once bereft/ Of wet and of wilderness? Let them be left,/ Oh let them be left, wildness and wet;/ Long live the weeds and the wilderness yet.'[37] In his 2010 celebratory account of *Weeds*, Mabey cites Hopkins's 'famous couplet' as a celebration of 'maverick independence . . . though his weeds are just commonplace plants of all kinds'. Weeds are for Mabey 'vagabond plants' whose 'cussedness and refusal to play by our rules makes them subversive, and the very essence of wildness'.[38] 'Inversnaid' also provided the title for photographer Simon Roberts's 2017–20 project *The Weeds and the Wilderness*, inspired by Hopkins's idea of 'inscape', showing winter images of ancient broadleaved woodland, tangles of mossy branches. Roberts also took Hopkins's 'Inscapes' for the title of a Sussex project commissioned to accompany a 2019 exhibition of Ivon Hitchens's landscape paintings.[39] Roberts walked the Downs, finding woodland inscape scenes, some of trees in open country, others of mossy entanglement, human eye meeting arboreal growth in intricate green.

Roberts also found in *The Weeds and the Wilderness* a national message:

> Many Britons no longer have any daily connection with its woods. Mostly we go about our lives sealed from the wild. At the same time, these landscapes touch upon themes such as conservation, ownership, history, magic and myth, climate change, childhood fears, and our current obsession with what is 'native' or 'alien'. They also say something about Britishness and belonging.[40]

If Roberts took Hopkins's Scottish-set verse for meanings British and English, poet Andrew Motion made a more straightforward English claim in his outgoing 2015 Presidential speech to the Campaign to Protect Rural England on 'Poetry and the English Countryside'. Motion read 'Inversnaid', finding it 'a poster poem for CPRE', the braes and the burn by Loch Lomond gathered into the English rural, in sentiment if not formal jurisdiction.[41]

Even in the Anthropocene, and perhaps especially in the Anthropocene, the wild, the weed, the wilderness retain categorical value for those taking stock of the natural: sometimes for consolation; sometimes for a sense that even if the human marks everything, qualities beyond the human remain; sometimes to challenge modes of thought. We may never have been wilderness, but even in an epoch defined by the imbrication of the human and natural, the wild remains in play.

England Rewilded

'Inversnaid' citations invoke a landscape left to go its own way, a self-willed ecology, untended, untidied, unweeded. Such qualities also inform projects to 'rewild' landscape, the term 'rewilding' carrying a particular inflection in a land without wilderness. Removing human intervention, and reintroducting 'lost' species at one time native, including the beaver, rewilding projects have appeared across the UK, initially upland in location and charity-led, including on Dartmoor and in Ennerdale in the western Lake District. 'Wild Ennerdale' brought together Natural England, the National Trust, the Forestry Commission and United Utilities to restore the valley to something other than a conifer plantation.[42] Rewilding has lately spread to lowland locations under private ownership, meeting different farming practices and cultures of property and thus becoming entwined with the historic iconography of rural England. Virginia Thomas notes that the 'domestication' of rewilding in 'England's green and pleasant land' has often tended to drop the 're', to become simply 'wilding': 'rewilding is being adapted to exist alongside people in England as compared to other countries where it has lower tolerance for human intervention and a tendency to exclude humans.'[43] Released into English landscape, (re)wilding gathers the tensions of English land management; of public goods and private preserves, ecological sustainability and commercial viability.

English places are as ever remade via connections elsewhere, and a significant elsewhere for rewilding is the Dutch polder of

Oostvaardersplassen, overseen since the 1980s by ecologist Frans Vera as an experiment in wilding, exploring the influence of herbivores in shaping plant ecology and introducing the necessary carnivores to maintain species balance.[44] Vera's artifice of the wild, with agricultural land formerly reclaimed from the sea reclaimed again for wilding, offers a model for contained experiment. In *Nature Cure* Mabey admired Dutch wilding work, with Vera's 'nature-culture preserve' a productive paradox.[45] On a local Suffolk fen, Mabey similarly found introduced Konik ponies had somehow 'conjured up a wilderness' in an 'artfully stage-managed landscape'.[46]

The most prominent lowland England rewilding case is Knepp Castle Estate in West Sussex. Owner Charlie Burrell inherited Knepp in 1987 and, after efforts at farm intensification and diversification proved unprofitable, chose a different direction in the early 2000s. Burrell's wife Isabella Tree recounts the Knepp story in *Wilding*, with Hopkins's 'Inversnaid' providing the book's epigram.[47] Burrell and Tree visited Oostvaardersplassen in 2002 after reading the 2000 English translation of Vera's book *Grazing Ecology and Forest History*, and Vera was later invited onto Knepp's Wildland Advisory Board.[48] *Wilding* is a story of longhorn cattle, Exmoor ponies and Tamworth pigs introduced, and turtle doves and purple emperor butterflies attracted, as Knepp is redeemed from intensive farming to wood pasture through a kind of organic non-farming (though specialist meat is sold): 'the biggest change of all came from simply not drenching the land with fungicides and pesticides.'[49]

The Knepp experiment wraps rewilding within English landscape themes of family, property and social class. Knepp has been owned by the Burrell family since 1787, and the first rewilding steps were taken in the estate's parkland, laid out in the early nineteenth century in the style of Humphry Repton. Allusions to upper-class life appear in *Wilding*, as when an Exmoor pony colt causes concern: 'He would gallop onto the practice polo field in front of the house, straight through the spectators, to investigate his strange cousins chasing a ball.'[50] Rewilding also met local scepticism, neighbouring farmers wary of emergent scrubby waste, threatening a reweeding of their land. Knepp's scrub, presented as ecological virtue, challenged assumptions as to what the Sussex Weald should be: 'It was not surprising, then, that locals who had gazed all their lives on what they considered the epitome of English landscape, the picture postcard of resolute agricultural endeavour, were outraged when Knepp was invaded by scrub.'[51]

Knepp rewilding is also informed by connections and allusions to Africa, just as nature conservation in the 1960s was shaped by colonial and post-colonial experience. *Wilding* invokes personal intercontinental biography, Burrell's early life spent in Rhodesia where his father farmed tobacco and cotton before independence: 'For Charlie, the imprint of Africa was deep in his bones.'[52] The 'gentle burbling' of Knepp's turtle doves, arriving from West Africa as summer migrants, 'takes him back to the African bush'.[53] Tree and Burrell had undertaken wildlife safaris in southern Africa, and Oostvaardersplassen too has African connections, Tree noting that Vera was inspired by 1979 studies of Serengeti grazing ecology. *Wilding* sets Africa, the Netherlands and Sussex in exchange, with Vera's Dutch 'model for Europe' being 'as tightly cropped as Kenya's Maasai Mara': 'For sheer biomass Charlie and I had seen nothing like it this side of Botswana's Okavango Delta.'[54] Knepp itself conjures 'The Serengeti Effect', as fallow deer brought from Petworth in Sussex settle: 'by summer they were wandering quietly through the landscape like herds of impala in the Serengeti.'[55] Sussex appears African to shame modern England; at the inaugural 2006 meeting of the Knepp Wildland Steering Group, 'The day's programme for "Establishing a Biodiverse Wilderness Area in the Low Weald of Sussex" began with a morning safari', while from 2014 the southern block of the estate hosted 'Knepp Wildland Safaris'.[56] Tree foresaw a wilder future Sussex: 'We dream of leading safaris from Knepp across rewilded land all the way to the sea.'[57] Knepp becomes a kind of Longleat for the English Anthropocene; if in the 1960s Lord Bath imported lions and other beasts to make a piece of Africa at Longleat safari park in Wiltshire, different African ecological connections shape twenty-first-century Sussex.[58]

Knepp, to adopt Mabey's phrase, offers an artfully stage-managed wild England. Rewilding as artful management also informs a musical work citing Knepp, Sam Lee's song 'Turtle Dove', on his 2020 album *Old Wow*, 'Dedicated to The Knepp Rewilding Estate, RSPB and all those who are working to save our disappearing species.' 'Turtle Dove' opens the 'earth' section of Lee's album, a traditional song, Lee's lyrics matching those collected as 'The Little Turtle Dove' in Cecil Sharp's 1905 *Folk Songs from Somerset*, with an added final verse. The tune follows Ralph Vaughan Williams's arrangement of a lyrically different

'The Turtle Dove', collected by him in Sussex in 1907.[59] Lee's 'Turtle Dove' enfolds migration stories of bird and human, and the love of a singer for a songbird and a motherly earth. Turtle doves also focused one of Lee's 'nature pilgrimages', a March 2019 BBC Radio Four programme conveying a Sussex 'turtle dove pilgrimage': 'the pilgrims sing as they progress towards the Knepp rewilding estate, where they hope to sing "The Turtle Dove" to the last remaining colony of turtle doves in Sussex.' Lee and the pilgrims find the bird, and hear its sound, 'a bird so utterly English and mythological'. Singing the song to the birds brings Lee 'catharsis': 'the song is now back where it needs to be, with the birds, with this bit of land with them singing to the land . . . it feels so right.'[60] The cover of *Old Wow*, painted by Alex Merry, shows the singer in a wood and pasture landscape, fauna proliferating, a refreshed ecology rewilding England, as Lee seeks to renew a country's old songs.[61]

The work of Knepp, and Tree's account of it, has become a standard reference point for those considering the possibilities of rewilding in lowland England. From 2010 Burrell chaired the Beaver Advisory Committee for England, which in 2015 oversaw the release of beavers into the River Otter in Devon, and from 2015 headed Rewilding Britain, established with the upsurge of rewilding interest following George Monbiot's 2013 book *Feral*.[62] Rewilding Britain aims for a million hectares rewilded over 100 years, 'to restore parts of the British Isles to wild nature and to allow lost creatures, like the lynx and beaver, the burbot, eagle owl and Dalmatian pelican, and, in our remotest places, elk and wolf, to live here once more'.[63] For Tree, rewilding could be cultural restoration, her response to criticism that rewilding erodes cultural landscapes being that such landscapes are often Victorian creations: 'If medieval wood pasture – our true "forest" is the baseline, rewilding is far from vandalistic. It restores to us a richer, deeper countryside that accompanied us for thousands of years.'[64]

Rewilding on an estate is one thing, extending the vision to a wider region another, and Lake District debates indicate potential English wilding turbulence, with in *Feral* Monbiot giving critical attention to Lakeland's ecological qualities. Monbiot promoted not wilderness but ecosystems 'self-willed: governed not by human management but by their own processes'.[65] Monbiot sought also a 'rewilding of human life', enhancing 'delight in the natural world', nature as ever an arena for arguments over human conduct.[66] Humans, as much as beavers or lynx, could be reintroduced to the English wild and Monbiot recounted his own formative experiences. Slinging a dead deer over his shoulders, Monbiot experiences 'a genetic memory', albeit one expressed through the language of a louche hotel: 'Civilisation slid off as easily as a bathrobe.'[67] *Feral* 'foresees large areas of self-willed land and sea, repopulated by the beasts now missing from these places, in which we may freely roam', and one of those large areas might be the Lake District.[68]

Monbiot argued for rewilding not on productive land but 'in the places – especially in the uplands – in which production is so low that farming continues only as a result of the taxpayer's generosity'.[69] Wild Ennerdale's single-valley rewilding was merely 'granting nature a kind of day release from the conservation prison', the rest of the Lake District showing conventional landscape values as an obstacle to a renatured land.[70] The Lake District World Heritage Site bid showed for Monbiot a disjuncture between cultural landscape and ecological virtue. The National Trust and others were official warders of 'The Conservation Prison', Monbiot's critical chapter on these headed by Hopkins's 'Inversnaid' weeds and wilderness quote.[71] Monbiot also targeted pastoral farming, with sheep as ruminant villains, reflecting an 'agricultural hegemony'.[72] When the World Heritage Site bid was launched in 2013, Monbiot commented on the Lakes:

> I see it as one of the most depressing landscapes in Europe. It competes with the chemical deserts of East Anglia for the title of Britain's worst-kept countryside.
>
> The celebrated fells have been thoroughly sheepwrecked: the forests which once covered them have been reduced by the white plague to bare rock and bowling green . . . This is the state which the bid would help preserve in perpetuity, preventing the ecological restoration of England's biggest national park.[73]

When World Heritage status was achieved, Monbiot lambasted a 'Lie of the Land', the region now 'officially designated a Beatrix Potter-themed sheep museum . . . sheep worship is the official religion in the Lake District':

> The Lake District's new designation is based on a fairytale: a fairytale with great cultural power. For 3,000 years this story

> has presented sheep farming as the seat of innocence and purity; an Arcadian refuge from the corruption of the city, an idyll in perfect harmony with the natural world . . . Sheep, by nibbling out tree seedlings and other edible species, are a fully-automated system for ecological destruction.[74]

Those speaking for pastoral farming unsurprisingly take another line, as indeed Monbiot acknowledges in *Feral* when recounting a sympathetic dialogue with farmer Dafydd Morris-Jones, for whom rewilding is 'post-romantic gardening'.[75] The ecological effect of sheep has been the subject of nuanced discussion within Lakeland, not least when the foot and mouth outbreak removed grazing from significant areas, allowing suppressed plant life to flourish. In 2003 the Friends of the Lake District and English Nature's *Flora of the Fells* project, coordinated by Martin Varley, highlighted rare plant life and the disappearance of 'colour, variety and diversity' under intensive grazing.[76] Botanist Jeremy Roberts described the 'untrammelled growth' after foot and mouth, and by 2002 the 'astonishing sight' of 'species reasserting themselves' after 'the epoch of over-grazing'.[77] *Flora of the Fells* also, however, sought the farmer's perspective, suggesting how reductions in grazing could produce not only a richer ecology but 'healthier' sheep.[78]

A reworked rather than removed sheep farming informs Rebanks's *A Shepherd's Life*, which presented proposals for 'destocking' the fells as 'a grave insult to the many folk who work this landscape because the loss of one flock, or its reduction, weakens the whole fell-farming system'.[79] Monbiot's critique of 'Lie of the Land' had indeed singled out Rebanks: 'From the beginning, the world heritage bid was slanted. The Lake District partnership commissioned its economic evaluation from a company called Rebanks Consulting. It is owned and run by James Rebanks, a Lake District sheep farmer. He was paid £30,000 to promote his own industry's interests.'[80] Rebanks by contrast presented a reworked sheep farming as an opportunity for environmental and social sustainability, redressing farming's 'twentieth-century excesses'.[81] Rebanks's 2020 book *English Pastoral* extended his arguments, envisaging 'agricultural diversity' such that his own practice would not appear some diversion from an intensive norm, and with a need for 'radical structural changes in our relationship with food and farming'.[82]

Matthew Kelly suggests that both Rebanks and Knepp serve as a reminder 'of how environmental debate is haunted by the fundamental that structures our society: the line that divides the propertied from the people without property'.[83] The scale of Rebanks's Lakeland and Burrell and Tree's Sussex properties may be rather different, but in both cases landownership enables the reshaping of a field. *English Pastoral* and *Wilding* both also draw on global reference points; Africa and the Netherlands at Knepp, while for Rebanks Australian and U.S. journeys put home in perspective. *English Pastoral* also acknowledges a visit to Knepp, hosted by Burrell and Tree, though Rebanks critiques those making sweeping proposals to rewild some areas while keeping others in intensive production. His Lakeland valley is 'a beautiful compromise', aiming 'to bridge the historic animosity between farmers and ecologists': 'We can build a new English Pastoral: not a utopia, but somewhere decent for us all.'[84] In the Lake District, as around Knepp in Sussex, different English landscape visions clash. Feral England meets English Pastoral, long and short horns locked.

If, with England as humanly natural landscape, we have never been wilderness, England has been here before in anxieties over the return of wild nature. Rewilding disputes carry a family resemblance to earlier fictional scenarios of a loss of control by diminished humanity, with from the late nineteenth century dystopian and science fictional accounts imagining the energies of nature released. To end this section, two literary examples can indicate the cultural genealogy of wilded England.

In 1885 Richard Jefferies's novel *After London, or Wild England*, southern England from Thames to Severn is under water, London is drowned, a noxious marsh takes the city's place and a lake backs up behind it, narrowing only at 'the straits of White Horse', the ancient chalk landmark at Uffington on the downs near Swindon surviving. After civilizational collapse, Jefferies presents 'The Relapse into Barbarism' (the title of part 1 of the book) producing a new old 'Wild England' (the title of part 2).[85] *After London* presented a southern England opposite to that in William Morris's 1890 *News from Nowhere*, where revolution produced a happy pastoral medieval-style English collective. In his introduction to a reissue of *After London*, John Fowles noted Jefferies's influence on Morris, but saw *After London* as exceeding *News from Nowhere* in its 'honesty'.[86] Fowles presented *After London* as a warning against the loss of 'all soul-life, all pagan greenness'.[87] In *After London*, drastic change produces a reverted land, where Jefferies's hero Felix Aquila adventures. Wilding initially involves the escape of exotic beasts from menageries, but these 'after a while entirely disappeared', with one exception, 'the beaver, whose dams are now occasionally found upon the streams'.[88]

Jefferies was a notable commentator on nature and the rural, with some of his work, including the autobiographic *The Story of My Heart* (1883), informed by a passionate nature-mysticism, with Jefferies in reverie on the downs and hill forts south of his Swindon home, at Liddington and Uffington.[89] The Uffington White Horse was part of Jefferies's enchanted England, but in *After London* it overlooks a country regreened, rewilded and relapsed:

> The old men say their fathers told them that soon after the fields were left to themselves a change began to be visible. It became green everywhere in the first spring, after London ended, so that all the country looked alike.
>
> The meadows were green, and so was the rising wheat which had been sown, but which neither had nor would receive any further care. Such arable fields as had not been sown, but where the last stubble had been ploughed up, were overrun with couch-grass, and where the short stubble had not been ploughed, the weeds hid it. So that there was no place which was not more or less green; the footpaths were the greenest of all, for such is the nature of grass where it has once been trodden on, and by-and-by, as the summer came on, the former roads were thinly covered with the grass that had spread out from the margin.[90]

Everything in England goes green, and civilization relapses. *After London* signals how stories of wilding or rewilding pivot on questions of control or its loss.

Adventure after catastrophe, and tensions over wild English nature similarly inform John Wyndham's 1951 *The Day of the Triffids*.[91] Wyndham's triffids are mobile carnivorous plants, with a deadly sting, farmed for their oil by humans. When the bulk of humanity is blinded by a brilliant display of green atmospheric radiation, the triffids escape their nurseries to dominate the planet. Green from the heavens blinds the human, green from their science kills, humanity's experiment with the natural world rebounding. Only a few, including miners who were underground on the night the lights came, and the hospitalized narrator Bill whose eyes were bandaged after an operation, retain sight.

Wyndham, as in other novels such as *The Midwich Cuckoos* (1957) and *Trouble with Lichen* (1960), refracts nature and Englishness, science fiction playing out in everyday spaces rather than fantasy worlds, recognizable from the reader's present.[92] *The Day of the Triffids* asks how social organization might recover, the cooperative or authoritarian roads that might be taken, the locations where life might rebuild. Six years after the change, Bill and his new partner Josella (who had slept through the green lights after a drunken party), inhabit a southern rural English triffid-free compound: 'Within the safety of our compound we continued to learn about agriculture, and life settled gradually into a routine.'[93] One day Bill and Josella journey to the coast, over roads 'growing so bad', and find an emptied town. Nature is taking England back, in the sense of both time and ecological reclamation:

> Viewed impressionistically from a distance the little town was still the same jumble of small red-roofed houses and bungalows populated mostly by a comfortably retired middle class – but it was an impression that could not last more than a few minutes. Though the tiles still showed, the walls were barely visible. The tidy gardens had vanished under an unchecked growth of green, patched in colour here and there by the descendants of carefully cultivated flowers. Even the roads looked like strips of green carpet from this distance. When we reached them we should find that the effect of soft verdure was illusory; they would be matted with coarse, tough weeds.
>
> 'Only so few years ago,' Josella said reflectively, 'people were wailing about the way those bungalows were destroying the countryside. Now look at them.'
>
> 'The countryside is having its revenge, all right,' I said. 'Nature seemed about finished then – "who would have thought the old man had so much blood in him"?'
>
> 'It rather frightens me. It's as if everything were breaking out. Rejoicing that we're finished, and that it's free to go its own way. I wonder . . . ?'[94]

Triffid dominance gives plant life free rein, and an 'unchecked growth of green' envelops England.

The Day of the Triffids presents a future challenge of dewilding. The initial scale for carving a future is local, and Bill and Josella join a 'colony' on the Isle of Wight, where triffids have been cleared. Resistance begins locally, but the aim is to clear the country, the novel ending:

> We think now that we can see the way, but there is still a lot of work and research to be done before the day when we, or our children, or their children, will cross the narrow straits on the great crusade to drive the triffids back and back with ceaseless destruction until we have wiped the last one of them from the face of the land that they have usurped.[95]

The cultural genealogy of the English wild encompasses dewilding as well as rewilding, both turning on the manner in which humans might shape the settings of their lives.

English Weather, English Climate

In 1972, as noted in Chapter Four, the Department of the Environment chose to preface their *Sinews for Survival* report with a Tolkien quotation, Gandalf proclaiming the need to manage the earth and uproot evils for those who are to come. The wizard notes, however, that the tides are beyond even his mastery and 'What weather they shall have is not ours to rule.'[96] Fifty years later, weather may still not be 'ours to rule', but the sense that we might have affected it has grown, anthropogenic climate change suggesting that unwitting human influence makes for unpredictability. Gandalf was in Gondor in *The Return of the King*, the final volume of *The Lord of the Rings*, addressing what Tolkien termed 'The last debate', a council of men and elves deciding how to counter Sauron such that the ring-bearing hobbit might have time to fulfil his quest, saving Middle Earth. As accustomed weather and climate shifts, a sense of twenty-first-century emergency has grown, with each COP meeting or IPCC convention billed as a last chance saloon, a final time to act. The terms of discussion have shifted from the 1970s, but the sense of crisis is reprised, in amplified form, as the designation of the Anthropocene as geological epoch matches anthropogenic climate change, both denoting the human remaking of the natural. While the Anthropocene is stratigraphic and climate change is atmospheric, the two enfold, and a common sense grows that humanity might be receiving that which is due to us, or at least due to some of us, 'due' here carrying meanings of both reward and responsibility.

Changeably English

Climate is lived at different geographical scales, with global process experienced intimately through local rain and flood, heat and drought. Established national stories about weather, especially powerful in England, are challenged by a breakdown of the distinction between climate as something fixed, and of broader scale, and weather as variable and local. The forecast for the Anthropocene is changeable for both, and an English cultural preoccupation with weather changeability is itself thus up in the air. Is an unusual downpour a mark of deep change, or another English weather quirk? Can images of national meteorological eccentricity hold? In 2010 the redesign of the passport for the United Kingdom of Great Britain and Northern Ireland featured weather symbols, temperature gauges and isobars across every inside page, as complex and unforgeable signs of national identity. Weather inscribed a document claiming solidity, certainty, but just however as freedom of movement became a matter of acute twenty-first-century national anxiety, so too did weather and climate. Alexandra Harris comments on the 2010 passport design: 'If our names and addresses and next-of-kin have been watermarked by the weather we know and pretend not to love, how will we know ourselves without it?'[97]

In his 2013 study of 'living with the weather' in the 'quite mellow' climate of Britain, Richard Mabey suggested that 'What we really suffer from is a *whimsical* climate.'[98] Is, however, the whimsically changeable becoming dangerously capricious? Mabey suggested that even with 'that more sinister unpredictable, climate change', looking back might help domesticate 'maverick weather': 'Every extreme and nuance of weather has been experienced in Britain before, at least for a spell.'[99] Climate change may thus bring 'the traditional British weather as before, only worse and more muddled'.[100] When however in the 2019 revision of his book Mabey noted 27 February 2019 as the hottest February day since records began, where 'Swallows appeared, recklessly, in Dorset', any celebration of unseasonable sun was shadowed by 'ominous bulletins', with the 'premature spring' a likely 'collateral effect of global warming'.[101] The pleasantly warm signals something extreme, a world unbalanced.

Just as an understanding of late twentieth-century farming critiques demands appreciation of the preceding cultures of agricultural modernity, so consideration of contemporary national climate cultures benefits from exploring the mid-twentieth-century English weather world. In popular and scientific accounts, weather was presented as changeably English, the product of a temperate climate and shaping national identity; changeable, perhaps whimsical, but settled. Thus Stephen Bone's 1946 *British Weather* examined 'the results of weather and climate (which is average weather) on our surroundings and on ourselves', concluding: 'The weather is one of the few things in this world that we cannot influence in the slightest and which affects every one of us.'[102] Climate change would undercut the first half of Bone's statement, and ratchet up the second.

Changeability also marked geographer Gordon Manley's 1952 popular scientific Collins 'New Naturalist' account of *Climate and the British Scene*. Manley presented English and British weather as characterized by unthreatening variability:

> Shakespeare's intuitive appreciation of the qualities of his ideal island led him to put into the mouth of Caliban – the unlettered but sentient native – *Be not afraid, the isle is full of noises,/ Sounds, and sweet airs, that give delight and hurt not.* Yet there are but few days when this cannot equally be said of that English countryside which Shakespeare knew.[103]

Sixty years on, the same Shakespeare passage would frame the 2012 Olympic opening ceremony, spoken by Kenneth Branagh as Isambard Kingdom Brunel, as the ceremony's green and pleasant landscape setting was transformed by the Industrial Revolution, an event which in another telling would kick start the Anthropocene. *Climate and the British Scene* aimed 'to explain why the Englishman who contemplates his weather out-of-doors sees and feels what he does', offering a cultural meteorology:

> Nothing is more refreshing or reassuring to the English mind than the contemplation on a clear day of the pageant of the sky from rising ground overlooking a wide stretch of country. The restful changeability of the scene thus viewed has the same fascination as that of a river. There is a quiet underlying sense

> of purpose, a deeply-felt flowing rhythm beneath the fleeting disorderliness and variety of aspect. Faintly-apprehended overtones and harmonies abound to a far greater degree than in the brighter and more simplified American scene with its harsher outlines, its cruder contrasts, its strongly emphasised seasonal tom-tom, mitigated only where higher latitude and wider ocean begin to modify the behaviour of the air.[104]

English landscape told an English story, although *Climate and the British Scene* ranged across Britain, attentive to the national weathers within.

Colour photography by Cyril Newberry and others gave Manley's book visual atmosphere in both subject matter and effect. Captions registered quotidian sensory experience, as for Newberry's image of bus and bicycle in icy low-Fahrenheit commute: 'DERBY: January morning. Going to work in a Midland city. Characteristic coppery smoke-haze in the morning inversion layer following a clear night and light snow-cover. Temperature 22°.'[105] Weather shaped the yearly quotidian round:

> In the English Midlands some no doubt who take note of such things will remember mowing the lawn before the end of a mild March such as that of 1938 or 1945. Others will contrast the very slow oncoming of that inevitable suburban spring-song in the severely cold April of 1947.[106]

Manley's mower 'spring-song' denotes a changeably English weather soundscape.

When Mabey published his 2013 book on living with the weather he chose the title *Turned Out Nice Again*. The title phrase ends the book, Mabey suggesting a British conversational coping with climate change: 'And all the while waving *and* drowning, we will say to each other "It's turned out nice again".'[107] While Mabey's book carries a wide frame of cultural reference, it does not find room for the figure for whom 'Turned Out Nice Again' became a nationally famous catchphrase.[108] George Formby, hugely popular on stage and cinema screen either side of the Second World War, first used the phrase on stage at the Alhambra, Leicester Square, in August 1924 and it caught on, seemingly sunnily optimistic but deployed to distract from characteristic mishaps, melancholy and chirpiness two sides of an English comic

'DERBY: January Morning', photograph by Cyril Newberry, from Gordon Manley, *Climate and the British Scene* (1952).

coin. In 1941 *Turned Out Nice Again* became a film title, while Formby's 1939 song 'It's Turned Out Nice Again' (not featured in the eponymous film) found seasonal double meaning outdoors and indoors, in the weather and the bedroom. The chorus went through the seasons, all four sometimes happening together, but after all the unpredictability, it turns out nice again.

Thirteen years after Formby sang his seasonal song, the publisher's blurb for *Climate and the British Scene* stated, 'We often apologize for our climate, but in many ways it is the best in the world. No great extremes of heat and cold, no dreaded droughts, no destructive hurricanes, yet a marked seasonal rhythm with lots of little surprises – we owe much to our climate.'[109] Manley recorded the statistical extremes, including the harsh winter of early 1947, with February 1947 the snowiest month in two centuries, yet however remarkable, these were ultimately manageable. What happens though when reassuring changeability is overtaken, and weather ceases to, in Shakespeare's phrase, 'hurt not'?

The Summer of '76

The drought of 1976, and the great storm of 1987, pre-dated the emergence of climate change into popular public discourse, but both tapped into emerging concerns for long-term trends and put national weather stories in question. Just as an examination of mid-twentieth-century changeability helps in appreciating today's changed climate discourse, so does consideration of these late twentieth-century extreme events. The 1987 storm is examined below, but the summer of '76 would become the standard reference point for future English heat. When in summer 2022 intensely hot spells approached 40° Celsius, memories were enlisted of coping with drought and heat 46 years before.

The changing sense of what hot spells might mean, from 1976 to today, is conveyed in an annual English publication, *Wisden Cricketers' Almanack*, published yearly since 1864. Since 2018 *Wisden* has included annual 'Environment' reports by Tanya Aldred, who had put climate change on the *Almanack*'s agenda in a 2017 comment piece, 'Cricket and Climate Change: How Green is Your Sward?' Aldred presented cricket as a global game ignoring the most fundamental global change: 'there are few sports more intrinsically connected with their environment than cricket . . . cricket is defined almost entirely by the conditions. If they change, so does the essence of the game.' English cricket was especially vulnerable, its green qualities – seaming pitches, landscape symbolism – under threat:

> That is truest of all in Britain, land of Blake's pleasant pastures, the menacing cloud from across the moors, the Hove sea fret, the misty morning in the Quantocks. Here, there has been a tendency among writers and players of all abilities to romanticise the greensward, to link cricket with the pastoral and the pre-industrial. Yet there is a looming danger: traditional English conditions could be gone in 20 years.[110]

Aldred echoes the title of Michael Henderson's 2020 lament for the commercial disruption of the English summer game, itself taken from Larkin's 'Going, Going', *That Will Be England Gone: The Last Summer of Cricket*.[111] Henderson's 'last' summer was that before the scheduled introduction of the new 'Hundred' franchise format, but Aldred's threat is ecological rather than organizational: 'the assumptions that we make about English cricket, its landscapes and rhythms, will no longer apply. The ball may not move in 2025 the way it did in 1985, or even during that holy summer of 2005. The old-fashioned English seamer could be on his last legs.'[112]

In the 2023 *Almanack*, in a piece reflecting on connections of sponsorship and fossil fuel interests in cricket, Aldred noted the 2022 'joint-hottest summer since records began', with playing hours reduced on the hottest days, spectators sheltering under stands from sun and comparisons made with conditions in Abu Dhabi: 'Cricket's environment is changing fast, and with far-reaching consequences.'[113] Andrew Hignell's *Wisden* 2023 review of 'Weather in 2022' likewise noted the first ever Met Office extreme weather warning for heat in central England on 19 July: 'Five Championship matches were in the danger zone.'[114] At Derby, home bowlers toiled through a record Nottinghamshire partnership of 402: 'Hameed and Duckett were as merciless as the sun, which beat down on a true pitch as temperatures approached 40°c.'[115]

In 1977 *Wisden Cricketers' Almanack* looked back on 1976, but comment on hot and dry weather found only meteorological wonder, not climatic foreboding.[116] County summaries noted the benefits of heat, and in some cases, for County Championship winners Middlesex and fourth-placed Leicestershire, improved cricketing performance:

> it was the driest season since cricket's infancy that provided, literally, the perfect climate for Middlesex's supremacy. The sun-baked, arid pitches made spin the final key to the championship and Titmus, Edmonds and Featherstone enjoyed a sunshine wicket harvest.[117]
>
> With the Grace Road pitch as good as ever bowlers had no easy task but as the summer drought continued Illingworth was able to use his slow bowlers with more effect and mainly through their efforts Leicestershire's late challenge nearly succeeded.[118]

Norman Preston's 'Notes by the Editor' turned from England's recent victorious winter tour of India to recall the 1976 heatwave, surpassing the sunshine of 1975:

> **Another Wonderful Summer**
>
> Back in England, cricket certainly prospered in 1976. Following the wonderful summer of sunshine the previous year, all records were broken for spells of the hottest and coldest, the wettest and the driest weather. Unprecedented over the last 250 years in its length and intensity, was a spell of fifteen days in June and July. Up to the end of August there was the driest sixteenth [*sic*] month period since the record for England and Wales began in 1727. Small wonder that by midsummer most outfields resembled the Sahara desert and watering was prohibited except for limited quantities on the pitches. In many areas water was rationed with stand-pipes in the streets.[119]

Through the annual seasonal fixture of *Wisden*, the changing appreciation of English weather and climate, from the 1970s to the 2020s, from the wonderful summer to the danger zone, is apparent.

Not that 1976 had not prompted argument and reflection at the time. The year 1975 had been a hot summer, but 1976 combined heat and drought, and the weather became political, with a Drought Act rushed through in August and Sports Minister Denis Howell overseeing public measures to save water. The appointment of a Minister for Drought prefigured rain not long after, itself becoming a piece of weather folklore; Howell would in 1978–9 oversee a snow crisis, a 'Minister for Snow' hoping for similar political magic. The year 1976 brought the hottest summer and worst drought 'since records began', the latter phrase a weather cliché indicating modern meaningful variation, though before 'records' things might have varied more.[120] English children of the 1970s recall unrainy holiday play, unshivering sea dips, rationed baths and scorched grass, and now 1976 lingers in adult memory, possibly freighted with climatic change. Was this a joyful unknowing experience of things to come?

The dramatic weather of 1976 prompted grown-up climate change reflection at the time, as in director David Kenton's 1978 Anglia TV programme on 'Changing Climate', featuring the work of the University of East Anglia's Climate Research Unit, directed by Hubert Lamb. 'Changing Climate', which drew on written records, dendroclimatology and pollen analysis from ice cores, suggested 'what has happened at home during recent years really does indicate that we can no longer rely on what used to be called normal weather.' The implications of 1976 were open; on the one hand recent abnormality might prefigure a little ice age, a theory with which Lamb had been associated, but the CRU Director also acknowledged a 1976 warning from the World Meteorological Organization that human activity could drastically warm the earth and dramatically raise sea levels. Lamb, however, saw 'no clear sign yet': 'maybe we have time, but not very much time I think, to learn to control our activity.'[121]

Others, though, took 1976 as a definite sign of global warming. Jon Agar shows that while the 1970s Meteorological Office was sceptical of long-term change, some in government highlighted scientific warnings. In 1974 Cabinet Office civil servant P. T. Warren reported on a conversation with German climatologist Hermann Flohn at a meeting on European futures: 'there is a real likelihood that by the year 2100 the polar ice-caps will disappear if the increase in CO_2 in the atmosphere continued at its present rate.'[122] The government's Central Policy Review Staff were, notes Agar, 'drawn to climate change as a topic after the drought of 1976', concerned for the financial impact of extreme conditions in a warming future.[123] A report on 'A National Climate Programme' was issued in March 1978, and an Interdepartmental Group on Climatology met from October 1978, issuing a report on *Climatic Change* in February 1980. Publication was delayed by the change of government, with Margaret Thatcher initially cautious, and only becoming an advocate for action in 1988, with a speech to the Royal Society invoking 'a global heat trap which could lead to climatic instability': 'we have unwittingly begun a massive experiment with the system of this planet itself.'[124]

Thatcher's change of view was influenced in part by Crispin Tickell, who advised her informally from 1984. Tickell's 1978 study *Climatic Change and World Affairs*, written while a Fellow at the Harvard Center for International Affairs, presented climate change, alongside other environmental challenges, as an issue shaped by humanity, noting exponentially rising CO_2 emissions and the 'greenhouse effect'.[125] Polar ice melt could produce significant sea-level rise, and international monitoring and action were required. Tickell connected weather talk and climate science, commenting, 'For the United States the winter of 1976/77, simultaneously spreading crippling cold in the East and Middle West and withering drought in the West, was a fearful experience. Even earlier, small talk about the weather had turned into concern about the climate.'[126] From 1976, with its U.S. winter cold and UK summer heat, things might not turn out nice again.

Hurricane '87

The capacity of weather events to shape climate cultures is evident too in the storm of 16 October 1987. The storm passed across southern England, but became a national event – for being exceptional in strength for that region, for its newsworthy proximity to national reporting centres and for the landscapes it hit. The 1987 storm sat alongside that of 26–7 November 1703, recounted by Daniel Defoe in *The Storm*, with millions of trees toppled and over 8,000 dead on land and at sea, as something to be recorded and remembered.[127] In October 1987, 15 million trees still in leaf, in damp soil, toppled overnight, southern England waking, if it had slept, to a landscape transformed. While there was meteorological debate as to whether the storm was a hurricane, as captured in BBC weather forecaster Michael Fish's oft-replayed aside that there was no hurricane on the way, the term 'hurricane' stuck, registering the storm's extraordinary force. In his 1704 *Lay-Man's Sermon Upon the Late Storm*, Defoe had stated: 'In publick calamities, every Circumstance is a Sermon, and every thing we see a Preacher.'[128] What message from the fallen trees of 1987?

In Sevenoaks in west Kent, the storm blew down six of the seven oaks planted in 1902 to mark the town's name. Bob Ogley, editor of the *Sevenoaks Chronicle*, quickly published *In the Wake of the Hurricane*, a local record that sold 25,000 copies in the southeast. A 'National

Edition' followed in March 1988, mixing text and photographs, and making a national cultural weather story from the storm, with part of the proceeds donated to the National Trust's Trees and Gardens Storm Disaster Appeal. For Ogley, tree loss in a southern English landscape was cultural loss, and *In the Wake of the Hurricane* was an act of commemoration: 'October 16, 1987 is a date we shall all remember. It will be talked about by future generations as the time when nature's naked fury hurled itself at southern England and in many areas completely changed the face of the landscape.'[129]

Ogley deployed a wartime register, flying from Battle of Britain airfield Biggin Hill to aerially photograph a kind of nature blitz, with scenes 'like battlefields in the aftermath of an artillery bombardment'.[130] An image of Bodiam Castle is captioned, 'The dead and wounded lie all around'.[131] Nineteen-eighty-seven-as-1940 also gave Winston Churchill prominence, his Kent home at Chartwell suffering significant tree loss, and grandson Winston Churchill MP writing in Ogley's book on 'Re-planting Our Heritage', arguing that trees shaped the 'character' and 'Englishness' of Kent.[132] Ogley included a picture of the older Winston looking out on Chartwell's woods, contrasting with the flattened trees of today.[133] For grandson Winston, viewing the fallen, replanting was needed, 'not with little Scandinavian

'Chartwell, Kent. The View East from the Terrace', from Bob Ogley, *In the Wake of the Hurricane* (1988).

Front cover of Bob Ogley, *In the Wake of the Hurricane* (1988), photograph showing 'The View North from Emmetts House', Kent.

conifers but with the magnificent trees of Old England'.[134] Scenes of landed devastation also included National Trust estates, the book's cover showing fallen trees at Emmetts House, opening a new view of the North Downs. Arland Kingston of the National Trust reported 'a marvellous "wartime" spirit' in the immediate response, and looked to replanting, though with space left for natural regeneration, warning that 'the clinical clearance of the countryside could now do as much damage as the hurricane itself'.[135] *In the Wake of the Hurricane* showed the Trust's warden at Toys Hill talking to Prince Charles, 'who is carrying a copy of the first edition of this book'.[136]

Ogley presented an urban as well as landed story, of everyday life interrupted. An aerial view of Park Avenue, Orpington, showed trees blown down: 'Notice the milk float in the foreground and how its journey has been rudely interrupted.'[137] Storm debris marked suburb and seaside, country and town, with Sevenoaks providing a focal point, 'talked about as the town that epitomised the experiences of thousands of people in southern England'. Six of the seven oaks around the Vine cricket ground were toppled, an aerial view showing them fallen over the boundary fence, six going for six. Seven new saplings were planted, the eighth mature tree left as a symbol of the hurricane; Ogley's summary account is titled 'Eightoaks in Kent'. The saplings were planted at a 'Hurricane Fayre' on 6 December 1987, celebrity mother and daughter Gloria Hunniford and Caron Keating (then a *Blue Peter* presenter) helping out.[138] *In the Wake of the Hurricane* proclaimed resilience, nature's blitz defied, England regaining composure.

Ogley's narrative of arboreal devastation and cultural loss caught one 1987 landscape mood, with the storm as heritage destroyer and English landscape in need of restoration. Other stories could, however, emerge. Martin Newell's song 'Before the Hurricane', from the 1993 LP *The Greatest Living Englishman*, tells of a country town where time seems altered, now that trees are down and views are different. Hopes of restoration to how things were before are forlorn, and the song has accompanying bells chiming certainties passing, Newell adding a verse on the bomb for good measure. Newell plays on doubt, but others, as trees fell and prospects opened, found optimism in a storm landscape, natural forces opening a space for renewal. The hurricane might humble the human, and beyond some essential clearing to reopen highways and make buildings habitable, one option was simply to see what flowed.

For Richard Mabey, 'the great storm of 1987' was 'unquestionably one of the most important events in the history of southern English landscape for the past three hundred years', changing people's understanding of woods: 'It began by bringing a great sense of loss to people, but ended, I think, by reinspiring them with an understanding of the resilience of living things, and of how woods are capable of renewing themselves.' Mabey found 'more damage than was ever done by the storm was wreaked by humans attempting to manage their way out of the problems it created', especially when bulldozers cleared areas for replanting with new saplings.[139] Mabey criticized the initial responses of the Tree Council, who had proclaimed that 'Trees are at great danger from nature', and the National Trust, who held an art exhibition at Petworth of scenes of destruction, with a claim that 'The Great Storm desecrated the past and betrayed the future.'[140] A further storm in January 1990 would lead to a change in tree policy, the Trust letting the fallen lie.

After the storm, Mabey drove across southern England, seeing the 'apparent randomness of the damage', the devastated alongside the barely touched. While it 'was not pleasant for most people', Mabey registered sensory excitement:

> The whiteness of the broken trunks and dislocated branches was astounding. But it's the smell that has stayed with me, a cocktail of warm sap from the split wood and the tonic, almost vermouth-like aroma of myriads of crushed beech leaves. I have to confess that, entirely selfishly, I found the whole experience intoxicating. The whole landscape seemed sprung, as full of latent renaissance as Nash's Second World War paintings.[141]

Mabey's confession of excitement accompanied ecological analysis, with apparently dead wood showing life the next spring and ecologists excited at what effectively became a natural experiment:

> The storms of 1987 and 1990 had an impact far beyond the treescapes of southern England. They brought down, probably permanently, the idea that woods were settled places, whose behaviour could be tidily predicted in human models. They showed that natural disturbances were an entirely normal and well-tolerated part of a woodland's experience.[142]

Ecological disturbance might in turn put social aesthetic values in question, Mabey's preferred vernacular jumble edging out elite order: 'Out in the countryside, the elements seemed to be suggesting a different kind of aesthetic. The elegant landscape parks of the Garden of England were comprehensively rearranged.'[143]

The contrasting responses to the 1987 storm tapped different narratives of weather past and future. Ogley's *In the Wake of the Hurricane* includes an account of 'Some Famous Storms' from the twentieth century (1953, 1962, 1976, 1978), and 'The Tempest of 1703', where Ogley thanked 'the diligent journalist' Defoe, in effect his journalistic ancestor.[144] The year 1987 is registered within a pattern of English weather essentially changeable, occasionally wild, but ultimately containable, Ogley commenting, 'Where other countries have climates, we in Britain just have weather, a daily phenomenon that controls our lives, provides a perpetual topic of conversation and is totally unpredictable.'[145] As in the past, so today, and so in the future. Or did 1987 signal a new kind of predictability, of storminess from climatic shift? For Mabey, 1987 might not be just another wild episode; after the storm of January 1990, Mabey wrote, 'If the greenhouse effect (i.e., us) is to blame, then we can be reasonably sure that there will be more of the same in the years to come.'[146] The 1987 storm blew in at a moment when climatic naturalness was in question. Was this simply unusually windy for southern England, or a sign that English climate was newly defined by change?

England under Climate Change

In 1914, in the first issue of the Vorticist magazine *BLAST*, Wyndham Lewis diagnosed English climate as a problem:

> BLAST First (from politeness) ENGLAND
> CURSE ITS CLIMATE FOR ITS SINS AND INFECTIONS

For Lewis, temperate weather was England's curse ('OFFICIOUS MOUNTAINS keep back DRASTIC WINDS'), and even the ocean conspired, with its transatlantic Gulf Stream:

> A 1000 MILE LONG, 2 KILOMETRE Deep
> BODY OF WATER even, is pushed against us
> from the Floridas, TO MAKE US MILD.[147]

When climate change models consider effects on ocean circulation, one counter-intuitive possibility is that global warming could produce British cooling, should the Gulf Stream re-route. Lewis might have relished the prospect. Meteorological extremes might blast English temperament from the changeably temperate. The twenty-first century might indeed be a BLAST.

Most recent commentary on climate change would demur, seeing danger and vulnerability, as when George Szirtes's 2004 poem 'Climate' presents a country and a climate less changeable than changed. There is cloud and showers and lightning, mud under broken skies and no 'fixed point': 'It is England of course,/ not one of the dependable climates'. Szirtes's poem ends with a sense of an altered climatic state:

> It is as if there were some irresistible force
> blowing us over into a strange new century
> that billows beyond us, between our thin heart-beats.[148]

If the weather events of 1976 and 1987 prompted climate speculation, since 1987 climate change has become an obligatory reference point for any storm, downpour, heatwave or drought. The establishment in 1988 by the UN of the Intergovernmental Panel on Climate Change marked the entry of climate change and climate modelling into international and national politics, and for Mike Hulme experience of weather and climate thereby shift:

> in the new epoch of the Anthropocene people may have to learn to live without the idea of climate, at least without climate as an idea that brings order and stability to relationships between weather and culture. The 'new normal' of climate is simply that there can be no normal. And this is unsettling.[149]

Thinking about the mutual influence of people and climate is not new, but for Hulme climate change shifts the terms of exchange: 'In the Anthropocene there can be no climate in the old sense; only weathercultures, with people acting as weatherculturalists.'[150]

Global climate analysis thus meets and is translated through national weather cultures, and English changeability is tested and transformed. Exceptionally hot or dry or wet episodes become indicative of some coherently unpredictable global story, weather unusually changeable felt as climate change. As a pattern of weirdness becomes the norm, English landscape and its iconography serves as subject and medium for reflection and projection. In July 2022 two climate protesters from Just Stop Oil covered John Constable's *Hay Wain*, in the National Gallery, with a restyled version, an 'apocalyptic vision' showing 'the climate collapse and what it will do to this landscape'. In this altered England, the Hay Wain is stuck on double yellow lines on a concreted river, planes cross the sky, an industrial plant and a motorway take over the fields, rubbish is dumped, a car is burnt out and fires flame behind Willy Lott's cottage. The protesters glued themselves to Constable's frame, an English landscape mobilized against fossil fuels.[151]

A differently campaigning gesture, also indicative of climate's cultural reach, is the 2017 Ladybird book *Climate Change*, authored by the then Prince of Wales with Cambridge climate scientist Emily Shuckburgh and environmentalist Tony Juniper, former director of Friends of the Earth, who would from 2019 chair Natural England. Part of Ladybird's 'Expert' series, *Climate Change* was aimed at adult as well as younger readers, and followed the style of classic children's

Ladybirds, with text on one page and colour illustrations by Ruth Palmer on the other. *Climate Change* explored the means of mitigation to dampen disruption, including renewable energy, forest restoration, more organic farming and a zero-waste 'circular economy'.[152] The book had global coverage, but processes were brought home for UK readers via recognizably English landscapes. An original Ladybird illustration by mid-twentieth-century country artist Charles Tunnicliffe accompanied discussion of 'Food and farming solutions'; a tractor ploughs on a mixed farm, cattle look on and lapwings fly, with a church behind.[153] The 'New opportunities and improved quality of life' in 2017 are illustrated by Palmer's image of a nuclear family outside an ultra-low-energy country home, an electric car charging in the yard.[154]

Solutions and opportunities are, however, overshadowed by a sense of England in peril, the book's cover image showing flood. Derived from a press agency photograph, and also the illustration for 'Heatwaves, droughts, floods and storms', Palmer pictured a flooded high street, water halfway up the shop fronts, and flat dwellers taking refuge on the roof, a dinghy coming to the rescue.[155] A shop sign indicates 'Uckfield Pharmacy': the East Sussex town of Uckfield was flooded in October 2000 when the River Ouse burst its banks after 14 inches of rain in one night. A southern English market town signals global danger. Parched playing fields in 1976, Sevenoaks losing six oaks in 1987, Uckfield under millennial water, symbolic stations for England under climate change.

After clean-up and (where permitted) insurance claim, do flood waters deposit only future fear? Debate proceeds over the renewal of flood defences, on whether defence is possible and on changes in flood plain management to soak up new weather events. Alongside understandable anxieties, however, elements of hope appear. In their work on 'sustainable flood memory', Lindsey McEwan, Owain Jones and others examine, in the context of 2007 and 2014 river flooding in southwest England, the ways in which history and memory may foster resilience in traumatic times and how elements of joy alongside grief can confound prevailing expectations.[156] For some commentators, with an echo of Mabey's 1987 storm response, flood might prompt a necessary and hopeful conceptual transformation, an Anthropocene coming-to-terms with climate. Thus ecologist Brian Moss's 2001 popular scientific account *The Broads*, an East Anglian coastal wetland region of lakes and rivers, reedbed and grazing marsh, vulnerable to rising sea levels and river flooding, ended by imagining two future Broadlands under climate change. In 2025, 25 years ahead of when Moss wrote, a cyclone has devastated Britain, London is drowned, but Broadland has just about survived, and debate proceeds as to what should be done. Moss describes two 2050 Broadlands, both made in response to climate change, the first a negative heritage fantasy, the second a positive working landscape. In the first, concrete embankments line rivers and coast, guarding a defensive and exclusive region, a 'Broads Heritage Area' enjoyed by the rich in historic costumed style. In the second, the cyclone transforms ideas and power structures, with the sea allowed to reclaim the lower valleys as a tidal estuary, 'fortress' nature reserves abandoned and the region less rewilded than reworked. Moss imagines a new Broadland, something better than 'the doldrum years between 1960 and 2025', the cyclone jolting the place out of older conservationist modes, returning the country to ecological health.[157]

Prospects of flood increasingly preoccupy English landscape commentary, contemplating England as wet land, and scrutiny of one image can end this section. In 2017 Simon Roberts's book *Merrie Albion* gathered photographic landscape images from the preceding decade, including a February 2014 image of a family looking from Burrow Mump in Somerset over a deluged landscape, 'Flooding of the Somerset Levels, Burrowbridge'.[158] The flooded 'Albion' viewed from Burrow Mump carries its share of national iconography, of King Alfred at nearby Athelney, and the mythic Isle of Avalon. Burrow Mump is a smaller version of Glastonbury Tor, with the ruins of St Michael's church at its summit, the hill donated to the National Trust in 1946 by Major Alexander Gould Barrett as a memorial, a commemorative plaque stating, 'that the men and women of Somerset who died serving their country in the Second World War may be remembered here in time to come'.

Cultural, political and ecological elements enfold as Roberts's photograph overlays older iconography with twenty-first-century anxieties. Flood management had achieved newly political status in 2013–14, as a wet winter brought climate change and the future likelihood of extreme events to the fore. The government Environment Agency was accused locally of abandoning Burrowbridge to flood, and Royal Marines were brought in to reinforce defences. A line of white sandbags appears near the centre of Roberts's image. The embanked River Parrett flows in the middle distance beyond the A361, and has

Simon Roberts, 'Flooding of the Somerset Levels, Burrowbridge' (2014).

spilled into the fields to the west. The Quantock Hills are beyond, the river flowing left to right, north to Bridgwater and the sea.

Floods can be at once disaster and spectacle, and Roberts photographed others looking. Roberts's own perspective includes a family's perspective on altered landscape, his own tripod-mounted large format camera capturing the adult family members photographically recording events by phone. Seeing things becomes part of the view, and muddy foreground turf indicates that others too have been here to look, though Roberts recalls that on his visit Burrowbridge was 'eerily deserted', save for this one family.[159] As often in his images, Roberts, who would have been conspicuous on the bare hillside, appears to escape the attention of the observed, though the small child peering over the adult shoulder seems to catch his camera eye. What is that man doing?

Social stories also emerge from 'Flooding of the Somerset Levels, Burrowbridge'. We are led to assume this is a family group, and from dress, situation and lack of baggage they might be familiar with the place already, are not tourists, are possibly working people viewing a working landscape whose normal patterns of work have been suspended for the weather. Cars are parked behind the industrial buildings below, so indoors things seem to be proceeding, and roads are passable, but field working is out. The family may, like Roberts, have driven here for the view, or walked up from home, but either way they are here to see and to reflect. The inter-generational nature of the picture indicates not only spatial but temporal prospects, viewpoints forward as well as outward. Will this happen more as the children grow, as the adults age?

The flood waters of the Parrett are vividly brown with sediment, and the colour indicates dual process, on the one hand erosive disruption, on the other deposition for future fertility. Floods have made this landscape in the past, are what has made the Levels level. Will though their increased frequency and severity shift the present balance, becoming in human terms destructive rather than constructive? Roberts's image shows a habitat disrupted, yet also things being made. As the world enters the Anthropocene, as humanity marks the rock record, 'Flooding of the Somerset Levels, Burrowbridge' shows the River Parrett laying down future Anthropocene deposits.

Island Shores

Between 1972 and 1976 artist Susan Hiller collected 305 historic postcards, their photographers unknown, showing rough seas around the British coast, displaying them along with charts and maps in a work entitled 'Dedicated to the Unknown Artists', gathered in the publication *Rough Sea* (1976). In the year of the drought, Hiller displayed crashing waters, mapping the 'Locations and Distributions' of 'Rough Sea', annotating the British coastal outline with the sites of old seaside souvenirs.[160] If such postcards were reissued today, and sent by a twenty-first-century holidaymaker from Lowestoft or Gorleston, Whitby or Scarborough, Worthing or Southsea, Torquay or Teignmouth, would rough sea pictures carry meaning beyond the vagaries of English holiday weather?

The atmospheric process of climate change and the geological register of the Anthropocene meet on the shore, with accelerated erosion from rising seas. England's blue meets England's green, and the processes are various, depositional as well as erosive, but in recent years commentary has emphasized the latter, the sea nibbling and chomping at the land. Landforms are lost, things from past geological ages are exposed, buildings fall, wartime defences topple and sea eats into landfill, the coast styled 'the front line in the Anthropocene'.[161] The Met Office's *State of the UK Climate 2021* report, published in July 2022, found the rate of sea-level rise increasing, with a 3–5.2 mm increase per year, more than double the rate a hundred years ago, with the total rise since 1900 around 16.5 cm.[162] The forceful meeting of sea and land in England, whether cliffs undercut, beaches denuded or defensive walls battered, has long been a cultural and scientific preoccupation, and this section of the chapter considers the coast as a focus for Anthroposcenic stories, with older commentaries anticipatory of present concerns.

England and the Archipelago

England is not an island, with two national land-joins, but a sense of British islandness shapes argument about the English coast. England and Britain sit within a wider archipelago, and recent appeals to an 'archipelagic' identity set England, Scotland, Ireland, Wales, and all points from Guernsey to Shetland, Man to St Kilda in a relational exchange. Seas and coasts shape the kind of geographical imaginary conjured by the radio shipping forecast, with its roll call of sea areas and coastal stations, taking alert fishermen or tucked-up dozers clockwise around the islands.[163] Penny Woolcock's 2012 film *From the Sea to the Land Beyond*, compiled largely from British Film Institute archive footage, taps such a sensibility, gathering British coastal pictures of labour and leisure, civility and war, across the twentieth century. *From the Sea to the Land Beyond* presents English specificity alongside other national and subnational archipelagic entities, all edged and defined by the sea. The film's conclusion comments on sea-level rise, quoting a 1985 Peter Greenaway film for the Central Office of Information that at current rates, by the year 160000 the sea will be halfway up Nelson's Column. The figure, and the chronology, suggests a non-emergency, contrasting with more recent warnings.

England-in-the-archipelago also marks the soundtrack of Woolcock's film, by the group British Sea Power, whose 2005 song 'The Land Beyond' also gave Woolcock her film title. British Sea Power's work had registered the year before in another maritime display, when in 2011 the National Maritime Museum in Greenwich opened a new wing, and inscribed on an entrance wall a song lyric, 'The salt, the spray, the gorgeous undertow/ Always, always, always the sea/ Brilliantine mortality'. The quote is from British Sea Power's

2003 song 'Carrion', and carries the group's characteristic mix of the epic and prosaic, 'Brilliantine' suggesting both a quality of vividness and the name of a liquid hair product, something to keep a sailor's hair shipshape in the breeze. British Sea Power's work matched Woolcock's film in its evocation of the maritime and the national, with allusions on their 2003 debut album *The Decline of British Sea Power* to favourite English island shores ('Fear of Drowning') and tidal pulls from Scapa Flow to Rotherhithe ('Carrion'). When issued as a single, individual copies of 'Carrion' carried different British coastal features on the sleeve, while a launch event spelt out the song title in stones on top of the Seven Sisters cliffs in Sussex, not far from the band's Brighton base. Environmental themes register too, in early songs connected to the nuclear industry of group members' Cumbrian home region, while climate change also features, as in the 2005 'Oh Larsen B', to a collapsing Antarctic ice shelf, or the 2008 'Canvey Island', where the east coast floods of 1953, hitting low-lying Essex especially hard, are interwoven with the twenty-first-century's approaching storms and summer droughts. In 2021 the group dropped the 'British', operating henceforth as Sea Power, the 'wry humour' which they had sought in their name overtaken by newly 'antagonistic nationalism', such that their intentions might be misunderstood.[164] The name revised, the sea remains, though a wryly embedded take on national place, which still has its uses, may be lost.

From the Sea to the Land Beyond is archipelagic in scope, yet gravitates to English imagery, reflecting English cartographic and demographic dominance. England as non-island indeed sits awkwardly in the archipelago, tempted by its almost-surrounding seas to emphasize island distinction, but nonetheless joined to others. Perhaps some absurdist cartography, the Cheviots flipped over to make a northern channel, and Offa's Dyke inverted from bank to moat, could serve as a reminder of English non-islandness. As geopolitical shifts challenge historic equations of English and British interest, borderlines on land may gain significance. Archipelagic commentary often seeks out identities beyond the national, but the contested variety within all the archipelago's national components remains, whether at Scapa Flow or Rotherhithe, Essex marshes or Cornish cliffs, Cumbrian coast or Sussex chalk.

Anticipation

As island shores meet rising seas, conversation policy, scientific analysis and creative practice navigate tensions of coastal landscape, figuring what a future English coast might be. The National Trust is a significant coastal landowner, custodian of more than 780 miles of British coastline. In the early 1960s it owned just 200 miles, but holdings expanded following a 1960s reorientation of Trust campaigns from country house to coast. Enterprise Neptune, devised in 1962 and launched on St George's Day 1965 with bonfires on the site of Armada Beacons, was led by Conrad Rawnsley, grandson of Trust founder Hardwicke Rawnsley. It began with an appeal for £2 million fronted by the Duke of Edinburgh, and has since raised over £65 million, now as the Neptune Coastal Campaign.[165] The threat preoccupying the Trust in the 1960s was less marine erosion than leisure development, with fears over a Larkinesque coastal 'Going, Going', from car parks and caravan sites. The sea was a heritage ally, with valued seascapes at stake and the Roman marine god a fitting symbol for Trust action.

The twenty-first-century National Trust has rethought its coastal policy, the desire for protection reconciled with inevitable loss as seas rise. The Trust's 'Living with change: Our shifting shores' suggests working with sea power rather than defending holdings against it, with a likely loss of some valued human artefacts. Caitlin DeSilvey describes how at Mullion Cove in Cornwall the Trust has in effect become a curator of decay, deciding from 2006 that eventually, 'at an unpredictable date in the near or distant future', it would not be possible to protect the harbour sea wall from storms.[166] A heritage object formerly denoting stability, in its sea-defensive role and as a solid memorial to former fishing, will erode, in the process becoming a new kind of symbol, decommissioned to mark changing climate. The Trust's motto of 'For ever, for everyone' receives subtle revision; it might be for everyone, but sometimes it won't be forever. Island shores shift in the Anthropocene. From Enterprise Neptune to what might be labelled Operation Canute, a landholder underscoring its authority by recognizing and signalling the limits of its power.

At Mullion, DeSilvey reflects on transience, attending to schemes of preservation and profit which shaped the harbour, and the history of memory at the site, and aiming for an 'anticipatory history . . . at the intersection of the imagined future and the imagined past'.[167] The term 'anticipation' indicates that while for some, climate futures may be a matter of trepidation, and for a cautious accommodation with nature, for others there may be excitement over change and renewal, as in Brian Moss's projection of future Broadlands, discussed above. If such dimensions of climate change are often understandably downplayed given the prospects of disturbance to life and livelihood, the anticipation of loss may enable imaginative coping.

There may also be excitement of a kind in the capacity of disaster to become a morbid spectacle, a compellingly unavoidable sight. In 2001 George Szirtes, whose poem 'Climate' was noted above, produced 'An English Apocalypse', consisting of a prologue and five sets of five poems. The first set, 'Pastorals', begins with 'Jerusalem', presenting cultural tides ebbing and flowing, and identity in dissolution, the 'Old Jerusalem' a post-imperial 'forsaken garden/ where the sun is always about to set'.[168] Decay gathers pace through 'An English Apocalypse', and the final set, 'The Apocalypses', includes four 'Death by . . .' poems: by meteor, power cut, deluge and suicide.[169] 'Death by Deluge' presents eastern England attacked, with meaning coming 'to a full stop in mid-/ sentence' as the North Sea, 'rough/ and rising', cuffs the land, with cliffs down and the undersea bells of the lost Suffolk town of Dunwich ringing. There are enormous tides 'from Southend to Cromer', and a roll call of drowned inland towns: Peterborough, Ely, March, Cambridge, Royston, Stevenage. The Wash is nothing but water, and the Thames Valley 'filled to the brim', in a re-run of Jefferies's *After London*. Yet, as England drowns, the deluge itself attains an Englishness, 'Death by Deluge' ending: 'A slim/ line of high hills held out but all was water-colour,/ the pure English medium, intended for sky, cloud, and sea./ Less earth than you could shift with a spatula.'[170] Szirtes's apocalypse is English not only in its target, but its quality. After the flood, an England of sorts remains. Empire gone, decay ongoing, prospects of flood offer the country a new fable, England still, in that sense, fabulous.

England's Eastern Edge

'Death by Deluge' offers one example of the eastern English shore, with the North Sea meeting miles of often erodible cliffs, dunes and marshes, as a setting for the consideration of climatic pasts and futures. In the twenty-first century, eastern England has become an Anthropocene ground for the meeting of land and water, climate and Europe, registered in poetry and theatre, painting and archaeology.

Sometimes erosive flood can appear as welcome prospective alteration, the sea carrying away certain landed assumptions. In Sean O'Brien's 2011 poem 'Sunk Island', the poem's title acts as both general English metaphor and specific local reference. Sunk Island is an out-of-the-way Crown estate, on the north bank of the Humber east of Hull, reclaimed and enclosed for farming in the nineteenth century, with gabled farms and cottages, a school and church, a Victorian new England projecting a productive future. Outside the church, 'by the lych-gate', O'Brien meets a lady on a horse, looking down on him suspiciously as a loitering likely thief. The poet, though, only wants 'to read your graves, to stand and think,/ To hear the water taking back the frozen fields.' 'Sunk Island' offers 'a slow-motion replay of England', dreaming of future flood taking the landed lady, 'For your helmet to circle and sink like a moral'.[171] Whatever the charms of this unusual, dead flat, neatly enclosed part of the East Riding, 'Sunk Island' anticipates it sunk anew.

'Sunk Island' imagines the eventual failures of human engineering resetting class society, the sea acting as progressive social engineer. Future anticipations are more commonly ambivalent, as in Harriet Tarlo and Judith Tucker's nuanced investigation since 2012 of the north Lincolnshire coastal plotland site of Humberston Fitties. Tarlo's poetry and Tucker's painting present a landscape vulnerable to coastal change but cherished by residents for its makeshift qualities, the Fitties characterized by social and ecological adaptability, as a potential 'alternative, restorative form of simple seaside living', a place of emotional investment which, at present, 'will not be re-wilded'.[172] Local, regional and national attachments shape the Fitties landscape, Tucker's 2018 painting *We're All Very Close Round Here* showing shacks at night, lights on, a street lamp casting a shine, an England flag flying, shown in reverse.[173] Nature and England meet, for a particular variant of greenness: 'On one visit we glimpsed a fox darting in front of a stone crocodile dressed in England football regalia. The cement squirrel in the painting . . . looks up quizzically at the large England flag.'[174] Tarlo and Tucker note: 'There are conservationists on the Fitties, declared and undeclared and certainly unacknowledged.'[175] Humberston appears a place of green accommodation. Across the Humber estuary from Sunk Island, behind saltmarsh and dune, Tarlo and Tucker present a complex plotland Anthroposcenery; in its sea level situation, in the energy landscape

Judith Tucker, *We're All Very Close Round Here*, 2018, oil on canvas.

of the adjacent estuary with its oil terminals and wind farms, in its local and national affections, and in the former mining and industrial occupations of many plotland owners.

Elsewhere art styles the coast as a site of emergency. In Steve Waters's 2009 *The Contingency Plan*, paired plays present bleak theatrical prospects for low-lying eastern England. *On the Beach* is set on the north Norfolk coast, and *Resilience* in Whitehall, climate scientists and government officials responding to sea flood emergency, variously calling up wartime spirit, ideals of English nature and memories of the 1953 east coast floods. In *Resilience*, scientist Will addresses government minister Chris, predicting flood for the east coast and capital:

> Chris, 1953 was about a conjunction of circumstances. If it happened again, and I believe it is a question of when not if, it will be worse, far worse.
>
> A perfect storm, say.
>
> Sea level swollen from polar melt, warming and shifting currents, more vociferous storm surges, faster winds, higher tides – imagine that cold water rushing south east from

> Greenland, a great riptide blown and sucked and tugged across the Atlantic, gathering momentum as it goes, a mass of waters and turbulence, nothing forming an obstacle from Iceland to the Shetlands where high cliffs push it east like a ball flipped on a pinball machine, angering it further, and now, look, funnelled into the gap between the continent and the east coast, and my God, it's really ferocious now, and this is a spring tide, the sun and moon exerting their pull, sucking the currents into this great tower of water, down, down the eastern coast, smack into the rump of East Anglia and, yes, almost in reaction, sucked up the Thames Estuary and, yes, the Barrier may work, it may just work, but it may not and if, if the calculation made in a world of steady-state ocean patterns proves false then here it comes, up the Thames, and the Barrier proves as much a folly as the Maginot Line, and – well.[176]

As ice sheets melt, sea levels rise and storms frequent the coast, Waters dramatizes the lines of defence, the arguments for walls or wetlands as ways to meet the sea, and who might be responsible for alerting the country and the wider world. Theatre offers one means to sound the alarm.

Pictures offer another. Since the late 1990s Julian Perry has rendered the east coast in paint, art and erosion meeting in scenes of what a 1997 show of his work termed a 'Brittle England'.[177] Perry addresses a range of environmental concerns, including threats of arboreal disease, as in his 2015 show 'When Yellow Leaves'; his painting in general, but especially his works on coastal erosion, presents an English Anthroposcenery.[178] In 2010 Perry exhibited 'An Extraordinary Prospect: The Coastal Erosion Paintings', works in oil presenting Norfolk, Suffolk and Yorkshire coastal scenes.[179] The catalogue cover showed *Fanfare 34* (2010), a clifftop caravan eroded, 'Fanfare' being the model of caravan shown, but also perhaps suggesting a soundtrack for the humble caravan's entry into the frame of art. Perry pictures human dwellings, bungalows as well as caravans, hovering in mid-air, still grounded on grass and topsoil; elsewhere things *in situ* just cling on. These paintings do not in any sense look down on their objects, which gain elevated status as the ground is pulled from under them. The medium of oil paint, rather than, say, watercolour, allows ordinary objects to retain their substance as they contemplate, and make for, an extraordinary prospect. Their stilled life warns of what happens to things on unprotected soft cliffs, yet the paintings give caravans, chalets and bungalows an attention and value beyond the dismissal they often receive. If Larkin's poem 'Going, Going' had, in an echo of the National Trust's 1960s Enterprise Neptune, 'more caravan sites' denoting the cultural degradation of the English coast, Perry's caravans show something that was good, while it lasted.

A key site for Perry has been Happisburgh on the east Norfolk coast, a focus for coastal defence argument, with dispute over the degree to which existing coastal lines should be maintained, or policies of 'managed retreat' pursued. Perry's *Happisburgh Defences* (2010) and *Cliffs at Happisburgh* (2010) show wartime pillboxes eroding into mid-air, a defence never used in wartime receiving no protection now, wartime memory unable to stand firm. Erosion following the destruction and non-replacement of defences led to loss of the houses of Beach Road in the early twenty-first century, with local response mobilized through the Happisburgh Coastal Concern Action Group. Perry's 2013 painting *Happisburgh Scene* showed caravans still on site, yards from the eroding cliff edge, neatly curtained for the

Julian Perry, *Fanfare 34*, 2010, oil on panel.

Julian Perry, *Secular Altarpiece to the Assumption of* CO_2, 2021, oil on four panels.

view, maintaining decorum in the face of nothingness; by 2018 these had become, in another painting, *Abandoned Caravans Happisburgh*.

Happisburgh featured in the centrepiece of Perry's 2021 show at Southampton Art Gallery, 'There Rolls the Deep: The Rising Sea Level Paintings'. *Secular Altarpiece to the Assumption of* CO_2 (2021), presented as 'emblematic of Climate Breakdown', consisted of four panels showing sites in eastern England – Happisburgh, Benacre and Covehithe in Suffolk, and Skipsea in east Yorkshire – where long-standing processes of erosion were now wrapped in climate change stories.[180] The altarpiece showed, from left to right, Happisburgh sea defences no longer defending, a sycamore tree inverted after falling over the Benacre cliff and dairy buildings sliding over at Skipsea. Below, Perry painted a sun-bleached tree on Covehithe beach, an equivalent to the iconography of a dead Christ in religious altar art. While a 'devout atheist', Perry's titling of his work as an 'Assumption' altarpiece invoked theology, yet also pointed to the ways in which something – CO_2 – had come to assume inevitable narrative presence.[181] Just as medieval works could not but invoke God, twenty-first-century stories of environmental change begin to seem strange if they do not register a process deemed all-encompassing, climate change immanent if not transcendent. However local the cliff fall, carbon dioxide is assumed to be involved; even if the cliffs of Skipsea, Benacre, Covehithe or Happisburgh have fallen for centuries, a new narrative shadow falls.

Happisburgh is notable also for the intertwining of futures and pasts. As dwellings fell over cliffs, signs of older human life became apparent below. East Anglia has been a key site for the archaeological Ancient Human Occupation of Britain (AHOB) project, with Happisburgh findings including 800,000-year-old footprints in forest bed deposits exposed by erosion in May 2013, pushing back the story of human life in England. The Happisburgh image on the left side of Perry's CO_2 triptych shows the exposed footprint surface, found just behind the remaining defences. The 2014 scientific publication of findings hailed 'the earliest evidence of hominin footprints outside Africa', suggesting 'a group of at least five adults and juveniles walking along the mudflats of a large river'. The footprints were of varying length and depth, 'indicating that they were made by several people of different ages'.[182] While working in Norwich Castle Museum's archive a few years ago, on documents relating to historic east coastal erosion, natural history curator David Waterhouse showed me a resin cast of one of the Happisburgh footprints. Someone, or rather two people, had made this footprint shape; today's archaeologist casting their findings before marine action took them, and an earlier human walking a muddy surface. And did those feet? Yes.[183]

Happisburgh shows prehistory speaking to the present. Here is an ancient landscape for now, resonating in a way it did not fifty years ago. In 1973, in *The Unofficial Countryside*, urging people to be fascinated by the present, Richard Mabey commented, 'The fact that polar bears once splashed about in the Thames or mammoths grazed on the site of the M1 is not very relevant to our experience of nature now.'[184] Ancient fauna today, however, seem more compelling, climate change making longer environmental histories resonate. North Norfolk thus brands itself the Deep History Coast, its tourist logo a mammoth whose back echoes the map of the local coastline, where fossil mammoths have emerged from eroding soft cliffs.[185] The 2006 AHOB book *Homo Britannicus*, which reported early findings from Pakefield in Suffolk, opened with a landscape description of a river bed, hippos and elephants, and humans: 'This is not some scene from our ancestral African homelands of two million years ago . . . This is Suffolk, about 700,000 years before the recent emergence of evidence from sea cliffs near Lowestoft provided such a vivid picture of the landscape inhabited by the first Britons.'[186]

Another region, until recently unnamed, has also arisen from prehistory to speak to today's England. Under the North Sea lies an area now labelled 'Doggerland', on which the recent upsurge in commentary is notable.[187] Why the fascination? Doggerland chimes for its mix of climatic and European stories, and becomes an emblematic landscape for twenty-first-century England. In a period preoccupied with sea level, and with the British relationship to Europe, prehistory sends various messages: of British connection or insularity; of how lands have been lost before and might be again if extra care isn't taken; or of change as natural, with seas always rising and falling, maps thereby

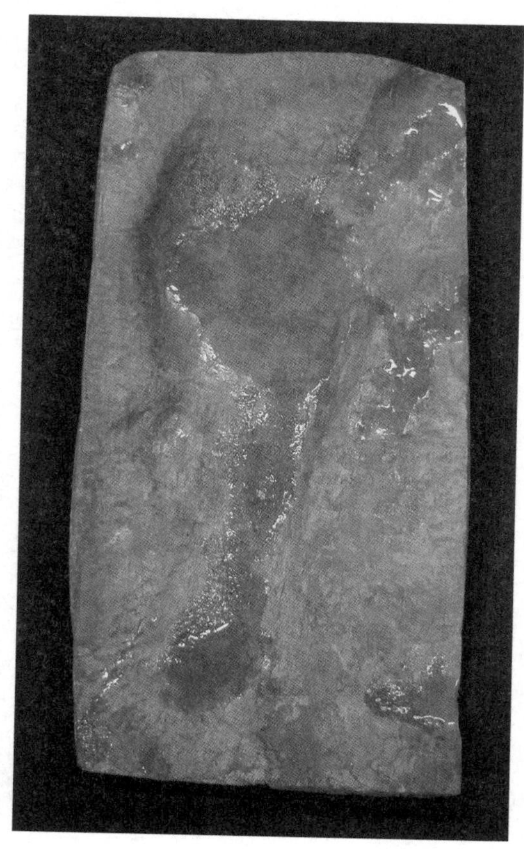

Resin cast of ancient Happisburgh footprint, Norwich Castle Museum.

shifting. The name Doggerland was coined by archaeologist Bryony Coles in 1998 in tribute to geologist Clement Reid, whose 1913 book *Submerged Forests* included a chapter on the Dogger Bank, now familiar from the shipping forecast sea area 'Dogger'.[188] In 1906, writing on coastal erosion, Reid had stated:

> If what I have said is correct, and since civilised man lived in Britain there has been a rapid change of sea-level, followed by a long rest, what are the prospects of a similar period of rapid change again setting in? . . . It is a problem of great importance, for a new rise or fall of the sea-level to the extent of a few feet would have most disastrous effects on all our coasts and harbours, and would seriously interfere with our inland drainage until things were again adjusted. Are we now living in a period of exceptional stability, both of sea-level and climate; or is it, as geology suggests, a mere interlude which may at any time give place to rapid change?[189]

Reid's interlude would seem to be closing.

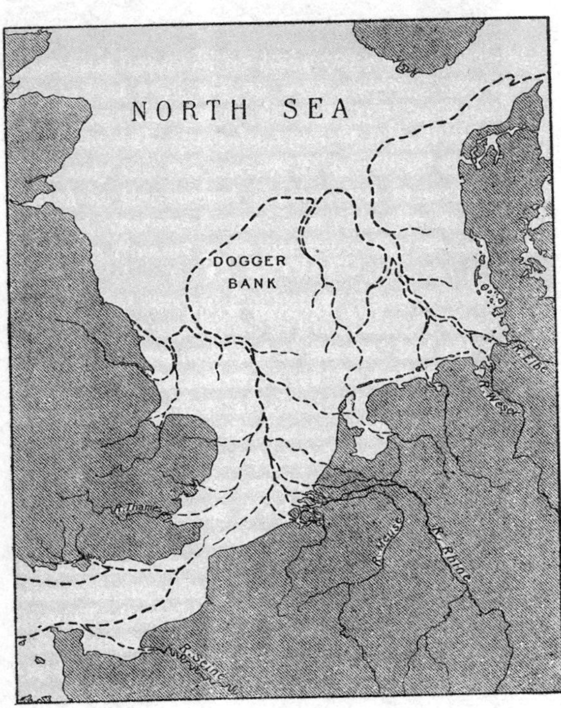

Map, 'Showing Approximate Coast-Line at the Period of the Lowest Submerged Forest', from Clement Reid, *Submerged Forests* (1913).

Coles's 1998 paper, entitled 'Doggerland: A Speculative Survey', shifted the archaeological narrative from ideas emphasizing a former land bridge between Britain and continental Europe to imagining Doggerland as itself 'a place to be'.[190] Maps showed how at 13,000 years BP the North Sea was merely an inlet between southern Norway and a northern European coast, but at 10,000 BP something like Scotland is clear and the North Sea extends south to the Dogger Hills. After 5000 BP Britain and Denmark appear, the East Anglian coast is defined and Dogger Island is stranded. The prevailing tone of Doggerland discussion, in England and elsewhere, has been counter-nationalist, highlighting what archaeologists Vince Gaffney, Simon Fitch and David Smith label 'Europe's Lost World' off the English east coast: 'Doggerland may well have had a significantly different character, in cultural and environmental terms, in comparison with Britain and possibly all the surrounding countries.'[191] The urge to define Doggerland as distinct resists any temptation to project current national territories outwards, to demarcate the lost undersea via such modern ideas as the nation state or territorial waters. Doggerland is thus not to be read as a lost England, or a lost Denmark. Paradoxically, though, the reluctance to claim Doggerland in effect reinforces the current boundaries of land and sea, and thereby current national territories, cutting them off from any sense that landscape, prehistoric or otherwise, might be a porous realm of movement. Taking archaeology instead as something blurring island edges might, however, prompt reflection on how remaining eastern areas are distinctive *within* England, part of a former lowland European territory now lost. Why look out to sea for European Doggerland? Look underfoot instead. And in the process reflect on the naming and claiming of national land, and the place of the sea.

The Anthropocene Inheritance

Doggerland connects not only to narratives of east coastal erosion but more general projections of submergence, rising seas steadily drowning low land, whether unpopulated or metropolitan. Themes of inheritance shape what Adam Trexler terms 'Anthropocene fictions', with drowned cities an especially powerful trope, the Anthropocene connecting past human actions and future planetary conditions.[192]

For Trexler, J. G. Ballard's 1962 *The Drowned World*, written 'years before the first novel about human-induced global warming', provides 'a strikingly stable archetype for subsequent fictions'.[193] In *The*

Drowned World, solar storms have caused earth to warm, and Triassic conditions return. Scientists in 2145 journey to a flooded, tropical London, where the waters of a lagoon are pumped out to reveal built structures intact, remembered by scientist Bodkin from his childhood there sixty years earlier. Ballard presents a 'gradual adjustment of life' over the first twenty years of warming, overtaken by rapid sea-level rise, defensive walls breached and 'the pole-ward migration of populations'. By 2100, 'fewer than five million people were still living on the polar caps.'[194] Imperial ventures haunt *The Drowned World*, the former British imperial metropolis an 'immense intact Atlantis', biologist Kerans's mission reprising tropes of imperial African exploration, venturing into a now tropical drowned England.[195]

Themes of imperial as well as environmental inheritance also structured a notable allegory of present-day coastal defence, David Dabydeen's 1993 novel *Disappearance*. Dabydeen tells a post-colonial story of a crumbling England, as the narrator, a young Guyanese engineer, stays with an older English woman, the widowed Mrs Rutherford, on the cliffs at Dunsmere in Sussex. Dabydeen presents coastal defence as a symbolic tale, of a particular kind of England defended, and as a globally entwined story. Mrs Rutherford's cottage is decorated with masks from an earlier life teaching in Africa, while the survival of Dunsmere is in the hands of a black man overseeing sea defence. The protagonists' relationship navigates sensitivities and sensibilities, Mrs Rutherford alert to histories of slavery and the colonial ignored by her compatriots, and the engineer ambivalent over what English recognition might denote. Mrs Rutherford declares that he has 'carved your name in our history', although readers of *Disappearance* remain ignorant, Dabydeen never naming the narrator: 'It was decent of Mrs Rutherford to claim that I now belonged to the heritage of England, but I knew that I had only been a transient worker.'[196]

Just as triffids anticipated English wilding, so John Wyndham's science fiction too prefigured Anthropocene coastal futures. Wyndham's 1953 *The Kraken Wakes* presents seas rising as intelligent aliens colonize ocean deeps. After atomic weaponry fails to dislodge them, the alien 'Bathies' take shipping, send sea-tanks ashore and melt the polar ice caps. Seas rise by 100 feet to drown coastal cities, with London under water and the east coast flooded, and the populations of the European North Sea lowlands migrate. Wyndham's key scientific character is an 'eminent geographer' and oceanographer, Alastair Bocker, who initially seeks cooperative communication with the 'Bathies', but eventually proposes destruction, having identified rising sea levels as the aliens' weapon, against which humans have no defence: 'I draw attention to the fact that in January of this year the mean sea-level at Newlyn, where it is customarily measured, was reported to have risen by two and a half inches.'[197] Weaponry ultimately destroys the aliens, but human population has been drastically reduced and climate changed.

As in *The Day of the Triffids*, Wyndham presents a man and a woman navigating the new geography for a new life. *The Kraken Wakes* ends with its leading protagonists, Phyllis and Mike Watson, escaping London by boat along the English Channel to their cottage in Constantine, Cornwall. Phyllis looks down from what was a hill, but is now an island:

> I was just thinking ... Nothing is really new, is it, Mike? Once upon a time there was a great plain, covered with forests and full of wild animals. I expect our ancestors hunted there. Then one day the water came in and drowned it all – and there was the North Sea ...
>
> I think we've been here before Mike ... And we got through it last time ...[198]

The as-yet-unnamed Doggerland ends *The Kraken Wakes*, as a consoling reference back.

Wyndham's 'we got through it last time' evokes communal endeavour; English, European, human. *The Kraken Wakes* was published a few months after the 1953 east coast floods, where 307 died and flood narratives highlighted communal experience and endeavour, a Blitz spirit reprised soon after the war.[199] Flood stories of the twenty-first century likewise mobilize the collective, though in different fashion, climate change and the Anthropocene connecting scalar identities from personal to local to regional to national to globally human.[200] The Blitz spirit remains, however, ready for national narrative mobilization, as in some responses to the 1987 hurricane, and as shown in the emergency stories of Covid-19, confirming the continuing narrative purchase of the Second World War.[201] Future Anthropocene events may test the continuing resonance of 1940, or 1953.

Wyndham's Phyllis offers reassurance that 'we've been here before'. If, in relation to the Anthropocene, we *haven't* been here before, it is in the sense that human processes are marking the rock record. The stratigraphic imagination of the Anthropocene nonetheless extends aspects of *The Kraken Wakes*: the unforeseen consequences of human technological capacity, the prospects for humanity under rising seas, the lessons and consolations to be drawn from the past. A notable dimension of the Anthropocene is that scientists have embraced rather than distanced themselves from cultural narrative, as in the popular scientific and part-science fictional writings of Jan Zalasiewicz, convenor of the Anthropocene Working Group reporting to the adjudicatory International Commission on Stratigraphy. Thus in Zalasiewicz's 2008 *The Earth After Us*, extraterrestrial visitors 100 million years hence explore human remains on a warmer earth, pondering the stratigraphic imprint. Wyndham and Ballard's descriptions of a drowning London, and the structural legacy it might leave, are echoed in *The Earth After Us*, where a contrast is drawn between futures of slow and gradually erosive sea-level rise, and rapid rise whereby 'landscapes may be drowned entire'.[202] Under rapid rise, England, like other lands, would be put 'beyond the reach of erosion . . . and into the kingdom of sedimentation. Our drowned cities and farms, highways and towns, would begin to be covered with sand, silt, and mud, and take the first steps towards becoming geology. The process of fossilization will begin.'[203]

Larkin's poem 'Going, Going', appearing in the Department of the Environment's *How Do You Want to Live?*, began Chapter Four's discussion of 'English Nature'. Another poem from Larkin's collection *High Windows* can conclude this section on Anthropocene inheritance. 'This Be The Verse', first published in *The New Humanist*, the journal of the Rationalist Association, in 1971, combines inheritance thoughts with a chosen coastal image, the third and final verse beginning: 'Man hands on misery to man./ It deepens like a coastal shelf.'[204] The shelf is the seabed area adjacent to a continent, Larkin choosing its gentle rather than plunging gradient to suggest an inheritance gradually, predictably, pulling under. The North Sea is all European coastal shelf, Doggerland included. Were they to have been written thirty years later, Larkin's coastal shelf lines might have been taken to indicate the vulnerabilities of land to rising sea, and the inter-generational responsibility and guilt of the Anthropocene.

There is a geological twist, in that in the mid-twentieth century a prominent environmental story, not least after the 1953 floods, was the tilting of Britain from post-glacial isostatic uplift. After the ice age, as glaciers melted and their weight was lifted, the northwest of the British island rose, while the southeastern parts tilted inexorably downwards.[205] Larkin might head east from Hull to the eroding Holderness coast, evoked for its 'unfenced existence' at the conclusion of his 1961 Hull poem 'Here', and find a gloomy ultimatum from times long past.[206] Tilting, however, was an absolutely non-human process about which nothing could be done, a slow doom with neither blame nor escape; perhaps a fitting image for Larkin in 1971. Climate change and the Anthropocene offer a different predicament, in both attribution and possible amelioration, and the dues of Larkin's verse thereby migrate. 'This Be The Verse' translates to the Anthropocene, with its first, familiar lines conveying ambiguous meanings of intended or accidental generation and anxieties handed down: 'They fuck you up your mum and dad./ They may not mean to, but they do.'[207] Going, going, eastern England erodes, Anthroposcenic on the European shelf.

Pits and Rivers

This chapter concludes with a particular spot, Attenborough to the west of Nottingham, discussed along with nearby Beeston in the companion volume to this book, *About England*, as a place carrying national stories, and noted in the second chapter of *England's Green* in connection with David Smith's photography of gravel extraction. Elements of Attenborough convey the Anthroposcenic, former gravel

Mural, Station Road, Beeston, Nottinghamshire, painted in 2018 by Qubek.

pits differently post-industrial to the landscape of Norman Nicholson's Millom. Alongside the pits, the River Trent carries the waters of Midland England, its fluctuations in level registering the weather.

On Station Road in Beeston, a wall shows reed, waters and bees, a mural by artist Qubek showing 'Beos Tun', the Saxon name for Beeston, meaning 'long grass settlement'. Imagery of flowers and insects, plant life and water, invokes for present-day Beestonians the landscape at Attenborough nature reserve, a couple of miles to the west.[208] The reserve is celebrated for its ecology and its social value, popular for birdwatching, walking and cycling, busy on a summer weekend but used the year round. The lakes of Attenborough are former gravel pits, their materials dug for construction work, making the world of the past century. Quarrying began in 1929, only ceasing a few years ago; some lingering bridge signs still warn of working waterways. Attenborough became the first nature reserve of the Nottinghamshire Wildlife Trust, leased in 1966 to forestall the threat of power station fly ash being dumped in disused pits, and opened by its coincidental namesake David Attenborough, who returned in 2005 to open a new visitor centre for the reserve. The Trust purchased the land and lakes from aggregate conglomerate Cemex in 2020.

Visitors to the Attenborough reserve take clear and well-surfaced paths between the lakes and along the riverbank, and people for the most part get along, with cyclist-walker or ornithologist-jogger tension minor. Birdwatchers occupy hides to view resident and migrant species, leisure and conservation cohabiting, although the leisure landscape has itself evolved since the 1960s. The 2005 opening of the visitor centre cemented a newly ordered space, with formerly bumpy and muddy paths resurfaced, leisure passage smoothed, and a diminished presence for angling, as the Wildlife Trust remade the place for nature. The Anthroposcenery of Attenborough featured in artist Kurt Jackson's project 'Place', where 32 writers (including Richard Mabey, Mark Cocker and Robert Macfarlane) were invited to choose a British place, which Jackson then visited to make work.[209] One of Jackson's authors was Jeff Barrett, co-founder of nature-attentive cultural journal and website *Caught by the River*, and also of independent label Heavenly Records in 1990, who chose Attenborough Nature Reserve.[210] Jackson showed three Attenborough pictures, with the emphasis on bird life reclaiming the industrial, but Barrett's accompanying text stressed Attenborough's changed social landscape, recalling growing up in

Attenborough, Nottinghamshire, 10 November 2019.

nearby Chilwell in the 1970s, fishing in the river near 'the gravs', with the pits a site for youthful free play.[211] The pits were then named after local factories, whose social clubs held angling leases. Barrett writes, 'Today there are no anglers. The factories are gone, the social club membership cards lie blank.'[212] Attenborough is thus post-industrial not only for its former extractive industry, but also in its lost industrial leisure society, the new nature space a lost social space. Moving into a world labelled 'Anthropocene', with the human geological mark on the world emphasized, these gravel grounds, like others in the Trent valley, and like the ironworks of Millom, become emblematic for their social as well as environmental complexity.

The pits and the river at Attenborough also register climate change, as rains gain intensity and floods are more frequent. The nature reserve is separated from Attenborough's village green and cricket ground by a high wall, built in 2012 as part of flood defence works after the Trent spilled into the village in 2000. The village gains flood protection, the reserve takes the waters. In 2019 heavy November rains fell after a wet autumn, and Trent floods followed. An old weather proverb hailed 'February fill dyke', with drainage channels full before spring, but here was November fill dyke, ground saturated and weather lore under review. The November river carried unusual momentum, flood debris finding its way into the lakes, a single plastic shoe calmly floating. Across the Trent, the chimneys and towers of the coal-fired power station at Ratcliffe-on-Soar looked over the hill, steam and smoke signalling operation.[213] Trent momentum, coal power, sodden land and the audible flow and lap of early winter spate made climate prospects vivid. Flood plains will of course flood, flood waters nurture fertility, and unusual wet spells do happen, but this felt like a November meeting point of climate and weather. And as the unusual becomes more frequent, and the once-in-a-hundred-year event turns decadal, this will likely re-happen, soon.

Past Attenborough, the path became narrower and a cycle ride along the north bank petered out into flood. On the far bank a few riverside houses held out above water. Boats moored outside, normally sitting well below the bank level, were lifted, blocking domestic views. Looking across, Anthroposcenic prospects met English history as a sign announced 'Restoration of Dunkirk Little Ship *Lady Sylvia*'. A well-kept craft, protected by an awning, was moored against the current, identified for anyone passing on the river, though no boats passed

Attenborough, Nottinghamshire, 10 November 2019.

that day. Wartime heroic rescue comes to Trentside, maritime memory tended inland. The Second World War tends to hover in the background, or lurch to the foreground, of any declared English crisis, and even here, cycling to view flood effects, war came into view. A Midland river in flood meets seaborne triumph-from-disaster. What prospects for *Lady Sylvia*, for England in the Anthropocene?

6
English Mystery

In 2007 Simon Armitage published a translation of the Middle English poem *Sir Gawain and the Green Knight*. The poem, likely written around 1400, gives an Arthurian tale. A green knight, green in skin, hair, attire and even with a green horse, arrives at Camelot at Yuletide, setting a challenge that anyone might strike him a blow, so long as he could hit back at the next new year. Gawain takes up the challenge and severs the green knight's head, only for the knight to pick up his head and depart. A year on, Gawain sets out for the 'green chapel', questing over the land, passing through parts of Wales and ending up in somewhere resembling the Cheshire and Staffordshire moorlands. Festive hospitality at a local castle sees Gawain resist temptations of the flesh while the lord is out hunting, his Christian chivalric standing confirmed, although acceptance of a protective green girdle from the lady, to guard against the green knight's blows, indicates a failure of loyalty to the hospitable lord. A self-questioning, self-questing Gawain finds the green knight, who turns out to be the local lord, greened-up. A year on from their Camelot meeting, Gawain escapes with a glancing blow. The whole local set-up is revealed to be magical, with Merlin's former pupil Morgan Le Fay resident in the castle, and Gawain returns to Camelot, lauded by all. The green girdle is adopted as a heraldic green belt by the Round Table knights, yet only serving to remind Gawain of his own minor failure of loyalty, not quite the perfect knight, though a little less naive, less green, than when he went away.

For Armitage the twenty-first-century resonance of *Sir Gawain and the Green Knight* was more Green than chivalric. Girdles, green or otherwise, and questing self-denial spoke less across six centuries than the Gawain poet's accounts of medieval nature. The Green and the mystical meet in the Green Knight, the green chapel, and the greenness of medieval landscape, as winter retreats and the spring lands 'wear a wardrobe of green'.[1] The Green Knight is for Armitage a 'green man',[2] a figure highlighted in recent commentary as a connecting symbol of nature and humanity, and denoting a relationship now lost, in Carolyne Larrington's terms 'a representative of all that the modern world undervalues, excludes or lacks'.[3] Sue Clifford and Angela King's entry on the Green Man in Common Ground's 2006 *England in Particular* included the Green Knight, alongside church carvings in stone and wood, and appearances in folk customs and on pub signs: 'As a historical presence the Green Man is enigmatic; as a future force he offers a positive face . . . The Green Man has emerged in our time as a symbol of reconnection with nature, of regeneration and hope.'[4]

The Green Knight is hardly however a benign spirit, 'but held in one hand a sprig of holly –/ of all the evergreens the greenest ever –/ and in the other hand held the mother of all axes'.[5] The 'green chapel' is where 'grisliness goes on', set within a gorge and marked by a mound by a stream, a hollowed 'bizarre hill', with moss and weed-matted walls, for Gawain 'the devil's lair'.[6] The Green of the Gawain poem signifies a complex enchantment, a vivid and alluring green world and a spell cast to entrap. For Armitage the complexity of this Green speaks to our present, Gawain's situation 'oddly redolent' of today's nature predicament:

> The Gawain poet had never heard of climate change and was not a prophet anticipating the onset of global warming. But medieval society lived hand in hand with nature, and nature was as much an enemy as a friend. It is not just for decoration that the poem includes passages relating to the turning of the seasons, or detailed accounts of the landscape, or graphic descriptions of our dealings with the animal kingdom. The knight who throws down the challenge at Camelot is both ghostly and real . . . Gawain must negotiate a deal with a man who wears the colours of the leaves and the fields. He must strike an honest bargain with this manifestation of nature, and his future depends on it.[7]

Should you be inclined, perhaps journey to the possible locations of the green chapel, and reflect on bargains with the future. 'Lud's Church', near the village of Flash in Staffordshire, by the jagged hills of the Roaches, is a popular candidate; the green chapel's surrounding hills have 'sabre-toothed stones'.[8] Visitors should however take care: the paths are uneven, and it may be slippery underfoot.

On the Mystical Geography of the English

England's Green, as this book has explored, may prompt appreciations of natural beauty, assessments of land work, variants of sustainability and renditions of the Anthroposcenic, but it also invokes mystery. *Gawain and the Green Knight*, rendered into the new millennium, takes its place within what Robert Macfarlane refers to as a twenty-first-century 'English eerie', a 'spectred rather than a sceptred isle', and what John Lowerson terms a long-standing 'mystical geography of the English', encompassing institutional and folk religion, paganism and earth mysteries, and representing 'major ways in which the English regard their physical and social landscapes'.[9] As noted above, Common Ground, whose work on nature and place was discussed in Chapter Four, have engaged with the mythic elements of a green country. Common Ground's 1986–9 project 'Trees, Woods and the Green Man', and their 1990 initiation of 'Tree Dressing Day' on the first weekend in December, celebrated arboreal spiritual significance, the December festival a kind of decorative nature Advent, sure that spring will be around the winter corner.[10] Clifford and King's work also inspired Kim Taplin's 1989 book *Tongues in Trees*, whose literary ecological moral was 'to remind ourselves of the primal relationship, which contains the possibility of living with trees, and within the whole of nature, lovingly. For if our sense of wonder were once to be fully awakened we should no longer be able to act sacrilegiously.'[11]

The natural and the mystical enfold in such work through placed accounts, whether the place is local or national, or a locale standing for nation, making up an English mystical geography. This chapter explores green English mysteries over the past six decades, with the environmentalism of the 1960s and '70s echoed in a spiritual and mystical counterculture, with its literary and musical evocations of a green England. Thus in 1967 Pink Floyd chose to name their first LP *The Piper at the Gates of Dawn*, after a chapter in Kenneth Grahame's 1908 *The Wind in the Willows* where the animals encounter Pan. Musical psychedelia corresponds with children's nature mysticism: 'Breathless and transfixed the Mole stopped rowing as the liquid run of that glad piping broke on him like a wave, caught him up, and possessed him utterly.'[12] Pan washes over Mole, echoing the sonic wash of *The Piper at the Gates of Dawn*'s longest track, the instrumental 'Interstellar Overdrive'. Pink Floyd, and singer and lyricist Syd Barrett, shared Grahame's capacity to swing from whimsy to intensity. Mystic England was framed too by Middle Earth, Tolkien a countercultural reference point, in part for his elves and wizards but also for the homely Shire, itself a place of folky hobbit song. Tolkien's Shire was an ordinary place where magic, destructive and redemptive, proceeded, an allegory for a natural life threatened by technological modernity, but which countercultural living might reclaim. Covent Garden's Middle Earth club opened in 1967, with Pink Floyd a featured group, while *Gandalf's Garden* magazine, produced in Chelsea by Muz Murray for six issues between 1968 and 1970, projected an Arthurian earth mysteries vision of Albion.[13]

Tolkien also crossed over to literary modernism, American poet Ronald Johnson's 1967 *The Book of the Green Man* journeying around sites of English visionary romanticism, the Lakes and the Wye, Southwell, Selborne, Shoreham and Cerne Abbas, 'And farther back in time,/ the lineaments clearly discerned of/ *Lothlorien* – '.[14] For Johnson: 'No work on England and mythology is complete, I reckon, without some mention of J.R.R. Tolkien's *Lord of the Rings*, the most magical imaginative work of the twentieth century.'[15] The ancient and the mystical achieved a new presence in counterpoint to modernity, in a manner which in retrospect would appear very much of its own late twentieth-century time.

English Festivities

From the late 1960s countercultural interest in the natural world, in alternatives to the present, and in England/Britain as an ancient Albion, found expression in festivities, some temporary and forgotten even by those who might have been there, some controversial and prompting state violence, and some now cemented as cultural fixtures in the seasonal round. To open the account, a festive memory of 1982.

On 3–4 July 1982 a 'Faerie Fair' was held near Lyng in mid-Norfolk, cheap to enter and free for experiment. In the summer after leaving school, we paid a visit to something styled as archaic, indeed something which by 1982 seemed archaic to anyone who might care about being up to date, its forms of self-fashioning by then unfashionable. On arrival, three men, amplified in a bare field, sounding like Hawkwind, played for themselves and anyone in wide earshot on a dull afternoon. Children hawked drugs, jesters improvised, there were fires after dark and tents to stumble round. An acoustic atmosphere prevailed, and the evening was gathered to a gentle end by Donovan, singing on a low stage, still doing a 1960s thing, in a field in Norfolk, on a green night. The stand-out memory remains the three men, amplified on bare soil, sounding like Hawkwind. Not everything in Faerie was gentle.

Lyng's Faerie Fair was one of the last of the Norfolk and Suffolk Fairs, documented in Richard Barnes's 1983 book *The Sun in the East*, with its title adapted from William Langland's fourteenth-century Middle English poem *Piers Plowman*, where 'I looked to the East, to the high sun', and saw 'a fair field full of folk'.[16] From Barsham Faire in 1972, 37 medieval-style fairs occupied East Anglian summers, with music, theatre, stalls, sideshows, puppetry, magic, games and more, shows of eccentric variety in field and wood. Some, as at Bungay in 1976 and 1977, mimicked earlier horse fairs in the area, their adaptation of the old echoing the way in which, as George McKay notes, the Notting Hill Carnival began in 1966 as a revival of a local traditional fayre, before gaining a Caribbean focus.[17] Attracting adults and children, families and non-families, enfolding past and present, the East Anglian Fairs were events for all ages. The non-place-name fair names conveyed an ethos: Mistletoe, Fantasy, Faerie, Green, Earth, Fire, Moon, Sun, Rainbow, Follye. From 1978 some were styled Albion Fairs, also the name of the coordinating body that took over the role from the East Anglian Arts Trust, set up by a group of friends to run the first fair in 1972. A related community newspaper, the *Waveney Clarion*, included a 'Coypu' comic strip, featuring a creature then being culled as a pest by the Ministry of Agriculture. The coypu, a South American rodent which had thrived in East Anglia after escaping from fur farms in the 1930s, served as a suitable dissident outlaw hero for the Albion Fairs.[18] The Trust committee recruited Suffolk author Adrian Bell, long connected to the organic farming movement, who noted in the Norwich-based *Eastern Daily Press* in May 1976, 'If I interpret

Front cover of Richard Barnes, *The Sun in the East: Norfolk and Suffolk Fairs* (1983).

them aright, they live by a faith in an organic England.'[19] Trust organizer Keith Payne noted that they 'made a point of only putting a fair on where the energy of the site was right, usually ancient sites'.[20]

Fair names conjured the visionary, the archaic, a chance to step aside into the otherworldly, spaces for experiment and renewal. A poster for the 1978 Wildream Albion Fair stated, 'Come as you would be'.[21] Entertainments shaped visionary festivity, offering a vaudeville of old Albion, with added extras: Morris dancers and Can Can dancers, puppetry and LSD. A photograph from the Alby Fair of 1981 shows 'England's Own Billy Bullshit', available for quackery and mendacity, '1p a Fib, 2p a Whopper'.[22] Comic and farcical elements leavened but did not diminish the utopic vision. An account of the third Barsham Faire in 1974 highlights the mix, noting that 'over thirty thousand people (never forgetting Walter Cornelius) joined in everything from dwile-flonking to the cosmic dance torchlight theatre.'[23] Dwile-flonking was an invented 1960s custom, under the auspices of the Waveney Valley Dwile Flonking Association, people hurling beer-soaked flannels in an event that was satisfyingly folk-parodic.[24] The never-forgotten Walter Cornelius, self-styled as 'The Birdman of Peterborough', was a regional news fixture for his charity attempts to fly across fenland waterways. Wings strapped to arms, a big run up, furious flapping, a few yards airborne and a big splash.[25] Being not too serious, the Fairs became inclusively vaudevillian, utopian capacity thereby gained rather than punctured, a capacious Albion, accommodating Coypu and Cornelius, whose absurdities deepened the sense that in all the entertainment there might be something profound.

The East Anglian fairs paralleled a free festival culture emerging in the early 1970s, espousing an anarchic, Blakeian ideal of Albion, as stated in the 1974 Albion Free State manifesto, '*Albion is the other England of Peace and Love* which William Blake foresaw in vision.'[26] Iconic English sites could stage this alternative national play, as in Windsor Great Park from 1972 to 1974, and at Stonehenge from 1974 to 1984, where around the summer solstice the stones became a camp for music, performance and the trading of alternative food, drink and drugs. Christopher Chippindale's *Stonehenge Complete*, navigating the many claims to Stonehenge and its meaning, shows how summer solstice celebrations had long included things beyond the formally Druidical: a pre-war jazz band, post-war sideshows and Morris dancers, crowds around and on top of the stones.[27] The Stonehenge free festival was therefore in one sense less a throwing off of convention than a formalization of earlier impromptu gatherings, an organized alternativeness, proclaiming its resistance to control.

Like the Green movement of which it was a loose part, festival culture styled itself through national as well as local and global referents. Windsor signalled a taking back of land from elite expropriation, Stonehenge an ancestral closeness to and knowledge of nature, as, weather permitting, the sun was seen to rise over the monument's heel stone at midsummer. Druid ceremony proceeded alongside free revels. Setting, sound and substances gave festivals a visionary quality, as places where mysteries might be encountered and even clarified. Some events were one or two-off happenings, while Stonehenge lasted a decade, but one festival became an iconic fixture of the English year. George McKay terms the Glastonbury Festival 'a very English fair', like the Albion Fairs part of 'the reconstruction of alternative traditions of Englishness'.[28] First held at Michael Eavis's Worthy Farm in 1970, the following year the event became a free 'Glastonbury Fayre', with its first pyramid stage. Arabella Churchill, Winston's granddaughter, was one of the organizers, and the 1971 event was filmed by David Puttnam and Nic Roeg. An informal free festival was held annually through the 1970s, but in 1979 Glastonbury became a commercial event, with profits to the UN Year of the Child and Genesis headlining. After a fallow year in 1980 the event became the Glastonbury CND Festival from 1981 to 1990, Worthy Farm also hosting an Ecology Party Summer Gathering in 1981 and a Green Gathering in 1982. The 'Green Field' was introduced at the festival site from 1984. Glastonbury connected music, performance and alternative environmental consciousness, playing on its local geography. Earlier Glastonbury festivals, such as those classical events organized in the town by Rutland Boughton from 1914, had harnessed Avalonian legends to articulate English mythologies, with in Boughton's case Arthurianism meeting socialism via religious and choral drama.[29] Eavis's events made the most of the views of Glastonbury Tor from Worthy Farm, and connected with the earth mysteries culture developing in Glastonbury from the 1960s, the 'Gothic Image' shop opening there in 1975.[30] As an annual festival on a working dairy farm in Avalon, the many facets of English pastoral met at Glastonbury, to visionary effect.

I attended Glastonbury once, in a muddy 1985, mainly for the music, with recollections of acts including the Style Council, Misty in Roots, The Triffids. Revisiting the programme shows I could have visited the Green Field, with its themes of Alternative Technology and Healing, and a 'Spirit of Peace' event featuring talks on the earth mother and Glastonbury's 10,000 years of visionary history. There was yoga and meditation, morning ragas and Sage Smudging. All this might go towards redeeming the world from the 'Countdown to Destruction':

> modern Man has made a rubbish tip of a paradise. He has multiplied his numbers to plague proportions, caused the extinction of 500 species of animals, ransacked the planet for fuels and now stands, like a brutish infant, gloating over his meteoric rise to ascendency, on the brink of a war to end all wars and of effectively destroying this oasis of life in the solar system.[31]

Festival culture, commercial or free form, attracted government attention as a novel phenomenon raising questions of regulation. The 1972 Department of the Environment report *50 Million Volunteers*, in its consideration of environmental themes, included a review of 'pop festivals': 'Since 1967 the tranquil British summertime countryside has been subjected on occasion to violent outbursts of throbbing music, barefoot children and "back to nature".' The Department noted that in four years there had been 'about fifteen large festivals (100,000–500,000), and perhaps three times as many smaller gatherings (5,000–50,000)'.[32] Here was a new cultural presence in English landscape, visible and audible, and controls and standards were advised: 'It is widely felt that pop festivals are an exciting development which should, if possible, be encouraged. Before this can happen, the basic problem of organisation must be overcome.'[33] An advisory committee of young people might aid central government.

50 Million Volunteers included an appendix outlining problems and challenges, and 'a cross-section of informed opinion'.[34] Notable here is a general positive tone, with experience diminishing fear. Straight demonization is evident only in parliamentary quotes: 'I spent two days at this festival incognito in my hippy outfit – and the scene both during and after the festival was one of indescribable squalor and filth.'[35] The quote was unattributed, but derived from a March 1971 parliamentary speech on the 1970 Isle of Wight Festival by local Conservative MP Mark Woodnutt.[36] Elsewhere, though, an approving tolerance comes through. A church representative noted:

> Those who attended come from a wide variety of backgrounds and although all may have been happy to accept the temporary label of 'hippy', the majority came from stable homes and occupations. They included bank clerks, civil servants, young mums, teachers, skilled and unskilled workers, students . . . and

> those still at school . . . Many came for a holiday and went home physically, mentally and spiritually refreshed.[37]

A 'Young Church organiser', in perhaps a twentieth-century equivalent of Gawain's chivalric denial, downplayed promiscuity: 'Semi-nudity of girls and total nudity of males . . . was totally unstimulating and unprovocative and occurred only for a few hours during the hottest days . . . Public parks and benches are dens of iniquity compared to the visible physical contact on site.'[38] *50 Million Volunteers* also noted that festivals required 'highly sophisticated organisation' while 'retaining spontaneity'.[39] If things have changed over the years, with Glastonbury becoming a corporate celebration of difference rather than its organizational manifestation, the Department of the Environment's report gives a reminder that these were always carefully organized spaces, where different forms and degrees of alternativeness met, and variously got along, before departing. Festivals, fairs and fayres staged versions of a free Albion, crafting spontaneity. Glastonbury's twenty-first-century evolution into a BBC summer television fixture, just before Wimbledon fortnight, has gathered Avalon into an official British mainstream, but Glastonbury Tor remains for long camera shots, signalling mysteries never quite figured.

Between the Department of the Environment's 1972 report and the BBC's embrace of Glastonbury, however, state bodies and festival bodies clashed. The final Windsor festival in 1974 was broken up violently by police, and in 1985 Stonehenge was sealed off to prevent the solstice free festival, the National Trust and English Heritage citing 'serious damage' in 1984. Two pastorals clash, a heritage ideal of a protected national monument, and an anarchic vision of a free Albion with access to land and its meaning. Barbed wire around the stones marked the distinction. The travelling 'Peace Convoy', a midsummer media fixture in the mid-1980s with its converted bus accommodation transgressing implicit rules of country life, and occasionally trespassing on rural property, aimed to reach the stones. On 1 June 1985 the Convoy was violently broken up by police in Wiltshire in what became known as the 'Battle of the Beanfield'.[40] Subsequent years saw repeat attempts to reach the stones, repeat injunctions and non-festivals.

In her 1990 photographic collection *Our Forbidden Land*, Fay Godwin showed Stonehenge, a site 'central to our culture', as a diminished place.[41] The visitors' underpass approach was an example

Fay Godwin, 'Nightguard, Stonehenge', from *Our Forbidden Land* (1990).

of 'theme park' heritage, while the shadow side of touristic framing was the summer solstice policing, with barbed wire as an example of 'twentieth century enclosures'.[42] Godwin photographed a solstice 1988 'Confrontation at the Heel Stone', festival goers facing riot-shielded police, and a demonstration to 'Free the Stones', where a hand-made banner showed a stone circle caged in barbed wire.[43] Godwin's image of 'Nightguard, Stonehenge' shows the circle in the background, a foreground stone acting as a sentinel for the walker's approach, but the stone is behind a wire fence, the walker cannot enter, and 'Nightguard' is the name on the security company sign, 'Guard Dogs Patrolling'.[44] Godwin was known for picturing ancient sites, her first photographic book work being in J.R.L. Anderson's celebratory 1975 guide to the prehistoric Ridgeway, *The Oldest Road*. Godwin photographed stones, barrows and hill forts, on a route designated in 1972 by the Countryside Commission as a long-distance path, and opened in 1973. For Anderson the Ridgeway offered readers an open ancient country, 'a wonderful journey through a landscape patterned by the feet of every generation from the Old Stone Age, and fashioned by digging-stick plough and tractor to make England'.[45] Modern

Stonehenge by contrast showed for Godwin the ancient traduced, the once-common view commodified, fenced-in.

The Peace Convoy formed part of a 'New Age Traveller' movement, transgressing the geographical structures of modern society. Government took a hard rhetorical and legislative line on such 'vagabonds', with their challenge to what Tim Cresswell terms the 'geography of normality'.[46] In the run-up to the 1994 Criminal Justice Act, Prime Minister John Major, speaking in Plymouth, stated: 'down here in the West Country, decent hard-working people are fed up with people invading their property and destroying their crops. In future, if these New Age travellers drive in, the police will have powers to drive them out.'[47] Major had earlier set out threats to property and land in his speech to the Conservative Party Conference on 9 October 1992:

> There's another problem we are dealing with – the illegal occupation of land by so called 'new-age travellers'.
>
> You will have seen the pictures on television or in the newspapers; if you live in the West Country and Wales you may have seen it on your doorstep. Farmers powerless. Crops ruined and livestock killed by people who say they commune with nature, but have no respect for it when it belongs to others.
>
> New age travellers? Not in this age. Not in any age.
>
> They say that we don't understand them. Well, I'm sorry – but if rejecting materialism means destroying the property of others, then I don't understand. If doing your own things means exploiting the social security system and sponging off others, then I don't want to understand. If alternative values mean a selfish and lawless disregard for others, then I won't understand. Let others speak for these new age travellers. We will speak for their victims.[48]

Major mocked travellers' claims to commune with nature, but missed another dimension that might have played to a Conservative conference audience, the travellers' claims to nation, to an alternative Englishness. Kevin Hetherington explores such non-nationalistic traveller 'visions of England', with the country a space of freedom and resistance, sites such as Stonehenge achieving 'shrine-like status', and the countryside in general a place of earth mysteries, an English holy land.[49] Nomadic rather than settled, in antithesis of the suburban

English life which many travellers had left, free festivals became meeting places, for something moving about England.

English festivities also framed a prominent early twenty-first-century English drama, which can act as a bridge to the remainder of this chapter, with its themes of ancient heritage and earth mystery, and signal forward to Chapter Seven, on folkloric England. In 2009 Jez Butterworth's play *Jerusalem* was hailed for its placing of rural English identity on the metropolitan stage, premiering at the Royal Court Theatre, staged on Broadway in 2011 and revived in London with its original cast in 2022.[50] *Jerusalem* centred on the marginal Johnny 'Rooster' Byron, played by Mark Rylance in the original production, living in a battered mobile home in a wood on the edge of Flintock in Wiltshire. Englishness is to the fore, with a faded cross of St George on the opening curtain and a flag of Wessex on Rooster's home. Phaedra, the soon-to-step-down fifteen-year-old May Queen, sings 'Jerusalem' for the play's prologue, and Act One's first stage direction is 'England at midnight'.[51] Byron is a Lord of Misrule, an anarchic figure whose wisdom channels folklore, drink, drugs and supposed inherited insight. Rooster has since been claimed as an icon for national rewilding, as when in *Feral* George Monbiot segues from a discussion of the wilder lives of Maasai tribes to Butterworth's *Jerusalem*, commenting on Rooster that the world 'cannot make room for him': 'There is no room for Johnny Byron in our crowded, buttoned-down land.'[52]

In *Jerusalem*, Kennet and Avon Council, supported by a residents' petition, seeks to evict Byron from their woodland, where he has camped illegally since 1982. Byron, his language veering between demotic and archaic, coarse and visionary, ends by calling the ghosts and giants of Albion to his aid. The sound of Flintock's Annual St George's Day Pageant and Wessex Country Fair is offstage, support characters moving to and fro, winning a goldfish, dancing the Morris. A variant of the May Song from Padstow in Cornwall recurs, Byron and friends finding spring joy and the eccentric Professor Ilchester toasting 'St George, and all the lost gods of England'.[53] Ley lines, discussed further below, run through the wood, and Byron claims to have met the giant that built Stonehenge. Butterworth sets an England of regulation, housing provision and planned rural celebration – the Pageant and Country Fair with its May Queen and Lord of the Rings float – against an anarchic, fantastic England of rebellious energy, deep in the woods. In Act Two, the one *Trivial Pursuit* answer Byron cannot instantly recall is the author of the words of the song 'Jerusalem', but after a severe beating from the father of the retiring fifteen-year-old May Queen in Act Three, it comes back: 'William Blake. It was William Blake.'[54]

The names in Butterworth's *Jerusalem* trigger associations. Byron's middle name is Winston, hinting at patriotic leadership but also Orwell's counter-totalitarian hero in *1984*. The surname conjures the Byronic, someone compelling yet dangerous. The Kennet and Avon local authority matches the actual Kennet Council, itself abolished in 2009 but covering the area of Wiltshire around Devizes and Marlborough, and including the stone circles of Avebury, discussed in the next section of this chapter, in its jurisdiction. As a village name, Flintock mixes the Hardyesque rural, as in Mellstock from Hardy's novel *Under the Greenwood Tree*, with flintlock gun deadliness, and perhaps even the all-round cricket energy of Andrew Flintoff, sportingly famous at the time of the play's writing, with boisterous qualities. And titling the play *Jerusalem* calls up all the many cultural and political associations carried by the poem and song, as detailed in an earlier chapter of *England's Green*. But especially it calls up the figure Byron takes care to remember, William Blake.

And then there is the name of the playwright, 'Butterworth', which itself could be taken to conjure English cultural associations. In another setting, perhaps another drama might be staged, 'The Butterworths', where playwright Jez, pastoral composer George and comic actor Peter meet to reflect on the performance of Englishness, carrying on up the banks of green willow.

Ancients' Places

> Our first sight of Stonehenge was when we came over a hill. From there it looked quite small. But when we drove alongside it looked very large . . . To get to Stonehenge we had to go through a subway. We had to pay 20p each to get into Stonehenge. When we got in we had a look around . . . After we had looked round I took some photographs. After that we found two holes in one of the stones. My friend's head and body fitted exactly into the holes.

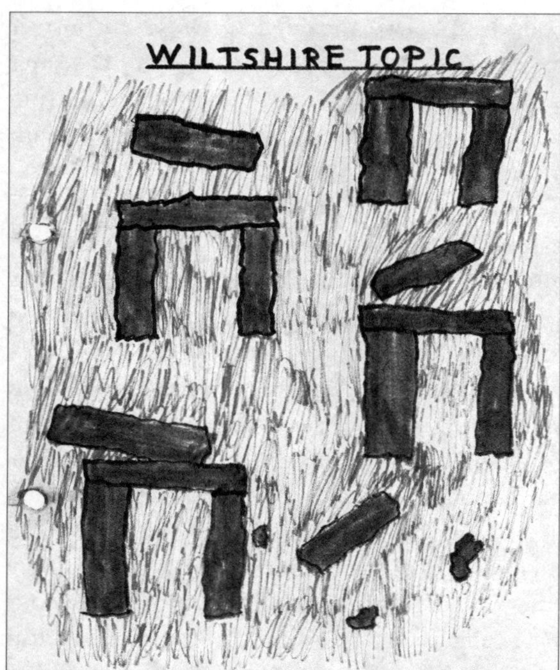

'Wiltshire Topic' front page, May 1975.

In 1975, on a junior school field trip, a week in Wiltshire, the first time away from home, I walked among the stones. The front page of my 'Wiltshire Topic' write-up showed a felt-tip drawing of Stonehenge, and inside the report gave another perspective, from a visit on 11 May. Stonehenge, ancient and modern, has generated much debate, but what did it mean to a late twentieth-century ten-year-old? The monument's landscape setting received comment, small in an open plain but large, indeed monumental, close-up. The incongruity of a modern subway was noted, and the novelty of being responsible, aged ten, for an entrance fee. In 1975 visitors were as free as free festivalers to explore the stones, and the child-fitting holes suggest some acting out of ancient ritual, a play at sacrificial mysteries. In an end-of-trip poll for favourite place visited, Stonehenge received three votes, well behind Bovington Camp Tank Museum and Longleat Safari Park, but nobody considered it 'The Place People Disliked Most'.

'Wiltshire Topic' described an exceptional piece of everyday life for a group of children, and a mystery is encountered. What were these things for? Did they have any connection for us? Could old stones in fields be simple matters of fact? Stonehenge was presented to us as an ancient monument of national importance, not something made by the English but surviving into something called England, and worth looking after. Stonehenge would become a World Heritage Site in 1986, its care deemed by UNESCO to be of global importance, and inscribed alongside the stone circles and avenues of Avebury, 25 miles to the northeast. The maintenance of Stonehenge has, as noted above, generated management controversy, including over nearby traffic, as when in late 2020 government approved a proposal, subsequently challenged and revoked, to tunnel the A303 under the monument. Tunnelling arguments saw a clash between those seeking, via road removal, to enhance the landscape composition of monument and setting, thereby restoring to some degree a Stone Age appearance, and those seeing the Stonehenge landscape as an underground-overground ensemble, where any road tunnel would destroy vital archaeology. Such arguments turn in part on how imaginative connection to the ancient might be made, and this section, through a selection of West Country journeys, considers how, since the mid-twentieth century, ancients' places have been presented as culturally close to or distant from the present. At Stonehenge, where solar alignments give evidence of ancient cosmology, various ancient-modern stories emerge: on the place of religion in ancient and modern societies; of parallel lines of reasoning between ancient and modern thinking people; of lost cosmological worlds whose nature wisdom needs to be regained. Sociological, scientific and visionary outlooks on English places of mystery generate different presences for the prehistoric.

Before the 1975 Wiltshire trip I had encountered Stonehenge through L. Du Garde Peach's 1961 Ladybird book *Stone Age Man in Britain*, where ancient belief was in effect contained through sociological assessment. The Ladybird Stonehenge was 'a great temple for the sun god', its construction requiring social organization and ingenuity, by people who 'were not savages', and a social and technological line could thus be traced from then to now, 'the dim beginnings of the modern civilisation in which you and all of us now live'.[55] The god worshipped may have been different, but these were 'our ancestors', nationally and intellectually.[56] Thinking through technology and religion, young twentieth-century readers could connect their English lives to ancient inhabitants of their land, via equivalent ways of being human, as problem-solving technicians on the one hand and believers in particular gods on the other.

The sociological, technological tone of the 1961 Ladybird was supplemented and sometimes contested in the late twentieth century by a visionary 'alternative archaeology', and a journey made seven years after the 1975 school trip can illuminate this cultural shift. In 1982 I walked part of the prehistoric Ridgeway with a friend, starting at Avebury. A train to Swindon, a bus to Avebury's stones, and a few days camping in downland before the hot weather became too much, getting only as far as Wantage before finding public transport home. H. D. Westacott's 1982 Penguin guide to *The Ridgeway Path*, bought for the trip, mapped the 'prehistoric trading route', and our camping spots and refreshment sites were recorded.[57] This was a practical guide for a practical walk, but there were visionary moments, in walk and guide. Aged seventeen, and with a head full of Tolkien, the Ridgeway carried ancient allure above other long-distance paths. Dismounting the service bus, browsing the stones, visiting Avebury's Red Lion, walking to Silbury

R. Hippisley Cox, *The Green Roads of England* (1914), front cover.

'Silbury', illustration by W. W. Collins, from R. Hippisley Cox, *The Green Roads of England* (1914).

Hill, ascending Avebury Down in the evening, camping in a field of sarsens by the ancient Herepath track, here was an ancient England. We were walking the path from west to east, but Westacott made some suggestions on what an east–west Ridgeway walker might find:

> Avebury can be regarded as a goal for the modern pilgrim. Such is the heightened awareness which several days on foot will induce that you would not be surprised to hear, as you make the final descent along the Herepath, the sound of celebration from within the sacred confines of the stone circle.[58]

Perhaps the 'several days on foot' were needed for the full effect, and so we followed the green road.

In 1914 R. Hippisley Cox had documented the Ridgeway as one of *The Green Roads of England*, with the hillside chalk carving of the White Horse of Uffington, east along the path from Avebury, on the book's cover. Hippisley Cox tracked the Ridgeway from Avebury to Streatley, passing the hill forts of Barbury, Liddington and Uffington, the burial mound of Wayland's Smithy, and the White Horse overlooking the vale, with the conical Dragon Hill below, a few years after our walk the site for Kate Bush's 'Cloudbusting' video. For Hippisley Cox, at Avebury the green roads of England converged, at a 'central gathering ground' and perhaps a 'seat of government', with the stone circles and avenues a 'sun temple'.[59] Hippisley Cox concurred with

'Mr. Cotsworth, of York' that the nearby 130-foot mound of Silbury Hill was a 'Shadow Hill' to mark the seasonal progress of the sun: 'Avebury would be an appropriate centre for the erection of a national Sun Temple and Shadow Hill, from which to issue edicts as to the proper seasons for seed-time and harvest.'[60] W. W. Collins's illustration showed Silbury with the downs behind.

So at Avebury in summer 1982, before ascending the Herepath, we wandered to Silbury, wondering what it was. A national Shadow Hill didn't come to mind, and by then other theories were in circulation, less visual than visionary. Westacott's *Ridgeway Path* guide noted the 'suggestion' that Silbury Hill 'represents the figure of the Earth Mother in the squatting or birth position . . . a spring issues from the side of the hill at certain times of year and some believe that this represents menstruation'.[61] Whether we concurred I forget, but Westacott's 'book list' included Michael Dames's 1976 *The Silbury Treasure*, subtitled 'The Great Goddess rediscovered', which had popularized Silbury and Avebury as a landscape evoking reverence for Mother Earth, an ancient green England to inspire a green future: 'the key to the Neolithic Age is the Great Goddess'.[62] Dames drew on popular works such as Robert Graves's *The White Goddess* (1948), but in effect revived a mainstream archaeological theory from thirty years before, out of academic fashion by the 1970s. As Ronald Hutton notes of Neolithic Goddess arguments by mainstream archaeologists such as Glyn Daniel, O.G.S. Crawford and Gordon Childe, 'Whether or not there ever was an Age of the Goddess in Neolithic Europe, there certainly was one among European intellectuals between 1951 and 1963.'[63]

The Silbury Treasure included photographs by Fay Godwin, picturing the hill in similar fashion to W. W. Collins's *Green Roads of England* illustration; Godwin had produced similar images in 1975 for Anderson's *The Oldest Road*.[64] While Anderson's Ridgeway guide had shied from alternative archaeology, Dames was a key practitioner and Silbury his sacred symbol: '*Silbury is the Great Goddess, pregnant.*'[65] For Dames 'the wisdom of the original designers is still accessible to us through the structure which they left behind': 'Properly read, Silbury conveys a splendid prehistoric philosophy, which is of exceptional relevance to the modern world.'[66] Dames presented Silbury as reaching back beyond an ancient patriarchal warrior society, and thereby pointing a way forward beyond a modern patriarchal warrior society. The spring mentioned in Westacott's Ridgeway guide was for Dames a key to the treasure, Swallowhead spring showing an ancient 'recognition of potent anthropomorphic qualities in the natural setting', feeding the River Kennet from underground.[67] Dames made some etymological anatomical speculation, with Kennet as 'Cunnit',[68] and found ancient southern England a goddess land:

> The reclining woman is to be found all over the English chalklands . . . For a society like the Neolithic, which saw life in terms of a Great Goddess, the compelling attraction of the chalklands is apparent, for there the people of the New Stone Age could walk on the torso of the divinity, explore her breasts, her armpits, the space between her thighs, or run the endless swell and ripple of her back for mile after mile, all the way from Dorset to East Anglia, or from Kent to the Yorkshire Wolds.[69]

The Silbury Treasure, published by a mainstream publisher, Thames and Hudson, generated new ecofeminist engagements with Silbury. Jon Cannon shows how Dames's work inspired a new ritual site at Swallowhead Spring, dressed from the early 1980s with ritual offerings.[70] Cannon notes the role of women from the Greenham Common peace camp, not far away near Newbury, who visited Silbury for an annual Lammas Day gathering; Dames had argued that the Hill was the focus for Lammas harvest rituals, with a 'total theatre' there on Lammas Eve as 'the goddess gave birth and gave birth *for all to see*.'[71] A new ritual landscape, with its own archaeological traces, emerges; modern earth consciousness, and modern environmental and gender politics, is made in connection with the ancient. In *Overlay*, her 1983 study of connections between contemporary and prehistoric art, Lucy Lippard discussed Dames's work and found Silbury a reference point for international ecofeminist art, as in Bristol-based Swedish painter Monica Sjoo's *The Goddess at Avebury* (1978), and U.S. artist Michelle Stuart's *Silbury Hill by Winterbourne Stream, Wiltshire, England* (1981), mixing black and white photography on rag paper and earth from the site.[72] *Overlay* itself begins and ends with photographs of Silbury, for Lippard Avebury's 'most affective monument'.[73]

So in 1982 we wandered through this landscape, not in search of an earth goddess, and unaware of Swallowhead, but nonetheless wondering about old mounds and stones and barrows, and finding them a fitting place for a cheap holiday. Our Westacott Ridgeway guide, despite its citation of Dames, set limits to the visionary:

> Those interested in fringe archaeology and earth mysteries will be disappointed. Prehistoric man probably looked at the world in a different way from us and some of his monuments may have a significance that escapes us, but the evidence put forward by those who believe in, for instance, ley lines and psychic archaeology seems to me unconvincing.[74]

By 1982, however, had we been so minded, and with a different guide, we could have walked the Ridgeway as a path to ancient wisdom. By the 1980s a popular, self-consciously alternative archaeology had rescripted ancient England, mapping ways to a different world. What if, for example, Janet and Colin Bord's *Mysterious Britain* had guided our experience? *Mysterious Britain* was first published in 1972 by the small Garnstone Press, but reissued by the mainstream Granada Publishing under their Paladin imprint in 1974, a sign of the commercial reach of visionary England by the mid-1970s.[75] With the Bords, we might have walked the green road to the hill forts, and reflected:

> the ancient men built upon the hills not for reasons of war but because the remoulding of the countryside was an integral part of their way of life; that by sculpturing the forms of the hills and downs they could enhance and magnify those currents of natural energies that flowed, and still do flow, through the body of the earth, and by the use of sound, movement, and above all thought, in the form of solemn and joyful ceremonies they could manipulate the vibrations in order to bring the bountiful and vital life force flowing through the land and the people.[76]

Ancient England becomes an artful place, as if the aesthetic of Lyng's Faerie Fair, which we had only recently attended, were projected on the downs.

Introducing *Mysterious Britain*, the Bords stated, 'The folklore and the theories we present stress the point that there is far more to our prehistory than appears on the ground or in history books, and, further, that we have much to learn from our ancestors and their way of life.'[77] Here was a life different from ours, but with which we could potentially connect. *Mysterious Britain*'s contents page indicates the portals to the past: ancient stones and earth works, holy wells, hill figures ('signals to the Gods?'), mazes and ley lines, paganism and the Holy Grail: 'such seemingly diverse studies as UFOs and morris dancing may lead to the elucidation of some of the enigmas of prehistory.'[78] Of the Uffington White Horse the Bords speculate: 'Could it be, as some have suggested, that it was intended to be seen from above, a signal from Neolithic man to his gods in their airborne craft who would then land on Dragon Hill?'[79] Another twenty years and crop circles might have made the Bords' list, possibly created by UFOs, if not by people with planks and ropes. All of this made for a country of mystery: 'Certain places have a "feel" about them; one remembers them for ever, the folk memory having been awakened for a moment. Some of them we put fences around and car parks nearby; others we keep for ourselves. Britain is uniquely rich in mysteries and mysterious places.' The Bords moved across Britain and indeed Ireland, current 'political divisions being ignored', English landscape's prehistoric message going beyond formal configurations of national heritage.[80]

A year before my 'Wiltshire Topic' title page, an aerial view of Stonehenge made the Bords' front cover. Here was a solar temple whose bluestones were brought from far, possibly by telekinesis, their particular properties required as part of 'a worldwide system for subtle energy transmissions'.[81] Avebury was an earlier 'great Sun temple', a 'spiritual powerhouse',[82] while around Glastonbury the Bords followed Katherine Maltwood's 1929 formulation of an Arthurian 'Glastonbury Zodiac', star signs outlined in landscape features, traceable on map and ground, an Avalonian 'Temple of the Stars' denoting 'mystic promise' in 'this Aquarian age of resurging sensibilities'.[83] *Mysterious Britain* also found some zodiac extras such as 'the Girt Dog of Langport', whose nose was the hill of Burrow Mump, 'while at the tail end of the figure is the hamlet of Wagg'.[84] Ancient England is barking, calling us home.

For the Bords, England was a spiritual palimpsest open to all, but especially to the sensitive, and 'psychometry' could allow 'those who are sufficiently sensitive, to tune into the vibrations retained in an ancient site or object'. The Bords speculated also on why non-psychics might want to explore the ancient, for example by walking the Ridgeway, with aesthetic fascination not seen as sufficient to explain the pull: 'The majority of people who have no knowledge of such matters, or may even retain a strong scepticism, are none the less receiving these psychic signals, albeit on a subconscious level. They, too, are attracted to these old stones.'[85]

And so we walked in a hot July as far as Wantage, and went home. If Westacott's guide was unconvinced by psychic archaeology, and if my Ladybird book on Stone Age Britain had implied that the ancients, with their religion reflecting their attention to the seasons, lived through a spatial delimitation of the sensible and numinous much like our own, alternative archaeologies offered a visionary ancient world, with reverence for nature pervasive. Prehistory showed an understanding lost in the modern world but which, through attention to ancient places, might be regained. One response to such visions could be ridicule, whether from archaeological doubts as to the evidential base of mysterious Britain, from a general sense that this might all be absurd, or from a questioning of the readiness of those seeking alternatives to set up new authorities and gurus. *Mysterious Britain* can here be usefully read alongside another 1970s vision of ancient England, the 1975 film *Monty Python and the Holy Grail*, an affectionate parody of grail questing that makes sense not only in the long line of Arthurian treatments from Malory and the Gawain poem onwards, but in the 1970s world of enthusiasm for mystery. *Mysterious Britain* had linked 'King Arthur and the Quest for the Grail' to the Glastonbury zodiac, where Arthur's ghost might still be seen: 'the mystic, esoteric and spiritual all meet here'.[86] Monty Python's Arthur, King of the Britons, played by Graham Chapman on an imaginary horse with his servant coconut-shell clip-clopping behind, declares his kingship as divinely ordained by the Lady of the Lake, raising Excalibur from the waters. The mystic, the esoteric and the spiritual meet, only for Michael Palin's peasant Dennis to retort, 'Supreme executive power derives from a mandate from the masses, not from some farcical aquatic ceremony.'

Energies in England

Standing stones had long stood as signs of an ancient country, but the 1960s brought new attention to the interconnection of ancient sites, via the rediscovery of a network posited forty years earlier. In the 1920s Herefordshire antiquarian Alfred Watkins had identified ley lines, 'old straight tracks' joining ancient sites, as an ancient transport system, previously undetected.[87] Archaeologists suggested the ley system had remained undetected because it never existed, but ley hunting became a genteel cult in interwar England. Watkins's leys were in origin prosaic, the ways in which ancient people got straight from A to B, but their detection could be styled as visionary. Watkins's 1925 *The Old Straight Track* ended:

> Out from the soil we wrench a new knowledge, of old, old human skill and effort, that came to the making of this England of ours.
>
> For as Puck, in Rudyard Kipling's tale sings:
>
> She is not any common Earth
> Water or wood or air,
> But Merlin's Isle of Grammarye,
> Where you and I will fare.[88]

In the 1960s Watkins's old tracks themselves went beyond the prosaic, turning into something numinous, as John Michell revisioned leys as earth energy lines, notably in his 1969 book *The View over Atlantis*.[89] As with the Bords, Michell entertained extraterrestrial possibilities, following Tony Wedd's 1961 book *Skyways and Landmarks* in order to posit a link between leys and UFOs, and producing his own *The Flying Saucer Vision* in 1967.[90] Michell's main emphasis, however, was earthly, the ley an energy system that ancient people had tapped, their awareness now lost. Ley rediscovery might reconnect modern humans. Archaeologists were again sceptical if not dismissive of 'earth mysteries', although from the 1990s attempts at dialogue across archaeological divides emerged, as in the 1990 collection *Who Owns Stonehenge?*, which brought together archaeologists such as Christopher Chippendale with Druid Tim Sebastian and earth mysteries writer Paul Devereux, and in Barbara Bender's 1998 attempt at 'making space' for the variety of narratives around Stonehenge.[91] Whether or not leys were earth energy lines, and whether or not archaeologists gave earth mysteries house room, the ley nonetheless struck a late twentieth-century human nerve, and a new popular countercultural ancient England emerged, warranting analysis for its aesthetic quality as much as historic accuracy. In *Overlay* Lucy Lippard commented, 'If the leys don't exist, then Alfred Watkins was a very good conceptual artist.'[92] Tracing leys across England, an earth energy map appears, almost as an alternative network to the motorways then under construction across the country.

Watkins's *The Old Straight Track* was reissued by Garnstone Press in 1970, with a note from Michell hailing Watkins as a 'true gnostic' and 'provincial visionary'.[93] In *Mysterious Britain* the Bords suggested that the sensitive might pick up the ley's energy as it connected ancient centres such as Avebury and Stonehenge:

> From these centres of power there stretched across the land leys or alignments of single standing stones, circles, dolmens, cairns, earthen mounds and other ancient sites, each with its particular function in the overall scheme of energy transmission. That the system has long fallen into disuse and the land and people have suffered accordingly there is no doubt, but like any great system based on natural principles, faint glimmerings of its original function occasionally activate some of the stones.[94]

Tapping old stones might redeem land and people, and all England becomes a potentially alternative landscape.[95] The reach of this new visionary geography was indicated when Nicholas Saunders's 1973 *Alternative London's Survival Guide for Strangers to London*, aimed at young visitors wanting 'to take part in the new culture', suggested a Glastonbury trip to investigate leys, zodiacs, UFOs and the Grail: 'There is a current re-awakening of English mysticism.'[96]

The View over Atlantis inspired the first pyramid stage at Glastonbury in 1971, Michell advising on its proportions, his book setting English leys within a global geometry, significant network nodes including the Great Pyramid of Giza:

> We all live within the ruins of an ancient structure, whose vast size has hitherto rendered it invisible. The entire surface of the earth is marked with the traces of a gigantic work of prehistoric engineering, the remains of a once universal system of natural magic, involving the use of polar magnetism together with another positive force related to solar energy.[97]

For Michell, geomancy, numerology, Aboriginal songlines and Chinese feng shui all indicated lost wisdom: 'At a time before the violation of the earth . . . men on earth must have exercised certain faculties which in us are now for the most part dormant.'[98] Watkins's original ley idea had been part of a challenge to an archaeological orthodoxy emphasizing the diffusion of civilized ideas from the Middle East across a primitive Europe, but in contrast Michell's revised ley set old England within a lost global civilization. Rediscovering the ley, returning to 'the natural sources of life', England could do its bit for the new global Aquarian age: 'Written across the face of the country in letters of earth and stone the cosmic knowledge of the ancient world is now within reach.'[99]

One ley, in its connection of prominent sites, became effectively the M1, or perhaps the L1, of the ancient system. Michell noted the 'St Michael line of traditional dragon sites in south-west England', tapping Christian associations of the Archangel and high places, but revealing an older force, from Land's End through St Michael's Mount to Burrow Mump and Glastonbury, to Avebury and across England to Bury St Edmunds before reaching the sea near Lowestoft.[100] Paul Broadhurst and Hamish Miller's 1989 *The Sun and the Serpent* traced the St Michael line, Miller's dowsing, conducted on foot or while driving, 'using only one rod, of course', identifying accompanying 'Michael' and 'Mary' currents of earth magnetism.[101] The Mary current was revealed at Avebury while dowsing Swallowhead Spring, and Michael and Mary waved about the line, making a corridor of certainty across southern England, with a ritual 'mating' of lines at Glastonbury Tor: 'The Mary energy formed a container which encompassed the Michael current and its bulbous projection around the tower. The symbolism was graphic. The female force enclosed the male energy in the form of a double-lipped cup. It was a chalice or Grail.'[102] Michell introduced *The Sun and the Serpent*, 'How lucky we are in England to inhabit such a diverse, mysterious, symbolically rich landscape.'[103]

Broadhurst and Miller, both based in Cornwall, presented *The Sun and the Serpent* as a two-year quest. The book opened with a Blake sun, moon and stars quote from the epic poem *Jerusalem*, asking 'Art thou Nature, Mother of all', and described an imagined Avebury Mayday in 2000 BC, marking the union of Sun God and Earth Goddess. On Mayday, as at Lammas, the Michael line aligned with sunrise: 'The fusion creates an enchantment over the land.'[104] The authors searched in ordinary as well as monumental spots, their narrative gaining from such variety. *The Sun and the Serpent* is also not without humour, as when, exasperated by dowsing tight curves of energy in Cornwall,

Broadhurst and Miller come to a farm: 'Just one word was painted on the sign. LEY. This was the second time the current had led through a place with this singular name. Perhaps, we thought, someone was trying to tell us something.'[105] The authors track the ley from Carn Les Boel, south of Land's End, to Hopton, between Lowestoft and Yarmouth: 'The Michael dragon left English soil incongruously at a breakwater on a beach behind a caravan park; the Mary parted company a short distance away.'[106] Fifteen years before the Ridgeway walk, my first caravan holidays had been at Hopton, tentatively paddling and making castles on the sand, oblivious to the dragons and currents, to Michael and Mary.

Just as Watkins's interwar ley hunting, as a walking, map-reading, picnicking popular prehistory, bore a family resemblance to popular cultures of outdoor leisure, so visionary ley geographies echoed popular cultures of landscape history shaped by the work of W. G. Hoskins and others, following the publication of Hoskins's 1955 *The Making of the English Landscape*.[107] Leys demanded topographic attentiveness as well as speculative spirituality, and their appeal could lie in both. Broadhurst and Miller comment:

> There can be little doubt that a quest such as this is one of the best ways to see the English countryside. The element of surprise sharpens the wits and the sense of adventure is always present; not only does one find oneself in the most exquisite backwaters of rural England, saturated with history and a mellow, unhurried peace, but the intimacy and atmosphere of the landscape affects the perceptions. It is easy to forget, while jostling with juggernauts on the motorway, that half-a-mile away a different world exists.[108]

In this different world, not far from the main road, you could tap another green world, arcane speculation aligned with diligent field study. Such grounded alternativeness is evident in regional studies such as those of Ian McNeil Cooke in west Cornwall, produced from his art studio near the Men-an-Tol monument, with its 'magical' holed stone. Cooke's study of 'ancient sites and pagan mysteries', archaeology and the 'old religion', is structured through walks across Penwith: 'it is only by experiencing the local landscape on foot that a deep and intimate acquaintance with this unique peninsula can be attained.'[109] Footwork lends depth, helps to suggest that these are not flights of fancy. Likewise in Shirley Toulson's 1979 walking of the 'ley lines and ancient tracks' of East Anglia, field study helps navigate folklore, energy lines, zodiacs and ancient socio-economic organization: 'Not that I find it wise to make any sharp distinction between practical and mystical matters.'[110] Toulson's other work included a guide to Derbyshire's ancient tracks, a landscape history of Welsh droving roads accompanying photographs by Fay Godwin, and the guide to farm museums discussed in Chapter Three above.[111] Toulson saw connection between ancient interests and current concerns, 'the self-sufficiency movements and the cults of organic farming, which are largely a response to synthetic twentieth-century living'. Prehistoric enquiry led people to 'take note of their natural surroundings, and in so doing to be aware of the elements which our prehistoric ancestors confronted. This leads them to become increasingly interested in the ways men worked with the forces of nature, both practically and spiritually.'[112]

The spiritual and the practical, the vision and the map reference, met too in singer Julian Cope's 1998 'pre-millennial odyssey through megalithic Britain', *The Modern Antiquarian*, a work also illustrating the pop cultural resonance, and commercial publishing possibilities, of archaeological mystery.[113] Cope and his family had moved to Wiltshire to be near to Avebury, *The Modern Antiquarian* taking shape through downland walks. Gazetteers cover three hundred sites by region, while Cope's introductory essay presents an ancient British mother landscape. Field accounts combine personal experience with access advice and map references, and a code on 'How to Behave in the Country'.[114] Antiquarian gnosis and fieldwork meet, with an opening off-beam citation of W. G. Hoskins's work on landscape as historical document: 'Hoskins appears to have been an early 20th-century scholar with a strong mystical bent.'[115] *The Modern Antiquarian* becomes a kind of magic *Making of the English Landscape*.

Cope's music had anticipated *The Modern Antiquarian*, from his 1992 LP *Jehovahkill*, with a plan of the Callanish stones on the Isle of Lewis on its cover, William Stukeley's 1724 plan of Avebury inside, a track called 'The Subtle Energies Commission' and sleeve notes telling of the ancient and why it was worth singing about. His album *20 Mothers* (1995) included 'Stone Circles 'N' You' and 'By the Light of the Silbury Moon', while *Interpreter* (1996) came with a 'mythological

Julian Cope, *Self-Portrait with Tripod; The Cove, Avebury*, postcard, July 1996.

mind map of the Marlborough Downs and surrounding area', crossed by the Michael line, though Cope is not in general enthusiastic for ley lines, *The Modern Antiquarian* noting them as 'wearisome and endless', the Michael Line excepted.[116] Cope recorded Part 1 of 'Paranormal in the West Country', on the album *Autogeddon* (1994), inside the chamber of West Kennet Long Barrow. Cope styled himself the 'Arch-Drude', a modern version of Stukeley's persona as 'Arch-Druid', mailing out postcards to his fan-base with news updates and megalithic photographs, as in 'Self-Portrait with Tripod; The Cove, Avebury', from 5 July 1996. For Cope, writing at a late twentieth-century time when Britishness and Englishness was under cultural and political scrutiny, Ancient Britain spoke to multiple modern identities, the English included: 'This book aims to give something back to the culturally dispossessed of Britain, be they white, black or green; Welsh, English or In-between.'[117] A pre-national land points to a plural modern culture, appreciative of difference across the island. Old English energies, or rather old energies which can be tapped in England as elsewhere, might help shape the country's future. Twenty years on, however, Cope would return to national matters with his 2022 album *England Expectorates*, in caustic despair at the political and cultural present, the title song finding a land where no European will go, and England bleak, however marvellous its ancient sites. The green of England gains a tinge of phlegm.

The Artful and the Ancient

> Last summer, I walked in a field near Avebury where two rough monoliths stand up, sixteen feet high, miraculously patterned with black and orange lichen, remnants of the avenue of stones which led to the Great Circle. A mile away, a green pyramid casts a gigantic shadow. In the hedge, at hand, the white trumpet of a convolvulus turns from its spiral stem, following the sun. In my art I would solve such an equation.[118]

From the 1960s and '70s ancient green England was also revisited for artful ends by those neither archaeologists nor alternative archaeologists, but nonetheless detecting significance. This section explores the attraction to stones and mounds of artists, filmmakers, authors and composers, some drawn by stories of earth energy, some in search of sites to realize alternative futures, but others simply, or not so simply, intrigued by the grounded abstractions of ancient shapes. The ancient attracts less by a promise of coherent wisdom than by some resonance in old English pattern, some landscape equation to ponder.

Artful late twentieth-century visitors to ancient sites were reprising engagements from before the war, as indicated in Paul Nash's description of an Avebury equation from 1934, quoted above.[119] In his 1937 essay 'Prehistory from the Air', John Piper had similarly juxtaposed an eighteenth-century engraving of Silbury Hill by Stukeley, a 1920s aerial photograph of the site by O.G.S. Crawford, and an abstract painting by Joan Miró, ancient and modern forms in conversation.[120] New met old again decades on, but in new circumstances, and with new stakes, tied to environmental anxieties, worries for the future and attempts to reconnect with land. Here were new variants on Nash's 1934 call that, just like William Blake, whose 'poetry literally came out of England', so 'we, today, must find new symbols to express our reaction to environment.'[121]

Lippard's *Overlay* highlighted parallel artistic engagements with prehistory across the world, with ritual, stone arrangement, maps, journeys and feminist earth work marking out new forms of green art. Lippard's own starting points were Dartmoor and its standing stones, encountered during a year spent on a Devon farm in 1977, and Avebury, where the field archaeology of Aubrey Burl and the works of Michael Dames could be complementary in 'bringing Stone Age culture to life'.[122] The artistic register identified by Lippard was global, but the fact that these were English landscapes, or pre-English landscapes in late twentieth-century England, nonetheless carried significance, becoming a point for reflection. Avebury certainly had a moment of resonance in 1970s England, in art, music and television. In early 1977, as Lippard began to investigate the English West Country, English children could tune to ITV and find the series *Children of the Stones*. Seven episodes, filmed at Avebury (renamed as Milbury), followed a scientist and his son studying the stone circle. The scientific and mystical enfold, as people are turned into stones and back again, and time recycles characters and events, aided by the conjunction of ley lines.[123] A few weeks later, on 9 March 1977, with interest in Avebury piqued, child viewers could have been taken, or dragged, to the Queen Elizabeth Hall in London for the London Sinfonietta's premiere of *Silbury Air* by Harrison Birtwistle, an ensemble piece presenting a ritual ancient sense of place. Birtwistle sought a balance of artifice and nature to match Silbury, which he termed 'an artificial but organic intruder of the landscape'.[124] Thematically, and musically, Birtwistle offered an equivalent to Stravinsky's modernist pagan ballet, a kind of rite of ancient English spring.[125] In Birtwistle's work, with its frequent landscape references, ancient places lend mystery to music determinedly modern. Fourteen years on, the grown-up 1977 children might have heard Birtwistle's 1991 opera *Gawain*, from the medieval Green Knight tale, ancient greenery given sonic potency.

Avebury offered a symbol for new times too in film, as Derek Jarman shot his ten-minute Super 8 silent yellow-filtered *A Journey to Avebury* (1971); Jarman also produced an 'Avebury Series' of paintings. *A Journey to Avebury* rapidly intercuts landscape views, grazing animals, tree clumps and trackways, the only identifiable humans a row of children on a wall, but lithic anatomy is present throughout, stones standing single, in formation, in silhouette or recumbent. Avebury stone anatomy also shaped poetry, in Richard Burns's 1972 sequence *Avebury*, fronted by Stukeley's 1724 plan of the site and with a 1722 Stukeley engraving on the cover. Burns reached across the 'matter of words/ word of matter', and simple page justifications were not worthy to figure these stones, lines set instead on the page in menhir shape.[126] Burns cut against the proliferation of Avebury myth, presenting instead stones 'defying discourse', the 'subversive stone' refusing easy narrative.[127] Material presence offered existential measure: 'anywhere centre/ say these stones/ of Avebury.'[128] The centre could be anywhere, though Burns is drawn to the very particular somewhere of Avebury to make the case.

A parallel geographical complexity, conjoining the anywhere and the somewhere, informs the art of Richard Long, who in the late 1960s and the '70s worked the traces of ancient England into the emerging green genre of land art. In 1971, in a spiral on the Whitechapel Gallery floor, Long brought Silbury to London: *A Line the Length of a Straight Walk From the Bottom to the Top of Silbury Hill* (1970).[129] Ancient measures, linear and spiral, are abstracted into London art space. A 1972 walking work combined text with an illustration of sunset behind Glastonbury Tor: 'On Midsummer's Day/ A Westward Walk/ From Stonehenge at Sunrise/ To Glastonbury By Sunset/ Forty Five Miles Following The Day'.[130] Maps registered Long's walks, in a fashion echoing alternative archaeology's line making, as in *A Walk By All Roads and Lanes Touching or Crossing an Imaginary Circle/ Somerset England 1977*.[131] Long's route is shown on an Ordnance Survey sheet centred on Ilminster, the black-lined pattern echoing the zodiac figures traced by Katherine Maltwood just to the north around Glastonbury. Arbitrary, or meaningful, or meaningful because arbitrary? A Dorset OS map has a photograph of the chalk carving of the Cerne Abbas Giant superimposed at the base, and a black lined network around Cerne Abbas at its heart: *A Six Day Walk Over All Roads, Lanes and Double Tracks Inside a Six Mile Wide Circle Centred on the Giant of Cerne Abbas/ Dorset 1975*.[132]

The walked line was a Long trope from his early work *A Line Made by Walking/ England 1967*, made by walking to and fro for a few yards in a field, having got off a train twenty minutes out of Waterloo to find a suitable spot.[133] Reference to any specific locale defers to a generalized 'England', a gesture echoed in a work simply titled *England 1968*, made in the public parkland at Ashton Court, Bristol. Long made an x shape in a field of daisies, picking the flowers along two lines, the x lasting until reflowering.[134] Calling this work *England* almost makes for an alternative flag, the red cross

Richard Long, 'England 1968'.

of St George tilted to a green x, marking a spot for the country. In March 1970 the work appeared in the art journal *Studio International*, part of 'Nineteen stills from the work of Richard Long', also registering pieces made in Dartmoor, Wiltshire, Krefeld in Germany and the summit of Mount Kilimanjaro. 'England' indeed appears in 'Nineteen stills . . .' alongside 'Africa', two x shapes made in different grassy contexts, a year apart: '2 lines walked through dust-covered grass, by the roadside. AFRICA 1969'/ 'A sculpture made by removing the daisy heads. ENGLAND 1968'.[135] Long's somewhere-anywhere practice drops equivalent signs across the world.

In the catalogue for Long's 1991 Hayward Gallery retrospective 'Walking in Circles', Anne Seymour asserted that 'there is nothing mystical or religious about Long's work'.[136] Long himself stated:

> I wouldn't make any claims to be mystical. I think I get my energy from being out on the road, having the world going past me. That's the time when I'm conscious of the energy in the world and in me. I suppose that's the idea that some places are more potent than others.[137]

Long, in exploring place potency, certainly however enacts ancient and mythic association, with England one potent place and select spots within it carrying a certain charge. Leaving lines and circles of stone in the landscape to mark his passage, Long's art, at Silbury and Glastonbury and Cerne, makes for and taps a mysterious England, just as it alludes to parallel mythic geographies elsewhere.[138] Long's anywhere-somewhere geographical imagination echoes that of alternative archaeology, the latter indeed registering in the catalogue for *Walking in Circles*, where Hamish Fulton's essay on Long recalls their 1972 visit to Peru's Nazca lines, mentioning the Glastonbury zodiac and a ley line along the Strand; lines in parallel across the world, and significantly somewhere.[139]

In 1997 Long published *A Walk Across England*, a book-length photographic and textual documentation of *A Walk of 382 Miles in 11 Days from the West Coast to the East Coast of England*, made in 1995 from the Atlantic near the Devon-Cornwall border to the North Sea in Suffolk. Broadhurst and Miller's countrywide St Michael ley quest, published eight years before, finds an aesthetic echo, though with a different relationship of prosaic and profound. Long's route, 'A walk across England as art', was not far off that of *The Sun and the Serpent*, inside cover maps showing the line, with eleven tent symbols marking night stops.[140] The eighteenth-century chalk hillside white horse at Westbury in Wiltshire appears on the book's cover, registering an iconic English landscape, but most of Long's photographs show prosaic scenes of path and lane, some with brief descriptive captions. There is a postbox still marked 'VR', a road sign for 'Glastonbury 8½', loose chipping signs, bridges and tree tunnels, bird droppings on tarmac, milestones and roadkill, field crops and weather scenes. Long ends on a Suffolk beach, where children play ball, inflatables bob and holes have been dug. Here is an English summer walk, coast to coast, ocean to sea. The quotidian is elevated via archetypal practice, Long walking east, though without the crutch of the Michael Line.

Artful quotidian encounters with old things, prehistoric or historic, continue to frame English landscape. *Detectorists*, a television comedy written by and starring Mackenzie Crook, ran for three series between 2014 and 2017, with occasional specials since, achieving a BAFTA-winning popularity often presented as surprising. Stories of people, especially men, in fields, somehow still fascinate. *Detectorists* also attracts the label 'English', for its qualities, characters and setting.

Crook's character Andy and older friend Lance, played by Toby Jones, are the lead metal detectorists, exploring the sub-surfaces of landscape and self. Keighren and Norcup, in their edited collection *Landscapes of Detectorists*, suggest the programme might itself serve as future cultural archaeology, 'a gift by which those who are yet to come will understand something of the cultures of Englishness in the early twenty-first century'.[141] Different archaeologies inform *Detectorists*, from Lance's heroic dream of the treasure of a Saxon ship burial to Danebury Metal Detecting Club president Terry's taxonomy of discarded buttons. Landscape can be a visionary portal, but also transports the detectorist to an older everyday England.

Detectorists is a romance, of a different kind to, say, *The Sun and the Serpent*, although it shares with Broadhurst and Miller's ley hunt a story of male companionship. The human presence is generally, like the humour, gentle. The search for treasure, eventually found after three series, entails conscientious scrutiny of finds, whether clay pipes, ring pulls, *Jim'll Fix It* badges or Saxon coins. There is reverence for the natural world, and for the history of human land work, and a precise evocation of East Anglian landscape, specifically that of Suffolk, where the series was filmed, and north Essex, where the fictional setting of Danebury is mapped precisely onto an Ordnance Survey sheet of the Maldon area. Maldon is the site of a tenth-century Anglo-Saxon versus Viking battle, commemorated in an Old English poem, 'The Battle of Maldon', taken by Tolkien as 'the last surviving fragment of ancient English heroic minstrelsy', for the basis of his 1953 'The Homecoming of Beorhtnoth Beorthelm's Son'.[142] *Detectorists* essays its own kind of landscape English heroism, with some minstrelsy along the way, in the programme's theme song and in the faltering musical efforts of Lance and Andy. Aside from odd finds, Lance's name is the closest the programme gets to weaponry.

Crook had played Ginger in the original production of Butterworth's *Jerusalem*, and Aimee-Ffion Edwards (Sophie in *Detectorists*) appeared in the play as Phaedra, Crook commenting on *Jerusalem* that 'during rehearsals we steeped ourselves in the myth and lore of the English landscape.'[143] Richard Smyth, commenting on its attention to birdsong and place, suggests that '*Detectorists* feels like a very English programme', with 'a habit of telling us back our own tales'.[144] Crook extended *Detectorists*' English tale in his subsequent remaking of Barbara Euphan Todd's *Worzel Gummidge* stories for television, discussed in Chapter Seven below. *Detectorists* shows another variant of an archaeological green England, different to Cope or the Bords in the distance kept from earth mysteries, but still allowing for numinous moments. And while cultural nationalism seems far from Crook's Danebury, England has some significance for the programme's characters and the pasts they explore.

A Mysterious English Dump

An earlier meeting point for the visionary and the prosaic, the artful and the ancient, can conclude this chapter. In a piece of children's literature from 1963, Clive King's *Stig of the Dump*, the ancient underfoot sparks time travel and English mystery.[145] *Stig of the Dump* has been a first portal to the archaeological for young readers, and can

Front cover of Clive King, *Stig of the Dump* (1963), illustration by Edward Ardizzone.

also serve as cultural shorthand for reminiscing adults, as when in Butterworth's *Jerusalem* Troy Whitworth curses Byron as 'Worzel Maggot, Stig of the Dump'.[146] Set around King's childhood village of Ash near Sevenoaks in Kent, *Stig of the Dump* begins with solitary modern jean-wearing eight-year-old Barney slipping into a disused chalk pit, where he finds Stone Age Stig, still down there in his cave, furnished Womble-style with modern rubbish. The pit, a place for discarding things, becomes a receptacle of memory. As ground gives way, imagination opens, Edward Ardizzone's cover design showing Barney following Stig into discovery.

Stig of the Dump brings past into present, and takes modern England back. Stig draws a hunt scene on his cave wall, and when Barney's sister Lou goes fox hunting they follow with one of Stig's spears. Seeing the fox, Barney reaches for the spear but Stig stays him, and the fox calmly goes to ground, Stig seeing no purpose in killing the inedible. The hounds come for Stig, but he sees them off and pursues an edible horse instead. Stig moves across current society, from the well-off hunt to the rough 'Snarget' boys whose common voices disturb Stig's pit peace. Reconciliation sees Woodbine cigarettes shared (Stig eats his) and jelly babies handed round. Stig initially treats the sweet as a ritual offering: 'he reverently stood the little sweetmeat in a niche in the chalk and stood and looked at it'.[147] King here echoes contemporary archaeology, notably the chalk 'goddess' figure held to have been discovered in a niche in the Norfolk Neolithic flint mines of Grime's Graves in 1939, though later suggested as a modern fake. The goddess was prominent in 1960s guides to Grime's Graves, and in Jacquetta Hawkes's 1951 book *A Land*, where it was suggested that carving the figure in chalk would 'at all times have recalled the flesh of the White Goddess'.[148] Stig's jelly baby, whatever its colour and flavour, briefly serves as goddess equivalent, until Barney eats it, and Stig too acquires the taste. After his first meeting with Stig, who knaps flint in his cave, Barney finds a flint 'in the left-hand pocket of his jeans', and muses, 'Something at the back of his mind was telling him that he'd seen pictures of chipped flints in books, and real ones in museums, and that they were made thousands of years ago by rough people who weren't alive any longer.'[149]

At the end of the book the dump is filling up, and Stig may be 'on the move', with reports of him recycling old cars, and mending chicken runs with wire mattresses 'in a back lane of that woody country at the top of the Downs'. Stig becomes a make-do-and-mind sprite, renewing for all times and perhaps to be on call for the twenty-first century as Stig of the Anthropocene.[150] *Stig of the Dump* also, though, involves visionary transports out of the modern, and here King's book echoes those tensions within 1960s cultures of archaeology noted earlier in this chapter, pulled between the excavation of ancient lives everyday like our own and an encounter with a mythic world we have lost. The final two chapters, 'Midsummer Night' and 'The Standing Stones', take Barney back in time, with sister Lou and dog Dinah. Under the midsummer moon, a stag is encountered ('But there *aren't* any stags here!'), and Stig's pit seems not yet to have been excavated. Time is travelled: 'It was then that the children went midsummer crazy.'[151] Stig is with his people, playing music, and pulling ropes in setting up a stone monument, still standing on the Downs in their modern present. The movement into the Neolithic, and out again at sunrise, takes the children to and from another England, or perhaps beyond anything called England; as Lou states, 'this doesn't seem to be England at all.'[152]

The past in *Stig of the Dump*, with its evidently English setting, characters and themes, does not offer national roots, rather a story of landscape then and now, and the capacity to cohabit with something and someone other, whose space this also turns out to be. Sun rises after the crazy midsummer night:

> and over the shoulder of the downs appeared a red spark, and the valley was flooded with light. It was sunrise. From the low mist in the bottom of the valley appeared the spire of a church, the tops of oast houses and electricity pylons. The solid forest was gone, and there were the squares of cornfield, orchard, and hop-garden. There were the villages, and the distant chimneys of cement-works, and the broad ribbon of the main road sweeping down the hill below.
>
> Barney looked round the hillside. The people of the tribe had disappeared. There were no huts, no sign of a camp fire. They had all vanished with the last shades of darkness. But one thing had not changed. The three stones with the great slab on top were still before his eyes – weathered now, with grey lichen growing on them. The mound was not there, but the stones stood just as they had done when he had let go the last of the rope.

Barney and Lou consider whether it may have been a dream, and wonder why they have woken on the hilltop: 'He walked round to the front of the stones, where the open side looked over the valley – and there, sitting in the entrance as if he was on his own front porch, was Stig.'[153] The children are back in their England, and Stig remains, a spirit of something, meaningful in 1963, and never yet out of print.

7
Folkloric England

In the early 1970s, in our suburban Norwich primary school, we country danced. Recordings of folk tunes were played, we clumped over the wooden hall floor, tried to follow patterns, held reluctant partner hands. Girls and boys circled, interchanging, lining up. At the summer fete, on the adjacent recreation ground, practised imperfections brought parental applause and general smiles. A few didn't join in, though, finding forced enrolment into something proudly archaic rather silly, refuseniks peeved at being a spectacle, at the holding hands business, at not remembering the moves. Let off, other things were done for a while. There was no objection to the organized modern bounce of a Spacehopper race, which made more Space Age sense.

Why were people doing this? Eighty years before, Cecil Sharp and other collectors had gathered English songs and tunes and dances, and fed them into the school curriculum, and so here we were. Most of us. What Sharp would have characterized as gently socialistic folk practice sparked a peculiar 1970s suburban childhood militancy against something cast as English. In an almost monocultural school, there was little doubt that we inhabited an English culture, whether that was manifest in sport, television, family war stories, holiday conventions and so on. On what basis did this intrusion into our everyday modern England claim a more profound cultural status?

The discussion of folkloric England in this chapter pursues this puzzle over recent decades, when many have sought and claimed answers, and attention to folk has undergone what Winter and Keegan-Phipps term a 'resurgence', commonly aligned with green values.[1] The environmental charity Common Ground, noted in the previous chapter for their interest in green myth, have likewise presented the folkloric as part of their green England. Sue Clifford and Angela King's 2006 A–Z of *England in Particular* has folkloric entries including:

> Abbots Bromley Horn Dancers, Britannia Coco-Nut Dancers, Castleton Garland Day, Cheese Rolling, Corn Dollies, Furry Dance, Grovely Rights Day, Haxey Hood Game, Maypoles, Morris Dancing, Mumming Plays, 'Obby 'Osses, Rush-Bearing, Straw Bear Day, Sword Dancing, Tar Barrel Rolling, Turning the Devil's Stone, Wassailing, Well Dressing.[2]

Around the country, through the year, things go on, and a folkloric England-in-particular could be extracted from Clifford and King's compendious work. In 2017 Common Ground, now directed by Adrian Cooper, sponsored Paul Wright's film *Arcadia*, made from a hundred years of British Film Institute archive material and presenting an 'old weird Britain' of strange ritual and mystery. Rather than an Arcadia of pleasant relaxation, educational dancing or pastoral escape, here was an Arcadia of uncanny depths. An electronic soundtrack by Adrian Utley of Portishead and Will Gregory of Goldfrapp accompanied a seasonal journey through common customs, harvest rites, fetes and fates. The lives captured by earlier filmmakers project a national culture showing a country which, lent weirdness through editing and soundtracking, becomes somehow more deeply English and British than the prosaic everyday, whether then or now. Common Ground celebrated the film's release with a commemorative poster by Stanley Dorwood, 'Vale of the White Horse', the Uffington landmark again watching over national proceedings. Common Ground's website presents appreciative *Arcadia* testimony, including from writer Paul Kingsnorth: 'Here is aboriginal Britain. You thought it was gone beneath a deluge of motorways and malls and screens and engines and scurrying human feet. Much of it is. But what remains? What remains, and what will you do with it?'[3]

An English Song and Dance

Folk had a curious presence in the 1970s English junior school, at once in and out of place. Outside of school, unless family or friends were enthusiasts, where would a growing child encounter such things, beyond acoustic singalongs on television programmes aimed at younger children, or occasional chart intruders on *Top of the Pops*? Seekers after folk would resort to seasonal events, specialist clubs, specialist shops, or might journey to Cecil Sharp House, London headquarters of the English Folk Dance and Song Society (EFDSS), with its Vaughan Williams Memorial Library. An EFDSS visit could combine library work and leisure, with the dance hall at Cecil Sharp House decorated in 1954 with a 6 × 21 metre modernist mural by Ivon Hitchens, depicting musicians and dancers in a mythical wood. In 1964, introducing his book on *English Folk Dancing*, Douglas Kennedy, EFDSS Director from 1925 to 1961 (and wartime member with Rolf Gardiner of the organic farming lobby group Kinship in Husbandry), advised, 'The searcher after more information must seek a fairly well-stocked library such as that at Cecil Sharp House with its books and its ever-expanding sound section containing film tracks, tapes and discs bearing the living evidence which can be seen, heard and felt.'[4]

In the digital new millennium other ways to see, hear and feel have emerged, which have intensified the at once in- and out-of-place sense of folk culture in England. Is this the real English life? Or just quaint fantasy? The EFDSS now offers 'The Full English', a digital archive presented as 'unlocking hidden treasures of England's cultural heritage'.[5] What can be found, and how might the manner of its finding shape understanding of a folkloric England? Online history here as elsewhere produces particular temporal effects, with manuscript collections from the late nineteenth and early twentieth-century folk revival searchable, and the gatherings of collectors including Cecil Sharp, Lucy Broadwood, Ralph Vaughan Williams, Maud Karpeles and George Butterworth downloadable. A couple of clicks and we are with Australian collector and composer Percy Grainger's notebook, the words and music for 'Rosemary Lane', taken from the singing of William Fishlock at Chiswick Ferry, Surrey, on 9 January 1908. Even the envelope in Grainger's hand, containing 'W Fishlock's Words', is on show.[6] 'Rosemary Lane' would become a folk staple, recorded by Bert Jansch on the 1971 LP of the same name; and that can also, of course, be heard online. The song's title suggests the bucolic, and perhaps 'The Full English' browser might click for that reason, but the lyrics convey folk's complexity, Rosemary Lane a poor part of dockland London, and the lyric one of pregnancy, abandonment and destitution.[7]

New seekers after twenty-first-century folk, more inclined to dance, could visit the website of the Morris Ring, coordinating affiliated Morris dance sides.[8] Notable here are films from the late twentieth century, where video technology can generate a sense of historical distance different from, and perhaps greater than, that conveyed by an Edwardian collector's notebook. The grain of video, the dress of spectators, the background cars going by; the dancers proceed in that other world of, say, 1983, just as they proceeded (with some variation) in the Edwardian period, and as they may still proceed (with different dress and vehicles, captured on higher quality phone video) today. Digital folk offers an uncanny connection to time and place, not that folk has ever been entirely canny, as the 1970s school fete suggested. Dancing and prancing and singing may say something about England, but whatever is articulated carries an incongruity, via movements and sounds and costumes which stand out.

This outstanding nature of folk was conveyed in 1989 by photographer Martin Parr, in his collection *The Cost of Living*, where Parr pictured 'Morris dancers' occupying a pedestrian zone outside McDonald's.[9] The dancers take the space for their practice, as shoppers pass, some looking on. A bystander's Mohican hairstyle almost blends in with the signage, while the dancers jingle from another time and place, no less distinctively or authentically folk for being outside McDonald's. Parr offers a multivalent picture, which might usefully supplement the EFDSS's 'Full English', filling it out with complications. 'Morris dancers' may convey an ironic juxtaposition of English tradition and global consumerism; or a picture of easy cohabitation facilitated by town centre pedestrianization; or an image of defiance, England dancing on regardless; or a joke, an absurd performance blocking the modern shopping way.

Appreciation of the iconic qualities of the folkloric should make allowance for those finding such practices awkward or comic. Folk-as-joke indeed characterized one line of twentieth-century commentary, as assertions of English tradition were met with sometimes dismissive humour. In their 1959 *Penguin Book of English Folk Songs*, gathered from the pages of the EFDSS *Journal*, Ralph Vaughan Williams and A. L. Lloyd felt obliged to insist that they offered more than 'mere clownish nonsense'.[10] It is as if Lloyd and Vaughan Williams were anticipating Kenneth Williams's 1960s comedy rustic 'Rambling Syd Rumpo', with his ludicrous folk-singing vocabulary of cordwanglers, moulies and grussetts, devised by *Round the Horne*'s scriptwriters Marty Feldman and Barry Took. Williams's parody may

Martin Parr, 'Morris dancers', from *The Cost of Living* (1989).

have been ultimately dismissive, but was affectionate. Others however pursued serious critique, challenging folk for nationalism, or for class condescension. For Dave Harker, in his 1985 polemical analysis *Fakesong*, folk needed proper demystification, with folksong and ballad 'intellectual rubble that needs to be shifted so that building can begin again . . . there is no point in attempting, as Bert Lloyd and others did, to rehabilitate such concepts'.[11] In 2012 a *New Penguin Book of English Folk Songs* was issued compiled by Steve Roud with Julia Bishop, Roud stating of Harker and others that 'the polemic that was produced has seriously warped the debate ever since, and it is time that it be relegated to a brief historiographical footnote concerned with the follies of the era.'[12]

Successive gatherings of English folk songs have sought to head off criticism and satire, the tradition sustained. Political commentary on folk, however, went well beyond Harker's work, indeed included A. L. (Bert) Lloyd, Vaughan Williams's co-author and one of Harker's *Fakesong* targets. Lloyd's 1967 *Folk Song in England*, written from the political Left, and informed by Marxism, integrated class analysis, attention to tradition and an interest in ritual and mystery.[13] Georgina

Boyes's 1993 history of folk revivals, *The Imagined Village*, likewise gave a critical cultural and political analysis going far beyond polemic, and with its own lasting impact, as discussed below, on folk practice.[14] Criticism, and indeed satire, might be taken as sources of renewal in their own right. Discussion of Lloyd's work, from his 1944 *The Singing Englishman*, based on a Workers' Music Association *William Morris Musical Society Bulletin* essay on 'The Revolutionary Origins of English Folk Song', to the influential and popular *Folk Song in England*, shows how the Englishness of folk could be subject to critique which, far from dismissive, complicated and enriched its national quality.[15]

Lloyd's *Folk Song in England* mixed realism and romance. For Lloyd, 'The mother of folklore is poverty,' and 'in England folk song is the musical and poetic expression of the fantasy of the lower classes – and by no means exclusively the country workers.'[16] Lloyd attended to the urban as well as rural, the industrial as well as agrarian, and promoted an evolving, non-monumental sense of tradition: 'A living tradition is not a stone column but a plant, hardy but sensitive to climate change.'[17] Thus, for Lloyd, 'the *creation* of folk music and poetry has, within the last hundred years or so, passed almost entirely into the hands and mouths of industrial workers.'[18] Recent youth enthusiasm for such song, 'the second folk song revival in England', a 'folk-song-with-teeth' and less polite than the Edwardian first revival, denoted a search 'for some less transitory satisfaction than is offered by the masters of mass entertainment', and 'something more relevant to their life-experience than the dim cloud-cuckoo land of the pops'.[19] Folk song offered relevance, and thus lasting pleasure. While critiquing the patriotic mobilization of folk song, Lloyd had no problem labelling songs as English, as songs and tunes moved between regions and countries, within the British Isles and beyond, the national and international mixing: 'A sort of patriotic mysticism inhibits this study to some extent. The notion is still prevalent that a folk tune must be the sacred property of a given country . . . Like other European countries, England has profited from the common fund of continental melody.'[20] Lloyd suggested that 'our English folk songs' emerged from a medieval 'general European complex' of songs, and only 'over slow centuries' took on 'their peculiar national and class character'.[21] So English folk song was not simply English, but *was* English, complexly. And if 'patriotic mysticism' was inhibiting, other kinds of mysticism were, as discussed below, admissible.

English folk has always denoted geographical complexity, echoing the geographical complexities of Englishness: the urban-rural-suburban traffic of Sharp's collecting, publication and dissemination; the transatlantic traffic of Sharp's collecting of English folk songs in Appalachia; the global work cultures of the sea shanty.[22] The geographical varieties of folk in England are conveyed too through Lloyd's contemporary Roy Palmer, in his works on Midland folk song and folklore. Two Palmer books from 1972, *The Painful Plough* and *Songs of the Midlands*, are indicative. *The Painful Plough*, one of a series for Cambridge University Press aimed at secondary schoolchildren, and with a related LP on influential folk label Topic Records, offered 'a portrait of the agricultural labourer in the nineteenth century'. A foreword by historian Edward Thompson, author of *The Making of the English Working Class* (1963) and also influential on *Folk Song in England*, presented the field labourer as an undervalued skilled worker, and Palmer prefaced each song with an extract from the 1898 autobiography of agricultural workers' union leader Joseph Arch (1826–1919), who 'had the qualities which, for many, epitomise the Englishman. He was sturdy, stubborn, self-reliant, and a champion of the underdog.'[23] *The Painful Plough* presented a former rural England with 1970s resonance, as Palmer aligned folk song and Left values of labour organization. Palmer's 1972 *Songs of the Midlands*, gathered from the urban and rural west Midlands, grew from the work of the Birmingham and Midland Folk Centre, drawing on old manuscripts and new gatherings, notably from Cecilia Costello (aged 88, Birmingham) and George Dunn (aged 85, Quarry Bank, Staffordshire). *Songs of the Midlands* presented the current folk music revival as 'a setting in which race, colour and creed can become less immiscible than behind the cherty partitions that our newspapers tend daily to buttress rather than demolish'.[24] Old songs could vault current barriers, whether songs of love and courtship, crime and punishment, social comment and 'seasonal and ritual songs'.[25] Midland teenagers even sustained folk practice, with the Tudor song 'The Best Bed', an accompaniment to singing games, surviving from one Elizabethan age to the next: 'Sung by a group of thirteen-year-old girls at Shenley Court Comprehensive School, Birmingham; collected by Roy Palmer, February, 1966.'[26] For Palmer, *Songs of the Midlands* made sense in and of today's England.

A sense of English folk song as not simply English, but complexly English, has shaped twenty-first-century folk enthusiasm, with England and Englishness rearticulated one more time in what Winter and Keegan-Phipps term a 'period of resurgence in the English folk arts'.[27] In 2007 an EFDSS tune book, *Hardcore English*, asked 'So What's England?'[28] The answer was that place mattered, though not as a source or sign of cultural purity, and as something which might move beyond a history bound up with the domination of others. Winter and Keegan-Phipps find folk arts constructing 'multiple Englands', pulling towards both the rooted and the cosmopolitan.[29] Sometimes Englishness is offered as a distinct and implicitly white identity, though happily inhabiting a multicultural country, sometimes as 'internally variegated', whether by ethnicity or regionality, and rooted in historical plurality.[30] As with Lloyd, and indeed Sharp and Vaughan Williams, this resurgent folk leans to the political left, actively distancing anything with a hint of right-wing nationalism, though happy with ideas of English indigeneity. Winter and Keegan-Phipps present a folk resurgence self-aware and self-critical, with an extended musical palette, and performatively English in its use of rural and nature imagery, as in Maggie Holland's 1999 song 'A Place Called England', winner of best song of 1999 in the Radio 2 Folk Awards, which evoked land and nature rather than flags and empire, a place open to all, as long as they loved English earth. Boyes's 1993 book *The Imagined Village* lent its title to a group whose eponymous 2007 debut album presented folk as multicultural endeavour. The Imagined Village, launched at the 2007 WOMAD festival, was led by Simon Emmerson, known for fusing musical genres from his work in Weekend, Working Week and Afro Celt Sound System. Winter and Keegan-Phipps see The Imagined Village as 'invested in both the rootedness and routedness of Englishness', with members including Chris Wood, Martin and Eliza Carthy, and Billy Bragg, whose 2006 book *The Progressive Patriot* had proposed a counter-reactionary English music.[31] For Winter and Keegan-Phipps one of the key folk 'resurgence' records was Eliza Carthy's 2002 *Anglicana*, issued on Topic Records and cemented in tradition via reference to EFDSS collections, the album for Carthy 'an expression of Englishness as I feel it'.[32]

Assertions of indigeneity make England familiar yet strange, a newly exotic element within the world of 'World Music', a forgotten treasure lying underfoot, forgotten by a people estranged from their traditions.[33] Thus in 2019 *Dancing England*, a theatre performance of traditional dance in Nottingham, previously held in Derby from

1979 to 1987 and revived from 2017, presented itself as 'a Celebration of England's dancing tribes'.[34] How might such indigenous qualities connect to the longer history of England's global engagement with tribal identities? In his 2004 book *After Empire*, Paul Gilroy finds Carthy's *Anglicana* and Holland's 'A Place Called England' having 'a precious ability to transport English ethnicity into the present'. Gilroy reflects: 'This little England owes something to its nativist predecessors. It certainly shares their commitment to the relocalization of the world, but it has expanded their horizons and overcome their xenophobia.'[35] Whatever events since 2004, the 'resurgence' documented by Winter and Keegan-Phipps in 2013 performs Englishness in that vein, including in its welcome of Black English performers, as in the work of Birmingham-bred, Cornish-based singer Angeline Morrison, with her 2022 Topic release *Sorrow Songs: Folk Songs of Black British Experience*.[36]

Back in 1972, the year of Palmer's *The Painful Plough* and *Songs of the Midlands*, a year after Jansch's *Rosemary Lane* and five years after Lloyd's *Folk Song in England*, and when at school I was being exposed to English songs and dances I had never known at home, a BBC film gave another take on English indigeneity, with folk culture one aspect of a critical, parodic reflection on place and race. *Black Safari*, directed by Colin Luke and written by Roy Lewis and explorer Douglas Botting, presented a 'Black Expedition' up the canals of Lancashire, 'to locate the geographical centre of the remote island of Britain', passing through 'the hidden parts of England, few black men had seen and lived to talk about'.[37] A parody of BBC2's *The World About Us* strand, and first broadcast on BBC 2 at 9.55 on Friday, 24 November 1972, *Black Safari* showed narrator Horace Ové journeying on board a boat, *The Queen of Spades*, with Yemi Ajibade, Merdel Jordine and Bloke Modisane. Botting appeared as their white 'loyal crew'. Ové was born in Trinidad in 1939, had lived in Britain since 1960 and was known from the late 1960s as a filmmaker, including his 1970 BBC television documentary *Reggae*. In 1973 Ové would direct 'King Carnival' on the Trinidad and Tobago Carnival for *The World About Us*.[38]

Black Safari presented Ové journeying into white Englishness, the end titles of *Black Safari* crediting Stanley, Livingstone, Scott and Park as inspiration, the film satirizing historic British self-importance. Explorers in African dress head for the heart of England, naming new topographic features after Kenyatta, Nyerere and Nkrumah as they go.

Tribal categorization is turned on the English, with one long-haired boat helper described as a 'picturesque fuzzy-wuzzy, of the nomadic hippy tribe'. The pejorative 'fuzzy-wuzzy' language of Corporal Jones in the hugely popular BBC1 comedy *Dad's Army*, as he recalls his time with Lord Kitchener in Sudan, is repurposed, rendering modern English hair quaintly peculiar. At a fete, where villagers' cooperative bemusement indicates they may not have been wholly in on the filming joke, the expedition's anthropologist measures local heads with callipers, the conclusion being, 'It is clear there is no such thing as a pure Englishman.'

The tribal centrepiece of *Black Safari* is a folk dance, as the Black Expedition reaches Bacup, where a 'local tribe', the 'Cloggies', meet them by the canal. The film's credits thank 'The Bacup Britannia Coco-Nutters', and the explorers watch their dance from the boat: 'here was a new mystery, their faces were black!' The dancers dance, and the explorers applaud politely, as 'we tried to conceal our real feelings', and so the dancers take applause as approval, and there is 'unfortunately' more dancing, with 'rather obscene fertility objects in their hands'. Ové talks to a dancer, asking 'why do you put this black stuff on your face?' The answer is ritual disguise, and an origin story of the Moors bringing the dance to Cornwall, from where slate miners brought it north. As the dancers dance away, Ové concludes:

> The mystery was explained. The Cloggies trotted away leaving us with the key to Britain's ancient history. The word moors is short for blackamoors, the old dialect word for Africans. This surely proved that British culture, degraded as it now is, was originally brought here by African missionaries and explorers, long long ago. So, in a sense we the British Expedition of 1972 were walking in the footsteps of our revered ancestors. Perhaps nothing in the whole expedition gave us such pride of race as this discovery.

The dancing faces of Bacup continue to be questioned, as part of arguments over who has control over local folk practice. Theresa Buckland indeed shows issues of ownership and control going back to 1929, with attempts by Maud Karpeles of the English Folk Dance Society to 'collect' the Bacup dance, and the Bacup dancers insisting on retaining rights over their practice, notably for the cultural and potential financial prestige acquired in regional and national competitions. Buckland documents a dance team long keen to retain independence.[39] In 2006 Clifford and King's *England in Particular* stated of the 'Britannia Coco-Nut Dancers', 'Blackened faces are a common disguise in folk custom, protection from recognition by evil spirits – or perhaps employer.'[40] Rights to the Bacup dance generated further controversy in the 2020s, with debate over whether face-blackening carries customary value or causes offence, the questions raised in *Black Safari* posed once more. Arguments over race at a time of statue toppling and the Black Lives Matter movement led to the Bacup dancers leaving the Morris Ring in 2020, after the latter deemed blackface unacceptable. The Britannia Coconut Dancers' public statement asserted blackface make-up as part of a 'unique mining tradition', which 'had no connection with ethnicity nor any form of racial prejudice': 'removing any part of our costume will take away the mystique of who we are.'[41]

Blackface had also been considered in 1964 by Douglas Kennedy, whose *English Folk Dancing* anticipated some of the complexities explored by *Black Safari*, and revisited in 2020. Buckland indeed notes of Bacup that as EFDSS Director Kennedy had 'provided an origin legend which the team has seen fit to repeat when an explanation of their activity is needed', though from *English Folk Dancing* any legend appears complex, and a clear argument for or against blackface would be hard to derive.[42] Kennedy reflected on the blacking of faces in Bacup and the wider origins of Morris, suggesting that 'blacking the face to disguise the person and turn him into a ritual actor is a device inherited from the Stone Age'. There may also, however, have been influence from 'close contact with the comparatively recent carnival entertainments popular in this part of England', by which Kennedy most likely meant minstrel shows. In different ways, then, blackface was, yet was not, about race. Kennedy suggested that the earlier Cotswold Morris had also involved face blacking (now not used), and that themes of disguise were also found in the masks and visors of winter mumming plays, such that blackface as dance practice therefore pre-dated racial classifications. Kennedy suggested, however, that the name 'Morris' was itself racially coded. While Kennedy marked his argument out from theories of 'Moorish' Iberian origin, he identified a more specific historical blackness, from an earlier imperious England of the seventeenth and eighteenth centuries: 'This disguising may have been the reason for the use of the name Morrice, or Morris, in England for the Spring-time dance custom. Two or three centuries ago the word negro for a black man was not current usage. A black man was a blackamoor.' Kennedy called Shakespeare in evidence: 'Shakespeare makes one of his characters speak of "leaping like a wild Morisco". This Morisco dancer could just as well be an English Whitsun-dancer as a Dervish in Morocco.'[43] Kennedy's *English Folk Dancing* thus presented an English dance type named for its dancers looking like a 'blackamoor', but where the reason for blackface painting was disguise, with blackface pre-dating empire and the assertion of racial hierarchy. Blackface was not about race, indeed nothing about the English Morris was really about skin colour: nothing except its name.

Green English Magic

In *Folk Song in England*, Lloyd noted the annual Horn Dance in the large Staffordshire village of Abbots Bromley:

> The famous Abbots Bromley horn dancers were once midwinter creatures who perambulated the countryside with a good deal of obscene horseplay on Twelfth Day. The shift of their season to September occurred in fairly recent times, probably in the same period, *c.* 1893, when the local parson put a check on the phallophoric displays, and his wife sacrificed the vicarage curtains to make the prototype of the present costumes worn by the dancers, tame ghosts of their old wild and ribald selves.[44]

The Abbots Bromley Horn Dancers take reindeer skulls and antlers, stored all year in the parish church, on a 20-mile early September circuit around the parish, walking the streets and lanes, pausing to dance in facing rows, to and fro and through and back again, accompanied by accordion and triangle, beginning at the church, out into the country and the grounds of Blithfield Hall and back again by the evening. Processing around a set route, social history and social mystery meet. Lloyd's account noted changes in timing and costume, traditions reinvented, but traditional nonetheless, the Horn Dance going back a long way, in Ronald Hutton's phrase, 'a single living reminder of north Midland winter revelry half a millennium ago'.[45] In 1966 the dancers appeared, with a replica set of horns, at the EFDSS's Albert Hall Festival, and would appear in the 1979, 1980 and 1987 *Dancing England* shows, along with the Bacup dancers, and again at the 2019 *Dancing England* event, as 'a dance tradition rooted in medieval times, there's nothing quite like this anywhere else'.[46] I visited once, on 10 September 2001, arriving for the afternoon return to the village, seeing the dance in old streets and new cul-de-sacs, out of time in its continuity, antlers moving back and forth, outside someone's modern home.

The Horn Dance is a common citation for those finding something green and magical in folk, though its meaning varies. Thus in 1941 Abbots Bromley was one of Christina Hole's 'pagan survivals' in *English Custom and Usage*, while Dames's 1976 *The Silbury Treasure* included a horn dance photograph as a harvest custom, representing 'the survival of a ceremony originating in the Neolithic Age'.[47] In 1982 Janet and Colin Bord identified the Horn Dance as one of their 'earth rites': 'In the seventeenth century the dance took place around Christmas, and this suggests that originally it was a winter solstice custom designed to renew the vigour and fertility of the dormant natural world.'[48] Dodie Masterman's dustjacket design for Reginald Nettel's 1954 *Sing a Song of England* showed the horn dance, Nettel's

Front cover and spine of Reginald Nettel, *Sing a Song of England* (1954), jacket design by Dodie Masterman.

book beginning with a 'Pagan Introduction', on song and dance as 'once a matter of life and death'.[49] *Sing a Song of England*'s chapter on 'The Green Man' started in Abbots Bromley, where the 'dance and its characters summarize everything in English folk-dance, but in an individual way'.[50] Nettel's book, like Lloyd's work, stressed the material roots of folk culture, indeed for Nettel songs of transportation showed that, 'In the theatres England's glory was never sullied, but in folk-songs the glory and the shame intermingle.'[51] For both Nettel and Lloyd, though, mystery accompanied history, the Horn Dance suggesting something supra-material.

In 1965 Lloyd provided sleeve notes for The Watersons' LP *Frost and Fire: A Calendar of Ritual and Magical Songs* on Topic Records. Lloyd emphasized songs' origins in sympathetic regenerative earth magic, especially those associated with winter ritual. The Watersons sang around the year from midwinter wassail to midwinter wassail, pausing at Easter, harvest and Christmas, with the pagan and Christian interleaved. Here were songs for the 'green calendar of spring', and at the turn of October–November for the dead close by. Through song and custom, Lloyd suggested, people 'tried to bind the potency of nature to themselves', though behind it all was 'nothing more mysterious, nothing less realistic, than the yearly round of work carried out in the fields'.[52] The songs signified human concerns carrying across to today: 'To our toiling ancestors they meant everything, and in a queer irrational way they can still mean much to us.' In *Folk Song in England* Lloyd would also stress the enfolding of ritual and livelihood: 'A remarkable number of folk ritual songs have survived in twentieth century England, not so much due to any mystical connection as to their close relation to the work-processes and the economic life of men . . . but some of the original content shows through however mistily.'[53]

Materialist commentators on folk song have expressed frustration with Lloyd and his 'queer irrational' meanings, Vic Gammon noting *Folk Song in England*'s emphasis on archaic survivals as an example of a 'lingering influence of this tradition in an otherwise excellent writer'.[54] Lloyd, however, found in folk a ritual materialism, in part through attention to another seemingly transhistorical theme, the erotic:

> the erotic folklore of the soil . . . with its clean joy and acceptance of the realities of virginity and desire, passion and pregnancy, belongs to a country people living an integrated

> deeply-communal life, in tune with natural events, with the cycle of the seasons, seed-time and harvest . . . For them, a love affair is not simply established within the couple, nor even between the couple and the community, but extends beyond that to the whole natural environment as an echo, however faint, of an ancient ritualistic way of looking at the world.[55]

Boyes notes Lloyd as a performer from the late 1950s of folk songs with erotic themes, thereby evoking 'the dream landscape of Englishness', with Lloyd moving from his 1946 dismissal of archaic survivals as 'a lot of dark anthropological hoo-ha' to his re-embrace of Sharp's ideas in *Folk Song in England*.[56]

Folk as ritual indeed reawakened in the late 1960s to meet another narrative, that of environmentalism, itself linked to narratives of a lost past and a fallen present. Boyes records nine folk clubs in England in 1959, around 1,700 by 1979, the second 'Revival' partly driven by an interest in industrial song, but also entailing the revisiting of the first Revival's rural focus. The final chapter of Boyes's *The Imagined Village* is 'Anthems from Eden', the title adapted from Shirley and Dolly Collins' 1969 LP *Anthems in Eden*. Their sleeve notes told of 'The lyric and glee songs put together like icons by shepherds and farm workers', asking how such 'icons' might speak to the 'special generation' of 'today's England', newly educated, inheriting 'the best of the tradition', and 'with a clear historical and prophetic vision of themselves, enough now to continue the story'.[57] The Collins' 'Eden' was the countryside before 1914, the first side of *Anthems* comprising 'A Song-Story', a medley, with instrumentation mixing folk and early music, conveying the breaking of life by the First World War. Such evocations, whatever their historical sociological accuracy, resonated in 1968, still only fifty years after the armistice, but *Anthems in Eden* also signalled the musical purchase of English pastoral at an ecological moment. Through English folk dance and song, cultural and environmental authenticity could join hands.

In his 2011 book *Electric Eden: Unearthing Britain's Visionary Music*, Rob Young documents the arcadian, pastoral musical culture of the 1960s and '70s, in folk, progressive folk and psychedelia, with English landscape a common preoccupation and outlooks from the seriously profound to the affectionately parodic.[58] To give one not especially prominent example, earnest affection characterized acoustic progressive folk band Amazing Blondel, noted for their use of medieval instruments and who had played the first Glastonbury Festival. Tracks on the 1972 Amazing Blondel LP *England* included 'Springtime', 'Seascape' and 'Landscape', the latter's chorus finding splendour, beauty and spiritual value as the seasons turned. Elsewhere, folk performers parodically evoked old England, not to diminish the country, but inhabiting English cliché to new ends. Thus Pentangle founder John Renbourn's 1968 solo LP, mixing folk guitar and early music, and with a brass-rubbed knight on the sleeve, was entitled *Sir John A lot of Merrie Englandes Musyk Thyng & ye Grene Knyghte*. Comic profundity, the former not diminishing the latter, also characterized *Morris On* (1972), founded by Ashley Hutchings (also co-founder of Fairport Convention and Steeleye Span) as an electro-acoustic folk accompaniment to Morris dance, sticks and bells included. The sleeve of *Morris On* showed musicians in archaic/modern gear; a chimney sweep with vacuum cleaner, a hobby horse by a chopper bike, the latter rather than the former the height of early 1970s riding fashion.[59]

Morris On included guest singer Shirley Collins, then married to Hutchings, singing the 'Staines Morris', reprised from *Anthems in Eden*. Collins's work is in general indicative of a meeting of folk culture and green Englishness and mystery, and can serve also as a bridge from the mid-twentieth century to the present. Collins's first LP, *Sweet England*, was released in 1959, its opening title song recalling England from a migrant's exile in America. As with 'Rosemary Lane', a bucolic title belies a hard story, 'Sweet England' the cry of the rural poor migrating overseas, dreaming of returning to a sweet home. A mixture of roots and routes – of migration, of military service, of vagrancy, of homecoming – characterized Collins's recordings of traditional song, and her explorations of early music, folk rock and, with guitarist Davy Graham on the 1964 *Folk Roots, New Routes*, jazz and raga. Collins was awarded an MBE in 2006, appointed EFDSS President in 2008, and in 2012 curated the collections on Southern English traditional and Romany song in Topic Records' 'Voice of the People' series, *You Never Heard So Sweet: Songs by Southern English Traditional Singers* and *I'm a Romany Rai: Songs by Southern English Gypsy Traditional Singers*, both from recordings made in Sussex and Hampshire by Peter Kennedy and Bob Copper between 1951 and 1963.[60] Collins returned to recording in the 2010s after a thirty-year hiatus, releasing *Lodestar* (2016) and *Heart's Ease* (2020), both recorded in her Lewes cottage, the latter reprising one element of *Anthems in Eden*'s 'A Song Story' medley, the song 'Whitsun Dance', 42 years on from the 1968 LP, 102 years on from the armistice. The album *Archangel Hill* followed in 2023, its cover a painting by Peter Messer of the titular Sussex downland.

England and English landscape remain central to Collins's work. *Lodestar*'s first line is 'Awake awake sweet England', the song 'Awake Awake' collected in Herefordshire by Vaughan Williams in 1909, a penitential ballad originally from 1580 calling for national repentance after an earthquake toppled part of St Paul's Cathedral. Rob Curry and Tim Plester's 2018 documentary film *The Ballad of Shirley Collins* marked Collins's return, with film of the *Lodestar* recording, seasonal festivals in Lewes and Hastings, and inland and coastal Sussex scenes.[61] Curry and Plester show Collins walking her childhood street in Hastings, Athelstan Drive, as if streets named from Anglo-Saxon kings might have preordained English preoccupations. Collins states that her earlier work sought to convey 'the essence of English song', and that her sister Dolly, accompanying Shirley on pipe organ on many recordings, understood 'the Englishness of the music'. The year 2018 also brought Collins's memoir *All in the Downs: Reflections of Life, Landscape and Song*, a follow-up to her 2004 *America over the Water*, which had alternated a memoir of her Hastings childhood with accounts of her 1959–60 American trip with U.S. folk collector Alan Lomax. On her return from America in 1960, Collins states that 'deep down I realised that I belonged to England, that I wanted to be an *English* singer of *English* songs.'[62]

In *All in the Downs*, the Sussex Downs provide a backdrop to childhood, but are only fully explored in Collins's thirties, on returning to Sussex from London. Collins concludes, 'folk music reflects the landscape it's written in.'[63] Collins presents herself as 'the conduit' for the 'old singers' encountered through Cecil Sharp House: 'my working-class, semi-rural background wasn't an obstacle but an advantage . . . I felt I was part of them and of the music of England.'[64] On the 'familiar "Englishness"' of folk songs heard at primary school, Collins reflects:

> But back to why 'Englishness' should be so important? And what is it? I wonder why my family had such a deep feeling for England as a country. They weren't wearing rose-coloured spectacles: their lives had never been easy . . . They loved England, but weren't ignorant of its dark history.[65]

Landscape and song gain value in mutual personification: 'The countryside and the songs are as one to me; the safeguarding of them equally important, both so vulnerable.'[66] A metaphor from downland geology might characterize Collins's recording career, her twenty-first-century re-emergence akin to a bourne, a seasonal chalk stream whose bed empties as the water table lowers, but which may return in spate as ground fills. Through *Lodestar*, *Heart's Ease* and *Archangel Hill* the underground returns overground.

Another kind of underground helped Collins re-emerge. In 2004 *America over the Water* carried a foreword by David Tibet, founder of the group Current 93, whose early industrial/noise music had shifted from the late 1980s to an 'avant-folk' exploration of the mystic, Tibet developing a pastoral aesthetic, redemptively dwelling in joy and sadness, Arcadia and death. *The Ballad of Shirley Collins* is dedicated to Tibet. Why the confluence of Tibet and Collins? Tibet and Current 93 are key characters in David Keenan's 2014 study *England's Hidden Reverse*, on 'a shadowy English underground scene whose work accents peculiarities of Englishness through the links and affinities they've forged with earlier generations of the island's marginals and outsiders'.[67] Tibet was born David Bunting in 1960 in colonial Malaysia, and sent to boarding school aged ten in Yorkshire, a child of late empire growing to nurture visionary Englishness. Collins features for Tibet alongside William Blake and Royalist civil war composer William Lawes, as figures mixing an innocence in their mode of delivery with a melancholy and mystical sense of a country passing: 'What I am always harking back to is a lost sense of innocence, so the thing about England that I love is the England of Shirley Collins's *Anthems in Eden*.'[68] Tibet contacted Collins and reissued a compilation of her work, *Fountain of Snow* (1992), on his Durtro record label, beginning what Collins termed her 'renaissance'.[69] Collins made speaking and singing guest appearances on Current 93 records such as *The Starres are Marching Sadly Home* (1996), singing 'All the Pretty Little Horses', and *Black Ships Ate the Sky* (2006), singing 'Idumea'. Tibet's associates Stephen Thrower and Ossian Brown recorded *Lodestar* and *Heart's Ease*, Brown playing hurdy-gurdy on both records. Morris dancing and avant-rock met as *Lodestar* was recorded in Collins's Lewes cottage, the bells of Glen Rodman of Brighton Morris jangling as he danced 'Southover' indoors.[70]

Experimental engagements with folkloric England have proliferated in the third millennium, at a time of doubts over nation, doubts over nature and climate anxiety; Wright's 2017 *Arcadia* film, noted above, offers an 'old, weird Britain' for this moment. In 2006 Michael Cashmore, guitarist in Current 93 from 1990, released a solo album entitled *Sleep England*, instrumental electric and bass guitar pieces with titles signalling national reflection: 'Twilight Empire', 'Dream England', 'Broken Seas', 'Sleep England'. From *Sweet England* to *Sleep England* across five decades. From 23 to 25 May 2003 the EFDSS had hosted a 'Visionary Landscapes' event at Cecil Sharp House, a weekend of 'folk, film, landscape', part of the 125th anniversary celebrations of the Folklore Society, while in 2011 the British Film Institute, in partnership with the EFDSS, issued a DVD collection *Here's a Health to the Barley Mow: A Century of Folk Customs and Ancient Rural Games*, showing 'folk traditions' as 'powerful and enduring'. The BFI's compilation of dance, drama and sport was lent an air of mystery, showing a strange anthropology close to home. From between the wars, the horn dancers of Abbots Bromley dance in a farmyard, while in 1930 the Coconut Dancers of Bacup, their faces not blackened, are caught on film and both find their way onto twenty-first-century DVD. Older folk life appears in touch with nature, and a longer-term England, lasting through changes, the 'Green England' evoked by John Fowles in his 1964 essay 'On Being English but Not British', an 'emotional' rather than 'intellectual' concept: 'Deep, deep in those trees of the mind the mysteries still take place; the green men dance, hunt, and run.'[71]

Folkloric England is met as a twenty-first-century green uncanny, a strangeness at home; something you didn't expect to find, but to which you might belong. In 1912, in a lecture on 'English Folk Songs', Ralph Vaughan Williams stated, 'I am like a psychical researcher who has actually seen a ghost, for I have been among the more primitive people of England and have noted down their songs.'[72] Vaughan Williams here anticipates the century-later turn to 'hauntology', Simon Reynolds's 2006 coinage for musical explorations revisiting earlier electronic sounds to make the past resound in the present and where folk was a key reference point.[73] For Reynolds, the folkloric runs alongside, indeed to an extent gathers in, a wider 1960s and 1970s cultural archaeology of radiophonic electronics, children's television soundtracks, advertising tunes and library music. Reynolds highlighted those artists associated with the Ghost Box record label,

'Belbury', from CD booklet of Belbury Poly, *The Owl's Map* (2006), released by Ghost Box Records, designed by Julian House.

founded by Julian House and Jim Jupp, notably The Focus Group (House) and Belbury Poly (Jupp), as combining folkloric investigation with nostalgia for earlier future visions. Belbury Poly's 2006 album *The Owl's Map*, electro music with folk and film samples interwoven into 'briskly melodious ditties',[74] accompanied its soundworld with mock mid-twentieth-century book design artwork by House, outlining a 'Field Guide to British Towns and Villages. Volume 7'. Belbury and environs includes modernist libraries, haunted manors, the Iron Age hill fort of Belbury Hill and 'the nearby Neolithic stone circle, Thornwood Ring . . . Some feel that Belbury is an uneasy mix of ancient and modern, but it is, nonetheless, a fascinating town to visit for the casual tourist and amateur historian alike.'[75]

In his folk collecting and arrangement, encountering the 'primitive people of England', Vaughan Williams navigated questions of class and cultural translation within England, and parallel questions arise for twenty-first-century hauntology, as singers gathered by early twentieth-century revivalists are manifest in new ghost boxes. Belbury Poly's 'Caermon' on *The Willows* (2004) sampled a recording of Joseph Taylor, a Lincolnshire folk singer known for singing and recording 'Brigg Fair', its tune turned to early twentieth-century classical form by Percy Grainger and Frederick Delius. 'Wetland' on *The Owl's Map* does the same for mid-twentieth-century Norfolk folk singer Harry Cox.[76] Traditional singers are here not only placed in an electronic out-of-context but subtly warped in speed and pitch.[77] Is this the manipulation of the ghosts of the English primitive? Taylor and Cox were hardly 'primitive' performers, both adept in the recording studio, hence their captured voices, as well as in the pub. A reprise of Vaughan Williams's psychic moment risks however rebadging them as eerie, reinterring them in a primitive box, as slightly weird old out-of-time Englishmen. Sampling old singers cannot help but resurrect old cultural questions, which early twenty-first-century Ghost Box practitioners seek to navigate, while at the same time maintaining a careful distance from any hint of cultural nationalism. Jupp reflects on his fascination for 'a particular period of time in British history – more or less 1958–78. All this might be tied up with a special kind of national identity, nothing to do at all with jingoism, flags, sports, borders, anthems.'[78] Nothing jingoistic, but as with Shirley Collins, or Amazing Blondel or Bert Lloyd, nationally English nonetheless.

Pagan Places

Folkloric interest in the mysteries of England's green goes beyond stone circles and folk traces to encompass gods and the occult, touching another cultural and spiritual formation revived in the late twentieth century, paganism. Ghost Box releases indeed approach the pagan. The Focus Group's 2007 *We Are All Pan's People* puns in part on the former Top of the Pops dance troupe, but also gestures to earth belonging, with its 'Willowedge Vision', 'Pan Calling' and 'Albion Festival Report', and quotes from Arthur Machen's cult 1894 novella *The Great God Pan*.[79] In 2009 The Focus Group collaborated with the group Broadcast to produce *Witch Cults of the Radio Age*, Trish Keenan offering incantatory vocals evoking ritual and seance, and James Cargill and Julian House's electronica adding wrappings of mystery. Keenan stated, 'It makes sense to me that if the witches of the Seventeenth

Century made music it would have been playful and hypnotic and made with indecipherable sounds, not music made with pitch perfect, well-tempered instrumentation.' Music becomes memorial practice: 'It seems to me that the past is always happening now, all previous events have positioned us here philosophically, geographically, and in the present we are always in memory.'[80]

The occult and the pagan as musical subject was, as Young notes, prominent in the 1960s and '70s, a means to remagic the world.[81] In *All in the Downs* Collins reflects on her fascination for the 'subtle mysteries' in song, suggesting that 'not everything has to be explained' and recounting personal and familial experience of ghosts and UFOs.[82] While not sharing the late 1960s folk interest in 'fairies and transformations', Collins notes that some saw the moody cover of her and Dolly Collins's 1970 album *Love, Death and Lady* as suggesting they might be witches: 'it wasn't, and isn't true.'[83] The reader of *All in the Downs* might make the same false reading of the cover photograph of Collins seated holding a wooden staff. *The Ballad of Shirley Collins* films a homely guru, and ends at the Lewes Bonfire festival, Collins sat by the fires singing, 'Awake awake sweet England', conjuring the old anew.

The occult and folkloric meet in the UK's only dedicated Museum of Witchcraft, in Boscastle in Cornwall, run since 2013 by Simon Costin, who in 2009 inaugurated the Museum of British Folklore, initially via a touring caravan show. Costin took over the Boscastle museum from Graham King, renaming it the Museum of Witchcraft and Magic in 2015. The Museum of British Folklore, still in want of a building, carries an Abbots Bromley horn dance photograph on its homepage 'Manifesto', and curates 'Morris Folk', a collection of dolls showing the costumes of different Morris sides, and folkloric events such as 'Waking the Giant' in February 2020, exploring the 'sleeping giant of Dover'.[84] The Museum of Witchcraft and Magic, by the River Valency as it flows into a rocky harbour, came to Boscastle with founder Cecil Williamson in 1960, after previous incarnations in Stratford-upon-Avon and the Isle of Man. King bought the museum in 1996, inspired to leave the business world after meeting the new age travelling Dongas tribe in their horse-drawn wagons on the Marlborough Downs, 'eco-travellers' who 'changed my life': 'I walked the 200 miles to Boscastle from Hampshire and the Museum ownership transferred from Cecil Williamson to me at midnight on 31st October 1996.'[85] King made Boscastle a focus for occult reflection and pagan identity, celebrated in a 2011 sixtieth anniversary 'magical history'.[86] The museum was badly damaged in the 2004 Boscastle flood, but the collections survived and the building was restored. In keeping with the pagan emphasis on connection to place, Cornish objects and Cornish identity are prominent, alongside material from Britain and beyond. A museum 'Friends' group raises funds and awareness, with Ronald Hutton, key historian of British paganism and witchcraft, acting as Patron.[87] Hutton's works, including *The Pagan Religions of the Ancient British Isles* (1991), *The Stations of the Sun: A History of the Ritual Year in Britain* (1996) and *The Triumph of the Moon: A History of Modern Pagan Witchcraft* (1999), give a critical appreciation of his subjects, attentive to historical continuities, discontinuities and self-conscious reinventions, not least by figures such as Williamson and the founder of the twentieth-century Wicca religion Gerald Gardner. The scepticism of a critical historian cohabits with an affirmation of paganism's cultural significance and value, Hutton becoming both chronicler and shaper of pagan stories.

The pagan concern for place can invoke a specifically English green spiritual tradition. In 1990 Evan John Jones, with Doreen Valiente, published *Witchcraft: A Tradition Renewed*, presenting witchcraft as the old religion, Valiente asserting pagan roots deeper than Gardnerian Wicca.[88] Witchcraft here carries English nature at its heart. Jones presents the 'Old Faith', with its worship of the Mother Goddess and Horned God, as understanding that 'there are powers which were once the birthright of humanity, later to be lost in our so-called advance of material civilization.'[89] Humanity's 'divine spark', however, remained, the Old Faith having strongholds in the countryside, with people unable to 'stand apart from their environment. They were an intrinsic part of it.'[90] While Celtic myths might represent 'the main root-source of modern British paganism', they were 'not English witchcraft':

> The true English witchcraft spanned the gap between the old Anglo-Saxons and the general acceptance of Christianity by the population as a whole.
>
> This is the faith that was lost. Belittled and scorned by the Church, preached against and its god turned into a devil. This is the knowledge that was shattered; and with it, part of the spirit of both race and land. For in the spirit of the land were the rhythms of the English roots.[91]

Some stories nonetheless came through, and Robin Hood as Green Man was one trace of 'the matter or lore of England'.[92]

Robin Hood as Green Man was familiar in 1990 not only via secret occult practice but popular television, paganism having leapt to the mainstream via the 1984–6 ITV series *Robin of Sherwood*. Immensely popular and distinctly mystic, soundtracked by Irish folk group Clannad, and with accompanying novelization by series writer Richard Carpenter, *Robin of Sherwood* presented a magic English hero. Robin, played by Michael Praed, with his magic sword 'Albion', effectively becomes a Green Man, affiliated in the series to Herne the Hunter.[93] In *Witchcraft*, Jones noted Herne as god of hunting and fertility, haunting the Great Oak of Windsor Great Park around Candlemas.[94] *Robin of Sherwood* promoted the ancient, with contemporary styling, a paganism for early evening ITV, mystic and hairsprayed.

Ten years earlier a different television drama had rendered paganism a vital sign of English marginality. One of the speakers at the 2003 EFDSS 'Visionary Landscapes' event was playwright David Rudkin, accompanying a screening of his 1974 BBC1 'Play for Today' *Penda's Fen*, directed by Alan Clarke and produced at Pebble Mill Birmingham, where the Regions Television Drama Department, established in 1972, allowed a creative freedom beyond London headquarters.[95] For Rob Young in 2021, *Penda's Fen* signalled 'the lingering pagan presence in the British landscape, and by extension, the soul of the nation'; for Roger Luckhurst in 2019, 'this is England's dreaming, in multiple time signatures'.[96] According to Rudkin, in the *Radio Times* on 14 March 1974, 'I wanted to write something that grew out of the landscape.'[97] The year before, Rudkin ascribed 'contradictions in my temperament' to his being 'half English, half Irish . . . Contrary to popular superstition in this matter, the demonic-romantic-mystical element in my work springs from my Saxon side.'[98]

Penda's Fen presented teenager Stephen Franklin discovering himself and his country anew. At the outset Stephen is a conservative patriot, playing *Jerusalem* on the organ in the grammar school assembly, and a devotee of Elgar, whose music plays over shots of nearby Malvern landscape. By the conclusion of *Penda's Fen*, and with the help of an angel, who appears by the river and on a Malvern hillside, and a bedside demon, Stephen realizes his homosexuality and adopted family status, and finds new complexities in Elgar, an aged version of whom he meets in a derelict cottage. Another kind of landscaped patriotism forms, distinctly pagan.

Penda's Fen was set and filmed in the village of Pinvin in Worcestershire, the name presented as derivative of Pinfin, Pendefen, Penda's Fen. Under the fen a new nuclear bunker is unleashing buried horrors, local playwright William Arne asserting that top secret construction means 'the land is hollow'. The disturbance of solidity stirs the *genius loci*, one kind of secret power provoking another. Walking in Pinvin fields, Stephen's parson father, himself a seeker of buried truths in the Christian story, evokes the older gods, and the meaning of 'pagan' as 'belonging to the village': 'Man may yet in the nick of time revolt and save himself: revolt from the monolith, come back to the Village.'[99] Stephen's father wonders about Penda, the 'last pagan king in England': 'King of Midland England . . . What mystery of this land went down with him for ever?'[100]

Stephen's awakening to his sexuality, and his awareness of having non-English birth parents, accompanies the re-awakening of Mercian king Penda, killed in battle in AD 655. Things repressed return, for good. In the final scene Stephen rejects those seeking to put a conservative claim on him as a 'true English boy', declaring his 'mixed' nature in race and sex: 'nothing pure. I am mud and flame!'[101] Penda appears, robed and throned on the Malvern ridge, his face obscured but his message clear. Stephen is entrusted to 'cherish the flame', to be 'impure and dissonant':

> Stephen. Our land must live. This land we love must live. Her deep dark flame must never die.
>
> Night is falling. Your land and mine goes down into a darkness now; and I, and all the other guardians of her flame, are driven from our home, up out into the wolf's jaw. But the flame still flickers in the fen.[102]

Stephen looks up, but Penda has gone, and he descends England's small mountains green, as the credits roll. Penda's Fen offers a different heart of England, the green fen magic of a queer sort of place.

Take One, Take Two, Take Several

> It takes all sorts to make a world – anthropologists, antiquaries, trained musicians, folk-singers and dancers, people who like a good tune and those who can't tell God save the weasel from Pop goes the weasel; if folk-songs and dances are to be considered in relation to social history we must take the English as we find them, look at them in the round.[103]

Taking the folkloric in the round, in all its sorts, it spins out from collecting and singing and dancing, and from ritual and green mysteries, into other orbits. Folkloric varieties germinate beyond the nurturing remit of dedicated institutions such as the EFDSS, the 'Full English' becoming fuller still, various and lively. Folkloric England interweaves the mythic and prosaic, the meditative and the knockabout, and this section examines selected musical, artistic and televisual treatments, expanding the folkloric remit, before returning to the junior school classroom of the 1970s.

In 2005 Jeremy Deller and Alan Kane's *Folk Archive* project, with exhibitions and a photographic book, set common understandings of folk within a wider set of British vernacular arts. Deller's art has often questioned national memory, as in his works on military and industrial conflict or archaeological heritage.[104] In the 2012 Olympic year, 'Sacrilege', a replica Stonehenge bouncy castle, travelled the country, while Deller's 2013 installation for the Venice Biennale was entitled *English Magic*, combining myth and folklore with cultural and political history. *Folk Archive* worked a seam of folk and popular arts, with customs conventionally labelled as 'folk' part of a broader prospectus. A 'Diary of Selected Events' presented a customary calendar, Padstow's May Day alongside the Oxford May Morning, the Nutters Dance at Bacup alongside the Battersea Park Easter Parade, the Horn Dance alongside Blackpool Illuminations.[105] Folk-popular art encompasses the creativity of protest left and right, the self-styling of tattoo and fancy dress, commercial signage and grotesque exuberance, sandcastles and scarecrows. Introducing the project, Deller and Kane apologized to anthropologists for a 'misuse' of the term 'archive', and admitted their approach to 'folk' might also seem cavalier: 'For all involved in the folk or vernacular cultural scenes we must similarly apologise for the cheap "folk" shot and a fly-by-night plundering of whole worlds.'[106]

If plundering can be respectful, *Folk Archive* aims for that, stretching the category for a celebratory cultural harvest, where all is gathered in, if not entirely safely.

The folkloric is likewise stretched, given a workout, in the records of Richard Dawson, labelled as a 'folk', or 'avant-folk' singer and guitarist, with varied accompaniment. The opening words of Dawson's 2017 album *Peasant*, in the song 'Ogre', set things in the ancient kingdom of Bryneich, in sixth-century proto-Northumbria. Songs about the ancient region are sung in an audibly northeastern voice. If some of Dawson's work, as in the 2019 album *2020* or the 2014 *Nothing Important*, is set in a current world of work grind, social tension and flooding, the past is commonly present, as in *The Glass Trunk* (2015), ballads made out of archival material in the Newcastle Discovery Museum. *Peasant* presents a folklore of occupations in what is now northeast England, lives from an older kingdom: 'Soldier', 'Weaver', 'Prostitute', 'Shapeshifter', 'Scientist', 'Beggar', 'Masseuse'. Clay houses shelter lives, with curses and cures, hardship and battle, and occasional joys, in a world cornucopic with beasts and birds. Sounding the elemental, *Peasant* reclaims earlier Northumbrians, and the word 'peasant', from condescension. In temporal contrast, Dawson's 2022 album *The Ruby Cord* is future folkloric, telling of a Northumbria where cities have crumbled, motorways are greened over and survivors live in a fashion akin to Jefferies's *After London*. This future does retain memory, the song 'Museum' set a dozen centuries hence, displays conjuring distant memories of soldiers and shoppers, sports fans and schoolchildren, climate protesters and astronauts. One day, 'Museum' implies, today's lives will be as folkloric as those of the kingdom of Bryneich.

The category 'folk' is thus malleable, and subject to adaptation. Another take comes in the modern classical works of Michael Finnissy, where what Christopher Fox terms musical 'modernism with an English accent' refracts the folkloric.[107] In Finnissy's *Kemp's Morris* (1978), for 'pianist wearing Morris-bells', knuckle bells reproduce the effect of feet jingling, with nine sections representing Shakespearean actor Will Kemp's reputed nine-days' dance in 1600 from London to Norwich; a Norwich Morris side, formed in 1956, is called Kemp's Men. Finnissy frames his 1998 *Folklore* collection with citation of Lloyd's *Folk Song in England*, a work 'wisely and clearly expounded',[108] while elsewhere he hails the 'irregular barring' of Percy Grainger's notations of English folk music over the more rigid style of Cecil Sharp.[109] The preface to the score of *Folklore* (1993–5), whose reference points cross the world, includes the statement, 'England: insular and conservative, institutionalized, de-spiritualized, tawdry and corrupt.'[110] Folklore is not necessarily therefore a realm of affection, but a means to ponder anxieties of affiliation.[111]

Finnissy's sounds and titles alight on aspects of this and the previous chapter: folklore, archaeology, English sonority. The 1976 chamber piece *Pathways of Sun and Stars* thus 'relates to leylines and magic squares'.[112] *English Country-Tunes* (1977, revised 1982–5) is stated in the 1978 first edition of the score to have been 'written in celebration of the Silver Jubilee of Her Majesty Queen Elizabeth II, in 1977', although it gives unorthodox fanfare.[113] For Fox, *English Country-Tunes* has 'Englishness its very audible focus', with the folkloric a stepping point to dissonance.[114] Eight pieces are named from folk tunes (including 'Green Meadows', 'Midsummer Morn' and 'The Seeds of Love'), but with only fleeting sonic resemblance to anything in the EFDSS collections. Any occasional melodic moment contains, in Jonathan Cross's phrase, 'the very seed of its own destruction', with the final piece, 'Come beat the Drums and sound the Fifes', signalling that 'nature, England even self, are all destroyed, but ultimately regenerated, in a final primitive ritual'.[115] Finnissy comments, 'Across the still and snow-swept landscape a deep chasm opens. BAM! The sun disappears behind a cloud. A hurricane suddenly tears across southern England at two in the morning. Relish the unpredictability of such events – even while lamenting the terrible destruction. They should render us somewhat more humble.'[116] Reflecting on remaining in England, for all its 'bigotry, racism, fear and ignorance', Finnissy states, 'For me the landscape is still a potent contexualisation for music.'[117] The mythic dissonance of Penda, the regenerative force of the 1987 hurricane, find musical echo.

If Finnissy queers the English pitch in one fashion, pop culture offers other tangents, evident in the history of the folk song 'Strawberry Fair'. The EFDSS's 'Full English' site provides access to several versions of the song, with its refrain, 'As I was going to Strawberry Fair/ Singing, singing, buttercups and daisies'.[118] 'Strawberry Fair' appeared in Rev. Sabine Baring-Gould and Cecil Sharp's 1906 *English Folk-Songs for Schools*, and in *Folk Song in England* Lloyd noted how Baring-Gould took 'his pruning-knife to the songs he heard', cutting euphemisms of suspect morality:

Anthony Newley, in duet with a scarecrow, still from *The Strange World of Gurney Slade* (1960, episode three).

> 'Strawberry Fair', for instance, as he first heard it, was not the mawkish thing of buttercups and daisies that has wearied generations of primary school children for the last half-century. When it was sung to him in a Devon pub, he liked the tune, but said later: 'The text is unsuitable and I've been constrained to rewrite it. The words turn on a *double entendre* that is quite lost – fortunately so – on half the old fellows who sing the song.' And what was this daring *double entendre* (whose significance wasn't lost on the parson, by the way)?[119]

The offending lines, which appear on *The Full English* in Baring-Gould's notebooks, concerned a lock and key, the girl having a lock but lacking a key and asking a man if he might have one.[120]

The Full English restores the faintly bawdy, but finds no place for perhaps the most heard twentieth-century version of 'Strawberry Fair', Anthony Newley's 1960 No.3 hit recording. Can *The Full English* be full in its absence? Newley turned 'Strawberry Fair' to uptempo pop, the lyrics starting out folk-faithful but gathering current vernacular as they rolled along. Newley's London showbiz voice gives folk a variety twist, initial flowery courtesies turning to 'buttercups and oojahs'.[121] In the same year as 'Strawberry Fair', ITV screened Newley's *The Strange World of Gurney Slade*, a programme whose six episodes subverted televisual conventions almost before they had been established. Newley's title character, named after a Somerset village, took peak-time viewers to a surreal England. In the third episode, set in the country, and featuring a signpost to Gurney Slade the village, Gurney talks to ants, wanders farms and lanes, and talks to a cow, voiced by Fenella Fielding. On a hillside Gurney hum-duets 'Greensleeves' with a scarecrow, although neither can find the words. A Tudor tune, made famous through Vaughan Williams's setting, is not quite voiced in Newley's off-kilter country. Gurney's green English hillside mystery offers a whimsical counterpoint to the Malvern meeting of Stephen and King Penda.

Episode five of *The Strange World of Gurney Slade* included a performance of 'Strawberry Fair', as children and parents visited 'Gurneyland', an imagined world inside Gurney's mind, finding Newley-as-Newley singing the song. Piano and percussion accompany Newley, as Newley-as-Gurney watches on: 'I should have thought that would have driven them out, I always thought I sung better than that.' *Gurney Slade* began its run on 22 October 1960, episode five broadcast on 19 November, though by then the programme had been rescheduled from primetime 8.35 to 11.10 p.m., after audience puzzlement. 'Strawberry Fair' would chart on 30 November. A capaciously full tracing of sonic folk Englishness would embrace such varieties. If folk song attracts in part for its variations of tune and text, here are some more, broadcasting folk beyond the territory of standards.

Young listeners in the 1960s and '70s would have known Newley's 'Strawberry Fair', and his 1961 swinging version of 'Pop Goes the Weasel', a hit in the UK and USA, from programmes such as BBC Radio's 'Junior Choice'.[122] If for Reginald Nettel, in the 1954 passage that opened this section, it took 'all sorts' to make a singing and listening world, these were the versions my sort could recognize. We could also spot the difference from the dose of folk we received at school, whether dancing for the fete or singing in the hall. The 1970s BBC broadcast radio and television schools programmes, with music a focus for primary schools lacking instrumentation and/or teacher capability. Sometimes a programme might be watched, for example 'Music Time' with Mari Griffith and Ian Humphris, while others were heard, for joining in. On Monday mornings at 11.00, *Singing Together* broadcast folk songs, the children provided with songbooks, showing the words and the music. We were all to sing along, the national enrolment in listening making for a kind of children's educational version of the BBC's earlier adult show *Music While You Work*, with its origins in the boosting of wartime factory output.[123] *Singing Together* too had begun as a wartime morale-booster, running from 1939 until the mid-1990s, and showing children a British Isles musical culture, with distinct English, Scottish, Welsh and Irish components, alongside some global tunes. Collective singing would signal collective belonging, and so we sang along.

In November 2014 Jarvis Cocker presented a fond Radio 4 tribute programme, *Singing Together* seen to have shown the value of singing in general, and folk song in particular, to various children now grown, though not without occasional political and cultural controversy.[124] My memory, however, is more of bemusement, songs of highwaymen and sailors saying nothing to me about my life and implying that modern life was not really worth a song. *Top of the Pops*, and indeed *Junior Choice*, made sense as entertainment, even as transgressive inspiration, but *Singing Together* jarred, in part for the songs, in part for the togetherness. Occasional giggles, however, helped get us through, as when the song 'Mountain Duel', from *Singing Together*'s Autumn 1974 collection, included in its sprightly, lyrically congested setting of frustrated love in the Welsh mountains the line: 'Mountain path was hawthorn prickly'. Something about the phrasing tickled, not, aged ten, for euphemisms attached to 'prickly', but for the archaic sentence construction. Words were being mangled, and all for the sake of a rhyme: 'Yet my love had said, "Come quickly"' followed. Why, in 1974, were young tongues twisting for old songs? The seriousness of folk seemed silly, something less grown up than our modern selves. Giggles could signal modernity, even maturity, for the suburban young. As the introductory chapter of *England's Green* noted, folkloric England has happily accommodated the documentation of child's play, with the green games of Iona and Peter Opie's 1969 collection *Children's Games in Street and Playground*. Could however a full folkloric England admit children laughing at itself?

On English Scarecrows

Newley's 'Greensleeves' scarecrow duet indicates one form of playful folkloric England. While in Gurneyland the song's words could not be found, and the scarecrow stuck at humming, scarecrows have managed to articulate various messages about England and greenery. As figures bringing together the folkloric and the agrarian, and subject to all kinds of weather, scarecrows can serve to conclude this chapter, and connect back to earlier discussions in *England's Green* of climate, nature and farming. Scarecrows also carry a telling mix of the serious and the comic, and school play again offers a starting point.

Alongside its green games, hunting games, catching games and racing games, Iona and Peter Opie's *Children's Games in Street and Playground* also recorded the chasing game 'Scarecrow Tig'. The Opies noted this as a name used in 'many places' for a game elsewhere known as 'Stuck in the Mud'. In 'Scarecrow Tig', a chaser's touch immobilizes the player, who stands upright with arms outstretched, shouting to others for assistance, until a free player touches and releases them, 'Meanwhile the chaser attempts to touch and transfix the rest of the players.' The successful chaser leaves a field of immobilized child scarecrows: 'The game ends, or rather begins again, if the chaser manages "to get all the players with their arms outstretched", or if one of the players has been twice caught and released, and is then caught for a third time.'

The Opies remarked on Scarecrow Tig's sinister undertones, the game ending almost as if in a mass crucifixion, without a bright side of life to look on: 'British children are not alone in finding the game uncanny. In Berlin, where it is known as 'Hexe geh – Hexe steh', three witches do the chasing.'[125] Boria Sax notes that scarecrows, like the crows they deter, are presented as 'somewhat scruffy, a little mischievous, and closely associated with supernatural powers', with their use 'as much a matter of magic as practicality'.[126] Three years after the Opies' survey, the Hex air of Scarecrow Tig was echoed in Lal and Mike Waterson's 'The Scarecrow', from the 1972 LP *Bright Phoebus*. Walking out one summer morn, a windblown scarecrow is seen to worry the crows, so that corn can grow. As the verses proceed the scarecrow figure turns to an old man hanging, or a baby tied to a stake, ritual scenes with a family resemblance to the Opies' immobilized playground, but with added hints of sinister sacrifice for a fertile land. *Bright Phoebus* ends with the shining smiling sun of the title track, as if the anxieties of earlier songs have been resolved, but the scarecrow, the second song on side one, stands for the cares of the world, for seasonal cycles where some things die so that others shall live.[127]

At a time of concern over the ecological effects of modernized farming, the scarecrow could stand out, and appeal, as archaic. The scarecrow in part attracted as a picturesque charm, something ramshackle lingering after its time, but also as a magical charm. At a time when field labour had diminished, and it was increasingly rare to see a human in an English field, a few mock humans lingered, attracting stories variously quirky and sinister. Scarecrow Tig and the scarecrow of *Bright Phoebus* may have entertained and/or unnerved their particular local audiences, but in 1979 a particular English scarecrow, already well known, would become very famous, a national green icon. From 1979 to 1981 the ITV company Southern Television produced four series of *Worzel Gummidge*, written by Keith Waterhouse and Willis Hall, filmed in rural Hampshire, and starring Jon Pertwee as Worzel and Una Stubbs as Aunt Sally. Both were familiar television faces with appeal to adults and children, Pertwee having appeared as Dr Who from 1970 to 1974. Worzel Gummidge is the scarecrow of Scatterbrook Farm, befriended by two children, John and Sue. Only they know that Gummidge is a walking, talking scarecrow, and adventures follow, Pertwee's scarecrow a gurning creature played for laughs and sentiment.

The English scarecrow achieved mainstream cultural presence, Worzel an old charmer matching interests in traditional crafts and historic farming at a time when modern agriculture was leaving such things behind. The ITV series were adaptations of books originating in an earlier moment of doubt and crisis. Barbara Euphan Todd's first Worzel book, the 1936 *Worzel Gummidge or The Scarecrow of Scatterbrook*, was reissued in 1941 by Penguin as the first book in the influential children's Puffin Books imprint.[128] The human as well as the scarecrow story resonated, with John and Sue sent to the country from London to recuperate from whooping cough, their tale matching a general narrative of rural health and urban unhealth in the 1930s, but also a specific wartime story of the evacuation of children from city to country away from bombing danger, the experience of almost 1.5 million children in September 1939.[129] Todd described a scarecrow country just before the next agricultural revolution, and her work could therefore appear in the 1970s as an account of a lost ecology, where enchantment lingered and things came to life, Worzel's daft intuitions carrying forward as signs of magic from another age. Todd presents Worzel, with his three birthdays, one for each body part, as standing outside conventional time, a figure 'all manner of ages', with robins nesting in his coat.[130] Coming to Scatterbrook, Sue is 'sure there was something magic about the place, even in the winter-time'.[131] Magic here signifies a power more than simply quaint, and the children exercise scarecrow caution. Worzel is 'a kind of wizard as well. They felt afraid': 'Magic is ordinary enough in a book, but it seems a queer thing in real life.'[132]

Through Todd's books and the ITV series, strange scarecrow stories become ordinarily folkloric in an age of popular children's literature and mass television. Worzel's magic is further heightened in the recent television adaptation of Todd's stories, again hugely popular, by Mackenzie Crook, *Worzel Gummidge* the next TV project for Crook after *Detectorists*. Worzel, played by Crook in make-up accentuating his own distinctive angular, quizzical features, was first broadcast in two BBC1 episodes at Christmas 2019, with sequels at Christmas 2020 and 2021, and also a bonfire night 2021 special. Crook presented the stories as 'set in the countryside amongst nature, myth, and legend', a Worzel for the green twenty-first century.[133] Gummidge and his fellow scarecrows are here made by and under the protection of the Green Man, who appeared in the second Christmas 2019 episode, played by Michael Palin; in the 1979 version the creator had been a 'Crowman'. The sense of a country diverse in spirit is paralleled in Crook's diversity of casting, John and Susan now non-white children, Thierry Wickens and India Brown taking the roles played in 1979 by Jeremy Austin and Charlotte Coleman. Crook also commissioned a folk soundtrack, with prominent folk group The Unthanks singing of nature, and of how the scarecrow knows, as the tales unfold. Worzel is a scarecrow for an age of climate change, noting the seasons going awry and voicing old saws for today. For Jacob Smith, Crook offers 'biosemiotic television', with Worzel 'a kind of environmental sensor'.[134] As noted above, Crook's *Detectorists* was in part inspired by his role in Butterworth's *Jerusalem*, and its concern for myth and lore. When in *Jerusalem* Troy Whitworth curses Rooster Byron as 'Worzel Maggot, Stig of the Dump', it is Gummidge being invoked alongside Stig, and the Worzel adaptations might be viewed as Crook's retort to the insult, just as *Detectorists* reclaimed the archaeological spirit of King's story.[135] Worzel becomes a gentle, U-rated Rooster Byron, the presiding spirit of Scatterbrook.

So the English scarecrow speaks to different times and altered climates, through novels, songs, television series and playground games. The word 'Worzel' too migrates across fields, finding other meanings, and a diversion around Worzel and its related spellings

– Wurzel, Wurse – illustrates other aspects of folkloric England, and projects back across *England's Green* to matters of farming and rurality. In 2022 PJ Harvey published a long Dorset dialect poem, *Orlam*, a month-by-month cycle through the seasons, inspired by William Barnes's nineteenth-century Dorset dialect glossary and poems. In *Orlam*, and on Harvey's 2023 album *I Inside the Old Year Dying*, which struck a musical match for the book, the mythic meets pop musical vernacular, and pagan and Christian symbolism enfold. Harvey's April poem 'Lwonesome Tonight', one of several Elvis Presley references in *Orlam*, begins, 'Hark the greening of the eth/ Curl-ed ferns yet to uncurl'.[136] Reaching October, the reader encounters 'Wurse', given glossary meaning as 'devil, arch-fiend, a variation of "Ooser"'.[137] In Gore Woods, in Orlam's home village of Underwhelem, there is something disturbing, and it is not unlike a scarecrow: 'sack of jute with arm-hole rips/ a guise with head and horns complete/ stinking elder dressed with meat'. Charms again move from pleasantries to peculiars. The third quoted line here is noted as 'a remedy for warts', with raw beef rubbed on a wart and hung in the elder.[138] If this seems outlandish, similar remedies applied in 1970s suburban Norwich, with raw beef rubbed and then buried in the garden, rotting as the wart decayed, in sympathetic magic. In un-idyllic *Orlam*, Worzel meets Wurse, and the magic turns devilish, with powers less benign than Crook's Gummidge. In April 2022, ahead of *Orlam*'s publication, Harvey gifted Dorchester's Dorset Museum, founded by William Barnes, a proof copy and a signed photograph of her wearing traditional Dorset buttons. Harvey viewed items from the collection, including a wooden replica 'Ooser' or 'Wurse', as carved in 1975 by John Byfleet for the Wessex Morris Men, and still carried in Morris performances, and at May Day celebrations at Cerne Abbas.[139] The 1970s revival of green English magic lingers.

Alter the Worzel spelling a little further, and other 1970s associations, rustic and musical, arise. From Worzel to Wurzel, the Somerset group The Wurzels achieved fame in 1976, bringing 'Scrumpy & Western' (the title of a 1967 EP) to the charts, trading on an image of rural folk, with vocals clearly accented, embedded in place.[140] The Wurzels' career in general, and their '70s fame in particular, casts a tangential light on the folkloric and the agrarian, and indeed the meteorological. Two Wurzels hits, 'Combine Harvester' and 'I Am a Cider Drinker', bookended 1976's hot summer, 'Combine Harvester' charting for thirteen weeks from mid-May, 'Cider Drinker' for nine weeks from early September. Fine weather for the harvest, and a thirst-quenching anthem to follow. Both borrowed their tunes from pop hits, 'Cider Drinker' from Jonathan King's 1975 'Una Paloma Blanca', 'Combine Harvester' (which had been a number one in Ireland in 1975 for Brendan Grace) from Melanie's 1972 hit 'Brand New Key', the latter's brand new pair of rollerskates replaced by a new combine. 'Cider Drinker', with lyrics by the band, hymned a distinctive Somerset drink. 'Combine Harvester', with lyrics by Brendan O'Shaughnessy, described a farming affair with a view to marriage, compliments traded with mild innuendo, machinery assessed and acreages compared. It is as if Gainsborough's iconic eighteenth-century marriage portrait of *Mr and Mrs Andrews*, on Mr Andrews's Suffolk estate, had been translated across the centuries, moving down from polite society to something rougher, but still a story of affection, property and land.

The Wurzels' fame lingered but chart success petered out, the third and final hit a minor one, 'Farmer Bill's Cowman', a reworking of the First World War 'I Was Kaiser Bill's Batman', peaking at number 32 in June 1977. The related LP was entitled *Give Me England*, the title track the theme song for British sex comedy *Confessions from a Holiday Camp*, and also including a comic song of new farming technology, 'Nellie the Bionic Cow', nodding to the 1970s bionic human TV favourite *The Six Million Dollar Man*, with animal machines a matter less for moral outrage than absurd comedy. As of 2023, The Wurzels still perform, the 1970s membership intact. The group had begun, though, in the 1960s as Adge Cutler and the Wurzels, 'Drink Up Thy Zider' scraping the national chart for a week at number 45 in February 1967, the group content with and/or stuck in regional popularity until Cutler's death in a car accident in 1974. The Cutler-Wurzels songs hymned aspects of Somerset life; the quiet of the village ('Down the Nempnett Thrubwell'), the lively Pill ferry across the mouth of the Avon ('Pill Pill') and jaunts 'All Over Mendip'.[141] The latter might have provided an alternative locals' soundtrack for Peter Nichols's 1968 TV play *The Gorge*. National family-entertainment fame eluded Cutler's Wurzels, the songs too locally embedded, the humour too crude. Cutler could indeed have served as a contemporary regional example for Bert Lloyd as he sought in 1967 in *Folk Song in England* to rescue erotic folk song from the 'prudence' and 'prudery' of earlier collectors.[142] Cutler's Wurzel muck and filth went beyond the dirt of farming; had

James Ravilious, 'Scarecrow in a Barley Field Near Iddesleigh', from *The Heart of the Country* (1980).

an earlier collector found themselves in a north Somerset pub in the late 1960s, and heard Cutler singing 'My Threshing Machine' (1967), they might have noted: 'while the song gave the appearance of agrarian subject matter, the titular machine was primarily euphemistic (do not publish)'. Like Newley's 'Strawberry Fair', 1966 recordings of Cutler upstairs in the Royal Oak, Nailsea, might usefully be gathered into the EFDSS's 'Full English'.[143]

These West Country diversions through Dorset and Somerset find an end point in Devon, with a return to the scarecrow. In the summer of 1976, by a field of barley not yet combined, during the drought and possibly in the brief fallow window between the Wurzels' two summer hits, James Ravilious photographed a scarecrow. Ravilious had moved to north Devon in 1972 with his wife Robin, whose family had owned a small estate there since the 1680s, and his photographic work, carried out for the Beaford Arts Centre, archived the locality; the resultant Beaford Archive included 80,000 images taken between 1972 and 1991, a photographic residency in the colloquial rather than artistic sense.[144] 'Scarecrow in a barley field near Iddesleigh' appeared in Ravilious's first book, *The Heart of the Country*, published in 1980 with a foreword by

Suffolk rural writer Ronald Blythe and text by Robin Ravilious. The scarecrow appears in a section on 'The Land', with the caption:

> A lonely landscape – like many in North Devon. No village is visible in the whole sweep of this view, and what houses there are are concealed by trees. The hedges have been mechanically trimmed, and the corn will be combine-harvested, but at this moment it is a scene that Thomas Bewick might have engraved some two hundred years ago.

The preceding image in the book showed 'Iddesleigh in the drought', with fields bleached 'to a slivery pallor', in weather which 'dessicated even this waterlogged country'.[145]

The scarecrow, and its caption, look across *England's Green*, catching themes running through the preceding chapters of this book. The agricultural scene carries a mixed time signature, of continuity and tradition in the present view, but only because the machines are not working at the photographic moment. It won't be long until the combine comes, modern farming proceeding. Seasons cycle on, but this is 1976, and the drought has challenged farming norms, and England reflects on exceptional weather, some beginning to wonder whether it might not be so exceptional in the future. The scarecrow views the signs of things to come. An archaic coat-and-hat-and-head-on-a-pole stands still, as what Anthropocene scientists will term the Great Acceleration gathers pace. Elsewhere in *The Heart of the Country* Ravilious documents traditional practice hanging on, his Devon pictures documenting a country on the cusp. 'Scarecrow in a barley field near Iddesleigh' shows the scarecrow, having done its job, the corn grown, standing folkloric over the barley, the only figure in the scene.

And what might the scarecrow be looking forward to? Devon farmers had worked under the Common Agricultural Policy since 1973, UK membership of the Common Market having been confirmed in the 1975 referendum, with Devon voting 72 per cent to stay in. The 'Village Life' section of *The Heart of the Country* includes a picture of a village tree in Newton St Petrock, with a Notice of Poll for the 1975 vote and a poster urging 'Keep Britain in Europe'. Does the scarecrow look forward to the opportunities of modern farming, the regulations and the subsidies, the profits to be made, the mechanized bird scarers available? Three years later, with TV exposure, the 'Worzel' name will stick to any

Scarecrow in a field near Iddesleigh, seen from the B3217 to Dowland, taken from Google Earth street view, images captured April 2010, accessed February 2023.

scarecrow, whether or not they resemble Pertwee, and 43 years later the label will return. By the time of Crook's 2019 Worzel, Devon has voted Leave, with the Torridge constituency, home of Beaford and just north of Iddesleigh, registering 60.8 per cent against remaining in the European Union in the 2016 referendum. The Iddesleigh scarecrow's successors, whether retained for traditional, magical or bird-scaring value, look over a farming shaped legislatively from London rather than Brussels, control of sorts taken back to Westminster, with white papers and Acts shaping the country, grappling with global forces, navigating different deals.

Driving round Iddesleigh on Google Earth in February 2023, through virtual fields un-updated since 2009 and 2010, on B-roads with passing places, the scene is chiefly permanent pasture and arable is uncommon. As in 1976 this is a predominantly pastoral region. Head though for Dowland on the B3217, the pictures from April 2010, and on the right, cresting a hill, is a ploughed field. In its bare middle stands a scarecrow. This is not Ravilious's field, but it is not far off, and while it may not be overseeing barley, the scarecrow guarding the reddish soil could be 1976's descendant. Scarecrow 2010 keeps watch over a changing England, standing in the red, waiting for the green.

8
To Green Possibilities

In Alan Garner's 1976 Cheshire-set story *The Stone Book*, a stonemason father inducts his daughter into the mysteries of place via a walk under a hill, to the mined seams of 'galena, cobalt and malachite', following the geological grain.[1] An underground cave shows bull paintings, fossil bird footprints, her father's mason marks, and ancestral footprints, and Mary touches a handprint which somehow matches her own, in 'the most secret place she had ever seen'.[2] Father carves daughter a stone 'prayer book', opening to something like a fossil, 'two fronds of a plant': 'the stone book that had in it all the stories of the world and the flowers of the flood'.[3] Just as Swinnerton's *Fossils* opened up a Carboniferous green England, so, by mineral seams and the grain of rocks, Garner's *Stone Book* germinates an unlikely, mysterious green.

Seams and Grains

The Stone Book opens, for consideration, seams and grains of green. *England's Green* has run from the Wellow maypole to the Ravilious scarecrow, from Trent gravel to red Devon soil, from sprayed fields to Googled fields. How has the green served as a connecting seam, or a running grain, through accounts of land, farming, nature, the Anthropocene, mystery and the folkloric?

A green 'seam' might indicate an underlying pattern, as in the seams of rock across a geological map, to be tapped for possible human value. Or a seam might help keep things in shape, holding garment threads fast, the green a binding agent, connecting humanity to the natural world, whether through livelihood, emotional affinity or spiritual value. In keeping with Peter Bishop's attention to the varieties of green, and their 'subtlety, contrast and paradox', a green grain might be identified, with grain a metaphor both mineral and vegetable.[4] *England's Green* has tracked a variously green English grain, echoing in this sense William Carlos Williams's 1925 prose work *In the American Grain*, with its articulation of American voices to amplify a country various and contested.[5] 'Grain' here can suggest a running pattern, as in wood, whether growing or cut for timber. The green English grain, with its running patterns of the green and pleasant, the green and anxious, thereby registers contrasting emotions; the seeming continuities and cycles of nature, or the break in continuity marked by the Anthropocene; the hope of renewal, or fears of ecological doom. A green grain might also signal germination, and all the varieties which might follow; vigorous critiques of modern ways, a lively defence of agrarian living, the folkloric observance of mystery, the contemplation of the Anthropocene weather.

Looking back through *England's Green*, we can make out farmers, growers, politicians, ecologists, oil tankers, puppets, naturalists, poets, rewilders, scientists, painters, festival goers, archaeologists, alternative archaeologists, singers, dancers, witches, scarecrows, all with their own green hues. This concluding chapter reviews the parade, before ending with a projection of future green possibilities.

Concluding through *England's Green*

England's Green has explored a six-decade variegated green episode, the green carrying a complex time signature. The book has been: a study in the decadal, with moments of correspondence between, say, 1965–75 and 2015–25; a consideration of the fifty-odd years, whether viewed as an interlude, or something cruelly cut short, of European political affiliation; an account of the resonance of specific histories in recent times, whether eighteenth-century enclosures or lost Anglo-Saxon kingdoms; a reflection on the cyclical time of traditional agrarian and/or folkloric practice; a record of the cultural work done by a sense of an eternal green nature, outside of historical time; an analysis of the geologically epochal time of the Anthropocene.

The green and national meet over six decades in provisional contested variety, forward and/or backward looking, with pleasant or anxious greenery informing political visions conservative and radical.

The green may suggest a comfortable keeping of things as they have been, or a transformative energy, an injection of renewal. Green England appears variously affirmative, critical or contrarian, the range of cultural and political associations present in the genealogy of Blake's green and pleasant Jerusalem playing out across the decades. The introductory excursion around the green in this book emphasized green varieties, ending with Raymond Briggs's green English Bogeydom, with its settled, happily decaying life. What further varieties have populated *England's Green*?

The late twentieth century saw the accustomed green of farmed England jolted. The modern green harmonies of post-war agriculture turned to discord, chemical and welfare anxieties claiming green values against modern farming, with dying falcons, battery hens and grubbed-up hedgerows the dystopic evidence. Green becomes the language of critique, with longstanding tropes of the natural as something beyond property mobilized against prevailing structures of ownership. The green and pleasant counters the present, yet also becomes a resource of hope for a different green future. Present landed interests retort with a different green, of stewardship and intimate knowledge gained through ownership and/or labour, the pursuit of animals through hunting shown as evidence of land care rather than domineering cruelty. Shuttling between the claims of rural and urban, the green is entangled and evoked in parliamentary dispute, metropolitan marching and carcass pyres. At the same time, people look back to other times, collecting old ploughs, eating organics, growing their own, making green selves in a no-longer-green world. England's Green is recast through contested takes on land.

In the 1960s and '70s the green becomes Environment, political stakes raised through the diagnosis of crises; of resources, of pollution, of qualities of living eroded by modern trends. Government seeks to take things in hand, prompted yet also overtaken by events, as tankers sink and oil prices inflate. Between the *Torrey Canyon* and the OPEC price hike, a discourse of attempted environmental governance is fashioned. A Green movement, and a Green politics, shapes itself by claiming a crisis diagnosis more realistic, and a politics more radical, signalling emergency themes which continue to shape the political Green. Nature values appear also through popular entertainment, children and accompanying grown-ups taking in the green adventures of Clangers and Wombles, underground and overground messages broadcast in the mainstream. Naturalists, notably Richard Mabey, likewise project a green world, something to be appreciated in part for its human affinities, something close to home rather than a far-away wonder. England's Green is refigured through the humanly natural, as a nature suffering from human treatment, yet whose values might be conserved by another configuration of the human.

By the twenty-first century, with anthropogenic climate change and the emergence of the Anthropocene, concerns planetary, national and local are refracted through England's Green. Sites more or less obviously green, in ecological value or colour, appear Anthroposcenic, emblematic of a newly diagnosed epoch. The humanly natural English green twists to new formulations of an earth marked indelibly by the human, even to its rock record. The wild is reworked, in a country without wilderness, and dispute follows, over the rewilding of land, and matters of property and ecological propriety. The naturalness of earth and air and rain is jarred, late twentieth-century drought and hurricane acting as cultural appetizers for climate change. Anthropocene England is marked by flood, eroded by rising seas, England's blue nibbling England's green. Past dues are received and futures hang, like one of Julian Perry's caravans, in the air.

The green brings together, and sometimes makes a clash of, matters often held apart: things landed, environmental, political, scientific, popular, creative. This green is complex and various enough, but then add further green associations of magic and spirit, green countercurrents running against a supposedly unmagical modern world. From the late 1960s, festivals at sites with mystic reputations nurture an England of green mystery, sometimes clashing with state power, confirming that something is at stake. Green values clash as ancient sites such as Stonehenge or Avebury are cast as energy-filled alternatives to a nature-eroding present. Green mystery takes the hand of the folkloric, longstanding alignments of folk culture and the national tapping environmental sensibilities. The mood here may be reverently serious or irreverently comic, and the two blend in excursions or safaris among the English. Dances with antlers, or scarecrow plays, carry hints of the numinous and/or pagan. Mystery and the folkloric even appear alongside, or within, the political and the governmental. In 1972, for the cover illustration of a report on the management of natural resources, the Department of the Environment choose William Blake. Through all the worries, the projections, the hopes, the fears, the policies, the protests, runs the grain of Blake's phrase, evident all ways: England's green and pleasant.

The meeting of green and national in England thus carries complex significance. In the green, the cultural, political, economic, scientific and spiritual meet, sometimes merrily, sometimes antagonistically. The green of England is shaped by particular geographies: the national iconographies of English landscape, accruing values of nature and/or the agrarian; the valorized local, whereby particular geographical distinctions add up to a variegated country; and a green shaped by the global, whether through end-of-empire conservation or the opening of a new global Anthropocene epoch marked by climate change. *England's Green* has traced such themes through the recent past. What might there be to look forward to?

England 2064: The Green Possibilities

> But the country dies hard. Billhooks and rabbit snares in an ironmonger's; and out of the towns the emptiness of the countryside is extraordinary. We try to use lanes wherever possible, and down them we drive for miles without passing other human beings or cars. I think this is owed to modern agriculture. There have never been fewer farm workers; and those that remain fight a sort of rearguard action against the town. But we are the last generation to know this old England. The population of 2064, with their three-car families and their autostrada and helicopters, will kill the England I love beyond all hope. And they won't even be able to imagine how lonely and peaceful much of it still is this year.[6]

This final section takes a forward look, from six decades ago to forty years hence. The passage quoted above, from John Fowles's journals for 1964, describes a Dorset part of 'Our little tour of the West' from 6 to 15 October.[7] The year 1964 also saw the publication of Fowles's essay 'On Being English but Not Being British', with its invocation of a 'Green England'.[8] Fowles travelled in Dorset in part 'to prospect for a house', and would move from London to Lyme Regis in 1965.[9] Fowles found a changing country, with even in Shaftesbury in Dorset a sense of how, while 'the unchangingness of the small provincial town is a shock', this was countered by new presences, in styles of dress, modes of transport, the television in the hotel lounge. But if the old country is eroded, 'it dies hard'.[10]

Fowles sets a changing rural England of 1964 against a new England of 2064. One hundred years on, Fowles imagines an England rather like those future visions transforming 1960s English townscape, as redevelopment schemes sought modern architectural forms fit for the motor age.[11] In Fowles's 2064, cars proliferate, families helicopter and the country is interconnected by motorways, a fossil-fuelled modernity killing Fowles's green 'England I love'. A few years on from 1964, however, such prospects would be undercut, and *England's Green* has shown the ebbing of such projections of techno-modernity, as other environmental visions achieved prominence. Between Fowles's 1964 projection and now, various forces have intruded; the rise of a popular environmentalism, critiques of modern farming that question the make-up of any green England and climate change as an inevitable frame for any future visions. Looking ahead from 2024, future prospects, whether optimistic or doom-laden, no longer envisage family lifestyles ever-more geared around driving and flying. For some, even getting to 2064 might be an achievement, as terms such as 'extinction' assume prominence in green debate.

To finish *England's Green*, sixty years on from Fowles's 1964 journal entry, what might be the prospects for 2064? Forty years on, what kind of Green England might there be? Three scenarios are given below, all carrying some plausibility, envisaging a changed English environment and with a hint of dramatic events. Scenario one suggests change navigated via new precision technologies, a country transformed but with a recognizable business-as-usual. Scenario two indicates a deeper transformation, a changed society, its nature renewed. Scenario three has something very dramatic happening, with things falling apart, producing an environment of just coping. Whether these scenarios are optimistic or pessimistic will depend upon the reader's diagnosis of 2024, and whether the present is seen as a challenge, an emergency or the prelude to extinction, should drastic action not be taken. These green possibilities appear as if written in 2064 by somebody old, who can remember thinking about such things forty years before.

England's Green, Precisely

Well, plenty has happened but we're still here, and it's nice that we can sit down of an evening with the television, built into the wall, low down, hearth style. 'It's that time of year', the announcers are saying, though it's only the third season, but we all enjoy *Harvest Race*. Nice for the BBC to get a surprise hit, first done for Great-Auntie's 140th anniversary in 2062 and one of those events where schedules still make sense. An instant TV fixture. People across the country, at the same time, can sit down and celebrate the productivity and skill of the farmer. The early sowing rounds, the county cup winners representing the shires through summer, the eliminators and semis whittling it down and the wheat final at the National Model Farm. It's a knockout programme. Two final rounds, the drone-guided and the hands-on, with points for speed and accuracy. Precision at pace, with maximums safely gathered in. Prestige, and a brand-new heritage self-binder, for the Farmer of the Year.

Some landed things have lasted through the changes. Owners may have shifted but ownership remains. Between the wild nature zones and the play lands, 'Precision England' rules apply. A lingering decades-old official slogan – 'Precision England!' Was it from the 2030s, something clutched at in the mess of that time, but which lasted? Crops for England, crops for export, artifice embraced, inputs targeted, outputs extended. Waste reduced, pollution minimized. Just as in older days, the English weather, with its new climate tricks, had to be tackled. Plans were hedged, with back-up varieties. Things no longer practical in England were jettisoned, while novelties bedded in.

Century storms turned to decadal storms, and so flood defences rose to the fight, rich lands kept dryish and waters channelled to wash zones. Some of the coasts went, so there's less England than there was, but while it's sad to see a castle topple, or a home, most places aren't coast, and the old saws of disaster and opportunity hold. Even the 'glean and glamp' boom of the thirties, tapping the new beachcombing craze, has proved sustainable. Who would have thought that old landfills could be an attraction? Anthropocene gatherers stalk the shore, picking the detritus of the plastic age and the odd proper fossil.

Of course the 2050 drought did for a lot. That all prompted an overdue taking-in-hand, and inter-regional pipes now keep the levels up, wet and dry balancing across the years. National Water is precisely channelled, good for government. Those markers sticking up from the surface to locate the underground pipe junctions have become quite the art form, shaped to celebrate their places, trying to win the 'Pipe Place' contests. Water junctions elevate their locality to importance, just like on the railways two centuries ago. Settlements thank the engineers, with totems to precision: towers, tree shapes, crop replicas. The oak of Oxton, the cucumber of Corpusty, the obelisk of Ware, find national renown.

Precise, zoned and ruled but quirky: this England in 2064. The national 'Land Song', sung by children at the start of the school year (and by the Farmers Choir on *Harvest Race*), captures sentiment:

We gambol on the play lands,
Safari on the wilds.
The English ox and beaver,
The joy of every child.

From sowing through to harvest
On farming we depend.
Precision is our lodestar,
Our fences we will mend.

By grape and golden barley,
By cauliflower and bean
By all the gifts around us
We sing of England's green.

England's Green, Naturally

So after all that, a cooperative England. Dug in, nationally retrenched after all that globalism. Selling and swapping between the counties and countries, settling down with nature as it resets. Our Local Scientist (every place has one) calls it the Great Deceleration, says the Anthropocene rocks will show a big human spike and then a fade. Our rotating capitals set some parameters, government perambulating the regions, but beyond that places get on, land held in community trust. Amazing no one died really, or at least not many, or not directly at anyone's hand, though you do hear stories.

Fields now have people in them, quite often. You would never see a human in an English field, save for the machine drivers and the odd migrant gang, but now there's plenty. Field Ergonomics are on the syllabus, for children and refreshing adults, for stylish repetitive movement. Gyms have died out with the new labour, though someone did set up a 'retro' one for dressing up, all comic heritage panting and puffing. Outdoors though it's hands-on England, planting and weeding, composting and picking, all safely gathering. Quite the range of festivals mark seasonal time, staggered between places as the cropping varies. Every weekend in May and September sees one, excuses for joy if excuses are needed.

Plenty of novelties, or what used to be novelties, grow in the new warmth, the new drought, the new storm. Varieties to avoid mildew, blight, desiccation, wilting; they even weathered the 2050 drought. Lucky things had shifted before that hit, or we might have starved. Down in the valley, stilted houses stand aloof from winter waters.

Depending where the geographical rotation of government lands, they hold the 'Local Flag' national final. Representatives of all England, gathered on the first September weekend. Any design as long as it's green. A friendly, unangry competition, the entered flags flying in their county schools for the year. The tenth anniversary 2064 theme was fruit, with all the varieties. Green grapes (Sussex), green apples (Lancashire), greengages (Nottinghamshire), green figs (Devon), all in the top five. Kent took the national pennant, with three limes in a row on a chalk background, a natural jackpot.

Cooperative, embedded, adaptive, celebratory: England in 2064. The national 'Nature Song', sung by children at the start of the school year (and at the Local Flag national final) captures the sentiment:

Green grows the country,
The forest and the fields,
Clean and bright and beautiful,
The scars begin to heal.

We fly the Local Flag
Painted all the colours green,
Returning to our nature
To make the English scene.

We're many and we're varied,
And all things in between.
Variety our watchword,
We sing of England's green.

England's Green, Incidentally

A decade or so ago, the world caught up with the old doomsayers. The rain went away for a long time, then came back for a long time, and that put the seal on it. The surviving old remembered predictions from childhood. There were bodies in the field. Powers lapsed, plugs were pulled, the net finally went. England turned back on itself, like everywhere else on its different course, not that we have time to worry about elsewhere. Bits of England make their way as they can, without much regard for nations or whatever. Some call up remembered wars, or old lockdowns, as stories for coping. We mostly get along. We can hardly afford not to.

Eating what's here, drinking what's here, swapping at the crossroads market, tasting the difference from over the hill. Plant what's best in each patch, and wish for the weather. Everything is a back-up for everything that fails. Most years this bit of country copes. In some ways we are fortunate, with the wood that's grown back and the stream and the fruits. There's plenty of wild. England's gone green, incidentally.

The capacity to smile remains. In one of the lazy weeks after harvest, some wander to the city, to take in what's left: the towers, the highways, the tottering bridges. Just like in those old books about the future. Happy occasions are marked, when summer is navigated and crops secured. We have a new traditional harvest feast: beaver stew, with greens. We're not short of beavers.

There wasn't a whole lot of singing through the changes, save for work dirges, but five years ago a harvest feast song took hold, a few valleys from here, and has spread. It is for children to sing, in unison:

Thanks to the ground for the things we have to eat
Thanks to the stream for the water
Thanks to the sun for the sunny summer heat
Thanks to the cloud for the rain

When summertime is over we will kick up all the leaves
And pick the twigs and branches for the fire
The winter will be here and we've made another year
We'll rest among the dark and start again

To think in five years it'll be the moon centenary. A very few very old ones recall the pictures, and the words, of whole earths and giant leaps. Small steps will do for now.

REFERENCES

1 Six Green Decades

1 On the history of Wellow maypole, see Frank E. Earp, 'May in Nottinghamshire: The Wellow Maypole', 29 May 2018, Nottingham Hidden History Team, www.nottinghamhiddenhistoryteam.wordpress.com, accessed 26 October 2023.

2 Abacus Lighting are based in nearby Sutton-in-Ashfield, specializing in mast construction, hence their maypole work.

3 'Wellow Maypole Celebrations', https://player.bfi.org.uk, accessed 26 October 2023. The same film appears on the website of MACE, the Media Archive for Central England, spliced with films from the late 1960s and early '70s of carnival parades in the nearby mining village of Ollerton: 'Ollerton Sports – 1965, 1966, 1967 Wellow Maypole', www.macearchive.org, accessed 26 October 2023.

4 'Jordan Castle Farm', *Countryside Classroom*, www.countrysideclassroom.org.uk, accessed 26 October 2023.

5 Roy Fisher, 'City' (1961), *The Long and the Short of It: Poems, 1965–2005* (Hexham, 2005), p. 43.

6 Such complexities of description and possession are also demonstrated in a recent work sharing this book's title, Zaffar Kunial's *England's Green* (London, 2022), which appeared only after this particular *England's Green* was drafted and titled. Kunial's *England's Green* is discussed here in Chapter 2.

7 David Matless, *Landscape and Englishness* (London, 1998, rev. 2016). On English pastoral, see also David Matless, *About England* (London, 2023).

8 The 'Cloudbusting' video is discussed by Rob Young in *Electric Eden: Unearthing Britain's Visionary Music* (London, 2010), pp. 571–2. Young notes the 'windswept landscape', but misses the specific setting at Uffington.

9 The Uffington white horse also appeared as the cover star of XTC's *English Settlement* LP in 1982. On Uffington, Chesterton and XTC, see Matless, *About England*, pp. 34–6.

10 Quotation from Harry Doherty, 'Enigma Variations', *Melody Maker*, 11 November 1978, cited on 'Oh England My Lionheart', *Kate Bush Encyclopedia*, www.katebushencyclopedia.com. On Bush's work, see

Young, *Electric Eden*, pp. 568–73; Michael Bracewell, *England is Mine: Pop Life in Albion from Wilde to Goldie* (London, 1997), pp. 160–61.

11 J. W. Robertson-Scott, *England's Green and Pleasant Land* (London, 1925; rev. Harmondsworth, 1947), p. 163.

12 Ibid., p. ix.

13 Ibid., pp. x and 168.

14 Ibid., p. 183.

15 The phrase could still be deployed in socio-economic critique, with Howard Newby's 1979 sociological analysis *Green and Pleasant Land? Social Change in Rural England* (London, 1979), suggesting the country did not live up to the ideal, or indeed to a stereotype of the rural idyll.

2 An Excursion around the Green

1 David Smith, *Industrial Archaeology of the East Midlands* (Dawlish, 1965).

2 David Matless, *About England* (London, 2023), pp. 249–50.

3 The coverage of extractive sites in *Industrial Archaeology of the East Midlands* focused on coal and gypsum, with neither seen as leaving a major built legacy.

4 University of Nottingham Manuscripts and Special Collections, MS 627: 'Vol. III, Part II – Other Mining and Quarrying'. One picture, on sheet 174, numbered 460 295, shows the Hilton Gravel works buildings, the other, on sheet 175, numbered 45 29, the worked area. Smith added, in an introductory text for 'Other Mining and Quarrying': 'The Trent Valley is an important source of gravel, the extraction of which has had its own distinctive effects on the East Midlands landscape. At Attenborough (between Beeston and Long Eaton) and Hemington (near Castle Donington) large areas of derelict land, most of it under water, mark the site of former gravel workings.' Smith completed a PhD on contemporary industrial location in the Department of Geography at Nottingham, and pursued industrial archaeology alongside this. His later work, mostly at Queen Mary College London, made a major contribution to social and welfare geography.

5 Matless, *About England*, pp. 283–7.

6 Tim Cooper and James Symonds, 'Gravel Extraction: History of the Aggregates Industry in the Trent Valley', in *Quaternary of the Trent*, ed. David Bridgland, Andy Howard, Mark White and Tom White (Oxford, 2014), pp. 235–42 (p. 242).

7 Hilton Gravel advertised their achievements in the 1957 *Stoke-on-Trent City Handbook*, reproduced online at www.thepotteries.org, accessed 26 October 2023.

8 Cooper and Symonds, 'Gravel Extraction', p. 238. Cooper and Symonds note that Hilton Gravel had been run since 1924 by 'the local squire', and was acquired by Blue Circle Aggregates in the mid-1960s.

9 Eleanor Parker, *Winters in the World: A Journey through the Anglo-Saxon Year* (London, 2022), p. 232.

10 E. M. Forster, 'The Abinger Pageant', in *Abinger Harvest* (1936) (Harmondsworth, 1967), pp. 369–84 (pp. 369–70).

11 Ibid., p. 371.

12 Ibid., p. 384.
13 For an extensive scholarly resource on such events, including those mentioned here, see Angela Bartie, Linda Fleming, Mark Freeman, Tom Hulme, Alex Hutton and Paul Readman, 'The Pageant of Abinger' and 'England's Pleasant Land', *The Redress of the Past: Historical Pageants in Britain*, www.historicalpageants.ac.uk, accessed 26 October 2023. See also Angela Bartie, Linda Fleming, Mark Freeman, Alex Hutton and Paul Readman, eds, *Restaging the Past: Historical Pageants, Culture and Society in Modern Britain* (London, 2020).
14 See David Matless, *Landscape and Englishness* (London, 1998, rev. 2016), Chapter 1.
15 Colin MacInnes, 'The Green Art: Gardening', in *Out of the Way: Later Essays* (London, 1979), pp. 201–10.
16 Ibid., pp. 201–2.
17 Ibid., p. 206.
18 John Fowles, *The Journals*, vol. I (London, 2003), p. 323; a footnote states that Fowles's only published work drawing on the Robin Hood theme was the story 'Poor Koko' in the 1974 collection *The Ebony Tower*.
19 The essay was republished as John Fowles, 'On Being English but Not British', in *Wormholes: Essays and Occasional Writings* (London, 1998), pp. 79–88 (p. 79); page references to quotations are taken from this republication. The essay was first published as John Fowles, 'On being English but not British', *Texas Quarterly*, VII (1964), pp. 154–62. In the contributors' notes for the *Texas Quarterly* Fowles explained that 'the present essay was sired by the ideas contained in *The Aristos* [Fowles's 1964 novel] and mothered by poems he was writing on the theme of the noble brigand as personified by Robin Hood, poems which began as semihistorical vignettes but gradually turned into definitions of what it is to be English' ('About the Contributors', *Texas Quarterly*, VII (1964), p. 176).
20 Fowles, 'On Being English but Not British', p. 82.
21 Ibid., pp. 82–3.
22 Ibid., p. 84.
23 Ibid., p. 86.
24 Ibid., p. 81.
25 Ibid., p. 87.
26 Ibid., p. 88.
27 John Fowles, *The Tree* (London, 1979), p. 80.
28 Zaffar Kunial, *England's Green* (London, 2022); Zaffar Kunial, *Us* (London, 2018).
29 Kunial, *England's Green*, pp. 60, 65 and 66.
30 Ibid., p. 63.
31 Ibid., p. 70.
32 Ibid., p. 5.
33 Ibid., p. 7.
34 Ibid., pp. 9–10.
35 Dudley Barker, *Green and Pleasant Land* (London, 1955). Barker was a novelist, a literary biographer of John Galsworthy, G. K. Chesterton and Arnold Bennett, and also wrote on Commonwealth issues. On

Winifred Holtby, *South Riding* (London, 1936), see Matless, *Landscape and Englishness*.

36 Jason Whittaker, *Jerusalem: Blake, Parry and the Fight for Englishness* (Oxford, 2022) p. 3. See also the essays in part four, 'Blake in Music', of Steve Clark, Tristanne Connolly and Jason Whittaker, eds, *Blake 2.0: William Blake in Twentieth-Century Art, Music and Culture* (Basingstoke, 2012), especially Keri Davies, 'Blake Set to Music', pp. 189–208.

37 Billy Bragg, *The Progressive Patriot* (London, 2006), pp. 16 and 4.

38 David Fallon, '"Hear the Drunken Archangel Sing": Blakean Notes in 1990s Pop Music', in *Blake 2.0*, ed. Clark, Connolly and Whittaker, pp. 248–62.

39 Jason Whittaker, 'Mental Fight, Corporeal War, and Righteous Dub: The Struggle for "Jerusalem", 1979–2009', ibid., pp. 263–73.

40 Matless, *About England*, pp. 33–4.

41 Quoted in Christopher Bryant, 'National Art and Britain Made Real: The 2012 London Olympics Opening Ceremony', *National Identities*, XVII (2015), pp. 333–46 (p. 334); Jason Whittaker, 'Blake and the New Jerusalem: Art and English Nationalism into the Twenty-First Century', *Visual Culture in Britain*, XIX (2018), pp. 380–92; Matless, *About England*, pp. 30–32.

42 John Higgs, *William Blake Now: Why He Matters More Than Ever* (London, 2019), p. 62.

43 *Jerusalem: An Anthem for England* was directed by Colm Martin. It was first broadcast on BBC4 on 8 September 2005, two days before the Last Night of the Proms, and repeated on 10 September just after the final Prom singalong. Figures from right and left, including Billy Bragg, conveyed a 'wider struggle to regain pride in English identity', at a time when 'Jerusalem' was being claimed by the British National Party.

44 George Revill, 'English Pastoral: Music, Landscape, History and Politics', in *Cultural Turns/Geographical Turns*, ed. Ian Cook, David Crouch, Simon Naylor and James Ryan (Harlow, 2000), pp. 140–58.

45 Higgs, *William Blake Now*, p. 7.

46 Ibid., p. 69.

47 Ibid., pp. 67 and 69.

48 Michael Bracewell, *England is Mine: Pop Life in Albion from Wilde to Goldie* (London, 1997), p. 30.

49 The dedication is on the single sleeve. The *Second Light* LP also included 'A Canterbury Tale', with samples from Powell and Pressburger's 1944 visionary English pastoral film of that title, and a melody shared with Vaughan Williams's *The Lark Ascending*. 'Little Britain' preceded by five years the radio and television programme of the same name, which used the phrase to less tolerant effect.

50 A shortened single version spent two weeks in the charts, peaking at number 59, relatively high for a Fall single. Bracewell, *England is Mine*, p. 183, comments: '"The Fall", in Blakeian terms, could be regarded as Smith's perception of England's fall from grace and descent into self-pity or fashionable liberalism – two sins of equal gravity in Smith's writing'. For thorough information see the unofficial Fall website at www.thefall.org, and the excellent collections of essays, Tessa Norton

and Bob Stanley, eds, *Excavate: The Wonderful and Frightening World of The Fall* (London, 2022), including Elain Harwood's 'Jerusalem to Prestwich', pp. 16-24.

51 William Blake, *Jerusalem* (London, 1904), p. 8. The *Dragnet* sleevenote relates to the song 'Spectre Vs Rector', whose story is prompted by M. R. James, and recounts a rector from Hampshire and spectre from 'Chorozina', a biblical allusion, to which the sleevenote refers.

52 Michael Horovitz, ed., *Children of Albion: Poetry of the 'Underground' in Britain* (Harmondsworth, 1969), pp. 320 and 317.

53 Ibid., pp. 337–8.

54 Ibid., p. 319.

55 The quotation on Blake is from a 1986 interview, published as Robert Sheppard, *Turning the Prism: An Interview with Roy Fisher* (London, 1986), p. 22, quoted in John Kerrigan, 'Roy Fisher on Location', in *The Thing about Roy Fisher: Critical Studies*, ed. John Kerrigan and Peter Robinson (Liverpool, 2000), pp. 16–46 (p. 26). The Levertov quotation is still used in promotion of Fisher's work, appearing on the website of Shearsman Books, publishers of work on and by Fisher, www.shearsman.com.

56 Horovitz, *Children of Albion*, pp. 77–8; Roy Fisher, *The Long and the Short of It: Poems, 1965–2005* (Hexham, 2005) pp. 39–40.

57 Roy Fisher in conversation with John Kerrigan, 'Come to Think of It, the Imagination', in *News for the Ear: A Homage to Roy Fisher*, ed. Robert Sheppard and Peter Robinson (Exeter, 2000), pp. 96–120; also in *Jacket*, 35 (2008), available at http://jacketmagazine.com. On Fisher and contemporary ecological poetry, see Matthew Sperling, 'Water', in *An Unofficial Roy Fisher*, ed. Peter Robinson (Exeter, 2010), pp. 161–8.

58 The last two blanks are 'bosom' and 'Spectre'; Blake, *Jerusalem*, pp. 35 and 69.

59 Blake, *Selected Poems*, p. 67.

60 Ibid., p. 123.

61 Blake, *Jerusalem*, p. 42.

62 Ibid., p. 96.

63 Ibid., p. 26.

64 Ibid., p. 99.

65 Ibid., p. 102.

66 Ibid., pp. 94 and 28.

67 Ibid., pp. 118–19.

68 See 'William Blake: The Blighted Corn', www.tate.org.uk; 'The Blighted Corn' is a wood engraving on paper, 34 × 73 mm, Tate T02120.

69 Martin Butlin, *William Blake, 1757–1827* (London, 1990).

70 Jonathon Porritt, *Seeing Green* (Oxford, 1984), p. 179.

71 Peter Bishop, *The Greening of Psychology* (Dallas, TX, 1990), p. 4.

72 Ibid., pp. 5–11.

73 Ibid., p. 18.

74 John Agard, *The Coming of the Little Green Man* (Hexham, 2018), poems noted respectively on pp. 30, 19, 27 and 37. Agard's 2022 collection *Border Zone* includes the long poem 'Love in a Sceptred Isle', which plays on the green and pleasant land of Blake's Jerusalem; John Agard,

Border Zone (Hexham, 2022). See also the green of Tim Dee, *Greenery* (London, 2020), an account of following the spring from Southern Africa to the Arctic, which emphasizes a positive green, where 'Green is almost always good and is everywhere the sign for go' (p. 5). Dee finds hope in the 'lit green fuse' (p. 13), yet even here an allusion may indicate a green more than just upbeat. In Dylan Thomas's 1933 poem 'The Force That Through the Green Fuse Drives the Flower', that which drives 'my green age' is also 'my destroyer'; Dylan Thomas, *Selected Poems* (London, 1974), pp. 34–5. Green shades from the straightforwardly good.

75 Patrick Wright, *On Living in an Old Country* (London, 1985), p. 109. On Butts, see also Nathalie Blondel, *Mary Butts: Scenes from the Life* (New York, 1998); Jane Garrity, *Step-Daughters of England: British Women Modernists and the National Imaginary* (Manchester, 2003), pp. 188–241; David Matless, 'A Geography of Ghosts: The Spectral Landscapes of Mary Butts', *Cultural Geographies*, xv (2008), pp. 335–58.
76 Blake, *Selected Poems*, pp. 139–40. For a memoir of Salterns, see Mary Butts, *The Crystal Cabinet* (Manchester, 1988).
77 Quoted in Blondel, *Mary Butts*, p. 290.
78 Mary Butts, 'Green', in *With or Without Buttons* (Manchester, 1991), pp. 71–84 (p. 79).
79 Ibid., pp. 76–7.
80 Ibid., p. 75.
81 Ibid., p. 74.
82 Iona Opie and Peter Opie, *Children's Games in Street and Playground* (Oxford, 1969), pp. 106–7. The Opies' archive, held at the Bodleian Library, is detailed at www.opiearchive.org.
83 Annie G. Gilchrist, 'Note on the "Lady Drest in Green" and Other Fragments of Tragic Ballads and Folk-Tales Preserved amongst Children', *Journal of the Folk-Song Society*, vi (1919), pp. 80–90 (p. 83).
84 Opie and Opie, *Children's Games*, pp. 106–7.
85 Ibid., p. 6.
86 Ibid., p. 16.
87 Raymond Briggs, *Fungus the Bogeyman* (London, 1977). The book has no page numbers but references below are given counting from the first illustrated page. Briggs' other environmental fables included the nuclear war story *When the Wind Blows* (London, 1982), and the magical Christmas fixture *The Snowman* (London, 1978).
88 Briggs, *Fungus the Bogeyman*, p. 12.
89 Ibid., pp. 28–9.

2 Life, Death and the Land

1 Information from Department for Environment, Food and Rural Affairs, 'Agricultural Workforce in England at 1 June', 29 September 2022, www.gov.uk, accessed 26 October 2023.
2 Paul Brassley, David Harvey, Matt Lobley and Michael Winter, *The Real Agricultural Revolution: The Transformation of English Farming, 1939–1985* (Martlesham, 2021), pp. 1–2.
3 C. S. Orwin, *Problems of the Countryside* (Cambridge, 1945), p. 1.

4 Ibid., p. 105.
5 Ibid., pp. 106 and 109.
6 For discussions of modern English agriculture, see Brassley et al., *The Real Agricultural Revolution*, and see the summary in Philip Conford, *The Development of the Organic Network: Linking People and Themes, 1945–95* (Edinburgh, 2011), Chapter 1, 'Agricultural Efficiency and Industrial Food'. Also Karen Sayer, 'The View from the Land, 1947–1968: "Modernity" in British Agriculture, Farm and Nation"', in *New Lives New Landscapes Revisited: Rural Modernity in Britain*, ed. Linda Ross, Katrina Navickas, Matthew Kelly and Ben Anderson (Oxford, 2023), pp. 156–81. Changes in agriculture and rural life are also conveyed well in David Kynaston, *On the Cusp: Days of '62* (London, 2021), Chapter Three, 'Things They Do Change'. See also Abigail Woods, 'Rethinking the History of Modern Agriculture: British Pig Production, *c*. 1910–65', *Twentieth Century British History*, XXIII (2012), pp. 165–91; Matthew Holmes, 'Crops in a Machine: Industrialising Barley Breeding in Twentieth-Century Britain', in *Histories of Technology, the Environment and Modern Britain*, ed. Jon Agar and Jacob Ward (London, 2018), pp. 142–60; Alun Howkins, *The Death of Rural England: A Social History of the Countryside since 1900* (London, 2003); Jeremy Burchardt, *Paradise Lost: Rural Idyll and Social Change in England since 1800* (London, 2002); and Alan Armstrong, *Farmworkers: A Social and Economic History, 1770–1980* (London, 1988).
7 See also David Matless, *About England* (London, 2023), pp. 155–7.
8 Shirley Morrison and Harry McGregor, *Gordon Murray's Camberwick Green Annual* (London, 1970).
9 Robert Newson, Peter Wade-Martins and Adrian Little, *Farming in Miniature: A Review of British-Made Toy Farm Vehicles Up to 1980*, 2 vols (Sheffield, 2012–14).
10 *Look and Learn*, 'Focus on the Farmer's Year', Issue 113, 14 March 1964, p. 4 (supplement).
11 David Matless, 'The Agriculture Gallery: Displaying Modern Farming in the Science Museum', in *Histories of Technology, the Environment and Modern Britain*, ed. Agar and Ward, pp. 101–22. A film recording of how the Agriculture Gallery looked in 2016 is available at www.sciencemuseum.org.uk, accessed 26 October 2023.
12 Lewis Holloway, 'Showing and Telling Farming: Agricultural Shows and Re-Imaging British Agriculture', *Journal of Rural Studies*, XX (2004), pp. 319–30.
13 Royal Norfolk Agricultural Association, *1975 Royal Norfolk Show Catalogue of Entries and Exhibitions* (Norwich, 1975).
14 Nan Fairbrother, *New Lives, New Landscapes* [1970] (Harmondsworth, 1972), pp. 236–7. On Fairbrother and wider questions of rural modernity see the excellent collection of essays in Linda Ross, Katrina Navickas, Matthew Kelly and Ben Anderson, eds, *New Lives, New Landscapes Revisited: Rural Modernity in Britain* (Oxford, 2023).
15 Ibid., p. 12.
16 Ibid., p. 231.
17 Ibid., pp. 235–6.

18 Ibid., p. 240.
19 Royal Norfolk Agricultural Association, *1975 Royal Norfolk Show Catalogue*, p. 152.
20 R. J. Hornby and P. W. Lambley, 'Farming Practice in Norfolk: Its Influence on Habitats', in Norfolk Naturalists Trust, *Nature in Norfolk: a Heritage in Trust* (Norwich, 1976), pp. 147–54 (p. 154). On the NNT, and nature in Norfolk, see David Matless, *In the Nature of Landscape: Cultural Geography on the Norfolk Broads* (Chichester, 2014).
21 Royal Norfolk Agricultural Association, *1975 Royal Norfolk Show Catalogue*, p. 2.
22 Nature Conservancy, *The Countryside in 1970* (London, 1964), p. 27.
23 Ibid., p. 38.
24 Ibid., pp. 74, 96 and 97.
25 John Sheail, *Pesticides and Nature Conservation: The British Experience, 1950–1975* (Oxford, 1985), pp. 68–73; John Sheail, 'Pesticides and the British Environment: An Agricultural Perspective', *Environment and History*, XIX (2013), pp. 87–108.
26 James Wentworth Day, *Poison on the Land: The War on Wild Life and Some Remedies* (London, 1957), p. 3. On Day, see Sean Nixon, *Passions for Birds: Science, Sentiment and Sport* (Montreal, 2022), pp. 139–46; David Matless, 'Versions of Animal-Human: Broadland, 1945–70', in *Animal Spaces, Beastly Places*, ed. Chris Philo and Chris Wilbert (London, 2000), pp. 115–40; Matless, *In the Nature of Landscape*.
27 Day, *Poison on the Land*, p. 7.
28 Nixon, *Passions for Birds*, p. 107. See Chapter 4 of Nixon's book for the impact of Carson's work in the UK.
29 Rachel Carson, *Silent Spring* (London, 1963), p. 3. Carson briefly discussed the UK in *Silent Spring*, pp. 101–3.
30 Ibid., pp. xiv–xvii.
31 Ibid., pp. xxi–xxii.
32 John Betjeman, *The Collected Poems* (London, 1974), pp. 350–51.
33 Sheail, 'Pesticides and the British Environment', p. 108.
34 Kenneth Mellanby, *Pesticides and Pollution* (London, 1967); Kenneth Mellanby, *Farming and Wildlife* (London, 1981). On the New Naturalist series see Peter Marren, *The New Naturalists* (London, 1995). Conford, in *The Development of the Organic Network*, pp. 264–5, notes the complexities of Mellanby's position, including his support for the work of the Soil Association, serving on its Council in the early 1970s. The first issue of *The Ecologist*, published in July 1970, included a letter from Mellanby at the Nature Conservancy headed 'Subsidised Erosion', seeking to 'clarify' the 'government subsidy on artificial fertilizers', but effectively critiquing the policy, noting that the lack of an equivalent subsidy on organic manures meant that the latter became a source of pollution instead of fertility; Kenneth Mellanby, 'Subsidised Erosion', *The Ecologist*, I (1973), p. 47.
35 Mellanby, *Pesticides and Pollution*, p. 11.
36 Ibid., pp. 191–2.
37 Ibid., p. 189.
38 Ibid., p. 15.
39 Sheail, 'Pesticides and the British Environment', p. 90.

40 J. F. M. Clark, 'Pesticides, Pollution and the UK's Silent Spring, 1963–1964: Poison in the Garden of England', *Notes and Records: The Royal Society Journal of the History of Science*, LXXI (2017), pp. 297–327.
41 Ibid., p. 302.
42 Ibid., p. 301.
43 Carson, *Silent Spring*, p. xv.
44 D. A. Ratcliffe, 'The Status of the Peregrine in Great Britain', *Bird Study*, x (1963), pp. 56–90 (p. 74); Derek Ratcliffe, *The Peregrine Falcon* (Calton, 1980), including Chapter 13, 'The Pesticide Story', pp. 304–32; Sheail, *Pesticides and Nature Conservation*, pp. 107–14; Helen Macdonald, *Falcon* (London, 2006), pp. 116–22; Nixon, *Passions for Birds*, Chapter 1.
45 Ratcliffe, 'The Status of the Peregrine', p. 76.
46 Macdonald, *Falcon*, p. 121.
47 Adam Searle, Jonathon Turnbull and William Adams, 'The Digital Peregrine: A Technonatural History of a Cosmopolitan Raptor', *Transactions of the Institute of British Geographers*, XLVIII (2023), pp. 195–212.
48 James Wentworth Day, *A Falcon on St Paul's* (London, 1935); on urban falcons see Macdonald, *Falcon*, Chapter 6.
49 J. A. Baker, *The Peregrine* (London, 1967), p. 13.
50 Helen Macdonald, *H is for Hawk* (London, 2016). In September 2011 Macdonald's play 'The Falcon and the Hawk', on her own goshawk and Baker's *Peregrine*, was broadcast on BBC Radio 4, produced by Tim Dee.
51 J. A. Baker, *The Peregrine, The Hill of Summer and Diaries* (London, 2011), p. 4; J. A. Baker, *The Hill of Summer* (London, 1969).
52 Hetty Saunders, *My House of Sky: The Life of J. A. Baker* (Beaminster, 2017); Robert Macfarlane, *The Wild Places* (London, 2007).
53 Baker, *The Peregrine*, pp. 14-15.
54 J. A. Baker, 'On the Essex Coast', in *The Peregrine, The Hill of Summer and Diaries*, pp. 227–31 (p. 428).
55 Ibid., p. 430; Baker also describes an oil-stricken diver in *The Peregrine*, pp. 76 and 121.
56 Sean Nixon, 'Vanishing Peregrines: J. A. Baker, Environmental Crisis and Bird-Centred Cultures of Nature, 1954–1973', *Rural History*, XXVIII (2017), pp. 205–26; Nixon, *Passions for Birds*, pp. 127–30.
57 Ratcliffe, *The Peregrine Falcon*, p. 15.
58 Saunders, *My House of Sky*, p. 118; on Ellis, see Matless, *In the Nature of Landscape*, pp. 153–6; Matless, 'Versions of Animal-Human'.
59 The quotation opens poem 35 in A. E. Housman, *A Shropshire Lad* (London, 1896), p. 54.
60 Baker, *The Peregrine*, p. 15.
61 Ibid., p. 41.
62 Betjeman, *Collected Poems*, pp. 350–51.
63 Lesley West, 'An Agricultural History Museum', *Agricultural History*, XLI (1967), pp. 267–74 (p. 272).
64 Letter, 18 January 1970, Science Museum archive, file Sc. M 100/2/39/1.
65 West, 'An Agricultural History Museum', p. 271.
66 J.G.S. Donaldson, Frances Donaldson and Derek Barber, *Farming in Britain Today* (Harmondsworth, 1969), p. 192.

67 Ibid., p. 189.
68 Ruth Harrison, *Animal Machines: The New Factory Farming Industry* (London, 1964), p. vii.
69 Ibid., p. viii; on Harrison and Carson's correspondence, see Claas Kirchhelle, *Bearing Witness: Ruth Harrison and British Farm Animal Welfare (1920–2000)* (London, 2021), pp. 95–124. Kirchhelle's biography also attends to Harrison's activism in the Campaign for Nuclear Disarmament, Quakerism, scientific thinking and politics.
70 Ibid., p. xi; Jennings also echoed concentration camp analogies made in the press, discussed ibid., pp. 127–47.
71 Ibid., p. 13. See also Karen Sayer, 'Animal Machines: The Public Response to Intensification in Great Britain, *c.* 1960–*c.* 1973', *Agricultural History*, LXXXVII (2013), pp. 473–501. Sayer also conveys the complexity and variety of debates around welfare and farm intensification in the period, for example around egg production. See also the discussion in Abigail Woods, 'From Cruelty to Welfare: The Emergence of Farm Animal Welfare in Britain, 1964–71', *Endeavour*, XXXVI (2012), pp. 14–22. Woods, 'Rethinking the History of Modern Agriculture', p. 168, notes that for pig production, factory-style units had existed from the 1930s, and that proponents of indoor intensive production themselves argued for their humane treatment of sentient creatures, with 'a romantic, moral view of the pig' being 'integral' to modern agriculture, not only mobilized in opposition to it.
72 Harrison, *Animal Machines*, p. 1.
73 Ibid., captions for figures 2 and 3, within 'The new factory farming – a pictorial summary', between pp. 98 and 99. For the 'traditional farm' Harrison used a photograph by Ronald Goodearl (1909–1998) of a Buckinghamshire farm. Goodearl was a professional freelance photographer from High Wycombe, often supplying images for the Bucks Free Press. On Goodearl see the 'Sharing Wycombe's Old Photographs' website: www.swop.org.uk/swop/swop.htm. I am grateful to Mike Dewey for information on Goodearl's work.
74 Countryside Commission, *New Agricultural Landscapes* (Cheltenham, 1974), p. i.
75 Ibid., p. 1.
76 Patrick Cormack, *Heritage in Danger* (London, 1976), p. 36.
77 Ibid., p. 43.
78 *The Observer*, 'Save Our Countryside', 9 December 1984, colour magazine, pp. 17–49.
79 Marion Shoard, *The Theft of the Countryside* (London, 1980), p. 9.
80 Ibid., p. 7.
81 Ibid., p. 9.
82 Ibid., pp. 9–10.
83 Ibid., p. 98.
84 Ibid., pp. 21 and 14.
85 Ibid., p. 29.
86 Ibid., pp. 152 and 202.
87 Graham Cox and Philip Lowe, 'Agricultural Corporatism and Conservation Politics', in *Locality and Rurality*, ed. Tony Bradley and

Philip Lowe (Norwich, 1984), pp. 147–66 (p. 160). On the Wildlife and Countryside Act see Matthew Kelly, 'Habitat Protection, Ideology and the British Nature State: The Politics of the Wildlife and Countryside Act 1981', *English Historical Review*, CXXXVII (2022), pp. 847–83.

88 Patrick Sutherland and Adam Nicholson, *Wetland: Life in the Somerset Levels* (London, 1986), pp. 136–7. On parallel conflicts on the Halvergate marshes in Norfolk in the early 1980s, see Matless, *In the Nature of Landscape*, pp. 189–92.

89 Graham Harvey, *The Killing of the Countryside* (London, 1997), p. 15.

90 The State of Nature 2023 report is available at www.stateofnature.org.uk, accessed 27 October 2023.

91 Mark Cocker, *Our Place* (London, 2018), pp. 9 and 286–7.

92 On live animal exports, see Alun Howkins and Linda Merricks, '"Dewy eyed veal calves": Live Animal Exports and Middle Class Opinion, 1980–1995', *Agricultural History Review*, XLVIII (2000), pp. 85–103.

93 Michael Woods, *Contesting Rurality: Politics in the British Countryside* (Abingdon, 2005), pp. 131–61; Howkins, *Death of Rural England*, pp. 109–12.

94 Fintan O'Toole, *Heroic Failure: Brexit and the Politics of Pain* (London, 2019), pp. 128 and 55–61.

95 Cocker, *Our Place*, p. 297.

96 Marion Shoard, *This Land Is Our Land* [1987] (London, 1997), pp. 364 and xvi–xvii. The second quotation is from Shoard's introduction to the revised 1997 edition.

97 Ibid., pp. 97, 106 and 126.

98 Ibid., pp. 394 and 127.

99 Ibid., pp. 213 and 217–18.

100 Marion Shoard, *A Right to Roam* (Oxford, 1999), p. 2.

101 Shoard, *This Land Is Our Land*, pp. 18–19.

102 Ibid., p. 483. See also a similar narrative on access and the 'roots of exclusion' in Shoard, *Right to Roam*, pp. 97–102.

103 Christopher Hill, 'The Norman Yoke', in *Puritanism and Revolution* (London, 1958), pp. 46–111 (p. 52).

104 Paul Kingsnorth, *Real England: The Battle Against the Bland* (London, 2008); Paul Kingsnorth, *The Wake* (London, 2014). *The Wake* is the first of three novels in Kingsnorth's 'Buccmaster' trilogy, the others being *Beast* (London, 2016) and *Alexandria* (London, 2020).

105 Kingsnorth, *The Wake*, pp. 356–8.

106 Shoard, *This Land Is Our Land*, pp. 36–8.

107 The film is available at 'Diggers 350 occupation – The Land Is Ours – St Georges Hill, Surrey – April 1999 – TLIO', www.youtube.com, accessed 27 October 2023. Christopher Hill, *The World Turned Upside Down* (London, 1972). Shoard's *This Land Is Our Land* book title also alludes to the song 'This Land Is Your Land' by Woody Guthrie, whose work is another common reference point for Billy Bragg.

108 Guy Shrubsole, *Who Owns England?* (London, 2019), pp. 271 and 5.

109 Fay Godwin, *Our Forbidden Land* (London, 1990); John Taylor, *A Dream of England: Landscape, Photography and the Tourist's Imagination* (Manchester, 1995), pp. 276–81.

110 Tom Stephenson, *Forbidden Land* (Manchester, 1989).
111 Fay Godwin, *Land* (London, 1985); Fowles's essay is reproduced as John Fowles, 'Land', in *Wormholes: Essays and Occasional Writings* (London, 1998), pp. 321–39 (p. 330). Godwin and Fowles had earlier collaborated on a study of the Scilly Isles; John Fowles and Fay Godwin, *Islands* (London, 1978).
112 Godwin, *Our Forbidden Land*, p. 99.
113 Ibid., quoted on p. 10.
114 William Wordsworth, *A Guide through the District of the Lakes in the North of England* [1835] (London, 1951), p. 127.
115 Fraser Harrison, *Strange Land* (London, 1982); Fraser Harrison, *The Living Landscape* (London, 1986).
116 Harrison, *The Living Landscape*, pp. 12 and 75.
117 Agrarian response to critique had occurred before, for example as Kirchhelle, *Bearing Witness*, pp. 98–100 notes, Harrison's *Animal Machines* had been countered in 1964 by the agricultural press and the NFU. The 1990s was, however, novel in seeing organized public actions that achieved national impact.
118 Woods, *Contesting Rurality*, pp. 1–22. See also Michael Woods, 'Deconstructing Rural Protest: The Emergence of a New Social Movement', *Journal of Rural Studies*, XIX (2003), pp. 309–25.
119 Woods, *Contested Rurality*, pp. 84–100.
120 G. K. Chesterton, 'The Secret People', in *The Collected Poems of G. K. Chesterton* (London, 1933), pp. 173–6. The poem is discussed further in the context of debates over devolution and Brexit in Matless, *About England*, pp. 101–2.
121 Woods, *Contested Rurality*, p. 3.
122 Allyson May, *The Fox-Hunting Controversy, 1781–2004* (London, 2014), pp. 182–3.
123 George Monbiot, 'Class War on the Hoof', *The Guardian*, 19 September 2004; quoted in May, *The Fox-Hunting Controversy*, p. 150.
124 May, *The Fox-Hunting Controversy*.
125 Garry Marvin, 'A Passionate Pursuit: Foxhunting as Performance', in *Nature Performed*, ed. Bronislaw Szerszynski, Wallace Heim and Claire Waterton (Oxford, 2003), pp. 46–60 (pp. 47–8); Martin Wallen, *Fox* (London, 2006).
126 Garry Marvin, 'Natural Instincts and Cultural Passions: Transformations and Performances in Foxhunting', *Performance Research*, V (2000), pp. 108–15 (p. 109).
127 Roger Scruton, *On Hunting* (London, 1998), p. 37; for parallel themes see Roger Scruton, *England: An Elegy* (London, 2000).
128 Scruton, *On Hunting*, p. 45.
129 Ibid., p. 161.
130 Ibid., p. 54.
131 Marvin, 'A Passionate Pursuit', p. 51.
132 Woods, *Contested Rurality*, pp. 152–8.
133 For the Watchtree reserve, including a copy of a DEFRA booklet on *The Birth of Watchtree Nature Reserve* (n.d. [*c.* 2004]), see www.watchtree.co.uk, accessed 27 October 2023.

134 Woods, *Contested Rurality*, p. 157.
135 See Gemma Edwards, *Representing the Rural on the English Stage: Performance and Rurality in the Twenty-First Century* (Cham, 2023); Gemma Edwards, 'This Is England 2021: Staging England and Englishness in Contemporary Theatre', *Journal of Contemporary Drama in English*, IX (2021), pp. 281–303.
136 *The Guardian*, 1 December 1995, p. 14.
137 James Rebanks, *The Shepherd's Life* (London, 2015); James Rebanks, *English Pastoral* (London, 2020).
138 Rebanks, *The Shepherd's Life*, p. 212.
139 Ibid., pp. 6 and xx.
140 Ibid., p. 114.
141 Wordsworth, *A Guide through the District of the Lakes*, pp. 101–2. Wordsworth's comment came within a section of his Guide on 'Aspect of the Country, As Affected by its Inhabitants', and even here change and memory was in play, Wordsworth evoking something which he said had lasted 'till within the last sixty years' (p. 101).
142 For an insightful essay on these themes and their connection with the World Heritage bid, see Susan Denyer, 'The Lake District Landscape: Cultural or Natural?', in *The Making of a Cultural Landscape: The English Lake District as Tourist Destination, 1750–2010*, ed. J. K. Walton and J. Woods (London, 2013), pp. 3–29.
143 Rebanks, *The Shepherd's Life*, p. 291.
144 Dominic Head, 'The Farming Community Revisited: Complex Nostalgia in Sarah Hall and Melissa Harrison', *Green Letters: Studies in Ecocriticism*, XXIV (2020), pp. 354–66. Melissa Harrison's 2018 novel *All Among the Barley* is discussed in Matless, *About England*, pp. 39–42.
145 Shirley Toulson, *Discovering Farm Museums and Farm Parks* (Princes Risborough, 1977), p. 59.
146 Ibid., p. 28.
147 Ibid., p. 50.
148 See Wright's autobiography, Philip Wright, *Country Padre* (Baldock, 1980); Philip Wright, *Traction Engines* (London, 1959); Philip Wright, *Old Farm Implements* (London, 1961); Philip Wright, *Old Farm Tractors* (Newton Abbot, 1974); Philip Wright, *Salute the Carthorse* (Shepperton, 1971).
149 Mellanby, *Pesticides and Pollution*, p. 82.
150 Toulson, *Discovering Farm Museums*, p. 3.
151 On a parallel culture around drink, especially beer, with the defence and promotion of 'real ale' from the early 1970s, see Matless, *About England*, pp. 181–9.
152 E. F. Schumacher, *Small Is Beautiful* (London, 1973).
153 On Schumacher, see Conford, *The Development of the Organic Network*, pp. 266–8; Meredith Veldman, *Fantasy, the Bomb and the Greening of Britain: Romantic Protest, 1945–1980* (Cambridge, 1994), pp. 273–99.
154 Philip Conford, '"Somewhere Quite Different": The Seventies Generation of Organic Activists and their Context', *Rural History*, XIX (2008), pp. 217–34.

155 Conford, *The Development of the Organic Network*; Philip Conford, 'Organic Society: Agriculture and Radical Politics in the Career of Gerard Wallop, Ninth Earl of Portsmouth (1898–1984)', *Agricultural History Review*, LIII (2005), pp. 78–96.
156 Rolf Gardiner, 'Nyasaland: From Primeval Forest to Garden Landscape', *African Affairs*, LVII (1958), pp. 64–9 (p. 68).
157 Rolf Gardiner, 'Nyasaland', in *Water Springing from the Ground: An Anthology of the Writings of Rolf Gardiner*, ed. Andrew Best (Fontmell Magna, 1972), pp. 215–35 (pp. 230–31).
158 Conford, 'Organic Society', p. 96; Veldman, *Fantasy*, pp. 258–7. On Jenks, see Philip Coupland, *Farming, Fascism and Ecology: A Life of Jorian Jenks* (London, 2017).
159 Armstrong, *Farmworkers*, p. 224.
160 On debates within the organic movement on food standards see Conford, *The Development of the Organic Network*, Chapter 5.
161 Conford, 'Somewhere Quite Different', p. 231.
162 H. J. Massingham, ed., *England and the Farmer* (London, 1941); Rolf Gardiner, *England Herself* (London, 1943).
163 Conford, 'Somewhere Quite Different', p. 230.
164 Rolf Gardiner, 'Speech to the Duke of Edinburgh's Conference "The Countryside in 1970"', in *Water Springing from the Ground: An Anthology of the Writings of Rolf Gardiner*, ed. Andrew Best (Fontmell Magna, 1972), pp. 264–5; Rolf Gardiner, 'Chronology', ibid., pp. 296–320 (p. 317).
165 Ibid., p. 322.
166 Patrick Wright, *The Village That Died for England* (London, 1995), p. 266; Matthew Jefferies and Mike Tyldesley, 'Epilogue: Rolf Gardiner: *Eminence Vert*?', in *Rolf Gardiner: Folk, Nature and Culture in Interwar Britain*, ed. Mike Tyldesley and Matthew Jefferies (London, 2010), pp. 169–75.
167 See www.springheadtrust.org.uk.
168 Rolf Gardiner, 'The Hesse Tour', in *Water Springing from the Ground*, ed. Best, pp. 236–45 (p. 241).
169 Rolf Gardiner, 'Harvest Thanksgiving: Cerne Abbas', ibid., pp. 289–94 (p. 290).
170 Ibid., p. 294.
171 Gardiner, 'Nyasaland', in *Water Springing from the Ground*, ed. Best, p. 235.
172 Sally Horrocks, 'Pyke, Magnus Alfred', *Oxford Dictionary of National Biography* (2004).
173 Magnus Pyke, *Man and Food* (London, 1970), p. 7; Magnus Pyke, *Townsman's Food* (London, 1952); Magnus Pyke, *Food and Society* (London, 1968).
174 Pyke, *Man and Food*, p. 246.
175 Amy Whipple, 'Murdered Bread, Living Bread: Doris Grant and the Homemade, Wholemeal Loaf', *Endeavour*, XXV (2011), pp. 99–106 (p. 100).
176 Ibid., p. 105.
177 Doris Grant, *Housewives Beware* (London, 1958), pp. 15 and 5. Grant, in association with the British Housewives League, also attended to 'water

and the chemical dragon', arguing against fluoridization as the unethical imposition of a 'toxic chemical'; ibid., p. 73. See Amy Whipple, '"Into Every Home, Into Every Body": Organicism and Anti-Statism in the British Anti-Fluoridation Movement, 1952–1960', *Twentieth Century British History*, XXI (2010), pp. 330–49.

178 Grant, *Housewives Beware*, p. 181.

179 Ibid., pp. 139–44.

180 Amy Raphael, ed., *Mike Leigh on Mike Leigh* (London, 2008), pp. 88–99; Tony Whitehead, *Mike Leigh* (Manchester, 2007), pp. 36–7; Andy Medhurst, *A National Joke: Popular Comedy and English Cultural Identities* (London, 2007), pp. 167–78.

181 Medhurst, *A National Joke*, p. 167; second quotation from Andy Medhurst, 'Mike Leigh: The Naked Truth', *Sight and Sound* (November 1993), available at www.bfi.org.uk, accessed 25 October 2023.

182 L.T.C. Rolt, *High Horse Riderless* (Hartland, 1988).

183 Conford, *The Development of the Organic Network*, pp. 269–73 and 362–3.

184 John Seymour, *The Fat of the Land* [1961] (London, 1974), p. 9.

185 Ibid., p. 21.

186 Ibid., pp. 39 and 9.

187 Ibid., p. 41.

188 Ibid., p. 164.

189 Ibid., p. 169.

190 Ibid., p. 163. John Seymour, *Self-Sufficiency* (London, 1973); John Seymour, *The Complete Book of Self-Sufficiency* (London, 1976).

191 The Agriculture Act 2020, House of Commons Library Briefing Paper CBP 8702, p. 6, available at https://commonslibrary.parliament.uk, accessed 27 October 2023.

192 Ibid., p. 18.

193 Department for Environment, Food and Rural Affairs, *The Path to Sustainable Farming: An Agricultural Transition Plan 2021 to 2024*, p. 7, 30 November 2020, www.gov.uk, accessed 27 October 2023.

194 Ibid., p. 4.

195 Ibid., p. 5.

4 English Nature

1 Department of the Environment, *How Do You Want to Live? A Report on the Human Habitat* (London, 1972).

2 Ibid., pp. x–xi.

3 Philip Larkin, 'Aubade', in *Collected Poems* (London, 2003), pp. 190–91.

4 Philip Larkin, 'Going, Going', in *Collected Poems* (London, 2003), pp. 133–4.

5 John Fowles, 'On Being English but Not British', in *Wormholes: Essays and Occasional Writings* (London, 1998), pp. 79–88 (p. 88).

6 Meredith Veldman, *Fantasy, the Bomb and the Greening of Britain: Romantic Protest, 1945–1980* (Cambridge, 1994); Denis Cosgrove, *Apollo's Eye: A Cartographic Genealogy of the Earth in the Western Imagination* (Baltimore, MD, 2001).

7 David Matless, *About England* (London, 2023), pp. 225–7.

8 Department of the Environment, *Sinews for Survival: A Report on the Management of Natural Resources* (London, 1972); Department of the Environment, *Pollution: Nuisance or Nemesis? A Report on the Control of Pollution* (London, 1972); Department of the Environment, *50 Million Volunteers: A Report on the Role of Voluntary Organisations and Youth in the Environment* (London, 1972).
9 Department of the Environment, *The Human Environment: The British View* (London, 1972), p. 6.
10 Ibid., p. 7.
11 Ibid., p. 26; the sentence quoted on England was followed by: 'Large areas of Scotland and Wales are strikingly beautiful.'
12 Matthew Kelly, Claudia Leal, Emily Wakild and Wilko Graf von Hardenberg, 'Introduction', in *The Nature State*, ed. Wilko Graf von Hardenberg, Matthew Kelly, Claudia Leal and Emily Wakild (Abingdon, 2017), pp. 1–15 (p. 1). See also Matthew Kelly, *Quartz and Feldspar: Dartmoor, a British Landscape in Modern Times* (London, 2015) for an illuminating regional study of parallel environmental and landscape issues on Dartmoor. For an excellent general account see Matthew Kelly, 'The Politics of the British Environment since 1945', *Political Quarterly*, XCIV (2023), pp. 208–15.
13 Department of the Environment, *The Human Environment*, p. 38.
14 David Matless, 'Checking the Sea: Geographies of Authority on the East Norfolk Coast, 1790–1932', *Rural History*, XXX (2019), pp. 215–40; James Winter, *Secure from Rash Assault: Sustaining the Victorian Environment* (Berkeley, CA, 1999).
15 J.R.R. Tolkien, *The Return of the King* (London, 1955), p. 185; quoted in Department of the Environment, *Sinews for Survival*, p. xi.
16 Department of the Environment, *Sinews for Survival*, p. 2.
17 Department of the Environment, *Pollution: Nuisance or Nemesis?*, p. 83.
18 Department of the Environment, *50 Million Volunteers*, p. 3.
19 Ibid., p. xiii.
20 Ibid., p. 18.
21 Ibid., p. xv.
22 Jon Agar, '"Future Forecast – Changeable and Probably Getting Worse": The UK Government's Early Response to Anthropogenic Climate Change', *Twentieth Century British History*, XXVI (2015), pp. 602–28.
23 Donella Meadows, Dennis Meadows, Jorgen Randers and William Behrens, *The Limits to Growth* (London, 1972).
24 Philip Larkin, 'Homage to a Government', in *Collected Poems* (London, 2003), p. 141.
25 Matthew Kelly, *The Women Who Saved the English Countryside* (London, 2022), p. 319.
26 Nature Conservancy, *The Countryside in 1970* (London, 1964), p. 96.
27 HRH The Prince Philip, Duke of Edinburgh, '"Countryside in 1970" Conference Opening Address', *International Journal of Environmental Studies*, I (1971), pp. 321–4 (p. 322).
28 Nature Conservancy, *The Countryside in 1970*, p. 29.

29 Matthew Kelly, 'Conventional Thinking and the Fragile Birth of the Nature State in Post-War Britain', in *The Nature State*, ed. Graf von Hardenberg, Kelly, Leal and Wakild, pp. 114–34 (p. 122).
30 Michael Dower, *The Challenge of Leisure* (London, 1965), p. 5.
31 Ibid., inside front cover.
32 Ibid., pp. 5 and 67.
33 Ibid., pp. 4–5.
34 J. Allan Patmore, *Land and Leisure* [1970] (Harmondsworth, 1972), pp. 304–6.
35 Ibid., pp. 103, 105 and 110.
36 Ibid., p. 111.
37 Ibid., plate 10, between pp. 162 and 163.
38 Ibid., p. 112.
39 Peter Nichols, 'The Gorge', in *The Television Dramatist*, ed. Robert Muller (London, 1973), pp. 71–148; quotations from pp. 73–5, which reproduces the 1968 preface to *The Gorge* by Nichols. In September 2023 a copy of 'The Gorge' was posted on YouTube by Billy Hamon, who played Mike in the film: www.youtube.com, accessed 27 October 2023.
40 Ibid., p. 129.
41 The debates here extended earlier arguments from before, during and after the Second World War; see David Matless, *Landscape and Englishness* (London, 1998, rev. 2016). Similar debates occurred around leisure and lockdown in the Covid-19 pandemic; see Matless, *About England*, pp. 92–4.
42 Nature Conservancy, *The Countryside in 1970*, p. 19; Colin Buchanan, *Traffic in Towns: The Specially Shortened Edition of the Buchanan Report* (Harmondsworth, 1964).
43 Nature Conservancy, *The Countryside in 1970*, p. 31.
44 Ibid., p. 30.
45 Garth Christian, *Tomorrow's Countryside: The Road to the Seventies* (London, 1966), p. 7.
46 Ibid., p. 6.
47 Ibid., p. 177.
48 Ibid., p. 6.
49 Ibid., facing p. 180.
50 Ibid., p. 61.
51 David Matless, Charles Watkins and Paul Merchant, 'Nature Trails: The Production of Instructive Landscapes in Britain, 1960–72', *Rural History*, XXI (2010), pp. 97–131.
52 'Report on the Public Use of East Wretham Heath Nature Reserve by the Warden', July 1970, East Wretham Heath Nature Reserve Management Committee file, Norfolk Wildlife Trust Archive; quoted in Matless et al., 'Nature Trails', p. 123.
53 Fairbrother, *New Lives, New Landscapes*, p. 101.
54 Timothy Luke, 'The World Wildlife Fund: Ecocolonialism as Funding the Worldwide "Wise Use" of Nature', *Capitalism Nature Socialism*, VIII (1997), pp. 31–61.
55 Richard Fitter and Peter Scott, *The Penitent Butchers: The Fauna Preservation Society, 1903–1978* (London, 1978).

56 Nature Conservancy, *The Countryside in 1970*, p. 94.
57 Ibid., p. 95.
58 Ibid., p. 97.
59 Anthony Clayton, 'Baring, (Charles) Evelyn, first Baron Howick of Glendale', *Oxford Dictionary of National Biography* (2004).
60 John Sheail, '*Torrey Canyon*: The Political Dimension', *Journal of Contemporary History*, XLII (2007), pp. 485–504; Anna Green and Timothy Cooper, 'Community and Exclusion: The *Torrey Canyon* Disaster of 1967', *Journal of Social History*, XLVIII (2015), pp. 892–909; Timothy Cooper and Anna Green, 'The *Torrey Canyon* Disaster, Everyday Life, and the "Greening" of Britain', *Environmental History*, XXII (2017), pp. 101–26; Simone Turchetti, 'The UK Government's Environmentalism: Britain, NATO and the Origins of Environmental Diplomacy', in *Histories of Technology, the Environment and Modern Britain*, ed. Jon Agar and Jacob Ward (London, 2018), pp. 252–70.
61 J. E. Smith, ed., *'Torrey Canyon' Pollution and Marine Life* (Cambridge, 1968), pp. 36–7.
62 Crispin Gill, Frank Booker and Tony Soper, *The Wreck of the Torrey Canyon* (Newton Abbot, 1967); D. J. Bellamy, P. H. Clarke, D. M. John, D. Jones, A. Whittick and T. Darke, 'Effects of Pollution from the *Torrey Canyon* on Littoral and Sublittoral Ecosystems', *Nature*, CCXVI (1967), pp. 1170–73.
63 Smith, *'Torrey Canyon' Pollution and Marine Life*, p. 184.
64 Ibid., p. 174.
65 Bellamy et al., 'Effects of Pollution', p. 1173.
66 Smith, *'Torrey Canyon' Pollution and Marine Life*, p. 73.
67 Ibid., p. 176.
68 Ibid., p. 16.
69 Ibid., p. 4.
70 Ibid., p. ii.
71 John Barr, ed., *The Environmental Handbook: Action Guide for the UK* (London, 1971), back cover.
72 Veldman, *Fantasy, the Bomb and the Greening of Britain*.
73 Max Nicholson, *The Environmental Revolution* (London, 1970).
74 Hughes reviewed Nicholson's book in summer 1970 for *Your Environment*, I, reprinted as Ted Hughes, 'The Environmental Revolution', in *Winter Pollen* (London, 1994), pp. 128–35 (p. 131).
75 The Ecologist, 'A Blueprint for Survival', *The Ecologist*, II/1 (1972).
76 The Ecologist, *A Blueprint for Survival* (Harmondsworth, 1972).
77 Ecologist, 'A Blueprint for Survival', p. 14.
78 Ibid., p. 15.
79 Ibid., p. 16.
80 William Morris, *News from Nowhere* (London, 1891).
81 William Morris, 'Prologue to *The Earthly Paradise*', in *News from Nowhere and Selected Writing and Designs* (Harmondsworth, 1986), p. 68.
82 Ecologist, 'A Blueprint for Survival', p. 17.
83 The Ecologist, 'And now, live from Cornwall . . .', *The Ecologist*, III/1 (1973), p. 9.

84 Henry Pool and John Fleet, 'The Conservation of Cornwall', *The Ecologist*, III/1 (1973), pp. 26–9 (p. 29).
85 Veldman, *Fantasy, the Bomb and the Greening of Britain*, p. 238, notes how at the Stockholm conference, Third World representatives would challenge the idea that development was the problem.
86 Quoted ibid., p. 235.
87 Ecologist, 'A Blueprint for Survival', p. 23. Survival International was set up in 1969 by explorer Robin Hanbury-Tenison, initially as the Primitive Peoples Fund.
88 Frank Fraser Darling, *Wilderness and Plenty* (London, 1970).
89 James Robertson, 'Goldsmith, Edward Rene David [Teddy]', *Oxford Dictionary of National Biography* (2013); Walter Schwarz, 'Edward Goldsmith obituary', *The Guardian*, 29 August 2009, p. 37.
90 Edward Goldsmith, 'Editorial', *The Ecologist*, I/1 (1971), p. 2.
91 Ibid., p. 5. Willson's cartoon was also reproduced as the frontispiece of Edward Goldsmith and Nicholas Hildyard, eds, *Green Britain or Industrial Wasteland?* (Cambridge, 1986), p. ii.
92 Rachel Moseley, *Hand-Made Television: Stop-Frame Animation for Children in Britain, 1961–1974* (London, 2016), p. 43.
93 Ibid., pp. 58–61 and 77–9; Oliver Postgate, *Seeing Things: An Autobiography* (London, 2000).
94 Postgate, *Seeing Things*, p. 273.
95 The soundtrack was issued in 2001 by Trunk Records as *Vernon Elliott, Clangers: Original Television Music by Vernon Elliott*.
96 Oliver Postgate and Peter Firmin, *The Sky-Moos* (London, 1993), no pagination.
97 Postgate, *Seeing Things*, p. 306.
98 *The Guardian*, 16 October 2006, p. 12.
99 Elisabeth Beresford, *The Wombles of Wimbledon* (London, 1976), quotation from author blurb inside back cover. On Beresford see the biography by her daughter, Kate Robertson, *The Creator of the Wombles: The First Biography of Elisabeth Beresford* (London, 2023).
100 Elisabeth Beresford, *The Wombles* [1968] (Harmondsworth, 1972, quotation from back cover. For one book, *The Wombles at Work* (1973) the Wombles moved to Hyde Park. In other books American, Russian and Chinese Wombles are also mentioned, but each Womble family is said to like to keep to itself. The television adaptations were very much focused on the Wimbledon burrow.
101 Beresford, *The Wombles*, p. 19.
102 Madame Cholet was not French in Beresford's books: 'She wasn't really French, but when years ago the time had come for her to choose her name, she had picked out a town in France because she had once heard that was the country where the cooking was wonderful'; Beresford, *The Wombles*, p. 68.
103 Garrett Hardin, 'The Tragedy of the Commons', *Science*, CLXII (1968), pp. 1243–8; Hardin's article was reprinted for Friends of the Earth in the anthology section of *The Environmental Handbook: Action Guide for the UK*, ed. John Barr (London, 1971), pp. 47–65. Hardin suggested the need for 'mutual coercion, mutually agreed upon by the majority of

the people affected' (p. 61), including in population control: 'The only way we can preserve and nurture other and more precious freedoms is by relinquishing the freedom to breed, and that very soon' (p. 64). *The Environmental Handbook* also included an extract from Kenneth Mellanby's *Pesticides and Pollution* (pp. 135–41), discussed in Chapter 3 above, and on farming also featured Michael Allaby on 'British Farming: Revolution or Suicide?' (pp. 143–50).

104 Beresford, *The Wombles of Wimbledon*, p. 24.

105 Beresford, *The Wombles*, p. 10.

106 Ibid., pp. 8 and 11.

107 J. Dodson and V. Wheelock, 'Letter to the editor', *Environmental Studies*, x (1977), pp. 196–7.

108 Jos Smith, *The New Nature Writing* (London, 2017), p. 1, opens by stating of Mabey: 'One figure, like no other, looms large in setting the ground for the contemporary form that has come to be called the New Nature Writing.' On the longer history of connections between the human and natural in England, see Keith Thomas, *Man and the Natural World* (London, 1983).

109 Richard Mabey, *The Unofficial Countryside* (London, 1973), p. 48.

110 Ibid., p. 50.

111 Kenneth Allsop, *Adventure Lit Their Star* (London, 1949), p. 9. On Allsop, see Richard Mabey, 'Kenneth Allsop', in *Turning the Boat for Home* (London, 2019), pp. 151–6.

112 Mabey, *The Unofficial Countryside*, p. 14.

113 Ibid., pp. 15–16.

114 Walter Benjamin, *Charles Baudelaire: A Lyric Poet in the Era of High Capitalism* (London, 1973), p. 36; Rebecca Solnit, *Wanderlust: A History of Walking* (London, 2001), pp. 196–213.

115 Mabey, *The Unofficial Countryside*, pp. 25–6.

116 Ibid., p. 77; on the giant hogweed, see also Richard Mabey, *Flora Britannica* (London, 1996), pp. 294–6.

117 Mabey, *The Unofficial Countryside*, p. 149; Richard Jefferies, *Nature near London* (London, 1879).

118 Mabey, *The Unofficial Countryside*, p. 140.

119 Ibid., p. 142.

120 Ibid., p. 172.

121 Richard Fitter, *London's Natural History* (London, 1945); Matless, *Landscape and Englishness*, pp. 314–16.

122 Eric Simms, *Woodland Birds* (London, 1971); Eric Simms, *The Public Life of the Street Pigeon* (London, 1979). On Metro-land, see also Matless, *About England*, pp. 125–7.

123 Mabey, *The Unofficial Countryside*, p. 14.

124 Marion Shoard, 'Edgelands of Promise', *Landscapes*, 1 (2000), pp. 74–93.

125 Paul Farley and Michael Symmons Roberts, *Edgelands* (London, 2011).

126 Richard Mabey, 'Introduction: Not On Speaking Terms', in *Class*, ed. Richard Mabey (London, 1967), pp. 7–18 (p. 17).

127 Kenneth Allsop, 'Pop Goes Young Woodley', in *Class*, ed. Richard Mabey (London, 1967), pp. 127–44 (p. 140).

128 Ibid., p. 133; the 'Young Woodley' title of Allsop's essay derived from a 1925 public school play.

129 Mabey, ed., *Class*, p. 174; Kenneth Allsop, *Hard Travellin': The Hobo and His History* (London, 1967).
130 Richard Mabey, *Food for Free* (London, 1972), p. 9.
131 Ibid., p. 11.
132 Ibid., p. 15.
133 Richard Mabey, *The Common Ground* (London, 1981), p. 30.
134 Ibid., p. 27.
135 Ibid., p. 22; on contemporary studies of Clare, see Matless, *About England*, pp. 53–5.
136 Mabey, *The Common Ground*, p. 13.
137 Ibid., p. 35.
138 Ibid., pp. 37 and 41.
139 Ibid., p. 43.
140 Gilbert White, *The Natural History of Selborne*, ed. Richard Mabey (Harmondsworth, 1977); Richard Mabey, *Gilbert White* (London, 1986).
141 Mabey, *The Common Ground*, p. 246. Hughes's poem was first published in *The Listener*, 16 May 1974, and appeared in his 1976 collection *Season Songs*; Ted Hughes, *Collected Poems* (London, 2003), pp. 315–16.
142 On Common Ground, see Matless, *About England*, pp. 166–73; Smith, *The New Nature Writing*, pp. 35–53.
143 Angela King and Sue Clifford, eds, *Trees Be Company* (London, 1989); Neil Sinden, *In a Nutshell* (London, 1989).
144 Richard Mabey, ed., *Second Nature* (London, 1984), p. x.
145 Smith, *The New Nature Writing*, p. 37.
146 Sue Clifford and Angela King, *England in Particular* (London, 2006).
147 Norman Nicholson, 'Ten-Yard Panorama', in *Second Nature*, ed. Richard Mabey (London, 1984), pp. 3–11 (p. 3).
148 Richard Mabey, 'Introduction: Entitled to a View?', in *Second Nature*, ed. Mabey, pp. ix–xix (p. xv).
149 Norman Nicholson, *Collected Poems* (London, 1994), p. 186.
150 Mabey, 'Introduction: Entitled to a View?', p. x.
151 Raymond Williams, 'Between Country and City', in *Second Nature*, ed. Mabey, pp. 209–19 (p. 209).
152 Ibid., pp. 215 and 219.
153 Sue Clifford and Angela King, eds, *Field Days: An Anthology of Poetry* (Totnes, 1998); Common Ground, *A Manifesto for Fields* (London, 1997), available at www.commonground.org.uk, accessed 27 October 2023.
154 Clifford and King, *England in Particular*.
155 Andy Goldsworthy, *Sheepfolds* (London, 1996), p. 16. Goldsworthy's late 1990s project 'Arch' took a red sandstone arch along former droving routes between southern Scotland and northern England, from the artist's Dumfriesshire home through Cumbria to Kirkby Lonsdale, the arch pictured popping up in fields, villages, towns, by country lanes and overlooking the M6, an incongruous form present in and speaking of and to regional agrarian history; Andy Goldsworthy and David Craig, *Arch* (London, 1999). On Goldsworthy, see David Matless and George Revill, 'A Solo Ecology: The Erratic Art of Andy Goldsworthy', *Ecumene*, 11 (1995), pp. 423–48.

156 Richard Mabey and Tony Evans, *The Flowering of Britain* (London, 1980), p. 16. Evans's previous work included Brian Rice and Tony Evans, *The English Sunrise* (London, 1972), on suburban architectural form; see Matless, *About England*, pp. 121–2.
157 Mabey and Evans, *The Flowering of Britain*, p. 20.
158 Ibid., p. 32.
159 Ibid., p. 16.
160 Mabey, *Flora Britannica*, p. 9. Mabey followed *Flora Britannica* by beginning work on an equivalent *Birds Britannica*, for which Mark Cocker became main author; Mark Cocker and Richard Mabey, *Birds Britannica* (London, 2005). This was followed by Peter Marren and Richard Mabey, *Bugs Britannica* (London, 2010).
161 Mabey, *Flora Britannica*, pp. 12 and 7.
162 Ibid., p. 10.
163 Ibid., p. 8; *Flora Britannica* includes a separate account by Peter Marren of Scottish vernacular plant names, pp. 450–55.
164 Ibid., p. 385.
165 Ibid., p. 40.
166 Jason Cowley, 'The New Nature Writing', *Granta*, CII (2008), pp. 7–12 (p. 10).
167 Richard Mabey, *Nature Cure* (London, 2005), p. 134.
168 Ibid., p. 102.
169 Ibid., p. 129.
170 Kelly, 'Conventional Thinking and the Fragile Birth of the Nature State'; Matless, *Landscape and Englishness*, pp. 304–17.
171 John Sheail, *Nature in Trust: The History of Nature Conservation in Britain* (London, 1976); John Sheail, *Nature Conservation in Britain: The Formative Years* (London, 1998); John Sheail, *An Environmental History of Twentieth-Century Britain* (London, 2002).
172 Quoted in the November 2021 press release for the Act: 'World-leading environment act becomes law', 10 November 2021, www.gov.uk, accessed 27 October 2023.
173 Helen Macdonald, *H is for Hawk* (London, 2016); Helen Macdonald, *Falcon* (London, 2006).
174 Macdonald, *H is for Hawk*, p. 207; T. H. White, *The Goshawk* (London, 1951); on Apple Day, see Matless, *About England*, p. 173.
175 There is a parallel here with Melissa Harrison, *All Among the Barley* (London, 2018), a novel set in 1930s rural England, which narrates a meeting of pastoral and hard right politics; see Matless, *About England*, pp. 39–42.

5 England and the Anthropocene

1 Paul Crutzen and Eugene Stoermer, 'The "Anthropocene"', *IGBP Newsletter* (May 2000), pp. 17–18.
2 Jan Zalasiewicz et al., 'The Working Group on the Anthropocene: Summary of Evidence and Interim Recommendations', *Anthropocene*, XIX (2017) pp. 55–60; Colin Waters et al., 'The Anthropocene is Functionally and Stratigraphically Different from the Holocene', *Science*,

cccli/6269 (2016), pp. 137–47; David Matless, 'The Anthroposcenic', *Transactions of the Institute of British Geographers*, xlii (2017) pp. 363–76; David Matless, 'Climate Change Stories and the Anthroposcenic', *Nature Climate Change*, vi (2016), pp. 118–19; David Matless, 'The Anthroposcenic: Landscape in the Anthropocene', *British Art Studies*, x, 29 November 2018, www.britishartstudies.ac.uk, accessed 25 October 2023; David Matless, 'Checking the Sea: Geographies of Authority on the East Norfolk Coast, 1790–1932', *Rural History*, xxx (2019), pp. 215–40.

3 Alec Finlay, 'From *A Place-Aware Dictionary*', in *Antlers of Water: Writing on the Nature and Environment of Scotland*, ed. Kathleen Jamie (Edinburgh, 2020), pp. 243–60 (p. 245).

4 Matless, 'The Anthroposcenic'; Matless, 'The Anthroposcenic: Landscape in the Anthropocene'.

5 H. H. Swinnerton, *Fossils* (London, 1960), p. xiv.

6 For a discussion of the twentieth- and twenty-first-century cultures of the Carboniferous, see Rebecca Solnit, *Orwell's Roses* (London, 2021), pp. 57–61.

7 Swinnerton, *Fossils*, p. 84. 'St George's Land' was used by other commentators, including geographer Dudley Stamp in a related New Naturalist volume; L. Dudley Stamp, *Britain's Structure and Scenery* (London, 1946), pp. 113–18. The area was later more commonly termed the Wales-Brabant Massif, or Wales-Brabant Island, stretching west–east across the present-day Midland England from either side.

8 James Secord, 'King of Siluria: Roderick Murchison and The Imperial Theme in Nineteenth-Century British Geology', *Victorian Studies*, xxv (1982), pp. 413–42; James Secord, *Visions of Science* (Oxford, 2014).

9 Doreen Massey, 'Landscape as a Provocation: Reflections on Moving Mountains', *Journal of Material Culture*, xi (2006), pp. 33–48.

10 Swinnerton, *Fossils*, p. 103.

11 Charles Lyell, *Principles of Geology*, vol. ii, 10th edn (London, 1866), p. 563.

12 Swinnerton, *Fossils*, p. 246. Swinnerton's comment on breaking into 'the precincts of geography' reflects his own institutional career, as Head of the Department of Geology and Geography at the University of Nottingham until Geography formed its own Department in 1934. This book has been written in that department, which outlasted Geology (now closed), and where a Swinnerton Laboratory acknowledges his founding role.

13 Jan Zalasiewicz, Colin Waters, Mark Williams, David Aldridge and Ian Wilkinson, 'The Stratigraphical Signature of the Anthropocene in England', *Proceedings of the Geologists' Association*, cxxix (2018), pp. 482–91 (p. 483).

14 Ibid., p. 490.

15 Ibid., p. 486.

16 Ibid., p. 488.

17 See Laura Devlin, 'Norfolk Beach Walker Finds Crisp Packet from 1960s', *bbc News East*, 16 May 2023, www.bbc.co.uk.

18 David Matless, *About England* (London, 2023), pp. 243–53.

19 M. John Harrison, *The Sunken Land Begins to Rise Again* (London, 2020), p. 198.

20 Ibid., p. 46.
21 Ibid., p. 108.
22 Norman Nicholson, *Provincial Pleasures* (London, 1959). See also the topographical account in Norman Nicholson, *Cumberland and Westmorland* (London, 1949). On Nicholson, see Kathleen Jones, *Norman Nicholson: The Whispering Poet* (Appleby, 2013); David Cooper, 'Envisioning "the cubist fells": Ways of Seeing in the Poetry of Norman Nicholson', in *Poetry and Geography: Space and Place in Post-War Poetry*, ed. Neal Alexander and David Cooper (Liverpool, 2013), pp. 148–60; David Cooper, 'The Post-Industrial Picturesque? Placing and Promoting Marginalised Millom', in *The Making of a Cultural Landscape: The English Lake District as Tourist Destination, 1750–2010*, ed. John K. Walton and Jason Wood (London, 2013), pp. 241–62; Andrew Gibson, '"At the Dying Atlantic's Edge": Norman Nicholson and the Cumbrian Coast', in *Coastal Works: Cultures of the Atlantic Edge*, ed. Nicholas Allen (Oxford, 2017), pp. 77–92.
23 Norman Nicholson, 'On the Closing of Millom Ironworks', in *Collected Poems* (London, 1994), pp. 297–8.
24 Norman Nicholson, 'On the Dismantling of Millom Ironworks', in *Collected Poems*, pp. 359–60. Nicholson's 1972 collection *A Local Habitation* includes, alongside 'On the Closing of Millom Ironworks', the poems 'Bee Orchid at Hodbarrow' (*Collected Poems*, pp. 276–8), and 'Hodbarrow Flooded' (*Collected Poems*, p. 279); there is also the anti-nuclear poem 'Windscale' (*Collected Poems*, p. 282). Millom could also be gathered under the category of 'edgelands', noted in Chapter Four above, and the former ironworks site would certainly register as Mabey's 'unofficial countryside'. For a photographic investigation of such themes in former industrial and other 'edgeland' sites around Peterborough, see Marc Atkinson and Ken Worpole, *Along the Outskirts* (Peterborough, 2016).
25 Richard Mabey, *Nature Cure* (London, 2005), p. 19.
26 Bruno Latour, *We Have Never Been Modern* (Hemel Hempstead, 1993).
27 Jonathan Raban, 'Second Nature: The De-Landscaping of the American West', *Granta*, CII (2008), pp. 53–85 (p. 55). On the entanglement of humans and birds, see Richard Smyth, *An Indifference of Birds* (Axminster, 2020). For insightful reflection on the Anthropocene and the Anthropogenic, see Laura Cameron, 'Resources of Hope: Wicken Fen Stories of Anthropogenic Nature', *Cambridge Anthropology*, XXXI (2013), pp. 105–18.
28 Tim Dee, 'Introduction', in *Ground Work*, ed. Tim Dee (London, 2018), pp. 1–14 (p. 1).
29 Ibid., pp. 1 and 6.
30 Tim Dee, *Landfill* (London, 2018), p. 11. Dee's nature writing began with his birding life in *The Running Sky* (London, 2009), followed by *Four Fields* (London, 2013) tracking birds and humanly worked land in the English Fens, Zambia, the USA and Ukraine: 'Without fields – no us. Without us – no fields' (p. 3). *Landfill* was published by Little Toller Books, whose publisher Adrian Cooper also heads Common Ground; on nature writing and the wild, see Jos Smith, *The New Nature Writing*

(London, 2017), pp. 71–102; Dominic Head, *Nature Prose: Writing in Ecological Crisis* (Oxford, 2022); David Matless, 'Nature Voices', *Journal of Historical Geography*, xxxv (2009), pp. 178–88.
31 Richard Mabey, *The Unofficial Countryside* (London, 1973), p. 162.
32 Dee, *Landfill*, pp. 14–15 and 11.
33 Ibid., p. 15.
34 Ibid., p. 130; Dee notes that this was a rare sighting he missed.
35 Niko Tinbergen, *The Herring Gull's World* (London, 1953); Tinbergen studied gull colonies on sandy coasts, but also noted: 'As scavengers, the gulls come to harbours and towns, where they devour refuse, often of the most appalling kind' (p. 28).
36 Mabey, *Nature Cure*, p. 212.
37 Gerard Manley Hopkins, 'Inversnaid', in *Poems and Prose of Gerard Manley Hopkins* (Harmondsworth, 1953), pp. 50–51.
38 Richard Mabey, *Weeds* (London, 2010), p. 20.
39 For Simon Roberts's *The Weeds and the Wilderness*, see www.simoncroberts.com, accessed 27 October 2023; Harriet Judd, 'Simon Roberts: Inscapes', in *Ivon Hitchens: Space through Colour*, exh. cat., Pallant House Gallery, Chichester (2019), pp. 100–105. It is notable that a detail from a Hitchens painting, *Warnford Water, 1960 First Variation*, had appeared on the cover of an earlier Penguin collection, Gerard Manley Hopkins, *Poems and Prose of Gerard Manley Hopkins*, ed. W. H. Gardner (Harmondsworth, 1953). The collection was reprinted almost annually from 1960. The Hitchens image appears on the front and back cover of my copy of the 1979 paperback reprint, and from a library copy was there in 1974, if not earlier.
40 Quotation from 'The Weeds and the Wilderness', www.simoncroberts.com.
41 A recording of Motion's CPRE reading is available at 'Sir Andrew Motion reads "Inversnaid" poem', www.youtube.com, accessed 27 October 2023.
42 Christopher Sandom and Sophie Wynne-Jones, 'Rewilding a Country: Britain as a Study Case', in *Rewilding*, ed. Nathalie Pettorelli, Sarah Durant and Johan du Toit (Cambridge, 2019), pp. 222–47; Kelly, *Quartz and Feldspar*, pp. 417–27; Richard Smyth, 'Human Nature', *Times Literary Supplement*, 19/26 August 2016, pp. 19–21.
43 Virginia Thomas, 'Domesticating Rewilding: Interpreting Rewilding in England's Green and Pleasant Land', *Environmental Values*, xxxi (2022), pp. 515–32 (p. 516).
44 Jamie Lorimer, *Wildlife in the Anthropocene: Conservation after Nature* (Minneapolis, MN, 2015), pp. 97–118; Jamie Lorimer and Clemens Driessen, 'Wild Experiments: Rewilding Future Ecologies at the Oostvaardersplassen', *Transactions of the Institute of British Geographers*, xxxix (2014), pp. 169–81.
45 Mabey, *Nature Cure*, pp. 73–4.
46 Ibid., p. 90.
47 Isabella Tree, *Wilding* (London, 2018).
48 Frans Vera, *Grazing Ecology and Forest History* (Wallingford, 2002).
49 Tree, *Wilding*, p. 113.
50 Ibid., p. 107.
51 Ibid., p. 129.

52 Ibid., p. 70.
53 Ibid., p. 1.
54 Ibid., pp. 70 and 57.
55 Ibid., p. 52.
56 Ibid., p. 150, and map p. xviv.
57 Ibid., p. 292.
58 On Longleat, see Andrew Flack, 'Lions Loose on a Gentleman's Lawn: Animality, Authenticity and Automobility in the Emergence of the English Safari Park', *Journal of Historical Geography*, LIV (2016), pp. 38–49; Matless, *About England*, pp. 202–5.
59 For 'The Turtle Dove', see the records of the English Folk Dance and Song Society at the Vaughan Williams Memorial Library, www.vwml.org.
60 'The Turtle Dove Pilgrimage', BBC Radio 4, 14 March 2019, available at www.bbc.co.uk, accessed 27 October 2023. Lee also held a three-night turtle dove event on 8–11 June 2023 'to "re-wild" one of Britain's ancient traditional songs back to the very birds that inspired the folk song'; www.samleesong.co.uk. On Lee's work, see also Lee Robert Blackstone, 'The Aural and Moral Idylls of "Englishness" and Folk Music', *Symbolic Interaction*, XL (2017), pp. 561–80. Blackstone discusses Lee as a Jewish singer growing up in England and engaging with English landscape, presenting connections of music and land through 'outsider communities' such as travellers, with folk the music of 'the unspoken classes', and 'so connected to the land', quotations from interview with Lee, p. 577.
61 Merry also produced the cover art for Shirley Collins's 2020 album *Heart's Ease*, a work discussed in Chapter 7 below.
62 George Monbiot, *Feral* (London, 2013).
63 Tree, *Wilding*, p. 10.
64 Ibid., p. 299.
65 Monbiot, *Feral*, p. 10; On Feral, see Smith, *The New Nature Writing*, pp. 93–6; Matthew Kelly, *The Women Who Saved the English Countryside* (London, 2022), pp. 327–31. Monbiot took issue with Vera's emphasis on wood pasture as a natural prevailing habitat, as 'overwhelmingly' not supported by evidence (*Feral*, p. 219), and instead promoted forest as a natural ecology.
66 Monbiot, *Feral*, pp. 10–11.
67 Ibid., pp. 32–3.
68 Ibid., p. 12.
69 Ibid., p. 11.
70 Ibid., p. 226; *Feral* makes the same argument for upland Wales as the 'Cambrian Desert', p. 64.
71 Ibid., p. 209.
72 Ibid., p. 154.
73 George Monbiot, 'Obstinate Questionings', *The Guardian*, 3 September 2013, also available at www.monbiot.com; see also Monbiot, *Feral*, pp. 153–66.
74 George Monbiot, 'The Lie of the Land', *The Guardian*, 12 July 2017, also available at www.monbiot.com.

75 Monbiot, *Feral*, p. 177.
76 Martin Varley, ed., *Flora of the Fells* (Kendal, 2003), p. 11.
77 Ibid., p. 12.
78 Ibid., p. 33.
79 James Rebanks, *The Shepherd's Life* (London, 2015), p. 121.
80 Monbiot, 'The Lie of the Land'.
81 Rebanks, *The Shepherd's Life*, p. 121.
82 James Rebanks, *English Pastoral* (London, 2020), pp. 178 and 187.
83 Kelly, *The Women Who Saved the English Countryside*, p. 330.
84 Rebanks, *English Pastoral*, pp. 274, 269 and 203.
85 Richard Jefferies, *After London, or Wild England* [1885] (Oxford, 1980).
86 John Fowles, 'Introduction', ibid., pp. vii–xxi (p. xvii).
87 Ibid., p. xviii.
88 Jefferies, *After London*, p. 14.
89 Richard Jefferies, *The Story of My Heart* (London, 1883).
90 Jefferies, *After London*, p. 1.
91 John Wyndham, *The Day of the Triffids* [1951] (London, 1999); Amy Binns, *Hidden Wyndham: Life, Love, Letters* (Hebden Bridge, 2019). *The Day of the Triffids* has a Cold War setting, Wyndham's triffids a product of Soviet experiment, and their seeds dispersed around the world after an air accident.
92 John Wyndham, *The Midwich Cuckoos* (London, 1957); John Wyndham, *Trouble with Lichen* (London, 1960).
93 Wyndham, *Day of the Triffids*, p. 206.
94 Ibid., pp. 206–7.
95 Ibid., p. 233.
96 Department of the Environment, *Sinews for Survival*, p. xi; Tolkien, *The Return of the King*, p. 185.
97 Alexandra Harris, *Weatherland: Writers and Artists under English Skies* (London, 2015), p. 384; on the 2010 passport design, see also Matless, *About England*, pp. 48–9.
98 Richard Mabey, *Turned Out Nice Again: On Living With the Weather* (London, 2019), pp. 10–11.
99 Ibid., pp. 11–12.
100 Ibid., p. 94.
101 Ibid., pp. 74–5.
102 Stephen Bone, *British Weather* (London, 1946), pp. 7 and 16.
103 Gordon Manley, *Climate and the British Scene* (London, 1952), p. 4; on Manley, see Georgina Endfield, Lucy Veale and Alexander Hall, 'Gordon Valentine Manley and His Contribution to the Study of Climate Change', *WIREs Climate Change*, VI (2015), pp. 287–99.
104 Manley, *Climate and the British Scene*, pp. 93–4.
105 Ibid., p. 94.
106 Ibid., pp. 180–81.
107 Mabey, *Turned Out Nice Again*, p. 104.
108 Sue Smart and Richard Bothway Howard, *It's Turned Out Nice Again!* (Ely, 2011).
109 Manley, *Climate and the British Scene*, inside front jacket.

110 Tanya Aldred, 'Cricket and Climate Change: How Green is Your Sward?', in *Wisden Cricketers' Almanack 2017*, ed. Lawrence Booth (London, 2017), pp. 65–70 (pp. 66–7).

111 Michael Henderson, *That Will Be England Gone: The Last Summer of Cricket* (London, 2020).

112 Aldred, 'Cricket and Climate Change', p. 67; Henderson's 'last summer' was itself followed by the Covid-19 pandemic, which put a stop to any county cricket-watching for 2020, and delayed the introduction of the Hundred by a year.

113 Tanya Aldred, 'The Environment in 2022: Taking a Stand', in *Wisden Cricketers' Almanack 2023*, ed. Booth, pp. 198–201 (p. 201).

114 Andrew Hignell, 'Weather in 2022: Spring Sleet, Summer Heat', in *Wisden Cricketers' Almanack 2023*, ed. Booth, p. 184.

115 'Derbyshire v Nottinghamshire', match report, in *Wisden Cricketers' Almanack 2023*, ed. Booth, p. 454.

116 This outlook found an echo in the 2023 *Almanack* in Geoffrey Dean's review of club cricket, back to its proper format after the pandemic, which 'at last enjoyed an unencumbered season, blest by some of the best weather since 1976', with 'parched outfields and plenty of high scoring'; Geoffrey Dean, 'ECB Club Leagues in 2022: Season in the Sun', in *Wisden Cricketers' Almanack 2023*, ed. Booth, pp. 749–51 (p. 749).

117 Norman Preston, ed., *Wisden Cricketers' Almanack 1977* (London, 1977), p. 490.

118 Ibid., p. 476.

119 Ibid., p. 110; the 1976 English summer included a five-Test series between England and the West Indies, the tourists winning 3–0 after the first two Tests were drawn.

120 Mike Hulme, *Weathered: Cultures of Climate* (London, 2017), pp. 57–8.

121 For the programme see 'Changing Climate', https://player.bfi.org.uk, accessed 28 October 2023.

122 Quoted in Jon Agar, '"Future Forecast – Changeable and Probably Getting Worse": The UK Government's Early Response to Anthropogenic Climate Change', *Twentieth Century British History*, XXVI (2015), pp. 602–28 (p. 608).; see also Jon Agar, *Science Policy under Thatcher* (London, 2019), pp. 221–60.

123 Agar, 'Future Forecast', p. 614.

124 Quoted in Agar, *Science Policy under Thatcher*, p. 240. Agar notes that climate became an arena for the assertion of British scientific and political leadership, in part through the Antarctic science given renewed funding after the Falklands War, although industrial interests helped shape the interpretation of evidence to emphasize uncertainty and doubt.

125 Crispin Tickell, *Climatic Change and World Affairs* (Oxford, 1978), p. 29.

126 Ibid., p. 11.

127 Daniel Defoe, *The Storm*, ed. Richard Hamblyn (London, 2003); Harris, *Weatherland*, pp. 170–74.

128 Defoe, *The Storm*, p. 186.

129 Bob Ogley, *In the Wake of the Hurricane* (Westerham, 1988), p. 3. Ogley would later publish a series of county 'weather books', on weather

history in Kent, Sussex, Hampshire and the Isle of Wight, Essex and Berkshire, and has also published works on war and local history.

130 Ogley, *In the Wake of the Hurricane*, p. 3.
131 Ibid., p. 94.
132 Ibid., p. 5.
133 Ibid., pp. 5 and 90.
134 Ibid., p. 5.
135 Ibid., p. 82.
136 Ibid., p. 133.
137 Ibid., p. 20.
138 Ibid., p. 36.
139 Richard Mabey, 'Wildness as an Aesthetic Quality', in *Arcadia Revisited: The Place of Landscape*, ed. Vicki Berger and Isabel Vasseur (London, 1997), pp. 180–93 (pp. 188–9).
140 Quoted in Richard Mabey, *Beechcombings: The Narratives of Trees* (London, 2007), pp. 244–5; Mabey, *Turned Out Nice Again*, pp. 98–9.
141 Mabey, *Beechcombings*, pp. 242–3.
142 Ibid., pp. 249–50.
143 Ibid., p. 243.
144 Ogley, *In the Wake of the Hurricane*, pp. 78 and 42.
145 Ibid., p. 14.
146 Richard Mabey, 'The Great Storm', in *A Brush with Nature* (London, 2010), pp. 84–5.
147 Wyndham Lewis, ed., *BLAST: Review of the Great English Vortex* (London, 1914), p. 14, available at https://repository.library.brown.edu, accessed 28 October 2023; Harris, *Weatherland*, pp. 331–2.
148 George Szirtes, *New and Collected Poems* (Hexham, 2008), p. 450.
149 Hulme, *Weathered*, p. 11; also p. 154.
150 Ibid., p. 153.
151 'Just Stop Oil "re-imagine" The Hay Wain', www.youtube.com, accessed 28 October 2028. On the conviction of the protesters, see 'Just Stop Oil: Protesters Guilty of John Constable Masterpiece Damage', *BBC News*, www.bbc.co.uk, 6 December 2022. On a previous use of the *Hay Wain* in anti-nuclear artistic protest by Peter Kennard, see Matless, *About England*, pp. 88–9.
152 HRH The Prince of Wales, Tony Juniper and Emily Shuckburgh, *Climate Change* (London, 2017), p. 44.
153 Ibid., p. 43. On Tunnicliffe, see Ian Niall, *Portrait of a Country Artist: Charles Tunnicliffe R.A. 1901–1979* (London, 1980). On Ladybird landscape illustrations, see Jeremy Burchardt, 'Ladybird Landscapes: Or, What to Look for in the What to Look For Books', *Rural History*, XXXI (2020), pp. 79–95. Tunnicliffe's Ladybird illustrations had included M. E. Gagg's *The Farm* (1958), and four seasonal 'What to Look For' books (1959–61).
154 Prince of Wales et al., *Climate Change*, p. 49.
155 Ibid., p. 11.
156 Lindsey McEwen, Owain Jones and Iain Robertson, '"A glorious time?" Some Reflections on Flooding in the Somerset Levels', *Geographical Journal*, CLXXX (2014), pp. 326–37; Joanne Garde-Hansen, Lindsey

McEwen, Andrew Holmes and Owain Jones, 'Sustainable Flood Memory: Remembering as Resilience', *Memory Studies*, x (2017), pp. 384–405; Lindsey McEwen, Joanne Garde-Hansen, Andrew Holmes, Owain Jones and Franz Krause, 'Sustainable Flood Memories, Lay Knowledges and the Development of Community Resilience to Future Flood Risk', *Transactions of the Institute of British Geographers*, XLII (2017), pp. 14–28. On flooded England, see also Edward Platt, *The Great Flood: Travels Through a Sodden Landscape* (London, 2019).

157 Brian Moss, *The Broads* (London, 2001), pp. 353–60; on the Broads and sea flooding, see also David Matless, *In the Nature of Landscape: Cultural Geography on the Norfolk Broads* (Chichester, 2014), pp. 182–214.

158 Simon Roberts, *Merrie Albion: Landscape Studies of a Small Island* (Stockport, 2017), p. 101; Matless, 'The Anthroposcenic: Landscape in the Anthropocene'.

159 Roberts, personal communication.

160 Ann Gallagher, ed., *Susan Hiller* (London, 2011), pp. 24 and 52–5.

161 Bruce Glavovic, 'On the Frontline in the Anthropocene: Adapting to Climate Change through Deliberative Coastal Governance', in *Climate Change and the Coast: Building Resilient Communities*, ed. Bruce Glavovic, Mick Kelly, Robert Kay and Ailbhe Travers (London, 2015), pp. 51–99. On the cultural history and geography of the sea, see Richard Hamblyn, *The Sea: Nature and Culture* (London, 2021).

162 Mike Kendon, Mark McCarthy, Svetlana Jevrejeva, Andrew Matthews, Tim Sparks, Judith Garforth and John Kennedy, 'State of the UK Climate 2021', *International Journal of Climatology*, XLII (2022), July Supplement, pp. 1–80.

163 On the archipelagic, see John Brannigan, *Archipelagic Modernism: Literature in the British Isles, 1890–1970* (Edinburgh, 2015), and the literary magazine *Archipelago*, published since 2007 by Andrew McNeillie at Clutag Press, www.clutagpress.com.

164 See the explanatory announcement, 'Goodbye British Sea Power, Hello Sea Power', *Sea Power*, 9 August 2021, www.seapowerband.com, accessed 28 October 2023.

165 Rawnsley's work and subsequent dismissal became a focus for internal debate on the future direction of Trust policy; see Sean Nixon, 'Trouble at the National Trust: Post-War Recreation, the Benson Report and the Rebuilding of a Conservation Organization in the 1960s', *Twentieth Century British History*, XXVI (2015), pp. 529–50.

166 Caitlin DeSilvey, 'Making Sense of Transience: An Anticipatory History', *Cultural Geographies*, XIX (2012), pp. 31–54 (p. 33).

167 Ibid., p. 35; Caitlin DeSilvey, Simon Naylor and Colin Sackett, eds, *Anticipatory History* (Axminster, 2011).

168 Szirtes, *New and Collected Poems*, p. 352.

169 Ibid., pp. 370–74; the fifth poem in the set is 'The Three Remaining Horseman of the Apocalypse'.

170 Ibid., p. 372.

171 Sean O'Brien, 'Sunk Island', in *Collected Poems* (London, 2012), p. 415.

172 Harriet Tarlo and Judith Tucker, 'Poetry, Painting and Change on the Edge of England', *Sociologica Ruralis*, LIX (2019), pp. 636–60 (pp. 639 and

654); on plotlands, see Denis Hardy and Colin Ward, *Arcadia for All: The Legacy of a Makeshift Landscape* (London, 1984); Matless, *About England*, pp. 176–81.

173 Tarlo and Tucker, 'Poetry, Painting and Change on the Edge of England', p. 646.

174 Ibid., p. 657; See also www.judithtuckerartist.com. The phrase 'We're all very close round/ here' appears in Tarlo's poem 'Fitties Voices 2016', within the set of poems 'Fitties 2013–2019', included in Harriet Tarlo, *Gathering Grounds* (Bristol, 2019), pp. 79–107 (p. 101). Tarlo notes: 'The Fitties Voices are all from conversations with inhabitants and visitors to the Fitties; they are all composed entirely of words spoken by individuals condensed and shaped into poems' (*Gathering Grounds*, p. 174).

175 Tarlo and Tucker, 'Poetry, Painting and Change on the Edge of England', p. 657.

176 Steve Waters, *The Contingency Plan* (London, 2015), p. 131. See also Waters's four seasonal BBC Radio 4 conservation dramas, *Song of the Reed* (2021–2), set on the Norfolk Broads, and part of a project to 'rewild drama', available at www.bbc.co.uk, accessed 28 October 2023. On *The Contingency Plan*, see William Boles, 'The Science and Politics of Climate Change in Steve Waters' *The Contingency Plan*', *Journal of Contemporary Drama in English*, VII (2019), pp. 107–22; Julie Hudson, '"If You Want to be Green Hold Your Breath": Climate Change in British Theatre', *New Theatre Quarterly*, XXVIII (2012), pp. 260–71.

177 Julian Perry, *Brittle England* (London, 1997).

178 Matless, 'The Anthroposcenic: Landscape in the Anthropocene'; David Matless, 'At the End of Beach Road', in Julian Perry, *There Rolls the Deep: The Rising Sea Level Paintings* (Southampton, 2022), pp. 70–81; Paul Gough, '"Cultivating dead trees": The Legacy of Paul Nash as an Artist of Trauma, Wilderness and Recovery', *Journal of War and Culture Studies*, IV (2011), pp. 323–40. Perry is part-based in Dunwich in Suffolk, a classic site for reflection on erosion, with the site of its medieval town now out to sea. On Dunwich, see Stefan Skrimshire, 'The View from Dunwich', *Environmental Humanities*, XIII (2021), pp. 264–71.

179 Julian Perry, *An Extraordinary Prospect: The Coastal Erosion Paintings* (London, 2010).

180 Perry, *There Rolls the Deep*, pp. 10–33 (p. 14).

181 Ibid., p. 11.

182 Nick Ashton, Simon Lewis, Isabelle De Groote et al., 'Hominin Footprints from Early Pleistocene Deposits at Happisburgh, UK', *PLOS one*, IX (2014), pp. 1–13 (pp. 2, 7 and 11). See also Simon Parfitt, Nick Ashton, Simon Lewis et al., 'Early Pleistocene Human Occupation at the Edge of the Boreal Zone in Northwest Europe', *Nature*, 466 (2010), pp. 229–33.

183 In his discussion of the Happisburgh footprints Richard Irvine cites archaeologist Clive Gamble stating that when he heard of the footprints it was 'like hearing the first line of "Jerusalem"'; Richard Irvine, 'The Happisburgh Footprints in Time', *Anthropology Today*, XXX (2014), pp. 3–6 (p. 6).

184 Mabey, *The Unofficial Countryside*, pp. 15–16.

185 John Davies and David Waterhouse, *Exploring Norfolk's Deep History Coast* (Cheltenham, 2023).
186 Chris Stringer, *Homo Britannicus* (London, 2006), p. vi.
187 Matless, 'The Anthroposcenic'; see, for example, Julia Blackburn, *Time Song: Searching for Doggerland* (London, 2019).
188 Clement Reid, *Submerged Forests* (London, 1913).
189 Clement Reid, 'Coast Erosion', *Geographical Journal*, XXVIII (1906), pp. 487–91 (p. 491).
190 Bryony Coles, 'Doggerland: A Speculative Survey', *Proceedings of the Prehistoric Society*, LXIV (1998), pp. 45–81 (p. 45).
191 Vince Gaffney, Simon Fitch and David Smith, *Europe's Lost World: The Rediscovery of Doggerland* (York, 2009), p. 138.
192 Adam Trexler, *Anthropocene Fictions: The Novel in a Time of Climate Change* (London, 2015).
193 Ibid., p. 87.
194 J. G. Ballard, *The Drowned World* [1962] (London, 2014), pp. 21–3.
195 Ibid., p. 120.
196 David Dabydeen, *Disappearance* (London, 1993), pp. 177–8; Dominic Head, *Modernity and the English Rural Novel* (Cambridge, 2017), pp. 162–7.
197 John Wyndham, *The Kraken Wakes* [1953] (Harmondsworth, 1955), pp. 46 and 199.
198 Ibid., p. 240.
199 Dorothy Summers, *The East Coast Floods* (Newton Abbot, 1978); Hilda Grieve, *The Great Tide: The Story of the 1953 Flood Disaster in Essex* (Chelmsford, 1959); Grieve's book was reprinted by the Essex Record Office in 2023.
200 Frank Furedi, 'From the Narrative of the Blitz to the Rhetoric of Vulnerability', *Cultural Sociology*, I (2007), pp. 235–54.
201 Matless, *About England*, pp. 90–96.
202 Jan Zalasiewicz, *The Earth After Us* (Oxford, 2008), p. 82.
203 Ibid., pp. 84–5.
204 Larkin, *Collected Poems*, p. 142. *High Windows* includes other sea poems, opening with 'To the Sea', evoking the holiday beach as a space of affectionate intergenerational care, its title a possible toast as well as a signpost; Larkin, *Collected Poems*, pp. 121–2.
205 Matless, *In the Nature of Landscape*, pp. 206–7.
206 Larkin, *Collected Poems*, pp. 79–80.
207 Ibid., p. 142. Larkin commented in an interview that: '"They fuck you up" is funny because it's ambiguous. Parents bring about your conception and also bugger you up once you are born,' quoted in John Haffenden, *Viewpoints: Poets in Conversation* (London, 1981), pp. 128–9.
208 For the adjoining murals on Station Road, showing notable Beeston figures, see Matless, *About England*, pp. 19–21. See 'Beeston Street Art', Beeston and District Civic Society, www.beestoncivicsociety.org.uk, accessed 29 October 2023.
209 Kurt Jackson, *Place* (Bristol, 2014). Jackson was also Mark Cocker's subject in *Granta*'s 2008 issue on 'New Nature Writing', observing Jackson in Cornwall as 'a man deeply embedded in his landscape'; Mark

Cocker, 'Encounter: The Visions of Kurt Jackson', *Granta*, CII (2008), pp. 22–6 (p. 22).

210 Jackson, *Place*, pp. 22–5; www.caughtbytheriver.net. *Caught by the River*'s attention to words, images and music, and its presence within the proliferation of niche festivals, have reflected and nurtured a form of nature self-fashioning.

211 Jackson's *Place* book includes three of Jackson's pictures alongside Barrett's text. Two showed flooded pits, with nature returning ('Duck, coot, goose' and 'Ducks and willows'), the other a 'Birds of Attenborough Nature Reserve' leaflet, with a tick list of birds to complete, and the logos of the Wildlife Trust and gravel-extractor Cemex below, overdrawn with Jackson's sketch of ducks, geese and coots.

212 Jackson, *Place*, p. 23.

213 On Ratcliffe-on-Soar power station, see Matless, *About England*, pp. 284–7. The images in this account were taken in the early afternoon of 10 November 2019.

6 English Mystery

1 Simon Armitage, *Sir Gawain and the Green Knight* (London, 2007), p. 29.

2 Ibid., p. 14.

3 Carolyne Larrington, *The Land of the Green Man: A Journey through the Supernatural Landscapes of the British Isles* (London, 2015), p. 232. Larrington includes discussion of Gawain's Green Knight as a manifestation of the Green Man, pp. 227–8.

4 Sue Clifford and Angela King, *England in Particular* (London, 2006), p. 209.

5 Armitage, *Sir Gawain and the Green Knight*, p. 14.

6 Ibid., pp. 97 and 100.

7 Ibid., pp. vii–viii.

8 Ibid., p. 100.

9 John Lowerson, 'The Mystical Geography of the English', in *The English Rural Community*, ed. Brian Short (Cambridge, 1992), pp. 152–74 (p. 152); Robert Macfarlane, 'Glimpses and Tremors', *The Guardian*, 11 April 2015; see also Rob Young, *The Magic Box* (London, 2021).

10 For details of the Common Ground trees projects, see 'Trees, Woods and the Green Man' and 'Tree Dressing Day', *Common Ground*, www.commonground.org.uk, accessed 29 October 2023.

11 Kim Taplin, *Tongues in Trees: Studies in Literature and Ecology* (Hartland, 1989), p. 26.

12 Kenneth Grahame, *The Penguin Kenneth Grahame* (Harmondsworth, 1983), p. 244.

13 Rob Young, *Electric Eden: Unearthing Britain's Visionary Music* (London, 2010), pp. 463–9.

14 Ronald Johnson, *The Book of the Green Man* (Axminster, 2015), p. 43.

15 Ibid., p. 83.

16 Richard Barnes, *The Sun in the East* (Kirstead, 1983), p. 9; George McKay, *Senseless Acts of Beauty: Cultures of Resistance since the Sixties* (London, 1996), pp. 34–44.

17 George McKay, *Glastonbury: A Very English Fair* (London, 2000), p. 8.
18 On the coypu, see David Matless, *In the Nature of Landscape: Cultural Geography on the Norfolk Broads* (Chichester, 2014), pp. 137–40.
19 Barnes, *The Sun in the East*, p. 33.
20 Ibid., p. 68.
21 Ibid., p. 19.
22 Ibid., p. 41.
23 Ibid., p. 10.
24 Matless, *In the Nature of Landscape*, p. 86. Regional television reports from 1966 and 1967 on dwile-flonking feature on the British Film Institute's 2011 DVD collection *Here's a Health to the Barley Mow: A Century of Folk Customs and Ancient Rural Games*.
25 Walter Cornelius was a 1940s Latvian émigré, a strongman who appeared on television on *Blue Peter*, and who worked as a lifeguard at Peterborough Lido, where he is commemorated by a Walter-shaped weather vane. See 'Walter Cornelius, Legend. 1923–1983', *Friends of Peterborough Lido*, www.friendsofpeterboroughlido.co.uk, accessed 29 October 2023.
26 McKay, *Senseless Acts of Beauty*, p. 11.
27 Christopher Chippindale, *Stonehenge Complete* (London, 1994), pp. 253–61. On the complex claims to and about Stonehenge, see Christopher Chippindale, Paul Devereux, Peter Fowler, Rhys Jones and Tim Sebastian, *Who Owns Stonehenge?* (London, 1990); Barbara Bender, *Stonehenge: Making Space* (Oxford, 1998).
28 McKay, *Glastonbury*, p. 21; see Young, *Electric Eden*, pp. 447–505, on pastoral, psychedelia and festivals.
29 Michael Hurd, *Rutland Boughton and the Glastonbury Festivals* (Oxford, 1993).
30 On the longer history of alternative archaeologies of Glastonbury, see Adam Stout, 'Grounding Faith at Glastonbury: Episodes in the Early History of Alternative Archaeology', *Numen*, LIX (2012), pp. 249–69.
31 Glastonbury CND Festival 1985, *Official Programme* (Pilton, 1985), p. 39.
32 Department of the Environment, *50 Million Volunteers: A Report on the Role of Voluntary Organisations and Youth in the Environment (London, 1972)*, p. 88; McKay, *Senseless Acts of Beauty*, pp. 27–8, discusses later positive government reports on festivals in the mid-1970s.
33 Department of the Environment, *50 Million Volunteers*, p. 90.
34 Ibid., p. 95.
35 Ibid., p. 97.
36 The speech was given on 18 March 1971 in connection with the Isle of Wight County Council Bill, and addressed 'the island's experience of three pop festivals'; see the report in Hansard, HC vol 813, cols 1789–863 (18 March 1971). The parliamentary debate gives a flavour of the varieties of official opinion on pop festivals, with a lengthy contribution from Labour member Tom Driberg, including the aside: 'I wish the hon. Member for Eastbourne [Sir Charles Taylor] would not keep interjecting "fornication" from a sedentary position. He seems obsessed with the subject.'

37 Department of the Environment, *50 Million Volunteers*, pp. 96–7. See also Maria Nita and Sharif Gemie, 'Counterculture, Local Authorities and British Christianity at the Windsor and Watchfield Free Festivals (1972-5)', *Twentieth Century British History*, XXXI (2020), pp. 51–78.
38 Department of the Environment, *50 Million Volunteers*, p. 98.
39 Ibid., p. 102.
40 McKay, *Senseless Acts of Beauty*, pp. 30–33; McKay, p. 43, also notes tensions between the Peace Convoy and the Albion Fairs, the former held at arm's length by the latter and blamed by some for the Fairs' demise. See also Tim Cresswell, *In Place/Out of Place: Geography, Ideology and Transgression* (London, 1996), pp. 62–96, on 'Stonehenge and the Hippy Convoy'; Kevin Hetherington, *New Age Travellers* (London, 2000).
41 Fay Godwin, *Our Forbidden Land* (London, 1990), p. 23.
42 Ibid., pp. 53–4.
43 Ibid., pp. 56 and 182.
44 Ibid., p. 183.
45 J.R.L. Anderson and Fay Godwin, *The Oldest Road* (London, 1975), p. 194.
46 Cresswell, *In Place/Out of Place*, pp. 82 and 94; Keith Halfacree, 'Out of Place in the Country: Travellers and the "Rural Idyll"', *Antipode*, XXVIII (1996), pp. 42–72.
47 'Mr Major's Speech to Conservative Central Council', 26 March 1994, https://johnmajorarchive.org.uk, accessed 29 October 2023.
48 'Mr Major's Speech to 1992 Conservative Party Conference', https://johnmajorarchive.org.uk, accessed 29 October 2023.
49 Hetherington, *New Age Travellers*, p. 30. See also the testimonies in Richard Lowe and William Shaw, *Travellers: Voices of the New Age Nomads* (London, 1993); Fiona Earle, Alan Dearling, Helen Whittle, Roddy Glasse and Gubby, *A Time to Travel? An Introduction to Britain's Newer Travellers* (Lyme Regis, 1994).
50 Jez Butterworth, *Jerusalem* (London, 2009); Gemma Edwards, 'This Is England 2021: Staging England and Englishness in Contemporary Theatre', *Journal of Contemporary Drama in English*, IX (2021).
51 Butterworth, *Jerusalem*, pp. 5–6.
52 George Monbiot, *Feral* (London, 2013), p. 48.
53 Butterworth, *Jerusalem*, p. 18.
54 Ibid., pp. 78 and 105.
55 L. Du Garde Peach, *Stone Age Man in Britain* (Loughborough, 1961), pp. 42–50.
56 Ibid., p. 10.
57 H. D. Westacott, *The Ridgeway Path* (Harmondsworth, 1982), p. 7.
58 Ibid., p. 9.
59 R. Hippisley Cox, *The Green Roads of England* (London, 1914), p. vii; the Ridgeway is discussed in Chapter 9 of the book.
60 Ibid., pp. 10–13; the reference would seem to be to calendar reformer Moses Cotsworth, with his interests in ancient calendars and the role of shadows, with the pyramids as effective sundials; Anna Cook, 'Moses B. Cotsworth', *Yorkshire Philosophical Society*, www.ypsyork.org, accessed 29 October 2023.

61 Westacott, *The Ridgeway Path*, p. 32.
62 Michael Dames, *The Silbury Treasure* (London, 1976), p. 49. Silbury had also been popularized by a 1968–70 excavation by R.J.C. Atkinson, filmed by the BBC. See also Adam Thorpe, *On Silbury Hill* (Toller Fratum, 2014), which begins 'The point about Silbury Hill is that she has no point' (p. 9), but examines in detail the ways in which points have been ascribed, even in parallels to very pointed pyramids.
63 Ronald Hutton, *The Triumph of the Moon: A History of Modern Pagan Witchcraft* (Oxford, 1999), p. 280; Robert Graves, *The White Goddess* (London, 1948).
64 Dames, *The Silbury Treasure*, pp. 20–21; Anderson and Godwin, *The Oldest Road*, pp. 54–5.
65 Dames, *The Silbury Treasure*, p. 54.
66 Ibid., p. 11.
67 Ibid., p. 99.
68 Ibid., p. 110.
69 Ibid., pp. 100–101.
70 Jon Cannon, 'New Myths at Swallowhead: The Past and Present in the Landscape of the Marlborough Downs', in *The Avebury Landscape*, ed. Graham Brown, David Field and David McOmish (Oxford, 2005), pp. 202–11. Thorpe, *On Silbury Hill*, includes a description of a pagan ceremony at Swallowhead, pp. 179–92.
71 Dames, *The Silbury Treasure*, p. 167; see also Michael Dames, *The Avebury Cycle* (London, 1977); Michael Dames, *Pagan's Progress* (London, 2017). The latter is billed as a 'Ge-ography primer' on British landscape, reinstating the goddess 'Ge', a visionary geography beyond conventional academic accounts.
72 Lucy Lippard, *Overlay: Contemporary Art and the Art of Prehistory* (New York, 1983), pp. 75 and 35.
73 Ibid., p. 214; the Silbury photographs are facing p. 1, taken by Lippard, and on p. 239, taken by Chris Jennings.
74 Westacott, *The Ridgeway Path*, p. 15.
75 Janet Bord and Colin Bord, *Mysterious Britain* (London, 1974). Westacott cited another of the Bords' works, Janet Bord and Colin Bord, *A Guide to Ancient Sites in Britain* (London, 1978). See also the examination of landscape and fertility in Janet Bord and Colin Bord, *Earth Rites: Fertility Practices in Pre-Industrial Britain* (London, 1982).
76 Bord and Bord, *Mysterious Britain*, p. 76.
77 Ibid., p. ix.
78 Ibid., p. x.
79 Ibid., p. 172.
80 Ibid., p. x.
81 Ibid., p. 5.
82 Ibid., p. 18.
83 Ibid., p. 221.
84 Ibid., p. 219.
85 Ibid., p. 3.
86 Ibid., p. 234; on the longer history of alternative archaeology in Glastonbury, see Stout, 'Grounding Faith at Glastonbury'.

87 Adam Stout, *Creating Prehistory: Druids, Ley Hunters and Archaeologists in Pre-War Britain* (Oxford, 2008); Tom Williamson and Liz Bellamy, *Ley Lines in Question* (Kingswood, 1983); Ronald Hutton, *The Pagan Religions of the Ancient British Isles* (Oxford, 1991), pp. 118–32; David Matless, *Landscape and Englishness* (London, 1998, rev. 2016) , pp. 119–23.
88 Alfred Watkins, *The Old Straight Track* [1925] (London, 1970), p. 218. On Watkins, see Ron Shoesmith, *Alfred Watkins: A Herefordshire Man* (Almeley, 1990).
89 John Michell, *The View over Atlantis* (London, 1969). On the countercultural ley, including disputes within the field, see Joanne Parker, *Britannia Obscura: Mapping Britain's Hidden Landscapes* (London, 2014), pp. 95–126.
90 John Michell, *The Flying Saucer Vision* (London, 1967); see also Michell's study of antiquarianism, John Michell, *Megalithomania* (London, 1982). Tony Wedd, *Skyways and Landmarks* (Chiddingstone, 1961).
91 Chippindale et al., *Who Owns Stonehenge?*; Bender, *Stonehenge*. See also Ronald Hutton, 'The Past and the Post-Modern Challenge', *The Ley Hunter*, cxxv (1996), pp. 5–8, and the 1996 'trial' of the various possible meanings of the Cerne Abbas giant, bringing together a range of commentators, including Bender and Hutton, in Cerne Abbas village hall to mull the past; Timothy Darvill, Katherine Barker, Barbara Bender and Ronald Hutton, *The Cerne Giant: An Antiquity on Trial* (Oxford, 1999).
92 Lippard, *Overlay*, p. 134.
93 Watkins, *The Old Straight Track*, p. xvi.
94 Bord and Bord, *Mysterious Britain*, p. 3.
95 Clare Cooper Marcus, 'Alternative Landscapes: Ley-Lines, Feng-Shui and the Gaia Hypothesis', *Landscape*, xxix (1987), pp. 1–10.
96 Nicholas Saunders, *Alternative London's Survival Guide for Strangers to London* (London, 1973), p. 202.
97 Michell, *The View over Atlantis*, cover quote.
98 Ibid., p. 126.
99 Ibid., pp. 126 and 146.
100 Ibid., pp. 64–7.
101 Paul Broadhurst and Hamish Miller, *The Sun and the Serpent* (Launceston, 1989), p. 29.
102 Ibid., p. 155.
103 Ibid., p. 14.
104 Ibid., pp. 17–18; on Cornwall and alternative archaeologies, see Rupert White, *The Re-enchanted Landscape: Earth Mysteries, Paganism and Art in Cornwall, 1950–2000* (Truro, 2017).
105 Broadhurst and Miller, *The Sun and the Serpent*, p. 58.
106 Ibid., p. 165.
107 W. G. Hoskins, *The Making of the English Landscape* (London, 1955).
108 Broadhurst and Miller, *The Sun and the Serpent*, p. 150.
109 Ian McNeil Cooke, *Journey to the Stones* (Bosullow, 1996), p. 5.
110 Shirley Toulson, *East Anglia: Walking the Ley Lines and Ancient Tracks* (London, 1979), p. 8.

111 Shirley Toulson, *Discovering Farm Museums and Farm Parks* (Princes Risborough, 1977); Fay Godwin and Shirley Toulson, *The Drovers' Roads of Wales* (London, 1977); Shirley Toulson, *Derbyshire: Exploring the Ancient Tracks and Mysteries of Mercia* (London, 1980).
112 Toulson, *East Anglia*, pp. 16–17.
113 Julian Cope, *The Modern Antiquarian* (London, 1998). Just as Broadhurst and Miller extended *The Sun and the Serpent* in their book *The Dance of the Dragon* (Launceston, 2000), tracing a 2,500-mile Apollo/St Michael line across Europe to the Middle East, so in 2004 Cope followed *The Modern Antiquarian* with *The Megalithic European* (London, 2004).
114 Cope, *The Modern Antiquarian*, p. 152.
115 Ibid., p. 3.
116 Ibid., p. 29.
117 Ibid., p. ix.
118 Paul Nash, 'Personal statement', in *Unit One,* ed. Herbert Read (London, 1934), pp. 79–81 (p. 81).
119 Jemima Montagu, ed., *Paul Nash: Modern Artist, Ancient Landscape* (London, 2003); Kitty Hauser, *Shadow Sites: Photography, Archaeology, and the British Landscape, 1927–1955* (Oxford, 2007); Alexandra Harris, *Romantic Moderns* (London, 2010).
120 John Piper, 'Prehistory from the Air', *Axis,* VIII (1937), pp. 3–11.
121 Nash, 'Personal statement', p. 81.
122 Lippard, *Overlay*, p. 180.
123 *Children of the Stones* was broadcast from 10 January–21 February 1977; see Young, *The Magic Box*, pp. 184–6; Peter Hutchings, 'Uncanny Landscapes in British Film and Television', *Visual Culture in Britain*, V (2004), pp. 27–40.
124 Harrison Birtwistle, quoted in the sleeve notes by Jonathan Cross to Harrison Birtwistle, *Secret Theatre*, a CD release including 'Silbury Air' alongside other works, NMC Recordings (2008).
125 Jonathan Cross, *Harrison Birtwistle: Man, Mind, Music* (London, 2000); Robert Adlington, *The Music of Harrison Birtwistle* (Cambridge, 2000).
126 Richard Burns, *Avebury* (London, 1971), p. 23.
127 Ibid., p. 20.
128 Ibid., p. 23. Burns was a pen name of Richard Berengarten, who also founded the Cambridge Poetry Festival. *Avebury* was reissued as by Richard Berengarten by Shearsman Books in 2016, and had also been collected in Richard Berengarten, *For the Living: Selected Longer Poems, 1965–2000* (Bristol, 2011). For 1970s poetic engagement with Wessex landscape, see also the work of Jeremy Hooker, with Paul Nash a key influence; Jeremy Hooker, *A View from the Source: Selected Poems* (Manchester, 1982).
129 Richard Long, *Walking in Circles* (London, 1991), p. 36.
130 Ibid., p. 46.
131 Ibid., p. 9.
132 Ibid., p. 38. Energies ancient and modern could also meet, as in Long's 1979 photographic piece 'Windmill Hill to Coalbrookdale', documenting a walk from ancient Avebury to Ironbridge in its bicentenary year;

Nicholas Alfrey, Joy Sleeman and Ben Tufnell, *Uncommon Ground: Land Art in Britain, 1966–1979* (London, 2013), p. 87.
133 Long, *Walking in Circles*, p. 26.
134 Ibid., p. 27; Alfrey et al., *Uncommon Ground*, pp. 80 and 117–18.
135 Richard Long, 'Nineteen Stills from the Work of Richard Long', *Studio International*, CLXXIX (1970), pp. 106–11 (p. 108). Long's labelling of a photograph as 'AFRICA' may appear to indicate an entire continent, but in appearing two pages after an image of Kilimanjaro, a particular region of Africa is implicitly signposted.
136 Long, *Walking in Circles*, p. 31.
137 Ibid., p. 105.
138 Lippard, *Overlay*, pp. 126–9.
139 Hamish Fulton, 'Old Muddy', in Long, *Walking in Circles*, pp. 241–6. Dames, *Pagan's Progress*, includes a critique of Long's art, specifically his 1970 Silbury spiral, as matching 'the instrumental rationalism adopted by most modern archaeologists in their studies of that monument' (p. 41), although later in the book Dames is more positive on the work's potential birth symbolism, p. 283.
140 Richard Long, *A Walk Across England* (London, 1997), quotation on back cover.
141 Innes Keighren and Joanne Norcup, eds, *Landscapes of Detectorists* (Axminster, 2020), p. 15. See also Joanne Norcup, '"All the Minorities Covered": Landscapes, Englishnesses, and Hopefulness in the TV Work of Mackenzie Crook', *Waiting for You: A Detectorists Zine 4* (2023).
142 J.R.R. Tolkien, 'The Homecoming of Beorhtnoth Beorthelm's Son', in *Tree and Leaf, Smith of Wootton Major, The Homecoming of Beorhtnoth* (London, 1975), pp. 147–75 (p. 152).
143 Keighren and Norcup, *Landscapes of Detectorists*, p. 10.
144 Richard Smyth, *A Sweet, Wild Note: What We Hear When the Birds Sing* (London, 2017), p. 178.
145 Clive King, *Stig of the Dump* (Harmondsworth, 1963).
146 Butterworth, *Jerusalem*, p. 80.
147 King, *Stig of the Dump*, p. 78.
148 Jacquetta Hawkes, *A Land* (London, 1951), p. 128. The Grime's Graves goddess also features in Lippard, *Overlay*, p. 16. On Grime's Graves, see David Matless, 'Properties of Ancient Landscape: The Present Prehistoric in Twentieth-Century Breckland', *Journal of Historical Geography*, XXXIV (2008), pp. 68–93.
149 King, *Stig of the Dump*, p. 19.
150 Ibid., pp. 156–7.
151 Ibid., p. 124.
152 Ibid., p. 127.
153 Ibid., pp. 153–4.

7 Folkloric England

1 Trish Winter and Simon Keegan-Phipps, *Performing Englishness: Identity and Politics in a Contemporary Folk Resurgence* (Manchester, 2013).

2 Sue Clifford and Angela King, *England in Particular* (London, 2006).

3 For details of *Arcadia*, Dorwood's poster and Kingsnorth's testimony see 'Arcadia', *Common Ground*, www.commonground.org.uk, accessed 29 October 2023.

4 Douglas Kennedy, *English Folk Dancing* (London, 1964), p. 9.

5 See 'The Full English Project', Vaughan Williams Memorial Library, www.vwml.org. The phrase 'The Full English', with its breakfast fry-up allusion, has also served as the title of a recent book exploring contemporary English identity, Stuart Maconie, *The Full English: A Journey in Search of a Country and Its People* (London, 2023), and a four-part 2023 Channel 4 television series, *Grayson Perry's Full English*, where artist Perry addressed similar themes, proceeding around England by region, and including attention to the mystical and folkloric.

6 See 'Percy Aldridge Grainger (1882–1961)', www.vwml.org.

7 'Rosemary Lane' is song 51 in Steve Roud and Julia Bishop, *The New Penguin Book of English Folk Songs* (London, 2012), pp. 124–5.

8 See *The Morris Ring*, www.themorrisring.org.

9 Martin Parr, *The Cost of Living* (Manchester, 1989), plate 46.

10 Ralph Vaughan Williams and A. L. Lloyd, *The Penguin Book of English Folk Songs* (Harmondsworth, 1959), p. 9.

11 Dave Harker, *Fakesong: The Manufacture of British 'Folksong' 1700 to the Present Day* (Milton Keynes, 1985), p. xii; see also the chapter on 'Fakesong', mainly focused on A. L. Lloyd and Ewan MacColl, in Dave Harker, *One for the Money: Politics and Popular Song* (London, 1980), pp. 146–58. For a counter-argument, discussing the identity of the singers of the songs collected by Sharp, see C. J. Bearman, 'Who Were the Folk? The Demography of Cecil Sharp's Somerset Folk Singers', *Historical Journal*, XLIII (2000), pp. 751–75. For a detailed social historical study of collecting, see Vic Gammon, 'Folk Song Collecting in Sussex and Surrey, 1843–1914', *History Workshop Journal*, X (1980), pp. 61–89.

12 Roud and Bishop, *New Penguin Book of English Folk Songs*, p. xviii. See also Steve Roud, *Folk Song in England* (London, 2017).

13 A. L. Lloyd, *Folk Song in England* (London, 1967); Dave Arthur, *Bert: The Life and Times of A. L. Lloyd* (London, 2012).

14 Georgina Boyes, *The Imagined Village: Culture, Ideology and the English Folk Revival* (Manchester, 1993).

15 A. L. Lloyd, *The Singing Englishman* (London, 1944).

16 Lloyd, *Folk Song in England*, pp. 13 and 24.

17 Ibid., p. 173.

18 Ibid., p. 320.

19 Ibid., pp. 395–7.

20 Ibid., p. 86.

21 Ibid., p. 91.

22 George Revill and John Gold, '"Far Back in American Time": Culture, Region, Nation, Appalachia and the Geography of Voice', *Annals of the Association of American Geographers*, CVIII (2018), pp. 1406–21; Stan Hugill, *Shanties from the Seven Seas* (London, 1961).

23 Roy Palmer, *The Painful Plough* (Cambridge, 1972), p. 6; E. P. Thompson, *The Making of the English Working Class* (London, 1963).

24 Roy Palmer, *Songs of the Midlands* (Wakefield, 1972), quotation on back cover.
25 Ibid., p. vii.
26 Ibid., p. 107.
27 Winter and Keegan-Phipps, *Performing Englishness*, p. 2; Lee Robert Blackstone, 'The Aural and Moral Idylls of "Englishness" and Folk Music', *Symbolic Interaction*, XL (2017), pp. 561–80.
28 Winter and Keegan-Phipps, *Performing Englishness*, p. 80.
29 Ibid., p. 130.
30 Ibid., p. 136.
31 Ibid., p. 152; Billy Bragg, *The Progressive Patriot* (London, 2006).
32 Winter and Keegan-Phipps, *Performing Englishness*, p. 134, quotation from Eliza Carthy's *Anglicana* sleeve notes.
33 Ibid., pp. 164–7.
34 See 'Dancing England 2019', www.youtube.com, accessed 29 October 2023.
35 Paul Gilroy, *After Empire: Melancholia or Convivial Culture?* (London, 2004), p. 104.
36 On folk and ethnicity, see also the November 2020 BBC Radio 4 series by Zakia Sewell, 'My Albion', available at www.bbc.co.uk, accessed 29 October 2023.
37 The film *Black Safari* can be viewed on the website of Zak Ové, son of Horace Ové: https://modernforms.org, accessed 29 October 2023.
38 *Black Safari* director Colin Luke was also a producer on 'King Carnival', and would in 1999 produce Martin Parr's BBC documentary exploration *Think of England*.
39 Theresa Buckland, '"In a Word We Are Unique": Ownership and Control in an English Dance Custom', in *Step Change: New Views on Traditional Dance*, ed. Georgina Boyes (London 2001), pp. 49–60; *Step Change* has a picture of a blacked-up Bacup dancer on the cover. Buckland does not mention blackface make-up, but another piece in the same volume considers another dance style characterized by blackened faces; Elaine Bradtke, 'Molly Dancing: A Study of Discontinuity and Change', ibid., pp. 61–86. Bradtke notes that the often disreputable East Anglian molly dance, with black face and cross-dressing for anonymity, died out in the 1930s, but was revived in the 1970s, often with mixed gender groups and with many groups still blackening faces.
40 Clifford and King, *England in Particular*, p. 57.
41 See 'The Official Britannia Coconut Dancers Press Statement – 30th July 2020', www.coconutters.co.uk, accessed 29 October 2023.
42 Buckland, '"In a Word We Are Unique"', p. 57.
43 Kennedy, *English Folk Dancing*, pp. 48–9.
44 Lloyd, *Folk Song in England*, p. 101.
45 Ronald Hutton, *Stations of the Sun: A History of the Ritual Year in Britain* (Oxford, 1996), p. 91.
46 See 'Dancing England 2019', www.youtube.com, accessed 29 October 2023.
47 Christina Hole, *English Custom and Usage* (London, 1941), pp. 8–10; Dames, *The Silbury Treasure*, p. 83.

48 Janet Bord and Colin Bord, *Earth Rites: Fertility Practices in Pre-Industrial Britain* (London, 1982), pp. 207–9.
49 Reginald Nettel, *Sing a Song of England* (London, 1954), p. 39.
50 Ibid., p. 42.
51 Ibid., p. 148.
52 Quotations from Lloyd's sleeve notes for *Frost and Fire*.
53 Lloyd, *Folk Song in England*, p. 101.
54 Gammon, 'Folk Song Collecting in Sussex and Surrey', p. 87.
55 Lloyd, *Folk Song in England*, p. 200.
56 Boyes, *The Imagined Village*, pp. 229 and 241.
57 On *Anthems in Eden* and remembrance, see also David Matless, *About England* (London, 2023), pp. 74–5.
58 Rob Young, *Electric Eden: Unearthing Britain's Visionary Music* (London, 2010). For an insightful reading of the music of Nick Drake in this context, see Nathan Wiseman-Trowse, *Nick Drake: Dreaming England* (London, 2013).
59 On *Morris On*, see Young, *Electric Eden*, pp. 276–8.
60 The Topic 'Voice of the People' series on English, Irish and Scottish traditional music had begun with 20 volumes in 1998, including *You Lazy Lot of Bone-Shakers: Songs and Dance Tunes of Seasonal Events* (Volume 16), which contained recordings of Bacup and Abbots Bromley.
61 Tim Plester had previously made the film *Way of the Morris* (2011) on Adderbury in Oxfordshire, on, as the film trailer put it, the lands and dances of his forefathers and ancestors.
62 Shirley Collins, *All in the Downs: Reflections of Life, Landscape and Song* (London, 2018), p. 105; Shirley Collins, *America over the Water* (London, 2004). Collins's U.S. trip with Lomax also featured in *The Ballad of Shirley Collins*, where the song 'Sweet England' is noted as having been collected in Kentucky.
63 Collins, *All in the Downs*, p. 144.
64 Ibid., p. 82.
65 Ibid., p. 159.
66 Ibid., p. 161.
67 David Keenan, *England's Hidden Reverse* (London, 2014), pp. 18–19; an expanded edition of Keenan's book appeared in June 2023. Alongside Current 93, Keenan considers the bands Coil and Nurse With Wound, all inspired by the 'industrial' music of Throbbing Gristle. This shadowy England could include the determinedly sinister. The cover of Throbbing Gristle's *20 Jazz Funk Greats* (1978) shows the group smiling on Beachy Head in the flowery grass, but the pastoral front is belied by grimness, the track 'Beachy Head' droning with faint seagulls and the pleasant scene a suicide spot. The rear cover carries a black and white version of the same photograph with added naked corpse.
68 David Tibet, quoted in Keenan, *England's Hidden Reverse*, p. 240.
69 Collins, *America over the Water*, p. 187.
70 Shirley Collins's *Lodestar* also featured drummer Alex Neilson, whose band Trembling Bells had from 2008 also shaped twenty-first-century reworkings of folk-rock, on releases such as *The Sovereign Self* (2015) and *Wide Majestic Aire* (2016).

71 John Fowles, 'On Being English but Not British', in *Wormholes: Essays and Occasional Writings* (London, 1998), pp. 79–88 (p. 87).
72 Ralph Vaughan Williams, quoted in Gammon, 'Folk Song Collecting in Sussex and Surrey', p. 83, from Ursula Vaughan Williams, *R.V.W.: A Biography of Ralph Vaughan Williams* (London, 1964), p. 100.
73 Simon Reynolds, 'Society of the Spectral', *The Wire*, November 2006, pp. 26–33; see also Reynolds's related blog piece, 'Haunted Audio: a/k/a Society of the Spectral: Ghost Box, Mordant Music and Hauntology', 14 May 2012, https://reynoldsretro.blogspot.com. On musical hauntology, see also Young, *Electric Eden*, pp. 594–607; Rob Young, *The Magic Box* (London, 2021). See also Stephen Prince, *A Year in the Country: Wandering through Spectral Fields* (London, 2018), and Prince's related works detailed at the extensive website https://ayearinthecountry.co.uk.
74 Reynolds, 'Society of the Spectral', p. 29.
75 Belbury Poly, *The Owl's Map*, sleeve notes.
76 On Harry Cox, see David Matless, *In the Nature of Landscape: Cultural Geography on the Norfolk Broads* (Chichester, 2014) , pp. 68–9; Christopher Heppa, 'Harry Cox and His Friends: Song Transmission in an East Norfolk Singing Community, *c.* 1896–1960', *Folk Music Journal*, VIII (2005), pp. 569–93.
77 Reynolds, 'Society of the Spectral', p. 31.
78 Quoted ibid., p. 30.
79 Arthur Machen, *The Great God Pan* (London, 1894)
80 Joseph Stannard, 'Potion of Sound', *The Wire*, 308 (October 2009), pp. 38–42; an unedited transcript of the interview on which the article was based, and from which the full quotations here are taken, is available at www.thewire.co.uk, accessed 29 October 2023. Trish Keenan died in 2011.
81 Young, *Electric Eden*, pp. 415–46.
82 Collins, *All in the Downs*, p. 201.
83 Ibid., p. 200.
84 See 'Manifesto', The Museum of British Folklore, www.museumofbritishfolklore.com.
85 Graham King, 'A Journey to Beyond', in *The Museum of Witchcraft: A Magical History*, ed. Kerriann Godwin (Boscastle, 2011), pp. 137–8.
86 Godwin, ed., *The Museum of Witchcraft*.
87 See Rupert White, 'Interview: Ronald Hutton on Cecil Williamson and Rewriting Wicca', *Enquiring Eye*, IV (2020), pp. 68–74.
88 Hutton, *Triumph of the Moon*, pp. 309–18.
89 Evan John Jones, with Doreen Valiente, *Witchcraft: A Tradition Renewed* (London, 1990), p. 23.
90 Ibid., p. 24.
91 Ibid., p. 53.
92 Ibid., p. 63.
93 Jason Connery took over the role of Robin after Praed left to join the cast of U.S. soap *Dynasty*.
94 Jones and Valiente, *Witchcraft*, pp. 116–17.
95 David Rudkin, *Penda's Fen* (London, 1975); Lez Cooke, *A Sense of Place: Regional British Television Drama, 1956–1982* (Manchester, 2012), pp. 135–9;

David Ian Rabey, *David Rudkin: Sacred Disobedience* (Amsterdam, 1997), pp. 63–8. On *Penda's Fen*, see also the excellent collection by Matthew Harle and James Machin, eds, *Of Mud and Flame: The Penda's Fen Sourcebook* (London, 2019), including the script of the play, and with contributions including a reflective piece by Rudkin ('Mongrel Nation: A Foreword', pp. 9–12), Joseph Brooker's insightful comparison with Raymond Williams ('Raymond's Fen', pp. 63–81), and Gary Budden's connection of the film and the 'landscape punk' of Current 93 and others, 'Gnostic Anarcho-Punk Anti-Pastoral Visions', pp. 123–30.

96 Young, *Electric Eden*, p. 415. Roger Luckhurst, 'Always Historicise? Penda's Fen in the 1970s', in *Of Mud and Flame*, ed. Harle and Machin, pp. 29–39 (p. 36).

97 The phrase is the title of a *Radio Times* article on *Penda's Fen*, discussed at the opening of Craig Wallace, 'The "Old, Primeval 'Demon' of the Place Opening Half an Eye": Penda's Fen and the Legend of the Sleeping King', in *Of Mud and Flame*, ed. Harle and Machin, pp. 185–96; David Rudkin, 'I wanted to write something that grew out of the landscape', *Radio Times*, 14 March 1974, p. 12.

98 David Rudkin, quoted in Rabey, *David Rudkin: Sacred Disobedience*, p. 9, from James Vinson, ed., *Contemporary Dramatists* (London, 1973), pp. 653–4.

99 Rudkin, *Penda's Fen*, p. 69.

100 Ibid., p. 71.

101 Ibid., pp. 79 and 81.

102 Ibid., p. 83.

103 Nettel, *Sing a Song of England*, p. 27.

104 Jeremy Deller and Alan Kane, *Folk Archive* (London, 2005). On Deller's First World War centenary work 'We're Here Because We're Here' (2016), see Matless, *About England*, pp. 78–9. For a memoir, see Jeremy Deller, *Art Is Magic* (London, 2023).

105 Deller and Kane, *Folk Archive*, pp. 154–6.

106 Ibid., p. 2.

107 Christopher Fox, 'Michael Finnissy: Modernism with an English Accent', in *Critical Perspectives on Michael Finnissy*, ed. Ian Pace and Nigel McBride (Abingdon, 2019), pp. 27–38.

108 Quotation from Michael Finnissy's sleeve notes to the CD *Folklore* (1998), issued by Metier, CD92010.

109 Michael Finnissy, 'Conversations with Michael Finnissy', in *Uncommon Ground: The Music of Michael Finnissy*, ed. Henrietta Brougham, Christopher Fox and Ian Pace (Aldershot, 1997), pp. 1–42 (p. 29).

110 Quoted in Ian Pace, 'The Piano Music', in *Uncommon Ground*, ed. Brougham, Fox and Pace, pp. 43–134 (p. 112).

111 History too is refracted in Finnissy's modernism, the 2003 choral work *This Church*, written for the 900th anniversary of St Mary de Haura's in Shoreham, Sussex, recounting episodes through past accounts, while *Maldon* (1991) commemorated the 1,000th anniversary of the Battle of Maldon in Essex, noted in Chapter 6 above, its text mixing fragments of Anglo-Saxon poetry with modern translation.

112 For details, see www.michaelfinnissy.co.uk, and the catalogue of works in Brougham et al., eds, *Uncommon Ground*, p. 360.
113 Quoted in Fox, 'Michael Finnissy: Modernism with an English Accent', p. 30, and in the catalogue of works in Brougham et al., eds, *Uncommon Ground*, p. 365.
114 Fox, 'Michael Finnissy: Modernism with an English Accent', p. 30.
115 Jonathan Cross, sleeve notes to the 1990 CD release of *English Country Tunes*, Etcetera Records, KTC 1091.
116 Finnissy, 'Conversations with Michael Finnissy', p. 30.
117 Ibid., pp. 25–6.
118 See 'The Full English Project', Vaughan Williams Memorial Library, www.vwml.org.
119 Lloyd, *Folk Song in England*, p. 202; Sabine Baring-Gould and Cecil Sharp, *English Folk-Songs for Schools* (London, 1906), pp. 56–7. 'Strawberry Fair' does not, however, appear in either Vaughan Williams and Lloyd, *The Penguin Book of English Folk Songs*, or Roud and Bishop, *The New Penguin Book of English Folk Songs*.
120 See 'Strawberry Fair', www.vwml.org.
121 On Newley, see Garth Bardsley, *Stop the World: The Biography of Anthony Newley* (London, 2003).
122 'Pop Goes the Weasel' also appears on the British Film Institute's *Here's a Health to the Barley Mow* DVD collection, sung and played on a fiddle by Sam Bennett in 1926 as a girls' dance in Ilmington, Warwickshire, with Bennett knocking his bow on the fiddle neck for the song's 'Pop'.
123 Keith Jones, 'Music in Factories: A Twentieth-Century for Control of the Productive Self', *Social and Cultural Geography*, VI (2005), pp. 723–44. *Music While You Work* lingered on the BBC Light Programme until channel reorganization in 1967.
124 For details of the programme, see 'Singing Together', BBC Radio 4, November 2014, available at www.bbc.co.uk, accessed 29 October 2023.
125 Iona Opie and Peter Opie, *Children's Games in Street and Playground* (Oxford, 1969), pp. 110–11.
126 Boria Sax, *Crow* (London, 2003), pp. 133 and 136. See also Hayden Lorimer, 'Scaring Crows', *Geographical Review*, CIII (2013), pp. 177–89.
127 'The Scarecrow' was also the title of a song on Pink Floyd's 1967 LP *The Piper at the Gates of Dawn*, Syd Barrett telling of a black and green figure in a barley field, resigned to his fate and not minding.
128 Barbara Euphan Todd, *Worzel Gummidge or The Scarecrow of Scatterbrook* [1936] (Harmondsworth, 1941).
129 David Matless, *Landscape and Englishness* (London, 1998, rev. 2016), pp. 247–53.
130 Todd, *Worzel Gummidge*, p. 19.
131 Ibid., p. 15.
132 Ibid., pp. 57 and 33.
133 Innes Keighren and Joanne Norcup, eds, *Landscapes of Detectorists* (Axminster, 2020), p. 12.
134 Jacob Smith, 'Mackenzie Crook's Biosemiotic Television', *Screen*, LXIII (2022), pp. 445–63 (p. 458).
135 Jez Butterworth, *Jerusalem* (London, 2009), p. 80.

136 PJ Harvey, *Orlam* (London, 2022), p. 115. 'Lwonesome Tonight' also forms a song on Harvey's 2023 LP *I Inside the Old Year Dying*. The album's twelve songs match twelve poems from *Orlam*, the texts sometimes identical but elsewhere amended or abbreviated, and with dialect glossaries accompanying printed lyrics.
137 Ibid., p. 296.
138 Ibid., p. 231.
139 See 'PJ Harvey visits Dorset Museum and gifts Orlam proofs and exclusive photograph to collection', *William Barnes Society*, www.williambarnessociety.org.uk; 'The Dorset Ooser', *Wessex Museums*, www.wessexmuseums.org.uk, accessed 29 October 2023.
140 Accented vocals also characterized Lal and Mike Waterson's 'The Scarecrow', the song registering the singers' Hull accents. On The Wurzels, see the informative website https://wurzelmania.co.uk.
141 'Down the Nempnett Thrubwell', with lyric by Cutler, was recorded for the 1976 *Combine Harvester* LP. 'Pill Pill' appeared on the 1967 'Scrumpy and Western' EP; the Pill ferry closed after the Avonmouth bridge opened in 1974.
142 Lloyd, *Folk Song in England*, p. 199.
143 Recordings from Nailsea are included on the EMI release, The Wurzels, *The Finest 'Arvest of The Wurzels* (2000).
144 Robin Ravilious, *James Ravilious: A Life* (London, 2017); Matless, *About England*, pp. 173–7.
145 James Ravilious, *The Heart of the Country* (London, 1980), n.p.; on Blythe, see Matless, *About England*, pp. 46–7 and 72–4.

8 To Green Possibilities

1 Alan Garner, 'The Stone Book', in *The Stone Book Quartet* (London, 1983), pp. 1–36 (p. 22).
2 Ibid., p. 30.
3 Ibid., pp. 35–6.
4 Peter Bishop, *The Greening of Psychology* (Dallas, TX, 1990), p. 18.
5 William Carlos Williams, *In the American Grain* [1925] (Harmondsworth, 1971).
6 John Fowles, *The Journals*, vol. I (London, 2003), pp. 616–17.
7 Ibid., pp. 616–20.
8 John Fowles, 'On Being English but Not British', in *Wormholes: Essays and Occasional Writings* (London, 1998), pp. 79–88.
9 Fowles, *The Journals*, pp. 619–20.
10 Ibid., p. 616.
11 Otto Saumarez Smith, *Boom Cities: Architect-Planners and the Politics of Radical Urban Renewal in 1960s Britain* (Oxford, 2019); David Matless, *About England* (London, 2023), pp. 228–33.

BIBLIOGRAPHY

Adlington, Robert, *The Music of Harrison Birtwistle* (Cambridge, 2000)

Agar, Jon, '"Future Forecast – Changeable and Probably Getting Worse": The UK Government's Early Response to Anthropogenic Climate Change', *Twentieth Century British History*, XXVI (2015), pp. 602–28

—, *Science Policy under Thatcher* (London, 2019)

Agard, John, *The Coming of the Little Green Man* (Hexham, 2018)

—, *Border Zone* (Hexham, 2022)

Aldred, Tanya, 'Cricket and Climate Change: How Green is Your Sward?', in *Wisden Cricketers' Almanack 2017*, ed. Lawrence Booth (London, 2017), pp. 65–70

—, 'The Environment in 2022: Taking a Stand', in *Wisden Cricketers' Almanack 2023*, ed. Lawrence Booth (London, 2023), pp. 198–201

Alfrey, Nicholas, Joy Sleeman and Ben Tufnell, *Uncommon Ground: Land Art in Britain, 1966–1979* (London, 2013)

Allsop, Kenneth, *Adventure Lit Their Star* (London, 1949)

—, 'Pop Goes Young Woodley', in *Class*, ed. Richard Mabey (London, 1967), pp. 127–44

—, *Hard Travellin': The Hobo and His History* (London, 1967)

Anderson, J.R.L., and Fay Godwin, *The Oldest Road* (London, 1975)

Armitage, Simon, *Sir Gawain and the Green Knight* (London, 2007)

Armstrong, Alan, *Farmworkers: A Social and Economic History, 1770–1980* (London, 1988)

Arthur, Dave, *Bert: The Life and Times of A. L. Lloyd* (London, 2012)

Ashton, Nick, Simon Lewis, Isabelle De Groote et al., 'Hominin footprints from early Pleistocene deposits at Happisburgh, UK', *PLoS ONE*, IX (2014), pp. 1–13

Atkinson, Marc, and Ken Worpole, *Along the Outskirts* (Peterborough, 2016)

Baker, J. A., *The Peregrine* (London, 1967)

—, *The Hill of Summer* (London, 1969)

—, 'On the Essex Coast', in *The Peregrine, The Hill of Summer and Diaries* (London, 2011), pp. 427–31

—, *The Peregrine, The Hill of Summer and Diaries* (London, 2011)

Ballard, J. G., *The Drowned World* [1962] (London, 2014)

Bardsley, Garth, *Stop the World: The Biography of Anthony Newley* (London, 2003)
Baring-Gould, Sabine, and Cecil Sharp, *English Folk-Songs for Schools* (London, 1906)
Barker, Dudley, *Green and Pleasant Land* (London, 1955)
Barnes, Richard, *The Sun in the East: Norfolk and Suffolk Fairs* (Kirstead, 1983)
Barr, John, ed., *The Environmental Handbook: Action Guide for the UK* (London, 1971)
Bartie, Angela, Linda Fleming, Mark Freeman, Alex Hutton and Paul Readman, eds, *Restaging the Past: Historical Pageants, Culture and Society in Modern Britain* (London, 2020)
Bearman, C. J., 'Who Were The Folk? The Demography of Cecil Sharp's Somerset Folk Singers', *Historical Journal*, XLIII (2000), pp. 751–75
Bellamy, D. J., P. H. Clarke, D. M. John, D. Jones, A. Whittick and T. Darke, 'Effects of Pollution from the *Torrey Canyon* on Littoral and Sublittoral Ecosystems', *Nature*, CCXVI (1967), pp. 1170–73
Bender, Barbara, *Stonehenge: Making Space* (Oxford, 1998)
Benjamin, Walter, *Charles Baudelaire: A Lyric Poet in the Era of High Capitalism* (London, 1973)
Berengarten, Richard, *For the Living: Selected Longer Poems, 1965–2000* (Bristol, 2011)
Beresford, Elisabeth, *The Wombles* [1968] (Harmondsworth, 1972)
—, *The Wombles of Wimbledon* (London, 1976)
Best, Andrew, ed., *Water Springing from the Ground: An Anthology of the Writings of Rolf Gardiner* (Fontmell Magna, 1972)
Betjeman, John, *The Collected Poems* (London, 1974)
Binns, Amy, *Hidden Wyndham: Life, Love, Letters* (Hebden Bridge, 2019)
Bishop, Peter, *The Greening of Psychology* (Dallas, TX, 1990)
Blackburn, Julia, *Time Song: Searching for Doggerland* (London, 2019)
Blackstone, Lee Robert, 'The Aural and Moral Idylls of "Englishness" and Folk Music', *Symbolic Interaction*, xl (2017), pp. 561–80
Blake, William, *Jerusalem* (London, 1904)
—, *Selected Poems* (Oxford, 1994)
Blondel, Nathalie, *Mary Butts: Scenes from the Life* (New York, 1998)
Boles, William, 'The Science and Politics of Climate Change in Steve Waters' *The Contingency Plan*', *Journal of Contemporary Drama in English*, VII (2019), pp. 107–22
Bone, Stephen, *British Weather* (London, 1946)
Bord, Janet, and Colin Bord, *Mysterious Britain* (London, 1974)
—, *A Guide to Ancient Sites in Britain* (London, 1978)
—, *Earth Rites: Fertility Practices in Pre-Industrial Britain* (London, 1982)
Boyes, Georgina, *The Imagined Village: Culture, Ideology and the English Folk Revival* (Manchester, 1993)
Bracewell, Michael, *England is Mine: Pop Life in Albion from Wilde to Goldie* (London, 1997)
Bradtke, Elaine, 'Molly Dancing: A Study of Discontinuity and Change', in *Step Change: New Views on Traditional Dance*, ed. Georgina Boyes (London 2001), pp. 61–86

Bragg, Billy, *The Progressive Patriot* (London, 2006)
Brannigan, John, *Archipelagic Modernism: Literature in the British Isles, 1890–1970* (Edinburgh, 2015)
Brassley, Paul, David Harvey, Matt Lobley and Michael Winter, *The Real Agricultural Revolution: The Transformation of English Farming, 1939–1985* (Martlesham, 2021)
Briggs, Raymond, *Fungus the Bogeyman* (London, 1977)
—, *The Snowman* (London, 1978)
—, *When the Wind Blows* (London, 1982)
Broadhurst, Paul, and Hamish Miller, *The Sun and the Serpent* (Launceston, 1989)
—, *The Dance of the Dragon* (Launceston, 2000)
Brooker, Joseph, 'Raymond's Fen', in *Of Mud and Flame: The Penda's Fen Sourcebook*, ed. Matthew Harle and James Machin (London, 2019), pp. 63–81
Bryant, Christopher, 'National Art and Britain Made Real: The 2012 London Olympics Opening Ceremony', *National Identities*, XVII (2015), pp. 333–46
Buchanan, Colin, *Traffic in Towns: The Specially Shortened Edition of the Buchanan Report* (Harmondsworth, 1964)
Buckland, Theresa, '"In a Word We Are Unique": Ownership and Control in an English Dance Custom', in *Step Change: New Views on Traditional Dance*, ed. Georgina Boyes (London, 2001), pp. 49–60
Budden, Gary, 'Gnostic Anarcho-Punk Anti-Pastoral Visions', in *Of Mud and Flame: The Penda's Fen Sourcebook*, ed. Matthew Harle and James Machin (London, 2019), pp. 123–30
Burchardt, Jeremy, *Paradise Lost: Rural Idyll and Social Change in England since 1800* (London, 2002)
—, 'Ladybird Landscapes: Or, What to Look for in the What to Look For Books', *Rural History*, XXXI (2020), pp. 79–95
Burns, Richard, *Avebury* (London, 1971)
Butlin, Martin, *William Blake, 1757–1827* (London, 1990)
Butterworth, Jez, *Jerusalem* (London, 2009)
Butts, Mary, *The Crystal Cabinet* (Manchester, 1988)
—, 'Green', in *With or Without Buttons* (Manchester, 1991), pp. 71–84
Cameron, Laura, 'Resources of Hope: Wicken Fen Stories of Anthropogenic Nature', *Cambridge Anthropology*, XXXI (2013), pp. 105–18
Cannon, Jon, 'New Myths at Swallowhead: The Past and the Present in the Landscape of the Marlborough Downs', in *The Avebury Landscape*, ed. Graham Brown, David Field and David McOmish (Oxford, 2005), pp. 202–11
Carson, Rachel, *Silent Spring* (London, 1963)
Chesterton, G. K., 'The Secret People', in *The Collected Poems of G. K. Chesterton* (London, 1933), pp. 173–6
Chippindale, Christopher, *Stonehenge Complete* (London, 1994)
—, Paul Devereux, Peter Fowler, Rhys Jones and Tim Sebastian, *Who Owns Stonehenge?* (London, 1990)
Christian, Garth, *Tomorrow's Countryside: The Road to the Seventies* (London, 1966)

Clark, J.F.M., 'Pesticides, Pollution and the UK's Silent Spring, 1963–1964: Poison in the Garden of England', *Notes and Records: The Royal Society Journal of the History of Science*, LXXI (2017), pp. 297–327

Clark, Steve, Tristanne Connolly and Jason Whittaker, eds, *Blake 2.0: William Blake in Twentieth-Century Art, Music and Culture* (Basingstoke, 2012)

Clayton, Anthony, 'Baring, (Charles) Evelyn, first Baron Howick of Glendale', *Oxford Dictionary of National Biography* (2004)

Clifford, Sue, and Angela King, eds, *Field Days: An Anthology of Poetry* (Totnes, 1998)

—, *England in Particular* (London, 2006)

Cocker, Mark, 'Encounter: The Visions of Kurt Jackson', *Granta*, CII (2008), pp. 22–6

—, *Our Place* (London, 2018)

—, and Richard Mabey, *Birds Britannica* (London, 2005)

Coles, Bryony, 'Doggerland: A Speculative Survey', *Proceedings of the Prehistoric Society*, LXIV (1998), pp. 45–81

Collins, Shirley, *America over the Water* (London, 2004)

—, *All in the Downs: Reflections of Life, Landscape and Song* (London, 2018)

Common Ground, *A Manifesto for Fields* (London, 1997)

Conford, Philip, 'Organic Society: Agriculture and Radical Politics in the Career of Gerard Wallop, Ninth Earl of Portsmouth (1898–1984)', *Agricultural History Review*, LIII (2005), pp. 78–96

—, '"Somewhere Quite Different": The Seventies Generation of Organic Activists and their Context', *Rural History*, xix (2008), pp. 217–34

—, *The Development of the Organic Network: Linking People and Themes, 1945–95* (Edinburgh, 2011)

Cooke, Lez, *A Sense of Place: Regional British Television Drama, 1956–1982* (Manchester, 2012)

Cooper, David, 'Envisioning "the cubist fells": Ways of Seeing in the Poetry of Norman Nicholson', in *Poetry and Geography: Space and Place in Post-War Poetry*, ed. Neal Alexander and David Cooper (Liverpool, 2013), pp. 148–60

—, 'The Post-Industrial Picturesque? Placing and Promoting Marginalised Millom', in *The Making of a Cultural Landscape: The English Lake District as Tourist Destination, 1750–2010*, ed. John K. Walton and Jason Wood (London, 2013), pp. 241–62

Cooper, Tim, and James Symonds, 'Gravel Extraction: History of the Aggregates Industry in the Trent Valley', in *Quaternary of the Trent*, ed. David Bridgland, Andy Howard, Mark White and Tom White (Oxford, 2014), pp. 235–42

Cooper, Timothy, and Anna Green, 'The *Torrey Canyon* Disaster, Everyday Life, and the "Greening" of Britain', *Environmental History*, XXII (2017), pp. 101–26

Cope, Julian, *The Modern Antiquarian* (London, 1998)

—, *The Megalithic European* (London, 2004)

Cormack, Patrick, *Heritage in Danger* (London, 1976)

Cosgrove, Denis, *Apollo's Eye: A Cartographic Genealogy of the Earth in the Western Imagination* (Baltimore, MD, 2001)

Countryside Commission, *New Agricultural Landscapes* (Cheltenham, 1974)
Coupland, Philip, *Farming, Fascism and Ecology: A Life of Jorian Jenks* (London, 2017)
Cowley, Jason, 'The New Nature Writing', *Granta*, CII (2008), pp. 7–12
Cox, Graham, and Philip Lowe, 'Agricultural Corporatism and Conservation Politics', in *Locality and Rurality*, ed. Tony Bradley and Philip Lowe (Norwich, 1984), pp. 147–66
Cresswell, Tim, *In Place/Out of Place: Geography, Ideology and Transgression* (London, 1996)
Cross, Jonathan, *Harrison Birtwistle: Man, Mind, Music* (London, 2000)
Crutzen, Paul, and Eugene Stoermer, 'The "Anthropocene"', *IGBP Newsletter* (May 2000), pp. 17–18
Dabydeen, David, *Disappearance* (London, 1993)
Dames, Michael, *The Silbury Treasure* (London, 1976)
—, *The Avebury Cycle* (London, 1977)
—, *Pagan's Progress* (London, 2017)
Darvill, Timothy, Katherine Barker, Barbara Bender and Ronald Hutton, *The Cerne Giant: An Antiquity on Trial* (Oxford, 1999)
Davies, John, and David Waterhouse, *Exploring Norfolk's Deep History Coast* (Cheltenham, 2023)
Davies, Keri, 'Blake Set to Music', in *Blake 2.0: William Blake in Twentieth-Century Art, Music and Culture*, ed. Steve Clark, Tristianne Connolly and Jason Whittaker (Basingstoke, 2012), pp. 189–208
Day, James Wentworth, *A Falcon on St Paul's* (London, 1935)
—, *Poison on the Land: The War on Wild Life and Some Remedies* (London, 1957)
Dean, Geoffrey, 'ECB Club Leagues in 2022: Season in the Sun', in *Wisden Cricketers' Almanack 2023*, ed. Lawrence Booth (London, 2023), pp. 749–51
Dee, Tim, *The Running Sky* (London, 2009)
—, *Four Fields* (London, 2013)
—, *Landfill* (London, 2018)
—, 'Introduction', in *Ground Work*, ed. Tim Dee (London, 2018), pp. 1–14
—, *Greenery* (London, 2020)
Defoe, Daniel, *The Storm*, ed. Richard Hamblyn (London, 2003)
Deller, Jeremy, *Art is Magic* (London, 2023)
—, and Alan Kane, *Folk Archive* (London, 2005)
Denyer, Susan, 'The Lake District Landscape: Cultural or Natural?', in *The Making of a Cultural Landscape: The English Lake District as Tourist Destination, 1750–2010*, ed. John J. Walton and Jason Wood (London, 2013), pp. 3–29
Department of the Environment, *50 Million Volunteers: A Report on the Role of Voluntary Organisations and Youth in the Environment* (London, 1972)
—, *How Do You Want to Live? A Report on the Human Habitat* (London, 1972)
—, *The Human Environment: The British View* (London, 1972)
—, *Pollution: Nuisance or Nemesis? A Report on the Control of Pollution* (London, 1972)
—, *Sinews for Survival: A Report on the Management of Natural Resources* (London, 1972)

DeSilvey, Caitlin, 'Making Sense of Transience: An Anticipatory History', *Cultural Geographies*, XIX (2012), pp. 31–54
—, Simon Naylor and Colin Sackett, eds, *Anticipatory History* (Axminster, 2011)
Dodson, J., and V. Wheelock, 'Letter to the editor', *Environmental Studies*, X (1977), pp. 196–7
Donaldson, J.G.S., Frances Donaldson and Derek Barber, *Farming in Britain Today* (Harmondsworth, 1969)
Dower, Michael, *The Challenge of Leisure* (London, 1965)
Du Garde Peach, L., *Stone Age Man in Britain* (Loughborough, 1961)
Earle, Fiona, Alan Dearling, Helen Whittle, Roddy Glasse, and Gubby, *A Time to Travel? An Introduction to Britain's Newer Travellers* (Lyme Regis, 1994)
The Ecologist, 'A Blueprint for Survival', *The Ecologist*, II/1 (1972); repr. (Harmondsworth, 1972)
—, 'And now, live from Cornwall . . .', *The Ecologist*, III/1 (1973), p. 9
Edwards, Gemma, 'This Is England 2021: Staging England and Englishness in Contemporary Theatre', *Journal of Contemporary Drama in English*, IX (2021), pp. 281–303
—, *Representing the Rural on the English Stage: Performance and Rurality in the Twenty-First Century* (Cham, 2023)
Endfield, Georgina, Lucy Veale and Alexander Hall, 'Gordon Valentine Manley and His Contribution to the Study of Climate Change', *WIREs Climate Change*, VI (2015), pp. 287–99
Fairbrother, Nan, *New Lives, New Landscapes* (Harmondsworth, 1972)
Fallon, David, '"Hear the Drunken Archangel Sing": Blakean Notes in 1990s Pop Music', in *Blake 2.0: William Blake in Twentieth-Century Art, Music and Culture*, ed. Steve Clark, Tristianne Connolly and Jason Whittaker (Basingstoke, 2012), pp. 248-62
Farley, Paul, and Michael Symmons Roberts, *Edgelands* (London, 2011)
Finlay, Alec, 'From *A Place-Aware Dictionary*', in *Antlers of Water: Writing on the Nature and Environment of Scotland*, ed. Kathleen Jamie (Edinburgh, 2020), pp. 243–60
Finnissy, Michael, 'Conversations with Michael Finnissy', in *Uncommon Ground: The Music of Michael Finnissy*, ed. Henrietta Brougham, Christopher Fox and Ian Pace (Aldershot, 1997), pp. 1–42
Fisher, Roy, in conversation with John Kerrigan, 'Come to Think of It, the Imagination', in *News for the Ear: A Homage to Roy Fisher*, ed. Robert Sheppard and Peter Robinson (Exeter, 2000), pp. 96–120
—, *The Long and the Short of It: Poems, 1965–2005* (Hexham, 2005)
Fitter, Richard, *London's Natural History* (London, 1945)
—, and Peter Scott, *The Penitent Butchers: The Fauna Preservation Society, 1903–1978* (London, 1978)
Flack, Andrew, 'Lions Loose on a Gentleman's Lawn: Animality, Authenticity and Automobility in the Emergence of the English Safari Park', *Journal of Historical Geography*, LIV (2016), pp. 38–49
Forster, E. M., 'The Abinger Pageant', in *Abinger Harvest* (1936) (Harmondsworth, 1967), pp. 369–84

Fowles, John, 'On Being English but Not British', *Texas Quarterly*, VII (1964), pp. 154–62; repr. in *Wormholes: Essays and Occasional Writings* (London, 1998), pp. 79–88
—, *The Tree* (London, 1979)
—, 'Introduction', in Richard Jefferies, *After London, or Wild England* (Oxford, 1980), pp. vii–xxi
—, 'Land', in *Wormholes: Essays and Occasional Writings* (London, 1998), pp. 321–39
—, *The Journals*, vol. I (London, 2003)
—, and Fay Godwin, *Islands* (London, 1978)
Fox, Christopher, 'Michael Finnissy: Modernism with an English Accent', in *Critical Perspectives on Michael Finnissy*, ed. Ian Pace and Nigel McBride (Abingdon, 2019), pp. 27–38
Fraser Darling, Frank, *Wilderness and Plenty* (London, 1970)
Fulton, Hamish, 'Old Muddy', in Richard Long, *Walking in Circles* (London, 1991), pp. 241–6
Furedi, Frank, 'From the Narrative of the Blitz to the Rhetoric of Vulnerability', *Cultural Sociology*, I (2007), pp. 235–54
Gaffney, Vince, Simon Fitch and David Smith, *Europe's Lost World: The Rediscovery of Doggerland* (York, 2009)
Gallagher, Ann, ed., *Susan Hiller* (London, 2011)
Gammon, Vic, 'Folk Song Collecting in Sussex and Surrey, 1843–1914', *History Workshop Journal*, X (1980), pp. 61–89
Garde-Hansen, Joanne, Lindsey McEwen, Andrew Holmes and Owain Jones, 'Sustainable Flood Memory: Remembering as Resilience', *Memory Studies*, X (2017), pp. 384–405
Gardiner, Rolf, *England Herself* (London, 1943)
—, 'Nyasaland: From Primeval Forest to Garden Landscape', *African Affairs*, LVII (1958), pp. 64–9
—, *Water Springing from the Ground: An Anthology of the Writings of Rolf Gardiner*, ed. Andrew Best (Fontmell Magna, 1972)
Garner, Alan, 'The Stone Book', in *The Stone Book Quartet* (London, 1983), pp. 1–36
Garrity, Jane, *Step-Daughters of England: British Women Modernists and the National Imaginary* (Manchester, 2003)
Gibson, Andrew, '"At the Dying Atlantic's Edge": Norman Nicholson and the Cumbrian Coast', in *Coastal Works: Cultures of the Atlantic Edge*, ed. Nicholas Allen (Oxford, 2017), pp. 77–92
Gilchrist, Annie G., 'Note on the "Lady Drest in Green" and Other Fragments of Tragic Ballads and Folk-Tales Preserved amongst Children', *Journal of the Folk-Song Society*, VI (1919), pp. 80–90
Gill, Crispin, Frank Booker and Tony Soper, *The Wreck of the Torrey Canyon* (Newton Abbot, 1967)
Gilroy, Paul, *After Empire: Melancholia or Convivial Culture?* (London, 2004)
Glastonbury CND Festival 1985, *Official Programme* (Pilton, 1985)
Glavovic, Bruce, 'On the Frontline in the Anthropocene: Adapting to Climate Change through Deliberative Coastal Governance', in *Climate Change and the Coast: Building Resilient Communities*, ed. Bruce Glavovic, Mick Kelly, Robert Kay and Ailbhe Travers (London, 2015), pp. 51–99

Godwin, Fay, *Land* (London, 1985)
—, *Our Forbidden Land* (London, 1990)
—, and Shirley Toulson, *The Drovers' Roads of Wales* (London, 1977)
Godwin, Kerriann, ed., *The Museum of Witchcraft: A Magical History* (Boscastle, 2011)
Goldsmith, Edward, 'Editorial', *The Ecologist*, I/1 (1971), p. 2
—, and Nicholas Hildyard, eds, *Green Britain or Industrial Wasteland?* (Cambridge, 1986)
Goldsworthy, Andy, *Sheepfolds* (London, 1996)
—, and David Craig, *Arch* (London, 1999)
Gough, Paul, '"Cultivating Dead Trees": The Legacy of Paul Nash as an Artist of Trauma, Wilderness and Recovery', *Journal of War and Culture Studies*, IV (2011), pp. 323–40
Grahame, Kenneth, *The Penguin Kenneth Grahame* (Harmondsworth, 1983)
Grant, Doris, *Housewives Beware* (London, 1958)
Graves, Robert, *The White Goddess* (London, 1948)
Green, Anna, and Timothy Cooper, 'Community and Exclusion: The *Torrey Canyon* Disaster of 1967', *Journal of Social History*, XLVIII (2015), pp. 892–909
Grieve, Hilda, *The Great Tide: The Story of the 1953 Flood Disaster in Essex* (Chelmsford, 1959)
HRH The Prince Philip, Duke of Edinburgh, '"Countryside in 1970" Conference Opening Address', *International Journal of Environmental Studies*, I (1971), pp. 321–4
HRH The Prince of Wales, Tony Juniper and Emily Shuckburgh, *Climate Change* (London, 2017)
Haffenden, John, *Viewpoints: Poets in Conversation* (London, 1981)
Halfacree, Keith, 'Out of Place in the Country: Travellers and the "Rural Idyll"', *Antipode*, XXVIII (1996), pp. 42–72
Hamblyn, Richard, *The Sea: Nature and Culture* (London, 2021)
Hardin, Garrett, 'The Tragedy of the Commons', *Science*, CLXII (1968), pp. 1243–8
—, 'The Tragedy of the Commons', in *The Environmental Handbook: Action Guide for the UK*, ed. John Barr (London, 1971), pp. 47–65
Hardy, Denis, and Colin Ward, *Arcadia for All: The Legacy of a Makeshift Landscape* (London, 1984)
Harker, Dave, *One for the Money: Politics and Popular Song* (London, 1980)
—, *Fakesong: The Manufacture of British 'Folksong', 1700 to the Present Day* (Milton Keynes, 1985)
Harle, Matthew, and James Machin, eds, *Of Mud and Flame: The Penda's Fen Sourcebook* (London, 2019)
Harris, Alexandra, *Romantic Moderns* (London, 2010)
—, *Weatherland: Writers and Artists under English Skies* (London, 2015)
Harrison, Fraser, *Strange Land* (London, 1982)
—, *The Living Landscape* (London, 1986)
Harrison, M. John, *The Sunken Land Begins to Rise Again* (London, 2020)
Harrison, Melissa, *All Among the Barley* (London, 2018)
Harrison, Ruth, *Animal Machines: The New Factory Farming Industry* (London, 1964)
Harvey, Graham, *The Killing of the Countryside* (London, 1997)

Harvey, PJ, *Orlam* (London, 2022)
Hauser, Kitty, *Shadow Sites: Photography, Archaeology, and the British Landscape, 1927–1955* (Oxford, 2007)
Hawkes, Jacquetta, *A Land* (London, 1951)
Head, Dominic, *Modernity and the English Rural Novel* (Cambridge, 2017)
—, 'The Farming Community Revisited: Complex Nostalgia in Sarah Hall and Melissa Harrison', *Green Letters: Studies in Ecocriticism*, XXIV (2020), pp. 354–66
—, *Nature Prose: Writing in Ecological Crisis* (Oxford, 2022)
Henderson, Michael, *That Will Be England Gone: The Last Summer of Cricket* (London, 2020)
Heppa, Christopher, 'Harry Cox and His Friends: Song Transmission in an East Norfolk Singing Community, *c.* 1896–1960', *Folk Music Journal*, VIII/5 (2005), pp. 569–93
Hetherington, Kevin, *New Age Travellers* (London, 2000)
Higgs, John, *William Blake Now: Why He Matters More than Ever* (London, 2019)
Hignell, Andrew, 'Weather in 2022: Spring Sleet, Summer Heat', in *Wisden Cricketers' Almanack 2023*, ed. Lawrence Booth (London, 2023), p. 184
Hill, Christopher, 'The Norman Yoke', in *Puritanism and Revolution* (London, 1958), pp. 46–111
—, *The World Turned Upside Down* (London, 1972)
Hippisley Cox, R., *The Green Roads of England* (London, 1914)
Hole, Christina, *English Custom and Usage* (London, 1941)
Holloway, Lewis, 'Showing and Telling Farming: Agricultural Shows and Re-Imaging British Agriculture', *Journal of Rural Studies*, XX (2004), pp. 319–30
Holmes, Matthew, 'Crops in a Machine: Industrialising Barley Breeding in Twentieth-Century Britain', in *Histories of Technology, the Environment and Modern Britain*, ed. Jon Agar and Jacob Ward (London, 2018), pp. 142–60
Holtby, Winifred, *South Riding* (London, 1936)
Hooker, Jeremy, *A View from the Source: Selected Poems* (Manchester, 1982)
Hopkins, Gerard Manley, 'Inversnaid', in *Poems and Prose of Gerard Manley Hopkins* (Harmondsworth, 1953), pp. 50–51
Hornby, R. J., and P. W. Lambley, 'Farming Practice in Norfolk: Its Influence on Habitats', in Norfolk Naturalists Trust, *Nature in Norfolk: a Heritage in Trust* (Norwich, 1976), pp. 147–54
Horovitz, Michael, ed., *Children of Albion: Poetry of the 'Underground' in Britain* (Harmondsworth, 1969)
Horrocks, Sally, 'Pyke, Magnus Alfred', *Oxford Dictionary of National Biography* (2004)
Hoskins, W. G., *The Making of the English Landscape* (London, 1955)
Housman, A. E., *A Shropshire Lad* (London, 1896)
Howkins, Alun, *The Death of Rural England: A Social History of the Countryside since 1900* (London, 2003)
—, and Linda Merricks, '"Dewy eyed veal calves": Live Animal Exports and Middle Class Opinion, 1980–1995', *Agricultural History Review*, XLVIII (2000), pp. 85–103

Hudson, Julie, '"If You Want to be Green Hold Your Breath": Climate Change in British Theatre', *New Theatre Quarterly*, XXVIII (2012), pp. 260–71
Hughes, Ted, 'The Environmental Revolution', in *Winter Pollen* (London, 1994), pp. 128–35
—, *Collected Poems* (London, 2003)
Hugill, Stan, *Shanties from the Seven Seas* (London, 1961)
Hulme, Mike, *Weathered: Cultures of Climate* (London, 2017)
Hurd, Michael, *Rutland Boughton and the Glastonbury Festivals* (Oxford, 1993)
Hutchings, Peter, 'Uncanny Landscapes in British Film and Television', *Visual Culture in Britain*, V (2004), pp. 27–40
Hutton, Ronald, *The Pagan Religions of the Ancient British Isles* (Oxford, 1991)
—, *Stations of the Sun: A History of the Ritual Year in Britain* (Oxford, 1996)
—, 'The Past and the Post-Modern Challenge', *The Ley Hunter*, CXXV (1996), pp. 5–8
—, *The Triumph of the Moon: A History of Modern Pagan Witchcraft* (Oxford, 1999)
Irvine, Richard, 'The Happisburgh Footprints in Time', *Anthropology Today*, XXX (2014), pp. 3–6
Jackson, Kurt, *Place* (Bristol, 2014)
Jefferies, Matthew, and Mike Tyldesley, 'Epilogue: Rolf Gardiner: *Eminence Vert*?', in *Rolf Gardiner: Folk, Nature and Culture in Interwar Britain*, ed. Mike Tyldesley and Matthew Jefferies (London, 2010), pp. 169–75
Jefferies, Richard, *Nature near London* (London, 1879)
—, *The Story of My Heart* (London, 1883)
—, *After London, or Wild England* [1885] (Oxford, 1980)
Johnson, Ronald, *The Book of the Green Man* (Axminster, 2015)
Jones, Evan John, with Doreen Valiente, *Witchcraft: A Tradition Renewed* (London, 1990)
Jones, Kathleen, *Norman Nicholson: The Whispering Poet* (Appleby, 2013)
Jones, Keith, 'Music in Factories: A Twentieth-Century Technique for Control of the Productive Self', *Social and Cultural Geography*, VI/5 (2005), pp. 723–44
Judd, Harriet, 'Simon Roberts: Inscapes', in *Ivon Hitchens: Space through Colour*, exh. cat., Pallant House Gallery, Chichester (2019), pp. 100–105
Keenan, David, *England's Hidden Reverse* (London, 2014)
Keighren, Innes, and Joanne Norcup, eds, *Landscapes of Detectorists* (Axminster, 2020)
Kelly, Matthew, *Quartz and Feldspar: Dartmoor, a British Landscape in Modern Times* (London, 2015)
—, 'Conventional Thinking and the Fragile Birth of the Nature State in Post-War Britain', in *The Nature State*, ed. Wilko Graf von Hardenberg, Matthew Kelly, Claudia Leal and Emily Wakild (Abingdon, 2017), pp. 114–34
—, *The Women Who Saved the English Countryside* (London, 2022)
—, 'Habitat Protection, Ideology and the British Nature State: The Politics of the Wildlife and Countryside Act 1981', *English Historical Review*, CXXXVII (2022), pp. 847–83

—, 'The Politics of the British Environment since 1945', *Political Quarterly*, xciv (2023), pp. 208–15
—, Claudia Leal, Emily Wakild and Wilko Graf von Hardenberg, 'Introduction', in *The Nature State*, ed. Wilko Graf von Hardenberg, Matthew Kelly, Claudia Leal and Emily Wakild (Abingdon, 2017)
Kendon, Mike, Mark McCarthy, Svetlana Jevrejeva, Andrew Matthews, Tim Sparks, Judith Garforth and John Kennedy, 'State of the UK Climate 2021', *International Journal of Climatology*, XLII (2022), July Supplement, pp. 1–80
Kennedy, Douglas, *English Folk Dancing* (London, 1964)
Kerrigan, John, 'Roy Fisher on Location', in *The Thing About Roy Fisher: Critical Studies*, ed. John Kerrigan and Peter Robinson (Liverpool, 2000), pp. 16–46
King, Angela, and Sue Clifford, eds, *Trees Be Company* (London, 1989)
King, Clive, *Stig of the Dump* (Harmondsworth, 1963)
King, Graham, 'A Journey to Beyond', in *The Museum of Witchcraft: A Magical History*, ed. Kerriann Godwin (Boscastle, 2011), pp. 137–8
Kingsnorth, Paul, *Real England: The Battle Against the Bland* (London, 2008)
—, *The Wake* (London, 2014)
Kirchhelle, Claas, *Bearing Witness: Ruth Harrison and British Farm Animal Welfare (1920–2000)* (London, 2021)
Kunial, Zaffar, *Us* (London, 2018)
—, *England's Green* (London, 2022)
Kynaston, David, *On the Cusp: Days of '62* (London, 2021)
Larkin, Philip, *Collected Poems* (London, 2003)
Larrington, Carolyne, *The Land of the Green Man: A Journey Through the Supernatural Landscapes of the British Isles* (London 2015)
Latour, Bruno, *We Have Never Been Modern* (Hemel Hempstead, 1993)
Lewis, Wyndham, ed., *BLAST: Review of the Great English Vortex* (London, 1914)
Lippard, Lucy, *Overlay: Contemporary Art and the Art of Prehistory* (New York, 1983)
Lloyd, A. L., *The Singing Englishman* (London, 1944)
—, *Folk Song in England* (London, 1967)
Long, Richard, 'Nineteen Stills from the Work of Richard Long', *Studio International*, CLXXIX (1970), pp. 106–11
—, *Walking in Circles* (London, 1991)
—, *A Walk Across England* (London, 1997)
Look and Learn, 'Focus on the Farmer's Year', Issue 113, 14 March 1964
Lorimer, Hayden, 'Scaring Crows', *Geographical Review*, CIII (2013), pp. 177–89
Lorimer, Jamie, *Wildlife in the Anthropocene* (Minneapolis, MN, 2015)
Lorimer, Jamie, and Clemens Driessen, 'Wild Experiments: Rewilding Future Ecologies at the Oostvaardersplassen', *Transactions of the Institute of British Geographers*, XXXIX (2014), pp. 169–81
Lowe, Richard, William Shaw, *Travellers: Voices of the New Age Nomads* (London, 1993)
Lowerson, John, 'The Mystical Geography of the English', in *The English Rural Community*, ed. Brian Short (Cambridge, 1992), pp. 152–74

Luckhurst, Roger, 'Always Historicise? Penda's Fen in the 1970s', in *Of Mud and Flame: The Penda's Fen Sourcebook*, ed. Matthew Harle and James Machin (London 2019), pp. 29–39
Luke, Timothy, 'The World Wildlife Fund: Ecocolonialism as Funding the Worldwide "Wise Use" of Nature', *Capitalism Nature Socialism*, VIII (1997), pp. 31–61
Lyell, Charles, *Principles of Geology*, vol. II, 10th edn (London, 1866)
Mabey, Richard, 'Introduction: Not On Speaking Terms', in *Class*, ed. Richard Mabey (London, 1967), pp. 7–18
—, *Food for Free* (London, 1972)
—, *The Unofficial Countryside* (London, 1973)
—, *The Common Ground* (London, 1981)
—, ed., *Second Nature* (London, 1984)
—, 'Introduction: Entitled to a View?', in *Second Nature*, ed. Richard Mabey (London, 1984), pp. ix–xix
—, *Gilbert White* (London, 1986)
—, *Flora Britannica* (London, 1996)
—, 'Wildness as an Aesthetic Quality', in *Arcadia Revisited: The Place of Landscape*, ed. Vicki Berger and Isabel Vasseur (London, 1997), pp. 180–93
—, *Nature Cure* (London, 2005)
—, *Beechcombings: The Narratives of Trees* (London, 2007)
—, *Weeds* (London, 2010)
—, 'The Great Storm', in *A Brush with Nature* (London, 2010), pp. 84–5
—, *Turned Out Nice Again: On Living with the Weather* (London, 2019)
—, 'Kenneth Allsop', in *Turning the Boat for Home* (London, 2019), pp. 151–6
—, and Tony Evans, *The Flowering of Britain* (London, 1980)
Macdonald, Helen, *Falcon* (London, 2006)
—, *H is for Hawk* (London, 2016)
McEwen, Lindsey, Owain Jones and Iain Robertson, '"A glorious time?" Some Reflections on Flooding in the Somerset Levels', *Geographical Journal*, CLXXX (2014), pp. 6–37
McEwen, Lindsey, Joanne Garde-Hansen, Andrew Holmes, Owain Jones and Franz Krause, 'Sustainable Flood Memories, Lay Knowledges and the Development of Community Resilience to Future Flood Risk', *Transactions of the Institute of British Geographers*, XLII (2017), pp. 14–28
Macfarlane, Robert, *The Wild Places* (London, 2007)
—, 'Glimpses and Tremors', *The Guardian*, 11 April 2015
MacInnes, Colin, 'The Green Art: Gardening', in *Out of the Way: Later Essays* (London, 1979), pp. 201–10
McKay, George, *Senseless Acts of Beauty: Cultures of Resistance since the Sixties* (London, 1996)
—, *Glastonbury: A Very English Fair* (London, 2000)
McNeil Cooke, Ian, *Journey to the Stones* (Bosullow, 1996)
Maconie, Stuart, *The Full English: A Journey in Search of a Country and Its People* (London, 2023)
Manley, Gordon, *Climate and the British Scene* (London, 1952)
Marcus, Clare Cooper, 'Alternative Landscapes: Ley-Lines, Feng-Shui and the Gaia Hypothesis', *Landscape*, XXIX (1987), pp. 1–10
Marren, Peter, *The New Naturalists* (London, 1995)

—, and Richard Mabey, *Bugs Britannica* (London, 2010)
Marvin, Garry, 'Natural Instincts and Cultural Passions: Transformations and Performances in Foxhunting', *Performance Research*, v (2000), pp. 108–15
—, 'A Passionate Pursuit: Foxhunting as Performance', in *Nature Performed*, ed. Bronislaw Szerszynski, Wallace Heim and Claire Waterton (Oxford, 2003), pp. 46–60
Massey, Doreen, 'Landscape as a Provocation: Reflections on Moving Mountains', *Journal of Material Culture*, xi (2006), pp. 33–48
Massingham, H. J., ed., *England and the Farmer* (London, 1941)
Matless, David, *Landscape and Englishness* [1998], revd edn (London, 2016)
—, 'Versions of Animal-Human: Broadland, 1945–70', in *Animal Spaces, Beastly Places*, ed. Chris Philo and Chris Wilbert (London, 2000), pp. 115–40
—, 'Properties of Ancient Landscape: The Present Prehistoric in Twentieth-Century Breckland', *Journal of Historical Geography*, xxxiv (2008), pp. 68–93
—, 'A Geography of Ghosts: The Spectral Landscapes of Mary Butts', *Cultural Geographies*, xv (2008), pp. 335–58
—, 'Nature Voices', *Journal of Historical Geography*, xxxv (2009), pp. 178–88
—, *In the Nature of Landscape: Cultural Geography on the Norfolk Broads* (Chichester, 2014)
—, 'Climate Change Stories and the Anthroposcenic', *Nature Climate Change*, vi (2016), pp. 118–19
—, 'The Anthroposcenic', *Transactions of the Institute of British Geographers*, xlii (2017) pp. 363–76
—, 'The Agriculture Gallery: Displaying Modern Farming in the Science Museum', in *Histories of Technology, the Environment and Modern Britain*, ed. Jon Agar and Jacob Ward (London, 2018), pp. 101–22
—, 'The Anthroposcenic: Landscape in the Anthropocene', *British Art Studies*, x, 29 November 2018, www.britishartstudies.ac.uk, accessed 25 October 2023
—, 'Checking the Sea: Geographies of Authority on the East Norfolk Coast, 1790–1932', *Rural History*, xxx (2019), pp. 215–40
—, 'At the End of Beach Road', in Julian Perry, *There Rolls the Deep: The Rising Sea Level Paintings* (Southampton, 2022), pp. 70–81
—, *About England* (London, 2023)
—, and George Revill, 'A Solo Ecology: The Erratic Art of Andy Goldsworthy', *Ecumene*, ii (1995), pp. 423–48
—, Charles Watkins and Paul Merchant, 'Nature Trails: The Production of Instructive Landscapes in Britain, 1960–72', *Rural History*, xxi (2010), pp. 97–131
May, Allyson, *The Fox-Hunting Controversy, 1781–2004* (London, 2014)
Meadows, Donella, Dennis Meadows, Jorgen Randers and William Behrens, *The Limits to Growth* (London, 1972)
Medhurst, Andy, 'Mike Leigh: The Naked Truth', *Sight and Sound* (November 1993), available at www.bfi.org.uk, accessed 25 October 2023
—, *A National Joke: Popular Comedy and English Cultural Identities* (London, 2007)

Mellanby, Kenneth, *Pesticides and Pollution* (London, 1967)
—, 'Subsidised Erosion', *The Ecologist*, I (1973), p. 47
—, *Farming and Wildlife* (London, 1981)
Michell, John, *The Flying Saucer Vision* (London, 1967)
—, *The View over Atlantis* (London, 1969)
—, *Megalithomania* (London, 1982)
Monbiot, George, 'Class War on the Hoof', *The Guardian*, 19 September 2004
—, *Feral* (London, 2013)
—, 'Obstinate Questionings', *The Guardian*, 3 September 2013
—, 'The Lie of the Land', *The Guardian*, 12 July 2017
Montagu, Jemima, ed., *Paul Nash: Modern Artist, Ancient Landscape* (London, 2003)
Morris, William, *News from Nowhere* (London, 1891)
—, 'Prologue to *The Earthly Paradise*', in *News from Nowhere and Selected Writing and Designs* (Harmondsworth, 1986), p. 68
Moseley, Rachel, *Hand-Made Television: Stop-Frame Animation for Children in Britain, 1961–1974* (London, 2016)
Moss, Brian, *The Broads* (London, 2001)
Nash, Paul, 'Personal statement', in *Unit One*, ed. Herbert Read (London, 1934), pp. 79–81
Nature Conservancy, *The Countryside in 1970* (London, 1964)
Nettel, Reginald, *Sing a Song of England* (London, 1954)
Newby, Howard, *Green and Pleasant Land? Social Change in Rural England* (London, 1979)
Newson, Robert, Peter Wade-Martins and Adrian Little, *Farming in Miniature: A Review of British-Made Toy Farm Vehicles up to 1980*, 2 vols (Sheffield, 2012–14)
Niall, Ian, *Portrait of a Country Artist: Charles Tunnicliffe RA, 1901–1979* (London, 1980)
Nichols, Peter, 'The Gorge', in *The Television Dramatist*, ed. Robert Muller (London, 1973), pp. 71–148
Nicholson, Max, *The Environmental Revolution* (London, 1970)
Nicholson, Norman, *Cumberland and Westmorland* (London, 1949)
—, *Provincial Pleasures* (London, 1959)
—, 'Ten-Yard Panorama', in *Second Nature*, ed. Richard Mabey (London, 1984), pp. 3–11
—, *Collected Poems* (London, 1994)
Nita, Maria, and Sharif Gemie, 'Counterculture, Local Authorities and British Christianity at the Windsor and Watchfield Free Festivals (1972–5)', *Twentieth Century British History*, XXXI (2020), pp. 51–78
Nixon, Sean, 'Trouble at the National Trust: Post-War Recreation, the Benson Report and the Rebuilding of a Conservation Organization in the 1960s', *Twentieth Century British History*, XXVI (2015), pp. 529–50
—, 'Vanishing Peregrines: J. A. Baker, Environmental Crisis and Bird-Centred Cultures of Nature, 1954–1973', *Rural History*, XXVIII (2017), pp. 205–26
—, *Passions for Birds: Science, Sentiment and Sport* (Montreal, 2022)

Norcup, Joanne, '"All the minorities covered": Landscapes, Englishnesses, and Hopefulness in the TV Work of Mackenzie Crook', *Waiting for You: A Detectorists Zine 4* (2023)

Norton, Tessa, and Bob Stanley, eds, *Excavate: The Wonderful and Frightening World of The Fall* (London, 2022)

O'Brien, Sean, 'Sunk Island', in *Collected Poems* (London, 2012), p. 415

The Observer, 'Save Our Countryside', 9 December 1984, colour magazine, pp. 17–49

Ogley, Bob, *In the Wake of the Hurricane* (Westerham, 1988)

Opie, Iona, and Peter Opie, *Children's Games in Street and Playground* (Oxford, 1969)

Orwin, C. S., *Problems of the Countryside* (Cambridge, 1945)

O'Toole, Fintan, *Heroic Failure: Brexit and the Politics of Pain* (London, 2019)

Pace, Ian, 'The Piano Music', in *Uncommon Ground: The Music of Michael Finnissy*, ed. Henrietta Brougham, Christopher Fox and Ian Pace (Aldershot, 1997), pp. 43–134

Palmer, Roy, *The Painful Plough* (Cambridge, 1972)

—, *Songs of the Midlands* (Wakefield, 1972)

Parfitt, Simon, Nick Ashton, Simon Lewis et al., 'Early Pleistocene Human Occupation at the Edge of the Boreal Zone in Northwest Europe', *Nature*, 466 (2010), pp. 229–33

Parker, Eleanor, *Winters in the World: A Journey through the Anglo-Saxon Year* (London, 2022)

Parker, Joanne, *Britannia Obscura: Mapping Britain's Hidden Landscapes* (London, 2014)

Parr, Martin, *The Cost of Living* (Manchester, 1989)

Patmore, J. Allan, *Land and Leisure* (Harmondsworth, 1972)

Perry, Julian, *Brittle England* (London, 1997)

—, *An Extraordinary Prospect: The Coastal Erosion Paintings* (London, 2010)

—, *There Rolls the Deep: The Rising Sea Level Paintings* (Southampton, 2022)

Piper, John, 'Prehistory from the Air', *Axis*, VIII (1937), pp. 3–11

Platt, Edward, *The Great Flood: Travels Through a Sodden Landscape* (London, 2019)

Pool, Henry, and John Fleet, 'The Conservation of Cornwall', *The Ecologist*, III/1 (1973), pp. 26–9

Porritt, Jonathon, *Seeing Green* (Oxford, 1984)

Postgate, Oliver, *Seeing Things: An Autobiography* (London, 2000)

—, and Peter Firmin, *The Sky-Moos* (London, 1993)

Preston, Norman, ed., *Wisden Cricketers' Almanack 1977* (London, 1977)

Prince, Stephen, *A Year in the Country: Wandering through Spectral Fields* (London, 2018)

Pyke, Magnus, *Townsman's Food* (London, 1952)

—, *Food and Society* (London, 1968)

—, *Man and Food* (London, 1970)

Raban, Jonathan, 'Second Nature: The De-Landscaping of the American West', *Granta*, CII (2008), pp. 53–85

Rabey, David Ian, *David Rudkin: Sacred Disobedience* (Amsterdam, 1997)

Raphael, Amy, ed., *Mike Leigh on Mike Leigh* (London 2008)

Ratcliffe, D. A., 'The Status of the Peregrine in Great Britain', *Bird Study*, x (1963), pp. 56–90
Ratcliffe, Derek, *The Peregrine Falcon* (Calton, 1980)
Ravilious, James, *The Heart of the Country* (London, 1980)
Ravilious, Robin, *James Ravilious: A Life* (London, 2017)
Rebanks, James, *The Shepherd's Life* (London, 2015)
—, *English Pastoral* (London, 2020)
Reid, Clement, 'Coast Erosion', *Geographical Journal*, xxviii (1906), pp. 487–91
—, *Submerged Forests* (London, 1913)
Revill, George, 'English Pastoral: Music, Landscape, History and Politics', in *Cultural Turns/Geographical Turns*, ed. Ian Cook, David Crouch, Simon Naylor and James Ryan (Harlow, 2000), pp. 140–58
—, and John Gold, '"Far Back in American Time": Culture, Region, Nation, Appalachia and the Geography of Voice', *Annals of the Association of American Geographers*, cviii (2018), pp. 1406–21
Reynolds, Simon, 'Society of the Spectral', *The Wire* (November 2006), pp. 26–33
Rice, Brian, and Tony Evans, *The English Sunrise* (London, 1972)
Roberts, Simon, *Merrie Albion: Landscape Studies of a Small Island* (Stockport, 2017)
Robertson, James, 'Goldsmith, Edward Rene David [Teddy]', *Oxford Dictionary of National Biography* (2013)
Robertson, Kate, *The Creator of the Wombles: The First Biography of Elisabeth Beresford* (London, 2023)
Robertson-Scott, J. W., *England's Green and Pleasant Land* (London, 1925; rev. edn Harmondsworth, 1947)
Rolt, L.T.C., *High Horse Riderless* (Hartland, 1988)
Ross, Linda, Katrina Navickas, Matthew Kelly and Ben Anderson, eds, *New Lives New Landscapes Revisited: Rural Modernity in Britain* (Oxford, 2023)
Roud, Steve, *Folk Song in England* (London, 2017)
—, and Julia Bishop, *The New Penguin Book of English Folk Songs* (London, 2012)
Royal Norfolk Agricultural Association, *1975 Royal Norfolk Show Catalogue of Entries and Exhibitions* (Norwich, 1975)
Rudkin, David, 'I wanted to write something that grew out of the landscape', *Radio Times*, 14 March 1974, p. 12
—, *Penda's Fen* (London, 1975)
—, 'Mongrel Nation: A Foreword', in *Of Mud and Flame: The Penda's Fen Sourcebook*, ed. Matthew Harle and James Machin (London, 2019), pp. 9–12
Sandom, Christopher, and Sophie Wynne-Jones, 'Rewilding a Country: Britain as a Study Case', in *Rewilding*, ed. Nathalie Pettorelli, Sarah Durant and Johan du Toit (Cambridge, 2019), pp. 222–47
Saumarez Smith, Otto, *Boom Cities: Architect-Planners and the Politics of Radical Urban Renewal in 1960s Britain* (Oxford, 2019)
Saunders, Hetty, *My House of Sky: The Life of J. A. Baker* (Beaminster, 2017)
Saunders, Nicholas, *Alternative London's Survival Guide for Strangers to London* (London, 1973)

Sax, Boria, *Crow* (London, 2003)
Sayer, Karen, 'Animal Machines: The Public Response to Intensification in Great Britain, *c.* 1960–*c.* 1973', *Agricultural History*, LXXXVII (2013), pp. 473–501
Sayer, Karen, 'The View from the Land, 1947–1968: "Modernity" in British Agriculture, Farm and Nation', in *New Lives New Landscapes Revisited: Rural Modernity in Britain*, ed. Linda Ross, Katrina Navickas, Matthew Kelly and Ben Anderson (Oxford, 2023), pp. 156–81
Schumacher, E. F., *Small Is Beautiful* (London, 1973)
Schwarz, Walter, 'Edward Goldsmith obituary', *The Guardian*, 29 August 2009, p. 37.
Scruton, Roger, *On Hunting* (London, 1998)
—, *England: An Elegy* (London, 2000)
Searle, Adam, Jonathon Turnbull and William Adams, 'The Digital Peregrine: A Technonatural History of a Cosmopolitan Raptor', *Transactions of the Institute of British Geographers*, XLVIII (2023), pp. 195–212
Secord, James, 'King of Siluria: Roderick Murchison and the Imperial Theme in Nineteenth-Century British Geology', *Victorian Studies*, XXV (1982), pp. 413–42
—, *Visions of Science* (Oxford, 2014)
Seymour, John, *The Fat of the Land* (1961) (London, 1974)
—, *Self-Sufficiency* (London, 1973)
—, *The Complete Book of Self-Sufficiency* (London, 1976)
Sheail, John, *Nature in Trust: The History of Nature Conservation in Britain* (London, 1976)
—, *Pesticides and Nature Conservation: The British Experience, 1950–1975* (Oxford, 1985)
—, *Nature Conservation in Britain: The Formative Years* (London, 1998)
—, *An Environmental History of Twentieth-Century Britain* (London, 2002)
—, '*Torrey Canyon*: The Political Dimension', *Journal of Contemporary History*, XLII (2007), pp. 485–504
—, 'Pesticides and the British Environment: An Agricultural Perspective', *Environment and History*, XIX (2013), pp. 87–108
Sheppard, Robert, *Turning the Prism: An Interview with Roy Fisher* (London, 1986)
Shoard, Marion, *The Theft of the Countryside* (London, 1980)
—, *This Land is Our Land* (1987) (London, rev. 1997)
—, *A Right to Roam* (Oxford, 1999)
—, 'Edgelands of Promise', *Landscapes*, I (2000), pp. 74–93
Shoesmith, Ron, *Alfred Watkins: A Herefordshire Man* (Almeley, 1990)
Shrubsole, Guy, *Who Owns England?* (London, 2019)
Simms, Eric, *Woodland Birds* (London, 1971)
—, *The Public Life of the Street Pigeon* (London, 1979)
Sinden, Neil, *In a Nutshell* (London, 1989)
Skrimshire, Stefan, 'The View from Dunwich', *Environmental Humanities*, XIII (2021), pp. 264–71
Smart, Sue, and Richard Bothway Howard, *It's Turned Out Nice Again!* (Ely, 2011)

Smith, David, *Industrial Archaeology of the East Midlands* (Dawlish, 1965)
Smith, J. E., ed., *'Torrey Canyon' Pollution and Marine Life* (Cambridge, 1968)
Smith, Jacob, 'Mackenzie Crook's Biosemiotic Television', *Screen*, LXIII (2022), pp. 445–63
Smith, Jos, *The New Nature Writing* (London, 2017)
Smyth, Richard, 'Human Nature', *Times Literary Supplement*, 19/26 August 2016, pp. 19–21
—, *A Sweet, Wild Note: What We Hear When the Birds Sing* (London, 2017)
—, *An Indifference of Birds* (Axminster, 2020)
Solnit, Rebecca, *Wanderlust: A History of Walking* (London, 2001)
—, *Orwell's Roses* (London, 2021)
Sperling, Matthew, 'Water', in *An Unofficial Roy Fisher*, ed. Peter Robinson (Exeter, 2010), pp. 161–8
Stamp, L. Dudley, *Britain's Structure and Scenery* (London, 1946)
Stannard, Joseph, 'Potion of Sound', *The Wire*, CCCVIII (October 2009), pp. 38–42
Stephenson, Tom, *Forbidden Land* (Manchester, 1989)
Stout, Adam, *Creating Prehistory: Druids, Ley Hunters and Archaeologists in Pre-War Britain* (Oxford, 2008)
—, 'Grounding Faith at Glastonbury: Episodes in the Early History of Alternative Archaeology', *Numen*, LIX (2012), pp. 249–69
Stringer, Chris, *Homo Britannicus* (London, 2006)
Summers, Dorothy, *The East Coast Floods* (Newton Abbot, 1978)
Sutherland, Patrick, and Adam Nicholson, *Wetland: Life in the Somerset Levels* (London, 1986)
Swinnerton, H. H., *Fossils* (London, 1960)
Szirtes, George, *New and Collected Poems* (Hexham, 2008)
Taplin, Kim, *Tongues in Trees: Studies in Literature and Ecology* (Hartland, 1989)
Tarlo, Harriet, *Gathering Grounds* (Bristol, 2019)
—, and Judith Tucker, 'Poetry, Painting and Change on the Edge of England', *Sociologica Ruralis*, LIX (2019), pp. 636–60
Taylor, John, *A Dream of England: Landscape, Photography and the Tourist's Imagination* (Manchester, 1995)
Thomas, Dylan, *Selected Poems* (London, 1974)
Thomas, Keith, *Man and the Natural World* (London, 1983)
Thomas, Virginia, 'Domesticating Rewilding: Interpreting Rewilding in England's Green and Pleasant Land', *Environmental Values*, XXXI (2022), pp. 515–32
Thompson, E. P., *The Making of the English Working Class* (London, 1963)
Thorpe, Adam, *On Silbury Hill* (Toller Fratum, 2014)
Tickell, Crispin, *Climatic Change and World Affairs* (Oxford, 1978)
Tinbergen, Niko, *The Herring Gull's World* (London, 1953)
Todd, Barbara Euphan, *Worzel Gummidge or The Scarecrow of Scatterbrook* [1936] (Harmondsworth, 1941)
Tolkien, J.R.R., *The Return of the King* (London, 1955)
—, 'The Homecoming of Beorhtnoth Beorthelm's Son', in *Tree and Leaf, Smith of Wootton Major, The Homecoming of Beorhtnoth* (London, 1975), pp. 147–75

Toulson, Shirley, *Discovering Farm Museums and Farm Parks* (Princes Risborough, 1977)
—, *East Anglia: Walking the Ley Lines and Ancient Tracks* (London, 1979)
—, *Derbyshire: Exploring the Ancient Tracks and Mysteries of Mercia* (London, 1980)
Tree, Isabella, *Wilding* (London, 2018)
Trexler, Adam, *Anthropocene Fictions: The Novel in a Time of Climate Change* (London, 2015)
Turchetti, Simone, 'The UK Government's Environmentalism: Britain, NATO and the Origins of Environmental Diplomacy', in *Histories of Technology, the Environment and Modern Britain*, ed. Jon Agar and Jacob Ward (London, 2018), pp. 252–70
Varley, Martin, ed., *Flora of the Fells* (Kendal, 2003)
Vaughan Williams, Ralph, and A. L. Lloyd, *The Penguin Book of English Folk Songs* (Harmondsworth, 1959)
Vaughan Williams, Ursula, *R.V.W.: A Biography of Ralph Vaughan Williams* (London, 1964)
Veldman, Meredith, *Fantasy, the Bomb and the Greening of Britain: Romantic Protest, 1945–1980* (Cambridge, 1994)
Vera, Frans, *Grazing Ecology and Forest History* (Wallingford, 2002)
Vinson, James, ed., *Contemporary Dramatists* (London, 1973)
Wallace, Craig, 'The "Old, Primeval 'Demon' of the Place Opening Half an Eye": Penda's Fen and the Legend of the Sleeping King', in *Of Mud and Flame: The Penda's Fen Sourcebook*, ed. Matthew Harle and James Machin (London, 2019), pp. 185–96
Wallen, Martin, *Fox* (London, 2006)
Waters, Colin, et al., 'The Anthropocene is Functionally and Stratigraphically Different from the Holocene', *Science*, CCCLI (6269) (2016), pp. 137–47
Waters, Steve, *The Contingency Plan* (London, 2015)
Watkins, Alfred, *The Old Straight Track* [1925] (London, 1970)
Wedd, Tony, *Skyways and Landmarks* (Chiddingstone, 1961)
West, Lesley, 'An Agricultural History Museum', *Agricultural History*, XLI (1967), pp. 267–74
Westacott, H. D., *The Ridgeway Path* (Harmondsworth, 1982)
Whipple, Amy, '"Into Every Home, Into Every Body": Organicism and Anti-Statism in the British Anti-Fluoridation Movement, 1952–1960', *Twentieth Century British History*, XXI (2010), pp. 330–49
—, 'Murdered Bread, Living Bread: Doris Grant and the Homemade, Wholemeal Loaf', *Endeavour*, XXXV (2011), pp. 99–106
White, Gilbert, *The Natural History of Selborne*, ed. Richard Mabey (Harmondsworth, 1977)
White, Rupert, *The Re-enchanted Landscape: Earth Mysteries, Paganism and Art in Cornwall, 1950–2000* (Truro, 2017)
—, 'Interview: Ronald Hutton on Cecil Williamson and Rewriting Wicca', *Enquiring Eye*, IV (2020), pp. 68–74
White, T. H., *The Goshawk* (London, 1951)
Whitehead, Tony, *Mike Leigh* (Manchester, 2007)
Whittaker, Jason, 'Mental Fight, Corporeal War, and Righteous Dub: The Struggle for "Jerusalem", 1979–2009', in *Blake 2.0: William Blake in*

Twentieth-Century Art, Music and Culture, ed. Steve Clark, Tristianne Connolly and Jason Whittaker (Basingstoke, 2012), pp. 263–73

—, 'Blake and the New Jerusalem: Art and English Nationalism into the Twenty-First Century', *Visual Culture in Britain*, XIX (2018), pp. 380–92

—, *Jerusalem: Blake, Parry and the Fight for Englishness* (Oxford, 2022)

Williams, Raymond, 'Between Country and City', in *Second Nature*, ed. Richard Mabey (London, 1984), pp. 209–19

Williams, William Carlos, *In the American Grain* [1925] (Harmondsworth, 1971)

Williamson, Tom, and Liz Bellamy, *Ley Lines in Question* (Kingswood, 1983)

Winter, James, *Secure from Rash Assault: Sustaining the Victorian Environment* (Berkeley, CA, 1999)

Winter, Trish, and Simon Keegan-Phipps, *Performing Englishness: Identity and Politics in a Contemporary Folk Resurgence* (Manchester, 2013)

Wiseman-Trowse, Nathan, *Nick Drake: Dreaming England* (London, 2013)

Woods, Abigail, 'From Cruelty to Welfare: The Emergence of Farm Animal Welfare in Britain, 1964–71', *Endeavour*, XXXVI (2012), pp. 14–22

—, 'Rethinking the History of Modern Agriculture: British Pig Production, *c.* 1910–65', *Twentieth Century British History*, XXIII (2012), pp. 165–91

Woods, Michael, 'Deconstructing Rural Protest: The Emergence of a New Social Movement', *Journal of Rural Studies*, XIX (2003), pp. 309–25

—, *Contesting Rurality: Politics in the British Countryside* (Abingdon, 2005)

Wordsworth, William, *A Guide through the District of the Lakes in the North of England* [1835] (London, 1951)

Wright, Patrick, *On Living in an Old Country* (London, 1985)

—, *The Village that Died for England* (London, 1995)

Wright, Philip, *Traction Engines* (London, 1959)

—, *Old Farm Implements* (London, 1961)

—, *Salute the Carthorse* (Shepperton, 1971)

—, *Old Farm Tractors* (Newton Abbot, 1974)

—, *Country Padre* (Baldock, 1980)

Wyndham, John, *The Kraken Wakes* [1953] (Harmondsworth, 1955)

—, *The Midwich Cuckoos* (London, 1957)

—, *Trouble with Lichen* (London, 1960)

—, *The Day of the Triffids* [1951](London, 1999)

Young, Rob, *Electric Eden: Unearthing Britain's Visionary Music* (London, 2010)

—, *The Magic Box* (London, 2021)

Zalasiewicz, Jan, *The Earth After Us* (Oxford, 2008)

—, et al., 'The Working Group on the Anthropocene: Summary of Evidence and Interim Recommendations', *Anthropocene*, XIX (2017), pp. 55–60

—, Colin Waters, Mark Williams, David Aldridge and Ian Wilkinson, 'The Stratigraphical Signature of the Anthropocene in England', *Proceedings of the Geologists' Association*, CXXIX (2018), pp. 482–91

DISCOGRAPHY

Songs and music mentioned in *England's Green*, referenced here as individual singles, tracks, works or (in italics) albums, as appropriate to their citation in the text.

A. C. Benson and Edward Elgar, 'Land of Hope and Glory' (1902)
Adge Cutler and The Wurzels, 'All Over Mendip' (1967)
—, 'Drink Up Thy Zider' (1967)
—, 'My Threshing Machine' (1967)
—, 'Scrumpy & Western' (1967 EP)
Amazing Blondel, *England* (1972)
Belbury Poly, *The Willows* (2004)
—, *The Owl's Map* (2006)
Bonzo Dog Doo Dah Band, 'The Intro and the Outro' (1967)
Billy Bragg, 'The World Turned Upside Down' (1985)
—, 'Jerusalem', from *The Internationale* (1990)
—, *William Bloke* (1996)
Harrison Birtwistle, *Silbury Air* (1977)
—, *Gawain* (1991)
British Sea Power, 'Carrion' (2003), from *The Decline of British Sea Power*
—, 'Fear of Drowning' (2003), from *The Decline of British Sea Power*
—, 'Oh Larsen B' (2005), from *Open Season*
—, 'The Land Beyond' (2005), from *Open Season*
—, 'Canvey Island' (2008), from *Do You Like Rock Music?*
Broadcast and The Focus Group, *Witch Cults of the Radio Age* (2009)
Kate Bush, 'Oh England My Lionheart' (1978), from *Lionheart*
—, 'Cloudbusting' (1985)
Eliza Carthy, *Anglicana* (2002)
Michael Cashmore, *Sleep England* (2006)
Shirley Collins, *Sweet England* (1959)
—, *Fountain of Snow* (1992)
—, *Lodestar* (2016)
—, *Heart's Ease* (2020)
—, *Archangel Hill* (2023)
Shirley and Dolly Collins, *Anthems in Eden* (1969)

—, *Love, Death and Lady* (1970)
Shirley Collins and Davy Graham, *Folk Roots, New Routes* (1964)
Julian Cope, 'The Subtle Energies Commission', from *Jehovahkill* (1992)
—, 'Paranormal in the West Country', from *Autogeddon* (1994)
—, 'Stone Circles 'N' You', from *20 Mothers* (1995)
—, 'By the Light of the Silbury Moon', from *20 Mothers* (1995)
—, *Interpreter* (1996)
—, *England Expectorates* (2022)
Current 93, *The Starres are Marching Sadly Home* (1996)
—, *Black Ships Ate the Sky* (2006)
Richard Dawson, *Nothing Important* (2014)
—, *The Glass Trunk* (2015)
—, *Peasant* (2017)
—, *2020* (2019)
—, *The Ruby Cord* (2022)
Dreadzone, 'A Canterbury Tale', from *Second Light* (1995)
—, 'Little Britain', from *Second Light* (1995)
Vernon Elliott, *Clangers: Original Television Music by Vernon Elliott* (2001)
Emerson, Lake and Palmer, 'Jerusalem', from *Brain Salad Surgery* (1973)
The Fall, 'Before the Moon Falls', from *Dragnet* (1979)
—, 'English Scheme', from *Grotesque (After the Gramme)* (1980)
—, 'Hard Life in Country', from *Room to Live* (1982)
—, 'Dog is Life/Jerusalem', from *I Am Kurious Oranj* (1988)
—, 'W.B.', from *The Unutterable* (2000)
Michael Finnissy, *Pathways of Sun and Stars* (1976)
—, *English Country-Tunes* (1977, rev. 1982–5)
—, *Kemp's Morris* (1978)
—, *Maldon* (1991)
—, *Folklore* (1993–5)
—, *This Church* (2003)
The Focus Group, *We Are All Pan's People* (2007)
Genesis, 'The Return of the Giant Hogweed', from *Nursery Cryme* (1971)
—, 'Aisle of Plenty', from *Selling England by the Pound* (1973)
—, 'Dancing with the Moonlit Knight', from *Selling England by the Pound* (1973)
Woody Guthrie, 'This Land is Your Land' (1944)
PJ Harvey, *I Inside the Old Year Dying* (2023)
Maggie Holland, 'A Place Called England' (1999)
Hot Butter, 'Popcorn' (1972)
Bert Jansch, 'Rosemary Lane', from *Rosemary Lane* (1971)
Jonathan King, 'Una Paloma Blanca' (1975)
Sam Lee, 'Turtle Dove', from *Old Wow* (2020)
Melanie, 'Brand New Key' (1972)
Morris On, *Morris On* (1972)
Angeline Morrison, *Sorrow Songs: Folk Songs of Black British Experience* (2022)
Martin Newell, 'Before the Hurricane', from *The Greatest Living Englishman* (1993)
Anthony Newley, 'Strawberry Fair' (1960)

—, 'Pop Goes the Weasel' (1961)
Hubert Parry, 'Jerusalem' (1916)
—, 'Jerusalem', orch. Edward Elgar (1922)
Pink Floyd, 'Interstellar Overdrive', from *The Piper at the Gates of Dawn* (1967)
—, 'The Scarecrow', from *The Piper at the Gates of Dawn* (1967)
John Renbourn, *Sir John A lot of Merrie Englandes Musyk Thyng & ye Grene Knyghte* (1968)
Paul Robeson, 'Jerusalem' (1939)
Throbbing Gristle, *20 Jazz Funk Greats* (1978)
Topic Records 'Voice of the People' series, *You Lazy Lot of Bone-Shakers: Songs and Dance Tunes of Seasonal Events* (1998)
—, *I'm a Romany Rai: Songs by Southern English Gypsy Traditional Singers* (2012)
—, *You Never Heard So Sweet: Songs by Southern English Traditional Singers* (2012)
Sex Pistols, 'God Save the Queen' (1977)
Trembling Bells, *The Sovereign Self* (2015)
—, *Wide Majestic Aire* (2016)
Vangelis, 'Chariots of Fire' (1981)
Rick Wakeman, *The Myths and Legends of King Arthur and the Knights of the Round Table* (1975)
Lal and Mike Waterson, 'The Scarecrow', from *Bright Phoebus* (1972)
The Watersons, *Frost and Fire: A Calendar of Ritual and Magical Songs* (1965)
Kenneth Williams, *The Best of Rambling Syd Rumpo* (1970)
The Wombles, 'The Wombling Song' (1973)
—, 'Wombles Everywhere' (1973)
—, 'Remember You're a Womble' (1974)
The Wurzels, 'Combine Harvester' (1976)
—, 'Down the Nempnett Thrubwell' (1976)
—, 'I Am a Cider Drinker' (1976)
—, 'Farmer Bill's Cowman' (1977)
—, *Give Me England* (1977)
—, *The Finest 'Arvest of The Wurzels* (2000)
XTC, 'Sacrificial Bonfire', from *Skylarking* (1986)
—, 'Season Cycle', from *Skylarking* (1986)
—, 'Summer's Cauldron', from *Skylarking* (1986)
—, 'Easter Theatre', from *Apple Venus, Vol. 1* (1999)
—, 'Greenman', from *Apple Venus, Vol. 1* (1999)

FILMOGRAPHY

Films and television programmes mentioned in *England's Green*.

Cinema

Arcadia (2017), dir. Paul Wright
The Ballad of Shirley Collins (2018), dir. Rob Curry and Tim Plester
Chariots of Fire (1981), dir. Hugh Hudson
From the Sea to the Land Beyond (2012), dir. Penny Woolcock
Here's a Health to the Barley Mow: A Century of Folk Customs and Ancient Rural Games (2011), British Film Institute DVD collection
A Journey to Avebury (1971), dir. Derek Jarman
Monty Python and the Holy Grail (1975), dir. Terry Gilliam and Terry Jones
Way of the Morris (2011), dir. Tim Plester

Television

Abigail's Party (BBC), 1977, dir. Mike Leigh
Black Safari (BBC), 1972
Camberwick Green (BBC), 1966
Changing Climate (ITV), 1978
Chigley (BBC), 1969
Children of the Stones (ITV), 1977
The Clangers (BBC), 1969–72
Dad's Army (BBC), 1968–77
Detectorists (BBC), 2014–17
Don't Ask Me (ITV), 1974–78
Don't Just Sit There (ITV), 1979–80
The Good Life (BBC), 1975-8
The Gorge (BBC), 1968, dir. Christopher Morahan
Grayson Perry's Full English (Channel 4), 2023
Jerusalem: An Anthem for England (BBC), 2005
Metro-land (BBC), 1973
Multi-Coloured Swap Shop (BBC), 1976–82
Music Time (BBC), 1970–91

Nuts in May (BBC), 1976, dir. Mike Leigh
Penda's Fen (BBC), 1974, dir. Alan Clarke
Robin of Sherwood (ITV), 1984–6
The Strange World of Gurney Slade (ITV), 1960
Survival (ITV), 1961–2001
Think of England (BBC), 1999
Trumpton (BBC), 1967
The Wombles (BBC), 1973–5
The World About Us (BBC), 1967–87
Worzel Gummidge (ITV), 1979–81
Worzel Gummidge (BBC), 2019–21

ACKNOWLEDGEMENTS

The School of Geography at the University of Nottingham has provided a supportive environment for my research since 1994, and work carried out by staff and research students in the Cultural and Historical Geography Research Group there has been a valuable source of ideas and critical reflection. Thanks to current and former colleagues within that Group and in the School, including Stephen Daniels, Charles Watkins, Susanne Seymour, Paul Merchant, David Beckingham, Mike Heffernan, Georgina Endfield, Steve Legg, Jake Hodder, Isla Forsyth, Gary Priestnall, Robert Hearn, Adam Swain and Andrew Leyshon. Undergraduate students, and those on the former MA in Landscape and Culture at Nottingham, have brought critical perspectives to the themes covered here, and all the PhD students I have supervised at Nottingham have been important in shaping the intellectual outlook of this book. Matthew Smallman-Raynor provided impeccable support as Head of School during the challenging years when this book was first drafted. Beyond Nottingham, thanks also to the support and collaboration of Laura Cameron, David Crouch, George Revill, Tim Boon, Mike Pearson, Tim Dee, Julian Perry and Colin Sackett. Conferences organized by Jon Agar and Jacob Ward (on technology and environment), Steve Waters (on re-wilding drama), Kate McMillan (on climate change and creativity), and Matthew Kelly, Ben Anderson, Katrina Navickas, Ian Robertson, Linda Ross and Ian Waites (on rural modernism and landscape in the twentieth century) provided valuable fora for the development of ideas. Thanks also to Ian Webster and Robert Lindsay for earlier field company. Staff in the Manuscripts and Special Collections department at Nottingham facilitated access to research papers, and the Hallward Library at the university and the public library in Beeston have also proved valuable sources of material. For support before, during and after the pandemic, thanks to the staff of Round Hill School, Beeston. My parents, Brian and Audrey Matless, have always given love and support, and helped nurture a particular attention to nature. Jo Norcup's companionship, knowledge and curiosity have shaped *England's Green* in many ways, and this book is dedicated to her and to our son, Edwyn.

PHOTO ACKNOWLEDGEMENTS

The author and publishers wish to thank the organizations and individuals listed below for authorizing reproduction of their work.

Cover illustration for *Stig of the Dump* by Clive King, illustrated by Edward Ardizzone, published by Puffin Books. Illustration © The Ardizzone Trust, reproduced by permission of David Higham Associates: p. 233; from *The Sun in the East: Norfolk and Suffolk Fairs* by Richard Barnes (compilation copyright: RB Photographic, 1983): p. 203; from *Fungus the Bogeyman* by Raymond Briggs © 1977, Raymond Briggs, published by Puffin. Extract reproduced by permission of Penguin Books: p. 42; © The British Library Board (photographs by Fay Godwin): pp. 70 (Source: FG176-7180-17/ Caption: Countryside of Brassington Derbyshire/Shelfmark: FG176-7180-17/ Author: Godwin, Fay/Artist/creator: Godwin, Fay/Credit: British Library), 208 (Source: FG6916-3-13/Caption: Night Guard; Stonehenge 1988/ Shelfmark: FG6916-3-13 Credit: British Library); from *Tomorrow's Countryside: The Road to the Seventies* by Garth Christian (John Murray, 1966): p. 108 top (photograph by V. Rogers) 108 bottom (photograph by S. J. Brown); © Julian Cope (with permission): p. 226; from *The Green Roads of England* by R. Hippisley Cox (Methuen & Co., London, 1914): pp. 214, 215 (illustration by W. W. Collins); *The Ecologist*: pp. 114 (1972), 118 (cartoon by Richard Willson, July 1970/courtesy of the British Cartoon Archive, University of Kent); © Ghost Box Records 2006 (with permission): p. 256; photograph by Ronald Goodearl, with permission of Friends of High Wycombe Library and *Bucks Free Press*: p. 60 top; Google Earth Street View: p. 275; from *Animal Machines* by Ruth Harrison (Vincent Stuart Publishers Ltd, 1964): p. 60 bottom; HMSO, London (Crown copyright, 1972): pp. 96, 101 top left, 101 top right, 101 bottom left, 101 bottom right, 102; © Richard Long. All Rights Reserved. DACS 2024: p. 230; from *Climate and the British Scene* by Gordon Manley (Collins, 1952): p. 161 (Photograph by Cyril Newberry); from *Gordon Murray's Camberwick Green Annual* (Purnell, 1970): p. 47 (detail from the front cover illustration by Harry McGregor); photographs by the author, David Matless: pp. 6, 8, 49 top and bottom, 76 top and bottom, 80, 122, 143 top and bottom, 187 (with the permission of David Waterhouse), 193, 194 top and bottom, 197, 212 (image from author's junior school homework); from *Sing a Song of England* by Reginald Nettel (Phoenix House, 1954): p. 249 (jacket design by Dodie Masterman); University of Nottingham Manuscripts and Special Collections, MS 627/1/3/174 and MS 627/1/3/175: pp. 19, 20; © Bob Ogley (with permission): pp. 167, 168; © Martin Parr (Magnum Photos): p. 241; © Julian Perry (with permission): pp. 184, 185; public domain: p. 38; 'Scarecrow in a barley field near Iddesleigh', photograph by James Ravilious © Beaford Arts digitally scanned from a Beaford Archive negative: p. 273; from *Submerged Forests* by Clement Reid (Cambridge University Press, 1913): p. 188; © Simon Roberts, *Flooding of the Somerset Levels, Burrowbridge, Somerset, 11 February 2014* from the series 'Merrie Albion', pigment print, 122 cm x 156 cm (with permission): p. 175; from *The Strange World of Gurney Slade* (ATV, 1960): p. 265 (Series directed by Alan Tarrant); from *Fossils* by H. H. Swinnerton: p. 158 (Collins, 1960); © Judith Tucker, *Night Fitties: we're all very close round here*, 2018, oil on canvas, 76 cm x 101 cm (with permission): p. 182; Estate of Maurice Wilson: p. 138 (Illustration from *Fossils* by H. H. Swinnerton, Collins, 1960).

INDEX

Page numbers in *italics* indicate illustrations